30119 027 927 85 6

KU-084-052

The Collected Poems
of Dylan Thomas:
The Centenary Edition

Also available from Orion

A Dylan Thomas Treasury
Portrait of the Artist as a Young Dog
Collected Stories
Dylan Thomas Omnibus
Selected Poems
The Love Letters of Dylan Thomas
Under Milk Wood

LONDON BOROUGH OF SUTTON LIBRARY SERVICE	
30119 027 927 85 6	
Askews & Holts	May-2016
821	

The Collected Poems of Dylan Thomas: The Centenary Edition

Edited and annotated by
JOHN GOODBY

WEIDENFELD & NICOLSON

A W&N PAPERBACK

First published in Great Britain in 2014 by Weidenfeld & Nicolson
This paperback edition published in 2016 by Weidenfeld & Nicolson,
An imprint of the Orion Publishing Group Ltd,
Carmelite House, 50 Victoria Embankment,
London EC4Y 0DZ

An Hachette UK Company

10 9 8 7 6 5 4 3 2 1

All rights reserved. No part of this publication may be
reproduced, stored in a retrieval system, or transmitted, in
any form or by any means, electronic, mechanical,
photocopying, recording or otherwise, without the prior
permission of the copyright owner.

Poems © The Trustees for the Copyrights of Dylan Thomas
Introduction and Notes © John Goodby 2014, 2016

The rights of Dylan Thomas and John Goodby, to be identified as the author and editor
of this work respectively, have been asserted in accordance with the Copyright, Designs
and Patents Act 1988.

A CIP catalogue record for this book
is available from the British Library.

ISBN 978-1-7802-2723-8

Typeset by Input Data Services Ltd, Bridgwater, Somerset

Printed in Great Britain by Clays Ltd, St Ives plc

The Orion Publishing Group's policy is to use papers that are
natural, renewable and recyclable products and made from wood
grown in sustainable forests. The logging and manufacturing
processes are expected to conform to the environmental
regulations of the country of origin.

www.orionbooks.co.uk

Note on the author and editor

Dylan Marlais Thomas was born in Swansea on 27 October 1914. After leaving school he worked briefly as a junior reporter on the *South Wales Evening Post* before embarking on a literary career in London, where he immediately established himself as one of the finest poets of his generation. He published four collections of poems, *18 Poems* (1934), *Twenty-five Poems* (1936), *The Map of Love* (1939) and *Deaths and Entrances* (1946), as well as the poetry chapbook *In Country Sleep* (1952). His *Collected Poems 1934–1952* appeared in 1952 to great acclaim. Throughout his life Thomas also wrote fictions; some were included in *The Map of Love*, and a short-story collection, *Portrait of the Artist as a Young Dog*, was published in 1940. During the Second World War, Thomas began a novel, *Adventures in the Skin Trade*, wrote film scripts and began working as an actor, broadcaster and writer for radio. His radio features are among his best-known works, and include 'Return Journey' and 'A Child's Christmas in Wales'. In 1950, 1952 and 1953 he gave reading tours in the USA, and worked on the radio 'play for voices', *Under Milk Wood*, which was first performed in New York in May 1953. It was in New York, during his fourth US tour, that he fell ill shortly after his thirty-ninth birthday, dying there on 9 November 1953. He is buried in Laugharne, Wales, where he had lived since 1949.

John Goodby is Professor of English at the University of Swansea. He has published widely on British and Irish poetry, and his work on Dylan Thomas includes the co-edited essay collection *Dylan Thomas: New Casebook* (2001), a monograph, *The Poetry of Dylan Thomas: Under the Spelling Wall* (2013), and *Discovering Dylan: A Companion to the Centenary Collected Poems*, the University of Wales Press (2016).

Contents

Appendices

Acknowledgements

I gratefully acknowledge the help and encouragement given me in the preparation of this edition by the following: my family, Nicola, Kate and George Goodby; friends, colleagues, students and fellow-Dylanites, including Rhian Bubear, Hannah Ellis, Aeronwy Thomas-Ellis, Victor Golightly, Barbara Hardy, Ivan Phillips, Neil Reeve, Jeff Towns, Steve Vine, Chris Wigginton and Dave Woolley. Of the institutions and individuals within them who have made this edition possible, I would like to thank the following: RIAH (Research Institute for Arts and Humanities), Swansea University; Sian Bowyer and the staff at the Manuscripts Collection at the National Library of Wales, Aberystwyth; the staff of the Department of Manuscripts at the British Library, St Pancras, London; Michael Basinski and the staff of the Special Collection Library of the State University of New York at Buffalo; Rick Watson and the staff of the Research Library at the Harry Ransom Research Center at the University of Texas at Austin; the staff of Swansea University Library; the Dylan Thomas Society of Great Britain; CREW (Centre for Research into the English Literature and Language of Wales), Swansea University; and Emily Klenin, UCLA. Thanks are due to Swansea University for sabbatical leave in 2010–11, during which a good deal of the preparatory work for this edition was carried out, and to the AHRC (Arts and Humanities Research Council of Great Britain) for the award of a Research Fellowship for the academic year 2012–13, during which the edition was prepared.

It is hard to know where my interest in Dylan Thomas's work began, and whether anyone in particular should be thanked for pushing it my way. However, many years ago I had the good fortune to be taught by an English master from Swansea. Peter Hellings had been a promising young poet when war broke out in 1939, and Thomas had even name-checked him approvingly in a letter to Vernon Watkins in 1940 – 'Peter Helling's got something, hasn't he? . . . "Got something", my God! Am I trying to be a Little Master?' Hellings's literary career, interrupted by the war and his work, never quite matched this flying start; but as a teacher he kindled in his pupils a love of literature, which included lending me the work of Dylan Thomas. When the chance arose for me to organise a conference on Thomas in 1998, this early memory was crucial in my acceptance, and the experience of the conference led to the work that gave rise to this edition. So while it may not be appropriate for a work such as this to be dedicated to any person but the poet himself, I hereby acknowledge a very particular debt of gratitude. If I never quite measured up to the aspirations my teacher entertained for me all those years ago, I hope this edition can nevertheless be taken as a fitting, if belated, tribute to his inspiration and his memory.

Introduction

Dylan Thomas today

Dylan Thomas is still valued today as the creator of one of the most distinctive and exciting of all poetic styles – sensuous, playful, rhythmically forceful and subtly musical, full of earworm-memorable lines and passages. He is that rarest kind of author, one who, like Hopkins, Shakespeare and Joyce, permanently bent the iron of English and expanded our sense of its possibilities. Thomas's broad appeal rests on his having written poetry which is considered to be poetic in the sense the word is popularly understood – that is, as writing distinguished from other kinds by its gestural qualities, its staking of everything on the power of its linguistic invention, music and imagery. This emphasis makes his work stand out from most twentieth-century English poetry, which is distinguished by a preference for plainer styles. A handful of Thomas's poems, among them 'Fern Hill' and 'Do not go gentle into that good night', remain anthology favourites, and are among the best-known poems in the language. Other works, notably his radio 'play for voices', *Under Milk Wood*, are established classics, and his writings have inspired work in, and been adapted for, many different media – rock, jazz and classical music, prints and paintings, film and television, cartoon, opera and the stage. Today, almost everything Thomas wrote is in print. He is one of the most Googled poets on the worldwide web, and the recent plethora of books and exhibitions, radio and television programmes to mark the centenary of his birth in 2014 all testify to the continuing resonance of his work over sixty years after his death.

Thomas's popularity is also, of course, indissolubly linked to his life and early death in New York in November 1953, at the age of thirty-nine. His meteor-like passing, flaring up in the grey, conformist Cold War world, immediately established him in the popular imagination as both rebel and victim, investing him with the aura of a folk hero (by 1962, for example, his spoken-voice LPs had sold over 400,000 copies). This was just the beginning of his transformation into a cultural icon, since his exuberant style and exemplary bohemian dissolution led to his adoption by the 1960s counter-culture; the favourite author of The Beatles, Peter Blake and Richard Burton, he lent his name to Bob Dylan, and became the tribal bard in Marshall McLuhan's electronic global village. He is still, indeed, the rock-, film-star and celebrity poet of choice, cherished by figures as diverse as Patti Smith, ex-US president Carter and Pierce Brosnan.

Yet Thomas's unusual visibility, as poets go, is qualified by the divergence between his popular reputation and his critical one. Until about forty years ago, these more or less matched each other. Despite attacks on his work, often by the Movement writers of the 1950s who defined themselves against their larger-than-life predecessor, many leading critics rated Thomas highly. He was honourably mentioned in Alvarez's seminal anthology *The New Poetry* (1962), appeared as a central figure in histories of British poetry, and was acknowledged as an influence on poets such as Sylvia Plath, Ted Hughes and W. S. Graham. Despite the continued suspicion of little-England and Welsh nationalist critics, by the twentieth anniversary of his death Dylan Thomas seemed to have found a place in the canon. But then, in the mid-1970s, what the US poet-critic Karl Shapiro called his 'impossible audience', of both academic and general readers, suddenly split. In Wales, critical activity continued, but elsewhere it fell away sharply, his critical reputation plummeting even as the popular one remained buoyed by the legend. In accounts of twentieth-century poetry he swiftly became marginal. From having a whole chapter devoted to him in A. T. Tolley's *Poets of the Thirties* of 1975, for example, he came to merit just a few passing (and derogatory) references in Valentine Cunningham's *Writers of the Thirties* of 1988.

This demotion needs to be set in context. In part, it reflected a natural adjustment: because he was hailed as a cultural icon, Thomas was over-exposed in the years following his death. However, this does not explain the depth and length of the neglect. A more likely cause was the re-evaluation of the 1930s as 'the Auden decade' by anglocentric critics in the late 1970s, and the consequent need to air-brush Thomas, Auden's main challenger for supremacy, from the period. Another factor was the sea-change in British poetic culture, one of the many instances of conservative backlash in British society in the late 1970s and 1980s. This led to a polarisation between modernist-influenced poetry, and an anti-modernist poetry of a plainer kind, with the latter coming to exclude the former kind from almost all mainstream attention and reward. A scene that had once taken Auden and Thomas seriously, and (just) tolerated poetry influenced by both Charles Olson and Philip Larkin, shrank in scope.[1] Thomas's offence was not just that he had modernist roots, however. He was also too excessive, his work too bound up in the legend, too anomalous to be easily pigeonholed. He had written 'Altarwise by owl-light', one of the most formidably difficult poems in English, and 'Fern Hill', once voted fourth-favourite poem ever by listeners of BBC Radio Four's 'Poetry Please'. Although, in the 1950s and 1960s, even the densest of Thomas's poems had been unravelled, in a divided poetry world this kind of divergence looked less like versatility than incoherence. It was easier to focus on an unrepresentative handful of late lyrics and argue that Thomas was a limited poet, and the bulk of his work merely obscure. It is this partial, simplified and rather sentimentalised version of Thomas which is prized, patronised or ignored today.

The process of simplifying and forgetting was abetted by the wild-man legend, which unhelpfully blurred the distinction between the life (or alleged life) of the poet and his work, suggesting that excessive personal behaviour meant slapdash, sound-before-sense poetry. Of course, the legend is what draws many readers to the poetry, and this is not, in itself, a bad thing. Unfortunately, because it is so potent, the legend also acts to limit interest only to work that seems biographical. And, because readers always know about the life in advance, many tend to feel they must already know what the poems mean; that they are direct expressions of Thomas's

1 For an account of these developments, see Andrew Crozier, 'Thrills and frills: poetry as figures of empirical lyricism', in Alan Sinfield (ed.), *Society and Literature 1945–1970*, Methuen, London, 1983, p. 227.

thoughts and feelings. Biography drives out poetry, when in reality the poetry is richer than the life – even if it is truer of Thomas than of most writers that, as Yeats put it, 'The poet who writes the poems is never the bundle of accident and incoherence that sits down to breakfast'. Thomas was, as he rightly described himself, 'a painstaking, conscientious, involved and devious craftsman in words', and his work explores the joyous and painful paradoxes of existence in profoundly satisfying verbal structures. To appreciate it fully, and to be able to take the poet seriously, we need to move beyond the colourful character and the limitations on our appreciation of his poems. This edition, therefore, aims to give readers, by whatever route they arrived at Thomas, the wherewithal needed to do exactly that. With just a little patience and guile, it is possible for any reader to make sense of almost any poem, and to confirm that, as Thomas once claimed, 'every line *is* meant to be understood; the reader is meant to understand every poem by thinking and feeling about it, not by sucking it in through his pores'. And however obscure the narrative sense of a Thomas poem might seem, the poem itself always rewards the attention paid to it, in an ingenious form repeated nowhere else, gorgeous verbal music, a twist of black humour, some vivid image, or merely an idiom memorably reminted; a renewed appreciation of words and poems, in fact.

Biography and development

If his legend has distorted our perception of Thomas's work, there is no doubt that an understanding of it has to start with his upbringing, on 'the uglier side of a hill' in the middle-class Uplands suburb of Swansea, where he was born during the opening weeks of the First World War, in October 1914. His father, D. J. ('Jack') Thomas, was an English master at the local grammar school, who through talent and hard work had risen from a humble background to achieve a First Class degree in English at Aberystwyth University. His mother, Florrie, was from a similar background, but in contrast to her stern, atheist husband was vivacious and a regular church-goer; on Sundays her son was bundled along to three services at the Paraclete Congregational Church in nearby Newton, where her brother-in-law was minister. 'From very early youth . . . the great rhythms [of the Bible] . . . rolled over me,' as Thomas later put it; and Welsh pulpit oratory also mixed with English poetry, including 'the quite incomprehensible magical majesty and nonsense of Shakespeare', which Jack Thomas was in the habit of reading aloud to his son well before he could understand it. From the earliest age, Dylan was given the run of his father's library, where he 'read indiscriminately, and with my eyes hanging out'. A word- and poetry-besotted child, he later claimed to have started writing poems when he was seven and a half. At school, he did badly in just about every subject, but was always first in English. He left, aged sixteen, to work on the local newspaper, but had already set his heart on a career as a writer.

What survives of Thomas's very early poetry is precocious, but conventional: comic verse, elegies for the war dead, imitations and exercises. Thomas sent Robert Graves a bundle of such poems when he was about fifteen; Graves answered, telling him that they were 'irreproachable, but that he would eventually learn to dislike them'. In April 1930, however, Thomas began the first of a series of notebooks (four would survive) in which he fair-copied poems in which he consciously tried to forge a modern voice. By this point, he was already acquainted with modern music, art and film, as well as poetry, thanks in part to his best friend, Daniel Jones, with whom he engaged in spoof radio broadcasts, cut-up word games and surrealist-style writing exercises.

The location of Swansea as a place 'in-between' shaped the writer Dylan would become. The town lies on the boundary between industrial and rural South Wales, and is also a port – it's no accident that so many Thomas poems are set on what he called its 'splendid-curving shore', the most elemental border of all. It was also at the furthermost point of anglophone South Wales, on the border with Welsh-speaking Carmarthenshire – a division that was also reflected in the Thomas family. Thomas's parents were Welsh speakers, but kept the language from their children because it was believed to be a bar to social advancement and was discouraged in the school system. But though he broke with his past in this way, D. J. Thomas compensated by giving his son the then almost unknown name of 'Dylan', which he found in *The Mabinogion*, a medieval Welsh text. Dylan ap Tôn (Dylan Son of the Wave) is a magical child who dashes into the sea immediately after his birth. Such borders and border-crossings, of culture, class and language, were highlighted when Dylan spent his summer holidays with Welsh-speaking relatives in rural Carmarthenshire. His hyphenated Anglo-Welshness was complex, but enabling, and he developed a hybrid nature, adept at empathy, parody and mimicry and relishing paradoxical states.

Thomas was on the border in other ways too. In an essay of 1929, for his school magazine, he defined the problem facing young would-be writers: 'No poet can find sure ground ... To-day is a transitional period.' It was a time when, although still intimidatingly impressive, the authority of Modernism was waning, and there was no obvious alternative model. His first two notebooks, running April 1930 to June 1932, found their 'sure ground' in largely undistinguished free verse, which was 'modern' but only in a rather dated way. But 1929 had also been the year of the Wall Street Crash. As the Great Depression deepened, modernist experiment seemed increasingly irrelevant. Domestic political crises and Hitler's seizure of power in January 1933 convinced other young poets, such as C. Day Lewis, W. H. Auden and Stephen Spender, that their generation had been betrayed, 'born into one war and fattened for another'.[2] Plain-style directness suddenly became the norm; collage was ditched in favour of traditional syntax, stanzas and rhyme, and reportage supplanted symbolist density.

Thomas was well aware of the crisis. He had been a journalist for sixteen months from August 1931, enjoyed the friendship of Bert Trick, a Labour councillor and socialist activist, and was involved in anti-fascist protests. His response, in late 1932, was irregularly rhymed lyrics, often using iambic pentameters as well as free verse, mixing social concern with personal angst, as in the poem 'Before the gas fades'. He had already discovered many of his future themes – bodies, sex, death, madness, faith – but his treatment of them was still inert, suggesting a future as a watered-down Welsh T. S. Eliot,

2 Francis Scarfe, *Auden and After: The Liberation of Poetry 1930–41*, Routledge, London, 1942, p. xiii.

or Auden. However, he was about to undergo a transformation that would underpin all of his subsequent work. Thanks to the notebooks, we know the date of this turning-point, mid-April 1933, and the poem in which it occurred – 'And death shall have no dominion'.

It was written in a friendly competition with Trick to see who could produce the best poem on the subject of 'Immortality'. Thomas used regular stanzas and rhyme scheme for the first time in his notebook poetry, perhaps because he did not take such a poem wholly seriously. Yet what he had done, inadvertently, was stumble on a way of achieving the cohesion his poems lacked, by fusing Eliot's intensities with Auden's retro use of form. 'And death' is modernist in its wordplay and sense of the inhuman vastness of the universe, but it mashes these into traditional stanzas, syntax and rhyme scheme. The straitjacket of strict form, paradoxically, liberates his voice. He also discovered another feature typical of the mature poetry. The message of the poem's biblical refrain – the promise of eternal life – and its emotive uplift coexists with, but never openly contradicts, the actual sense of the poem, which is that, after death, we simply push up the daisies. Revisions to the poem show that Thomas increased what we would now call the poem's 'cognitive dissonance', getting it to say two opposing things at once, equally forcefully. Almost by accident, then, he had hit on a style appropriate to his hybrid nature, a 'spider-tongued' way (as he calls it in the poem 'Especially when the October wind') of making language speak double. This became a basic, paradoxical principle of his work. Thomas's distance from London's literary force-field, his hyphenated Anglo-Welshness, had enabled him to combine the two leading poetic styles of the day with a version of his Welsh rhetorical inheritance.

At first Thomas seems not to have understood the significance of the breakthrough. Perhaps this was because 'And death' gave the lie to his long efforts to write in a self-consciously modern, free verse style. Whatever the reason, the next poem in the notebook, 'Within his head revolved a little world', is irregular. But Thomas was not able to ignore 'And death' for long. Evidently haunted by its success, by 13 May he was using regular stanza forms once more. In July, after a month's silence, they return: and, on 15 July, the notebook records '"Find meat on bones"', a poem which goes beyond 'And death' in dramatising the interrelatedness of all life. By the time of the fourth and final notebook, begun in mid-August 1933, we find Thomas extending the scope of his new style on a weekly, sometimes almost daily, basis. On 6 September he wrote 'Before I knocked', and a month later came 'The force that through the green fuse'. Over the winter of 1933–34 the notebook records brilliant lyric after brilliant lyric, and in April 1934 he ended it with 'I see the boys of summer' and 'If I were tickled by the rub of love'; poems of Shakespearean richness, written in a sensuous, modernist Metaphysical style. It was one of the most astonishing periods of growth on record of any poet since Keats's *annus mirabilis* over a century before.

18 Poems

Thomas's self-sufficiency and precocious development can make him seem an isolated figure. But as well as Trick and his political circle, he was active in local theatre and one of the group of Swansea artists and friends now known as the 'Kardomah Gang'. From September 1933 he was also in contact with another aspiring young writer, Pamela Hansford Johnson, who lived in London. Thomas's many letters to Johnson, written between late 1933 and late 1934, the product of a friendship which briefly became a love affair, shed much light on the evolution of his unique style, and reveal his deter-mination to establish himself on the poetry scene. His first London publication, 'And death', appeared in the *New English Weekly* in May 1933. Poems appeared in *Adelphi* and the *Sunday Referee* in September, and the *Referee* was also the outlet for 'The force that through the green fuse' on 29 October 1933, Thomas's calling card to literary London. In 1934, he consolidated his position with poems in *New Verse*, the *Listener* and Eliot's *Criterion*. On 22 April 1934, 'The force that through the green fuse' was judged the best poem the *Referee* had published in the preceding year, the prize being sponsorship of a poetry collection. Thomas gave this first volume, *18 Poems*, as much cohesion as possible by choosing thirteen of its poems from the fourth notebook. The 'black bomb', as Glyn Jones called it, was duly published on 21 December 1934. Thomas had recently moved to the capital to see it through the press, and stayed on – albeit the 'ragged life' he lived in London meant he would still sometimes return to Swansea to recuperate in the following year or two.

18 Poems was a success among poetry-lovers, who generally welcomed the return of Jacobean colour, concrete imagery and rhythmical vigour to the English lyric in such a compelling form. Most, however, were mystified as well as impressed, because his work seemed completely unlike other poetry of the time. And although the Bible, Joycean wordplay, Blake, Donne and Freud were rightly noted as influences, the poems' vitalism was often misread as adolescent in the negative sense, rather than it being understood that the poems used adolescence to explore the human condition more generally. Similarly, the rapid leaps of imagery were often attributed to automatic writing. This confusion was articulated by reviewers such as Louis MacNeice, who felt the 'cumulative effect' of the 'nonsense images . . . is usually vital and sometimes even seems to have a message', and that it was 'wild and drunken speech, but with the saving grace of rhythm'. (Strange as it now seems, the poems' regular syllable and rhyme schemes were usually missed.) But, using the notebooks, and the letters to Johnson and Thomas's Swansea friends, it is possible to discern the logical structure of the poetry, and to trace its development in this most formative period.

The process poetic

What contemporary reviewers needed, and what Thomas's readers still need, is some idea of the vision of the world he developed in his poems (and equally remarkable short stories) in 1933 and 1934. By the early 1940s critics had begun to define what this was; and the label that was eventually settled on, following Ralph Maud's study of 1962, was 'process', a word Thomas himself used in a poem of February 1934, 'A process in the weather of the heart'. The process vision is basically a belief in the unity of the universe, and the fact that it is subject to continuous change, manifested as a force of simultaneous creation and destruction active in all objects and events. The idea harks back to ancient beliefs and the panthe-ism of the Romantics, re-read in the light of modern discoveries in biology, physics and psychology. Thomas was au fait with the popular science of his time, having read Julian Huxley, Sigmund Freud and Alfred North Whitehead, the Stephen Hawking of his day, who had described his own 'philosophy of process' in 1920.

According to the 'process' view of the world, we are not merely born to die, or even know that we are dying as we live; conception itself is a death, 'the golden shot' of semen 'Storms in the freez-ing tomb' of the womb. The embryo dies in being born into the world, and elbows other beings into the grave; but their deaths are, conversely, 'entrances' into the life of decay and re-entry into the natural cycle. Thomas horrifyingly compresses what is ordinarily drawn out, as if in some time-lapse film, while continually contract-ing and expanding a poem's scale of reference from the microscopic to the cosmic. Fusing zygotes 'unwrinkle in the stars', 'clocking tides' pulse in the blood, manifesting the amoral 'force' which surges through the universe, and to which everything must submit. Linear time is yet another illusion; for Thomas it is as relative as anything else, and he finds equivalence between conception, gestation, ado-lescence and death in poems such as 'From love's first fever'. From cosmic flux to quantum foam, the only certainty is that there is no certainty: even energy is matter, matter energy, and time and space are spacetime.

A good guide to Thomas's poetic is William Blake's statement that 'Without contraries is no progression' from *The Marriage of Heaven and Hell*: life and death, dark and light, growth and decay, are all implicit and ceaselessly active within each other, and the role of poetry is therefore to present process as a 'progression' by such 'contraries', collapsing boundaries and continuously making over one state, or thing, into another. Poetry must reveal process by stripping away the illusory nature of reality, with the awareness that matter largely consists of a subatomic void, that the stable ego is a fiction, and that the hormonal soup of the blood mocks our pre-tensions to free will. This is why Thomas's poems have little use for the socio-political and sociological surfaces that preoccupy the

Audenesque poets, or for their irony and cerebralism. His is not a poetry of liberal humanism, but of agonising paradox. Contradictory states, as 'And death' showed, must be asserted with equal force, not moralised away. In 'I see the boys of summer', for example, 'the dogdayed pulse / Of love and light bursts in their throats', but 'bursts' is radically ambiguous. Is it aneurism or ecstasy, rupture or rapture? The context allows not just either / or, but both / and, deliberately exceeding the bounds of well-bred compromise. This is why the poetry focuses on precisely those points of human existence where process is most obviously at work – antenatal existence, dream, sex and death. Thomas's Egyptian, Welsh and Christian symbolic shorthand can make this seem odd, but in reality it is just a more hectic, pared-back version of the philosophies of recurrence used by other, older modernist writers, such as W. B. Yeats or James Joyce.

Bodies, sex, the Gothic-grotesque

Another aspect of Thomas's 'process' is the notion of the microcosm. As poems such as 'Ears in the turrets hear' show, Thomas felt cosmos, body and consciousness were linked, *were* each other, in some essential way. He informed Trevor Hughes that he hoped 'to prove beyond doubt to myself that the flesh that covers me is the flesh that covers the sun, that the blood that goes up and down in my lungs is the blood that goes up and down in a tree'. Such biomorphic mappings resemble the visual art of the time more than anything in English literature; the 'things of light' in 'Light breaks where no sun shines', for example, can be usefully likened to the protoplasmic blobs that crawl across paintings by André Masson, Hans Arp and Joan Miró. Bodies were central to Thomas's work because Welsh Nonconformism repressed them so severely. Like D. H. Lawrence, also from a Nonconformist background (the same revolt having taken place in England a generation before), Thomas placed sex at the heart of his work – or, to be more precise, what repression had done to sex. This is the source of poems such as 'Our eunuch dreams', which deal with onanism and sexual fantasy. However, Thomas is not limited by his own local circumstances;

one of the triumphs of his poetry is that it raises the struggle with the miseries of repression to a mythic, archetypal plane, making it part of a more universal struggle against determinism and towards self-knowledge.

The determinism the poetry wrestles with had a social content too, and Thomas incorporated this theme in a deeper sense than the poets who simply used pylons or aircraft to symbolise modernity. We find this in the cyborg overlappings of flesh and machine so common in the early poems, in their unsettling organic–inorganic compounds – 'mechanical flesh', 'oil of tears', 'brassy blood', 'petrol face', and so on – which touch on fears similar to those explored in Huxley's *Brave New World* or Chaplin's *Modern Times*. In focusing on the body so relentlessly, the poems also register the increase in control over bodies, most frighteningly apparent in the political violence and mass rallies of the totalitarian states. (As war loomed closer, in the later 1930s, many other writers would use imagery drawn from the body, the one irreducible constant of human existence, in order to express the hope for human survival: Thomas was ahead of the curve on this.) The almost medieval sense of mortality and 'fevered corporeality' of his poems of the time was personal – in September 1933 Jack Thomas was diagnosed with cancer of the mouth, which was treated, successfully, by inserting radium-tipped needles into the tumour. However, Thomas's Gothic-grotesque, repellent version of the body was chiefly a protest against the larger forces of control, and can be linked to William Empson's observation that his 'chief power as a stylist [is] . . . to convey a sickened loathing which somehow at once (within the phrase) enforces a welcome for the eternal necessities of the world'.

In a thematic sense the blood, bones, nerves, skulls, worms, mandrakes, Cadaver, vivisectionists, witches and psychopaths of his early poems and stories were drawn from favourite writers, such as John Webster and Caradoc Evans, and from the horror films the young Dylan had lapped up at the local flea-pit in the Uplands; a fan of *Dracula*, *Frankenstein* and *The Curse of the Mummy*, he could recite chunks of James Whales's *The Old Dark House* by heart. Rather than mere morbidity, these elements constitute a knowing form of Celtic Grand Guignol, a critique of Welsh society. Tony

Conran has noted, 'Modernism in Wales is most at home with the grotesque', and Thomas's monstrosities were an appropriately lurid outing of the deformed imaginings created by Nonconformist repression, as well as a counterblast to the bloodless hygiene, the denial of the messiness of the body and its suffering, in the work of the Audenesque poets.[3] But primarily they spoke of the terror and exaltation of being alive in a young body between two world wars. Thomas was as aware as his Swansea friends of the Wales of 'stubborn bankrupt villages, the children scrutting for coal on the slagheaps, the colliers' shabby allotments, the cheapjack cinema, the whippet-races, the disused quarries, the still pit-wheels'. His rebellion against this world did not take realist form but, as R. George Thomas noted, many readers understood that 'the febrile grotesqueness' and 'nightmare quality in the drift towards Hitler's War' were more accurately mirrored in his work than in that of other, more ostensibly realist writers of the time. '"The force that through the green fuse" was accepted as a . . . realization of unknown sources of physical suffering that must lie ahead of us, most probably in gas warfare or Guernica-like devastation. None felt uneasy about the macabre images . . . but all detected the mixed attitudes of confident exhilaration and wry acceptance of fate that were conveyed, without intellectual resolution, in the poem's tone and rhythm.'[4]

Twenty-five Poems

In 1935, Thomas developed his process style in even more radical and elaborate forms, in poems such as 'Now', 'Altarwise by owl-light' and 'I, in my intricate image'. Writing these densely intricate works slowed his output down by comparison with the winter of 1933–34. However, he was eager to consolidate the success of *18 Poems* as quickly as possible. He therefore turned back to the pre-process poems in his notebooks, hastily assembling *Twenty-five*

3 Tony Conran, *Frontiers in Anglo-Welsh Poetry*, Cardiff, University of Wales Press, 1997, p. 113.
4 R. George Thomas, 'Dylan Thomas and some early readers', in *Poetry Wales: A Dylan Thomas number*, 9:2 (Autumn 1973), p. 12.

Poems for publication in July 1936. Most reviewers of the collection welcomed what they saw as a movement away from obscurity towards the simplicity of poems such as 'I have longed to move away', unaware that these had been written before the work in *18 Poems*. The reviews were mixed, like the book itself, but one in particular had the effect of putting Thomas on the map in an even bigger way than *18 Poems* had. It was by Edith Sitwell, a leading national reviewer, and it appeared in the *Sunday Times*. Sitwell's advocacy of Thomas generated a large correspondence on modern poetry in the Letters page over the next two months, and his reputation rose from coterie *succès d'estime* to that of minor *cause célèbre*.

Religion

Although Sitwell did not mention it, one way in which *Twenty-five Poems* differed from *18 Poems* was in its greater use of biblical and religious material, as shown by poems such as 'This bread I break', 'Altarwise' and 'Incarnate devil'. Thomas's use of Christian allusion has led some to describe him as a religious poet in the traditional sense, one who wrestles with questions of faith and doubt. Although the first claim is untenable, the second is true enough; the relationship between the two might be said to be encapsulated in Thomas's claim, to John Malcolm Brinnin, that his poems were written 'in praise of God by a man who doesn't believe in God' (a more ambiguously accurate form of a similar statement in the 'Note' to the *Collected Poems* of 1952 [Appendix 5]). Thomas stated that process 'is the simplicity of religion', and in *Twenty-five Poems* he considers his religious inheritance from the viewpoint of process, subsuming it within its creative-destructive 'force'. Process now supplants religion, taking on its sacred status; its agents or indicators – time, snow, water, etc. – are often endowed with religious qualities. However, if he did not believe in an afterlife, Thomas did not feel that science had disproved what he called 'the kingdom of the spirit' either. He was fascinated with faith and the rhetoric of faith, and felt, like Blake, that rationalism easily became presumptuous: however much the phenomena of the universe are explained, the universe itself can never be *wholly* explained. Human beings can never be fully understood either, and the mystery of death cannot be argued away. In this sense, Thomas was a Metaphysical poet, fond of posing paradoxical questions ('What colour is glory?'); Christianity, which traditionally dealt with such existential issues, had therefore to be reinterpreted, its 'green myths' viewed through the lens of process.

Thomas's treatment of religion may owe something to the only figure of eminence in his family tree, his great-uncle Gwilym Thomas, a crusading Unitarian minister and minor poet whose bardic name Marles ('Marlais') was given to Dylan and his sister Nancy as a middle name.[5] There are several similarities between Thomas's take on Christianity and Unitarianism: for example, Unitarians believe in one God who is the primary power of the universe, but not in original sin, damnation and hell, miracles, the Trinity, virgin birth, predestination or the absolute truth of the Bible. They reject the doctrine of atonement, too; this meant that Jesus was not divine, nor the son of God except in a metaphorical sense, and his significance was to have realised, in an exceptional way, the potential for moral goodness innate in all human beings. But suggestive as the similarities are, Thomas's iconoclasm exceeds what any religious denomination would tolerate. The poems present Jehovah as a cruel, tyrannical patriarch, whose jealousy and remoteness were responsible for the Fall and Christ's crucifixion; guilty, according to 'Before I knocked' and 'Incarnate devil', of making Satan and Christ suffer for his own failures. 'Altarwise', likewise, blasphemously intertwines Thomas's own biography with that of Jesus, overcoming his castration by the official churches in a blatantly sexual way: Christ as 'stiff', the cross as 'rude, red' phallus. Even so, as 'Ceremony After a Fire Raid' puts it, 'the legend / Of Adam and Eve is never for a second / Silent in my service'; Christianity is what Thomas thinks with, even if his religious imagery is ambiguous and non-moralistic. Christ symbolises human potential, and Judgement Day represents the day of our death and re-immersion in process, no more or less.

5 For a fascinating account of the possible Unitarian influence on Dylan Thomas, see M. Wynn Thomas, *In the Shadow of the Pulpit: Literature and Nonconformist Wales*, University of Wales Press, Cardiff, 2010.

Language

The tougher poems in *Twenty-five Poems* were a reminder of Thomas's daring and unorthodox use of language in *18 Poems*: 'I, in my intricate image', for example, offered a verbal density which might daunt any reader, while some poems, such as 'Now', were regarded by many as mere nonsense verse (although they are, in fact, construable). As with religion, the reasons for this difficulty lie in process. If, Thomas reasoned, everything in the universe was subject to process, then his poems and the language they were written in must be too. And this meant that, rather than simply *describing* process, they would have to embody it in their syntax and verbal textures. Form and content must be one. This belief lies behind the one poetic principle Thomas would repeat throughout his life – that poetry should work 'from words', not 'towards' them (Appendix 1). Unlike most poets, who start with an idea or anecdote for which they then find words, Thomas felt the poet must develop a poem from an originating 'lump of texture or nest of phrases', as his friend Vernon Watkins called it, 'creat[ing] music' with his material, 'testing everything by physical feeling, working from the concrete image outwards'. One image produced other, contrary images, in what Thomas described to Henry Treece in a letter of 1938 as his 'dialectical' composition technique, an amoeba-like multiplication of image-cells which fought and multiplied, each containing 'the seed of its own destruction' (Appendix 2).

As well as having multiple centres, Thomas's poems try to apply process to language itself in the form of wordplay. The tendency of words to slip, slide and suggest others was crucial to Thomas because it revealed that language itself is not a fixed system but inherently changeable, subject to process. This is why, unlike many poets, Thomas didn't regret that words elude our attempts to tie them strictly to concepts or things. On the contrary, he revelled in and exploited the mismatch, and the surpluses this produces – he loved the fact that 'up to his ears' can become 'up to his tears', that 'capsized' has three different meanings, that he could take the 'v' out of 'drives' to make 'dries', revealing a contrary sense. For Thomas, poems ought to be a critical mass of words undergoing fission, with linguistic meltdown just held at bay by the rhymes, lines and stanzas inserted into the glowing core. Indeed, he deliberately created unstable verbal situations in order to be able to bring them under control.[6] And because he regarded language as a thing, he didn't just use concrete images, but made words palpable, using rhythm, stress and sonic repetitions to replicate the pulsions of the human body: breathing, walking, digestion, gestation, sex. Thomas wanted to evoke the pleasure we take in words as infants, before we know what they mean, and tried to get his word-music to reconnect us with that point in the past where pleasure and meaning overlapped (Appendix 4). He was not unaware of the risks, however; poems such as 'Especially when the October wind' dramatise the dangers, showing how his relish for language could push him to the point of feeling, as he admitted to Watkins, that he was just 'a freak user of words, not a poet'. As ever with Thomas, the swagger and bardic tone tell only half the story.

Surrealism

Such anxiety was at its greatest in 1935–37, as Thomas pursued his process poetic to its logical outcome. Poems such as 'Hold hard, these ancient minutes' and 'How soon the servant sun' confirm the accuracy of Watkins's description, 'symmetrical abstracts'; poems that try to do with words what musical compositions do with notes, and abstract paintings with paint. For many, they were (and are) a step too far – which is a pity, since English poetry of the time had nothing which stretched and explored its medium to a comparable degree (for an equivalent, one has to wait for the early work of Frank O'Hara and the New York School poets in the 1950s). After Thomas sent a batch which included the first six 'Altarwise' sonnets to Dent's, his new publisher, in October 1935, his editor,

6 'Grief thief of time', for example, originally had a standard grammatical form, with commas after 'grief' and 'time' in its opening line. Thomas removed these in order to make it possible to construe both 'grief' and 'thief' as adjective and noun; this meant that the poem enacted the interactions and fluidity of process more thoroughly, if at considerable cost to its transparency.

Richard Church, told him that he had detected the 'pernicious' influence of surrealism, which he 'abhorred', and baulked at publication. Thomas, with tongue firmly lodged in cheek, responded by denying any knowledge of surrealism, and refused to drop the poems. Church eventually gave way: 'I have decided to put myself aside and let you and the public face each other. I am accordingly taking steps to have the book set up in type.' It is possible to see what Church means, and even sympathise, without agreeing with him. Thomas was, in fact, up to his neck in surrealism: active in the International Surrealist Exhibition in London in the summer of 1936 (he toured the galleries with a tray asking visitors whether they would like a cup of boiled string, 'Weak, or strong?'), he was a friend of Max Ernst, Roland Penrose and other surrealist painters, and happy to read his poems alongside the French surrealist Paul Éluard. When we encounter the Daliesque scenarios of some of his poems, such as the opening of 'When, like a running grave', with its 'scythe of hairs' and 'turtle in a hearse', his denial becomes laughable.

Why, then, did he make it? Because, as we can now see, he did not want his conscious and highly crafted poetry to be associated with the merely automatic writing to which British public opinion had reduced surrealism. The real issue is what *kind* of surrealist Thomas was, not whether he was one. And the answer is that he was of the less well-known 'deep', or verbal, kind. Freud had described the ego as an ongoing struggle, or process, occurring between the id and the superego, with puns, jokes, verbal slips and wordplay revealing the inner workings of the mind. Thomas saw that this continual creation and de-creation of the self in language had implications for the lyric 'I'. He explained to Henry Treece how he wrote by 'mak[ing] one image, – although "make" is not the word, I let, perhaps, an image be "made" emotionally in me – ', and the very hesitancy of his account enacted, as much as it described, the imagination vacillating between conscious choice and the unconscious prompting prized by surrealists (Appendix 2). The writing of James Joyce in *Finnegans Wake* is the closest contemporary equivalent of Thomas's verbal surrealism (a kind which, with its Anglo-Welsh roots, can rightly be called 'surregionalism'). But by 1937, after two years of this style, Thomas realised he could take it no further: 'In the Direction of the Beginning' is its swansong. Having already complained to Watkins of suffering from 'crabbed' experimentalism and 'mad parody', Thomas now sought an escape from the impasse.

Changing styles: The Map of Love

The change in Thomas's style coincided with his marriage, in July 1937, to Caitlin Macnamara, whom he had met just over a year before in the Wheatsheaf pub in Fitzrovia. At the time they met, Caitlin was a companion-cum-mistress to the artist Augustus John; unlike Thomas, she was a genuine bohemian, intelligent, strong-willed, adventurous, and sharing his artistic interests. Their marriage was at first a very happy one, and in 1938 the couple moved to the Welsh seaside town of Laugharne, located in an area where an Anglo-Welsh literary colony was starting to establish itself around the journal *Wales*. Their first child, Llewelyn, was born in January 1939. But the outbreak of war, in September, dashed the hopes of a future in Wales. Work dried up, and the couple finally left Laugharne in 1941 under a cloud of debt, beginning a peripatetic existence which would last until their return in 1949.

It was during this first stay in Laugharne that Thomas assembled his third collection, *The Map of Love* (1939) (which also included seven of his early short stories), and wrote the short story collection *Portrait of the Artist as a Young Dog* (1940). In the latter he registers the recoil from extreme verbal densities; indeed, many of the *Portrait* stories are critiques of his earlier self, written in the comic, heightened realist style we recognise from Thomas's letters and conversation. The change in his poetry was less marked, but clearly discernible. *The Map of Love* included pieces as dense as those of the mid-1930s, such as 'It is the sinners' dust-tongued bell'; but others, such as 'After the funeral', written in spring 1938, revealed a new, more transparent, style. The second poem is an elegy for his aunt Ann Jones, who had died in 1932, and Thomas described it as his first poem about another human being. It works by setting up, then puncturing and finally reinflating its rhetoric, in order to redeem the emblems of Ann's dry piety, the stuffed fox and stale fern, with the pagan, loving force which she also possessed. 'Once it was the colour of saying', written later in 1938, formally announces this change in style but in typically ambiguous terms (the later poems would be more 'colourful' than their predecessors, not less). Both poems reflect the search for a more flexible, mobile style, and more varied subject matter than before. As well as poems written for Caitlin, there are several for the unborn Llewelyn, in which we find a tenderness new to Thomas's work. Both Caitlin and Llewelyn, or the prospect of Llewelyn, impelled Thomas to some of his finest work: although rather neglected today, 'How shall my animal', 'A saint about to fall', 'For Caitlin' (both versions) and 'Into her lying down head' are large-scale, ode-like lyrics in the most demanding forms, and contain some of his greatest poetry.

Deaths, Entrances and the Second World War

Neither of these two books, which form a stylistic 'hinge' in Thomas's career, did well, being published so close to the outbreak of the war. But the imminence of the conflict had propelled Thomas to the position of the leading young British poet. Auden's departure for the USA in early 1939 coincided with the publication of the New Apocalypse anthology, the manifesto of a group of Thomas's contemporaries who took their cue from him in fusing neo-Romanticism, mythopoeia and modernism. Thomas kept himself at arm's length from his acolytes, just as he met the declaration of hostilities with a less sublime, conflicted blend of facetiousness, comic bluff and mounting panic; attempting to organise a writers' forum to counter jingoism, he told one correspondent that he was going to 'declare myself a neutral state, or join up as a small tank'. His poor physical condition saved him from conscription, but it could not dissipate the nightmares of 'burning birdmen', invasion and silencing which now ensued. As a pacifist he declared 'my great horror's killing', but he was also a 'mental militarist', morally outraged by the Total War fought by the Allies as well as by Nazi barbarism, and given to provoking fights in pubs with off-duty servicemen who boasted of killing Germans. (After one such altercation, in 1944, a drunken SOE officer machine-gunned the bungalow in New Quay in which Thomas and his family were living.)

The poetry itself seemed to stumble uncertainly at this time, perhaps as a result of this moral queasiness as much as the stylistic gear-change Thomas was engaged in. 'When I woke' and 'Once below a time' are slightly awkward poems, groping towards the more shapely-syllabic 'The hunchback in the park' of a couple of years later. But it is one of the most admirable aspects of Thomas's poetry that he continued to develop, never repeating successes, abandoning a form after devising it, continually moving on. Nor was it just the war which disturbed him; 'Deaths and Entrances', 'On a Wedding Anniversary' and 'Into her lying down head' suggest that martial conflicts exacerbated marital ones, tracking as they did the flare-ups in his marriage to Caitlin. Passion, intrigue, jealousy and betrayal, real and imagined, were mapped on to the threatened territories of 'burning England' and 'many married London', while 'Love in the Asylum' takes 'asylum' in both its senses, as 'a haven' and 'a place for the deranged'.

These poems were created during the first period of Thomas's wartime poetry-writing, running from 1939 to 1941; a second began in spring 1944 and lasted until summer 1945. The gap has been explained by the fact that Thomas started writing film scripts in September 1941, his first regular paid employment since 1932. However, it is no coincidence that both periods coincide with the two main periods of the Blitz on British cities. Thomas's primary response to the war was one of moral outrage and profound shock at the violence inflicted on innocent and defenceless non-combatants. As the war continued, the figure of the burning child, simply a Gothic device in 'The Burning Baby', a story of 1936, became symbolic of the ultimate conceivable horror. It is the subject of Thomas's two greatest Blitz elegies, 'Ceremony After a Fire Raid' and 'A Refusal to Mourn the Death, by Fire, of a Child in London', the first attempting to find some consolation for the dead child by prophetically invoking a surge of sexuality and fecundity; the second more sombre and less tinged with the 'Blitz sublime', incorporating, with immense tact, allusions to the Holocaust. The reference to the 'long dead child' of memory in 'Poem in October', ostensibly a birthday lyric, suggests that in his wartime poems of childhood reminiscence,

Thomas was not just lamenting his own vanished childhood, or the actual deaths of children; the pathos in these poems, as in 'Fern Hill', lies in the death of the very idea of childhood.

At the same time, the war also ushered in a profound social revolution, and Thomas's work needs to be seen in relation to its effects on the arts in general. The 'hovel' and 'slum' torched by apocalyptic-regenerative fire in 'Ceremony' echo the themes of his film scripts, which urged post-war urban reconstruction ('New Towns for Old'), and helped create the climate that led to the Labour victory of 1945. Thomas was friendly with many artists in other media, and his work followed the broader impulse to adapt modernism to articulate the nation's wartime experience, as apparent in Graham Sutherland's paintings of Blitzed Silvertown or Michael Tippett's *A Child of Our Time* as in his own work. Henry Moore's famous drawings of those sheltering in London Tube stations (reproductions of which the Thomases pinned up on the walls of their Chelsea flat) also exemplify this trend, and like Moore's drawings Thomas's poems treat the child, living or dead, as the symbolic buried 'seed' of hope for a better future.

Faced with the atrocities of the era, and tempered by growing maturity, Thomas came to present the depredations of process in a mellower form in his wartime poems. The difference between the first and second wartime periods of poem-writing are well illustrated by the contrast between the priapically phantasmagoric 'Ballad of the Long-legged Bait' of 1941 and the erotic, calmly transcendent 'A Winter's Tale' of 1944, the two long narrative poems in *Deaths and Entrances* (1946), Thomas's fourth collection. Process is almost always negative in the early poems – 'I sit and watch the worm beneath my nail / Wearing the quick away', as 'Here, in this spring' puts it – but Thomas's vision of change grew more benign in wartime. 'The time dying flesh' is now cherished, and spawning and dying are accepted as necessary parts of the life-cycle, even as graced by a kind of heroic seediness. Faced with the ever-present danger of annihilation, the 'immortal hospital' of the sexual body is celebrated. The emotional amplitude of the poetry is greater, too; as the verbal textures grow less dense, ever more complex webs of subtle variation are woven. As John L. Sweeney noted, the 'meat-eating sun' of 'Twenty four years' of 1938 is a benevolent figure by the time of 'Holy Spring' in 1945, 'the visible father of the world, the dying and resurrected redeemer', its allusions bent towards rebirth as 'the father is reborn in the son' – and in the daughter, too, we might add, since Aeronwy Thomas had been born in 1943.

This mellower, humorous Thomas was even more apparent in the radio broadcasts which he began making for the BBC in 1943, and which would give him a modicum of national fame. As the war ended, and the womb and tomb coordinates of process were uncannily realised in the new Welfare State's promises of care 'from the cradle to the grave', Thomas looked like a writer who had made the transition from war to peace exceptionally well.

The later career: In Country Heaven

Thomas's later poetry begins with 'Poem in October' and 'Fern Hill' and their search for lost innocence, often realised in pastoral form. For nearly two years after 'Fern Hill', however, Thomas wrote no poems at all; then, in spring 1947, he produced the 'In Country Heaven' fragment. This was the touchstone for a projected sequence of poems which were to have been linked by 'In Country Heaven', as he hinted in a broadcast of September 1950 (Appendix 3). The sequence was to have formed a retrospective imagining of the joys and sorrows of the earth by its former inhabitants, following the atomic extinction of the planet. Thomas never completed the project, but three of its parts, with 'Lament', 'Do not go gentle' and 'Poem on his Birthday' (which may or may not have been intended for it), were published in the USA as the chapbook *In Country Sleep* for his second visit there, in 1952. Whatever the viability of the project, the individual poems it gave rise to are some of Thomas's most satisfying, and show once again his ability to reinvent himself. From 'A Winter's Tale' onwards, he had increasingly woven English pastoral poetry – allusions to Hardy, Arnold, Keats, Wordsworth, Meredith, Coleridge and others abound – into poems with ostensibly Welsh locations. It may be that his confidence in dealing with the canon became greater as his own work edged towards inclusion within it; certainly, he was deliberately, mischievously setting his poems on the border between the English and Anglo-Welsh traditions, undermining assumptions about belonging and identity.

Several of Thomas's champions present his career as that of a prodigal son: according to this, he suffered the 'capital punishment' of London (as he jokingly termed it), slowly learnt the error of his modernist ways, and returned to embrace realism, roots and community, in rural south-west Wales. But this is far from the truth; or, rather, is only a part of the overall picture. The later poems may be read, like so many before them, on several levels. On the one hand, they exude a strong sense of locale. But looked at closely, they are not so much poems of place (although we can take them as such if we wish) as poems that make us consider the place of 'place' in poetry, with their locations subtly adjusted to suit aesthetic rather than topographical ends. The 'sea wet church' in 'Poem in October', for example, cannot be the actual church in Laugharne, which is a mile inland. The beautiful, tenderly apocalyptic 'In the White Giant's Thigh', a proto-feminist elegy for its barren women, complexly interweaves the landscapes of Carmarthenshire-situated, but English-speaking, Laugharne with the Dorset-located, but Celt-created, figure of the Cerne Abbas giant.

All of this suggests the subtlety in the simplicity of the later works, which Derek Mahon has seen as the 'crowning glory' of Thomas's career. Certainly, their pastoral imagery is given an intenser glow, an eerie radiance from the threat of nuclear war in them – obviously in 'Over Sir John's hill', with its patrolling, bomber-like 'hawk on fire', and in 'Poem on his Birthday' with its 'rocketing wind'. Yet, as against this, 'In the White Giant's Thigh' has the spirit of one of Breughel's great bucolic panoramas of haymaking and feasting, and its gusto partakes, as *Under Milk Wood* does more obviously, of the carnivalesque energies of popular culture. As the later songs and verses also show, Thomas found himself completely at home in this milieu; there was serious talk of writing a radio comedy with Ted Kavanagh, one of the writers of the hit comedy show *I.T.M.A.* (*It's That Man Again*), and *Under Milk Wood*, with its utopian fantasy spiced with end-of-the-pier innuendo, lies on a spectrum somewhere between *The Goon Show* and *The Archers*. Thomas was a pioneer in interweaving (and to some extent eroding the barriers between) 'high-', 'middle-' and 'low-brow' cultures; he had the popular touch, and his various audiences instinctively understood that he did not patronise them, or stand on his reputation. It is revealing that, by the early 1950s, he was probably the only poet who had not only run the gamut of most literary forms (if we include his unfinished novel *Adventures in the Skin Trade*), but had also successfully worked in all available mass media forms – radio, feature and documentary film, LP record and even television (the two programmes he made for the BBC do not, alas, survive).

However, the years leading up to his death were increasingly difficult ones for Thomas; they saw the disintegration of his marriage to Caitlin, who was increasingly unwilling to be a domestic drudge while he spent his time in London watering-holes, or to tolerate his infidelities. At the end of 1952 came the death of his beloved father, so memorably marked in 'Do not go gentle into that good night'. To this was added the strain of three demanding American tours (with over 150 dates), his drink problem and tax difficulties (though these were caused by sheer incompetence rather than avoidance). The stress of holding writing and performing career together combined with a reckless disregard for his physical welfare to fatal effect in New York, in October 1953, on his fourth American tour. Whether Thomas would have continued to write poetry, had he lived, no one can say – although one suspects that the fascinating diffusion of his lyric gift into other forms and genres would have continued. In a sad yet somehow appropriate final irony, he had been due, after finishing his work in New York, to fly out to California, where he was to collaborate with Igor Stravinsky on an opera libretto; set after a nuclear war, it would have featured a boy and a girl who would, like Adam and Eve, begin all over again the task of inventing language and naming the world around them.

Conclusion

Dylan Thomas today is something of an anomaly. His popular reputation means that almost everyone has heard of him, but critics and poets are unable to quite say what his significance might be. Beyond a small number of poems and radio pieces, he is paradoxically almost unknown. And yet this is not just because he is seen, these few exceptions apart, as a 'difficult' poet. Until a generation ago, Thomas was better understood than he is today, and, once a few basic points about his vision and his poetry are grasped, most of what he wrote can be understood and enjoyed. The real stumbling block to this happening is institutional, and has to do with the fact that including him in the canon would threaten the dominant sense of what British poetry is and ought to be.

This is because his hybridity means that Thomas straddles British poetry's internal fault-lines, thrown up at the time of *The Waste Land* and still not fully acknowledged. Before today's cultural nationalism, when the idea of 'British' poetry still made sense, when anomalies and modernistic trends were not so actively sidelined, there was a space for his poetry. But the fault-lines became entrenched positions, and this makes it difficult to ask the kinds of question Thomas's poetry raises. They include: to what extent should poems work from, or towards, words? Is the speaking self in poetry fixed or multiple? How radical can poetry be if it has a conservative attitude to language? And beyond these lie others about the presumed centrality of Auden to the 1930s, or whether 1940s poetry is really as bad as it is said to be, or whether today's poetry world, as represented by metropolitan poetry publishers, national competitions and festivals, is too narrowly drawn. This is not just a problem for the mainstream poetry world. 'Alternative' poets also tend to look down on Thomas, partly because of his alleged selling-out to the entertainment industry. While Thomas himself mocked many of the mainstream poets of his time, he found the heroic myth of modernism suspect too; he did not set himself up as the judge of official structures, and in choosing 'the Rimbaud of Cwmdonkin Drive' as a title he poked fun at the self-styled avant-garde as well as himself.

Not that this should bother new readers overmuch, of course. It's enough to know that Thomas's poetry is a fabulous and strangely undervalued treasure, and that now is possibly the most exciting time to be reading it. Equipped with an accurate sense of his subtlety and an ethical regard for word and world, it is possible to see a renewed, powerful relevance in his poetry. Thus, Thomas's insistence on the body, and a poetry that 'comes to life out of the red heart through the brain', matches the recent rejection of behaviourism, and our modern, holistic sense of the inseparability of mind and body.[7] As the first great elegist of civilians under bombardment, Thomas is also a poet of the present, his work fit for mourning the dead of 'Shock and Awe' Baghdad, Fallujah and Homs as much as those of Swansea, Coventry and London during the Blitz. In his later pastoral masterpieces, which cherish the natural world in the face of the threat of nuclear weapons, he is one of the first and finest of our 'green' poets. In a world ever more monitored, increasingly more confined by authoritative plain style and micro-managerial jargon, his insistence on the anarchic pleasures of the signifier and the transformative power of poetry keeps alive the hope that language can be reclaimed from those who wish to subordinate it to purely instrumental ends. And, finally, Thomas is a poet who challenges the empirical and anecdotal basis of much British poetry, Welsh as well as English – one of the handful who, in an increasingly interconnected world, keeps it on the map. Superficially, he may seem to belong to a small, wet corner of Wales, the 'hymnal blob' with which he had an ambivalently affectionate relationship; but in reality, and however unwittingly, he was a great internationalist. He was the last British poet to have a significant impact on American poetry, the first to shine a spotlight on West African literature (in a famous *Observer* July 1952 review of Amos Tutuola's *The Palm-Wine Drinkard*), a poet appreciated by Paul Celan and admired by Tristan Tzara. His work has the generosity of spirit and the stature that accrue only to a poetry of genuine risk – it is a 'fire of birds in / The world's turning wood' – and exemplifies the nerve and verve which this ancient 'craft or sullen art' will need if it is to thrive in the twenty-first century.

Poem selection, previous editions and annotations

This centenary edition of the collected poems, verse and songs of Dylan Thomas aims to provide a more comprehensive and more varied selection of his work than has appeared before in a single

7 Dylan Thomas, *Early Prose Writings*, ed. Walford Davies, Dent, London, 1971, p. 165.

volume. Just over half of the items in it derive from the five collections Thomas published during his lifetime, which he collected in the 1952 edition of the *Collected Poems*. These ninety-one poems have been augmented by the poem Walford Davies and Ralph Maud added to their *Collected Poems 1934–1953* (1988), 'Paper and Sticks', which was published in Thomas's fourth collection, *Deaths and Entrances*, but which he left out of the 1952 *Collected* after having 'the horrors of it' at the last minute. Like Davies and Maud, I also include the two unfinished poems Thomas was working on at the time of his death – 'In Country Heaven' and 'Elegy' – although I have placed the original, longer version of 'In Country Heaven' in the body of the text, and the revision in the note to it. Taking inspiration from the other existing edition, Daniel Jones's *The Poems* (1971), I have added all the poetry, verse and songs I feel are worth including from other published texts – *The Notebook Poems 1930–1934* edited by Ralph Maud (twenty-nine poems); the short stories (three pieces of juvenilia and 'In the Direction of the Beginning'); the *Collected Letters* (eight poems); *Letters to Vernon Watkins*, ed. Vernon Watkins ('Poem [To Caitlin]'); *The Death of the King's Canary* (four of its eleven parodies); verses from the radio broadcast *Quite Early One Morning*; the verse film script *Our Country* and a verse passage from the film script *Wales – Green Mountain, Black Mountain*; songs, verses and a short passage from *Under Milk Wood*; six journal-published poems not collected by Thomas; *Letter to Loren*, edited by Jeff Towns, and the 'Redonda' verses. Many of these items were not included in the Jones edition or Davies and Maud. I have also included manuscript material, verses from the Veronica Sibthorpe Collection at the National Library of Wales, and the hitherto unpublished 'Song' (1951?), made known to me in September 2013, and included here with grateful thanks to its owner, Mr Fred Jarvis. I have been able to consult, and briefly quote from, variant and draft passages of poems held at the Harry Ransom Center Library at the University of Austin, the Special Poetry Collection at the Lockwood Memorial Library at the State University of New York in Buffalo, and at the British Library. The poems are all arranged in chronological order of composition as far as can be determined.

The idea of promiscuously mingling Thomas's different kinds of poetry in this way is in order to shed new light on it. The *Collected Poems* now sets the modernist ambition of poems such as 'Light breaks where no sun shines', with its grave and elliptical cadences, alongside the mocking, careerist sense of modernism of 'A Letter to my Aunt'; it allows a comparison of the two 'limit-texts' 'In the Direction of the Beginning' and 'I make this in a warring absence', and their astonishing textual-sexual journeys; it lets us see, for example, just how the lyrical impressionism of the film script for *My Country* is echoed in the apocalyptic, elegiac fervour of 'Ceremony After a Fire Raid'. This helps the reader gain important insights into how the poetry worked, feeding off itself, tackling similar problems and experiences in different ways. We also, perhaps, discover something of how Thomas himself worked, and felt about his work. However, to understand my selection more fully, it is necessary to briefly say something about its three predecessors, Thomas's own *Collected Poems 1934–1952* (1952), Jones's *The Poems* (1971) and Davies and Maud's *Collected Poems 1934–1953* (1988).

The 1952 edition simply assembles Thomas's five published collections. In a prefatory 'Note' he claimed it contained 'most of the poems I have written, and all, up to the present year, that I wish to preserve' (Appendix 5). The no-frills approach was adopted because Thomas was short of time and under stress; in the summer of 1952 his marriage was on the rocks, his father was dying, he was under pressure to finish *Under Milk Wood* and he was beset by money problems. As it was, he spent two months writing his verse 'Prologue' (which is one reason why the Note is so perfunctory). The book's ninety-one poems include almost all of his best, but less than a third of those in existence. This was made abundantly clear in 1967 when Ralph Maud published *Poet in the Making*, an edition of the four notebooks, previously accessible only to scholars, which Thomas had kept between April 1930 and April 1934. They contained 232 poems, and proved that not only were the notebooks the source of most of *18 Poems* (1934) but also of over twenty poems distributed across *Twenty-five Poems* (1936), *The Map of Love* (1939) and even *Deaths and Entrances* (1946), some reworked into completely different poems, others almost unchanged.

Daniel Jones's edition of 1971, *The Poems*, was a response to this. It offered a fuller sampling of Thomas's poetry, adding seventy-four poems from the notebooks and elsewhere. Crucially, given the revelations about Thomas's extensive use of the notebooks, it arranged the poems in chronological order of composition. A far better sense of Thomas's poetic range was given and also, for the first time, a sense of exactly how his work had evolved, and of the relationship between individual poems. Yet Jones was not an academic, and his edition did not have a proper editorial apparatus.

At the end of the 1980s, Dent replaced *The Poems* with two paperback volumes, the *Collected Poems 1934–1953* (1988) and a revised paperback edition of Maud's *Notebooks of Dylan Thomas* of 1967, *The Notebook Poems* (1989). All the notebook poems were now available, rather than just a selection of them, in paperback. But the *Collected Poems* itself reverted to the contents of the 1952 edition. Although the fifty or so notebook poems Jones had included were transferred to the other volume, the rest of his additional poems, two excepted, were dropped. Davies and Maud also reverted to the 1952 edition's non-chronological ordering. The advantage of their edition was its impeccable scholarly apparatus, which established definitive texts, gave punctuation, spelling and other variants, and publication histories.

Like the *Notebook Poems*, its companion volume, *Collected Poems 1934–1953*, is still essential reading for scholars. But as well as lacking the poems Jones had included from the stories, journals and letters, its abolition of chronology prevented readers from following Thomas's poetic development. Although a major advance on Jones, the annotations could be patchy, over-biographical, and they reflected only one critical viewpoint. Davies and Maud's case against Jones, which charged him with including 'trivial' poems and cited Thomas's 'all . . . I wish to preserve' claim, is also less than convincing today; criteria which applied decades ago are not binding on later editors, and certainly not in the case of a text for the general reader who may not wish to buy nine or ten more books and pamphlets in order to get hold of Thomas's other poems.[8]

8 Walford Davies and Ralph Maud, 'Concerns about The Revised New Directions Dylan Thomas', *P. N. Review*, 31:2 (November–December 2004), p. 67.

Davies and Maud's charge that Jones's chronological ordering made it difficult to know where some of the revised notebook poems fit in is more compelling. Even so, it is hard to see what any editor can do except follow his own informed judgement on this question. There is no absolutely objective way of determining the issue, and it seems to me that the benefits of chronological arrangement far outweigh its pitfalls. In this edition I have used, of necessity, a range of the potential responses to the issue, dealing with each poem pragmatically on a case-by-case basis. The original version of 'How shall my animal', for example, has been included (as one of the best very early notebook poems) as well as the later, quite different poem Thomas made of it. On the basis of the amount of revision Thomas carried out, I decided that 'Not from this anger' should move to its date of revision, in January 1938, whereas 'We lying by seasand' should stay in its original place in the third notebook. 'O make me a mask' and 'The spire cranes' move for the same reason as 'Not from this anger', while 'Foster the light', revised two or even three times after entering the fourth notebook in February 1934, appears at the date of its most substantial revision, in late summer/early autumn 1934. Details are given in the Notes for each poem affected in this way. For those who are interested, Thomas's (and Davies and Maud's) own arrangement of the *Collected Poems* may be found in Appendix 6. And, as my discussion suggests, in this edition I have adopted Jones's catholic, flexible approach to selection and arrangement, while aiming for Davies and Maud's high editorial standards.

Finally, how does one annotate Thomas's poems? In doing so, it is hard not to recall his own claim that 'I don't want to give the reader crutches, I want to give him a push'. Thomas's poems often seem designed to defeat paraphrase – in fact, this is an essential aspect of several of them. In his first three collections, even poem titles are spurned because they were felt to pre-empt the unmediated encounter between reader and poem Thomas desired. Yet Thomas also wanted his poems to be understood – 'craftsmen don't put their products in the attic', he once observed – and it is a fundamental assumption of this edition that annotation has a duty to recuperate the gist of past explications. In doing so, I have taken into account the substantial amount of work done on Thomas since the last *Collected Poems* – archive material and editions of the broadcasts and film scripts have been published, a DVD of the films issued, and new critical approaches, including those of feminism, Marxism and post-structuralism, have been brought to bear on Thomas's work for the first time.

For each poem, the dates and details of composition, first publication and book publication are given first. (It can be assumed that all poems published in individual collections appeared in the previous three editions, and that all notebook poems appeared in Maud's edition of the notebooks.) Editing or rewriting details then appear (since the priority in this edition has been to include the maximum number and range of poems, variant passages and poems will be included in a future *Companion*).[9] A brief account of the poem follows, followed in turn by line-by-line glosses of terms, cruxes, allusions, minor textual variants, puns, and so on. The most disturbing kinks in syntax and sense created by delayed and disguised verbs, appositive clauses, ambiguous punctuation, and so on, are also glossed.

Nicholas Moore claimed as early as 1948 that Thomas's poetry was 'almost silly with allusion', but allusion in his work is particularly difficult to spot, especially in the early poems, because it is concealed by context. Thomas has a habit of wrenching his materials sharply from their original contexts, although whether to strike a blow at authority or to avoid the pretentiousness of parading it is difficult to determine; whatever, the way allusion is used is part of what it is saying to us. Shakespeare – *Hamlet* in particular – furnishes the early poems with the devices of soliloquy and riddling speech, images of rotten states, suicide, sexual frustration and ghostly doubles. Other favourite poets include Blake, Lawrence, Donne, Herbert, Owen and Whitman, while less obvious ones – Stevens and Fulke Greville, for example – may be detected, as well as the odd prose writer, such as Sir Thomas Browne. The point is not the identification of all of these, so much as to suggest the layered richness out of which the work emerges, an indication of the considered

9 John Goodby, *Discovering Dylan: A Companion to the Centenary Collected Poems*, University of Wales Press, Cardiff, 2016.

nature of the poems, and Thomas's awareness of the criticism of Eliot and Empson, and their readings of the Metaphysical poets in particular. The elusive allusiveness of most of the poems is what explains the disconcerting sense of great originality and familiarity we often get when reading Thomas's poetry; a feeling that his voice is murmurous with other voices just beyond the horizon of identification. With the change in his poetry from 1938 on, Thomas drew other elements into his intertextual mulch, among them Djuna Barnes's novel *Nightwood*, while after 1944 we find a more overt form of allusion, often to 'smoother' and more canonical English poets than hitherto. In several of his final poems, Thomas uses a kind of homeopathic pastiche, conjuring up other poets, but in an idiom that remains entirely his own. 'Lament' and 'In the White Giant's Thigh', for example, remind us that Thomas told Watkins that he thought Yeats was the best poet of the century, and that his favourite was Thomas Hardy.

Note on the text

The text of the poems is based on that of *Collected Poems: 1934–1953* (1988), *Poet in the Making* (1968), *The Complete Screen Plays* (1995), *Under Milk Wood* (1995), *Letters to Vernon Watkins* (1957), *The Notebook Poems* (1989), *The Broadcasts* (1991), *The Collected Letters* (2000), *Collected Stories* (1993), and *Dylan Thomas & Redonda* (2003). Where possible, all poems have been checked against manuscript holdings and variants, and with each of the individual collections of Thomas's poems: *18 Poems*, *Twenty-five Poems*, *The Map of Love*, *Deaths and Entrances* and *In Country Sleep*. This paperback version of the new centenary edition also corrects errors in previous editions, and in its own earlier printings.

Table of Dates

1914

27 October: birth of Dylan Marlais Thomas at 5 Cwmdonkin Drive, Swansea, the second child of Florence and D. J. ('Jack') Thomas.

1925

December: Thomas's first published poem appears in the *Swansea Grammar School Magazine*, to which he will henceforth contribute regularly.

1927

14 January: first poem to be published in a newspaper, 'His Requiem', in the *Western Mail* (in 1971 this will be shown to be the work of Lillian Gard, purloined by Thomas from the *Boys' Own Paper*). A poem, 'The second best', appears in the *Western Mail* in February.

28 July: poem 'If the Gods had but given' also published in the *Western Mail*.

1929

10 October: two lines from a poem Thomas submits to a competition are quoted in the journal *Everyman*.

December: essay 'Modern Poetry', displaying wide acquaintance with contemporary poetry, is published in the school magazine, which Thomas now co-edits.

1930

27 April: starts the first of the four surviving notebooks into which

he will fair-copy his best poems until April 1934.

1931

July: leaves school and starts work as a reporter for the *South Wales Evening Post* in Swansea. Joins the Swansea Little Theatre, to which his older sister Nancy also belongs, acting in productions in the Swansea area over the next three years.

1932

16 December: leaves his job with the *Evening Post*.

1933

18 May: publication of 'And death shall have no dominion' in *New English Weekly* – his first appearance in a national poetry journal.

7 June: listed as one of twenty-eight winners (of 11,000 contestants) in a BBC poetry competition, with 'The Enchanted Isle' (now lost), broadcast on 28 June.

August: visits London to make literary contacts and place work with journals.

3 September: 'That sanity be kept', his first publication in the 'Poet's Corner' of the *Sunday Referee*. A letter of enquiry about the poem from Pamela Hansford Johnson begins one of Thomas's most important correspondences (Appendix 1).

29 October: 'The force that through the green fuse' published in the *Referee*.

October: his answers to a *New Verse* questionnaire published (Appendix 4).

1934

Visits London, trying to establish himself by contributing poems, short stories and reviews to *New Verse*, *Criterion* and other leading journals.

14 March: publication of 'Light breaks where no sun shines' in the

Listener prompts enquiries to the editor from T. S. Eliot.

22 April: wins 'Poet's Corner' annual prize, publication of a poetry collection.

10 November: moves to London, where he shares rooms with Swansea artist-friends Mervyn Levy and Fred Janes.

21 December: publication of *18 Poems*.

1935

Meets numerous literary figures and artists, but in March returns to Swansea briefly to recuperate; meets Vernon Watkins. Positive reviews of *18 Poems* in the *Listener*, *Morning Post*, *Spectator*, *TLS*, *Time and Tide* (Desmond Hawkins), *New Verse* (by William Empson). Spends time at cottage in Derbyshire owned by A. J. P. Taylor and his wife, Margaret Taylor, later his patron.

July/August: at Glen Lough, County Donegal, with Geoffrey Grigson, editor of *New Verse*; works on 'Altarwise' sonnets.

1936

Early April: introduced to Caitlin Macnamara by Augustus John.

8 April–20 May: living in Cornwall; has brief affair with Wyn Henderson before returning to London and beginning affair with Caitlin.

11 June: attends the opening of the International Surrealist Exhibition at the New Burlington Galleries in London.

26 June: poetry reading with Paul Éluard.

10 September: *Twenty-five Poems* published by Dent. Review by Edith Sitwell in the *Sunday Times* confirms his reputation as the leading poet of the post-Auden generation.

1937

January/April: affair with the US novelist Emily Holmes Coleman. 'We lying by seasand' chosen by W. H. Auden and Michael Roberts for English issue of *Poetry* (Chicago), Thomas's first US publication.

13 February: gives paper on 'Modern Poetry etcetera' at Cambridge.

21 April: first BBC recording, 'Life and the Modern Poet'.

April/May: brief affair with the artist Veronica Sibthorpe.

June: first issue of *Wales*, edited by Keidrych Rhys, features Thomas's story 'Prologue to an Adventure' on its cover.

11 July: marries Caitlin Macnamara at the Register Office in Penzance, Cornwall.

1 September: moves from Cornwall to live with his parents.

1 October: moves to his mother-in-law's house at Blashford, in Hampshire.

1938

23 March: letter explaining 'my dialectical method' to Henry Treece (Appendix 2).

April: moves from Blashford to his parents' house and then (in May) to Laugharne, Carmarthenshire. These will be their main homes for the next three years.

18 October: takes part in 'The Modern Muse', a BBC radio broadcast from Manchester, with W. H. Auden, C. Day Lewis, Louis MacNeice and others.

November: *Poetry* (Chicago) awards him its Oscar Blumenthal Prize.

1939

30 January: first child, Llewelyn, born at Poole, Dorset.

24 August: *The Map of Love* published by Dent; war declared on 3 September means the book is largely ignored.

20 December: *This World I Breathe*, selected poetry and prose by Thomas, published by New Directions Press in New York – his first US book.

1940

4 April: Dent publish *Portrait of the Artist as a Young Dog*, a collection of short stories.

6 April: registers for military service, and is turned down on medical grounds. Begins occasional freelance scriptwriting for the BBC; leaves Laugharne and moves, with Caitlin and Llewelyn, to the house of his friend John Davenport, at Marshfield in Gloucestershire. Collaborates with Davenport on the satirical novel *The Death of the King's Canary*.

24 September: US edition of *Portrait of the Artist as a Young Dog* published.

December: the Thomases leave Marshfield for Thomas's parents' house in Bishopston.

1941

April: agrees to sell the four 1930–34 notebooks, plus additional mss, to Bertram Rota, a London bookseller acting for the Lockwood Memorial Library, State University of New York at Buffalo. Works on novel, *Adventures in the Skin Trade*; abandoned after four chapters.

May/June: first Blitz ends; stops writing poetry. The Thomases live at various addresses in the capital, 'Blaencwm', the family-owned cottage in Carmarthenshire where his parents have moved, and elsewhere.

September: starts work as scriptwriter for Donald Taylor's Strand Films.

November: reads to the English Club at Oxford University.

1942

June: trip to northern England to work on film about the arts; meets the actress Ruth Wynn Owen, with whom he conducts a year-long romance.

July: trip to Scotland on film work with Caitlin, visiting Glasgow's South Street Art Centre; meets Hugh MacDiarmid and W. S. Graham.

20 August: joins Caitlin and Llewelyn in Talsarn, Cardiganshire, later moving to a flat in Chelsea. Talsarn, with other places in West Wales, is the main family base for the next two years.

1943

7 January: 'Reminiscences of Childhood' recorded for BBC Welsh Home Service. Beginning of consistent broadcasting work, with Thomas making friends among BBC personnel and actors such as John Arlott, Louis MacNeice and Michael Redgrave.

25 January: *New Poems* published by New Directions in New York.

3 March: daughter, Aeronwy, born in London.

1944

February: family moves to Bosham in Sussex to escape the 'Baby Blitz' of January–May 1944.

April: release of *Our Country*. Starts writing poetry again.

4 September: family moves to New Quay in Cardiganshire – the main model, with Laugharne, for the town of Llareggub in *Under Milk Wood*.

14 December: records *Quite Early One Morning*, a forerunner of *Under Milk Wood*, for the BBC Welsh Home Service.

1945

6 March: 'Majoda Incident', in which a bungalow containing Thomas and others is machine-gunned by a drunken off-duty soldier, the husband of a friend.

July: leaves New Quay, living in London until early 1946.

6 December: records 'Memories of Christmas' for BBC Welsh Service Children's Hour. Thomas is now a regular reader for the BBC.

1946

7 February: *Deaths and Entrances* published by Dent, to acclaim; beginning of Thomas's national reputation and appeal. Spends four days in St Stephen's Hospital, London, being treated for alcoholic gastritis.

April: the Thomases move to a summerhouse in the garden of Margaret and A. J. P. Taylor, at Holywell Ford, Oxfordshire; until May 1949 they live in or near Oxford.

13 May: reads 'Fern Hill', Lawrence's 'Snake' and Blake's 'The Tyger' at a Royal Command Performance at Wigmore Hall.

August: visits Ireland with Caitlin and friends.

Autumn: BBC Third Programme launched; Thomas in demand as actor, presenter and writer.

8 November: *Selected Writings* published in the US.

1947

10–12 February: in Swansea to research the BBC broadcast 'Return Journey', one of his finest radio features.

April–August: with his family, Thomas visits Italy funded by a Society of Authors award. Probably begins *Under Milk Wood*.

1948

Writing feature films for Gainsborough Films (*Rebecca's Daughters*, *The Beach at Falesá* and *Me and My Bike*; after 1948 film work falls off sharply).

1949

4–9 March: attends an artists' conference in Prague at the invitation of the Czech cultural attaché in London.

May: the Thomases move to the Boat House, Laugharne, bought for and rented to them by Margaret Taylor.

28 May: accepts invitation to visit the US on a lecture tour from

John Malcolm Brinnin, the director of the Poetry Center in New York City.

24 July: birth of third child, Colm.

1950

20 February–31 May: first US tour.

September: in London meets Pearl Kazin, with whom he had an affair in the US; Margaret Taylor reports their liaison to Caitlin, increasing the strain on the Thomases' marriage.

1951

8 January–14 February: visits Persia to write a documentary film script for the Anglo-Iranian Oil Company (the film is never made). Completes 'Lament', 'Poem on his Birthday' and 'Do not go gentle'. Gives the answers to student questions which form the so-called 'Poetic Manifesto' (Appendix 4).

1952

15 January: with Caitlin, sets sail on the *Queen Mary* on second US tour.

February: *In Country Sleep* published in a US-only edition. Thomas makes his first recordings for Caedmon Records.

16 May: the Thomases return to Britain from the US. Works on *Under Milk Wood* and proofs for his *Collected Poems*, writing a verse 'Prologue' and prefatory prose Note (Appendix 5).

10 November: *Collected Poems 1934–1952* published by Dent; acclaimed by Philip Toynbee in the *Observer* and Cyril Connolly in the *Sunday Times*. The UK edition alone sells 30,000 copies.

16 December: D. J. Thomas dies, aged seventy-six.

1953

20 January: receives the 1952 William Foyle Poetry Prize.

31 March: US edition of *Collected Poems* published by New Directions.

16 April–3 June: third US tour. Thomas's sister Nancy dies, in India, while he is en route to the US.

14 May: directs first performance of *Under Milk Wood*, at the Poetry Center in New York. Publication of his film script of *The Doctor and the Devils* in book form. Begins affair with Liz Reitell.

23 May: meets Igor Stravinsky in Boston to discuss collaboration on an opera.

August: records 'The Outing' for BBC television broadcast.

19 October: begins fourth US tour.

24 October–3 November: at the Chelsea Hotel, New York City. Despite drinking bouts, he is accompanied and supported by Reitell, and partly fulfils his obligations to rehearse *Under Milk Wood* (24 and 25 October); he takes part in symposium 'Poetry and Film' (28 October) and gives a reading (29 October). But he is ill and prone to mood swings.

4 November: ill and in pain from gout and gastritis, and possibly pneumonia, he is given three injections. After the last, half a grain of morphine sulphate, he falls into a coma and is taken to St Vincent's Hospital, where his condition deteriorates.

7 November: Caitlin Thomas flies to New York.

9 November, 12.40 p.m.: death of Dylan Thomas.

24 November: buried at St Martin's Church in Laugharne.

1982

1 March: memorial plaque laid in Poets' Corner, Westminster Abbey.

1995

Opening of Ty Llên, the Dylan Thomas Centre, Wales' national literature centre, in Swansea.

The lost poem:
A Dream of Winter ❧

Introduction to 'A Dream of Winter'

'A Dream of Winter' is not, strictly speaking, an unknown poem by Dylan Thomas, nor is it an unpublished one. However, it was 'lost' in the sense that it was almost completely forgotten and has never before been published as part of a collection. It is briefly footnoted by Paul Ferris in the *Collected Letters*, glossing a reference by Thomas in his letter to John Sommerfield of 6 January 1942: 'Glad you liked my winter verses, very quickly produced from my tame Swinburne machine'. As Ferris notes, Thomas was referring to this poem, then just published in the January 1942 issue of the journal *Lilliput*. But no one has ever acted on that cue, and 'A Dream of Winter' has been out of print since 1942. I myself only learnt of its existence earlier this year, thanks to my former teacher, Allan Wilcox.

Allan, a colleague of Peter Hellings (the dedicatee of this edition) in the 1970s, acted as an executor of Peter's estate following his death in 1994, and received as a thanks-offering from Peter's widow, Manon Hellings, a first edition of *Deaths and Entrances*, chosen from Peter's book collection. Inside it he discovered the carefully torn-out and folded pages containing the poem and its accompanying photographs. When he was given my *Collected Poems* twenty years later, for Christmas 2014, he naturally looked for 'A Dream of Winter'. Finding it was missing, he contacted me, generously sending me a copy of the poem and the fruits of his efforts to locate the relevant issue of *Lilliput* in the British Library.

Lilliput was a popular journal in the Forties, specialising in photojournalism and picture features, and Thomas wrote for it on more than one occasion. 'A Dream of Winter' was commissioned in late 1941 to accompany eight photographs of winter scenes, with Thomas producing tercets to go under each, all eight combining to make a complete poem. The feature is introduced by this short paragraph: 'Out of thousands of winter pictures we chose these eight because they seemed to us to have a curious dreamlike quality.

We showed them to the young poet, Dylan Thomas, and asked him if he would like to write some verses to go with them. Here are the pictures and here is his poem.'

The pictures, in sequence, show: a crescent moon over a semi-wooded hillside; a man standing on a frozen lake, about to hack at it with an axe; a steam-breathing polar bear on an icicle-fringed promontory in a zoo (Thomas, naturally, puns on the constellation); three men descending a misty hillside at night; a frost-etched classical statue of a half-draped female figure in a park; a canal between factories, reflecting a distant light; three alpinists ascending a glacier; and a man holding an umbrella standing in snow beside a busy, slushy London street. The photographers, among the best-known of the time, are credited as Brandt (1, 4 and 5), Fox (2 and 6), Darchan (3), Brassai (7) and Glass (8).

As so often, Thomas was being over-modest in describing one of his own poems. Although no masterpiece, 'A Dream of Winter' is a well-wrought and haunting work, which not only plays imaginatively with the images it was written to accompany, but stands as a beautiful lyric in its own right. In addition, it has stylistic and historical significance, replacing 'The hunchback in the park' as the last lyric Thomas wrote before the gap between the poems of the early war years and those of 1944–45. Its mesmeric weave anticipates those poems, and 'A Winter's Tale' in particular; indeed, it would not be too fanciful to see in 'A Dream of Winter' a trial run for that major work.

Swansea, 2015

A Dream of Winter

Very often on winter nights the halfshaped moonlight sees
Men through a window of leaves and lashes marking gliding
Into the grave an owl-tongued childhood of birds and cold trees,

Or drowned beyond water in the sleepers' fish-trodden churches
Watching the cry of the sea as snow flies sparkling, riding,
The ice lies down shining, the sandgrains skate on the beeches.

Often she watches through men's midnight windows, their winter
    eyes,
The conjured night of the North rain in a firework flood,
The Great Bear raising the snows of his voice to burn the skies.

And men may sleep a milkwhite path through the chill, struck still
    waves
Or walk on thunder and air in the frozen, birdless wood
On the eyelid of the North where only the silence moves,

Asleep may stalk among lightnings and hear the statues speak,
The hidden tongue in the melting garden sing like a thrush
And the soft snow drawing a bellnote from the marble cheek,

Drowned fast asleep beyond water and sound may mark the street
Ghost-deep in lakes where the rose-cheeked nightingale glides like
    a fish,
The Ark drifts on the cobbles, the darkness sails in a fleet,

Or, lying down still, may clamber the snow-exploded hill
Where the caverns hide the snowball's ivory splinter,
Fossil spine of the sea-boned seal, ice-print of pterodactyl.

Oh birds, trees, fish and bears, singing statues, Arkfloods and seals
Steal from the sleeper awake as he waits in the winter
Morning, alone in his world, staring at the London wheels.

The Poems ☙

Poems from 'The Fight'

i. Frivolous is my hate

Frivolous is my hate,
Singed with bestial remorse
Of unfulfilment of desired force,
And lust of tearing late;

Now could I raise   5
Her dead, dark body to my own
And hear the joyous rustle of her bone
And in her eyes see deathly blaze;

Now could I wake
To passion after death, and taste   10
The rapture of her hating, tear the waste
Of body. Break, her dead, dark body, break.

ii. Warp

Like suns red from running tears,
Five suns in the glass,
Together, separate yet, yet separately round,
Red perhaps, but the glass is as pale as grass,
Glide, without sound,   5
In unity, five tears lid-awake, suns yet, but salt,
Five inscrutable spears in the head,
Each sun but an agony,
Twist perhaps, pain bled of hate,
Five into one, the one made of five into one, early   10
Suns distorted to late.
All of them now, madly and desolate,
Spun with the cloth of the five, run
Widely and foaming, wildly and desolate,
Shoot through and dive. One of the five is the sun.   15

iii. The Grass Blade's Psalm

The frost has lain,
Frost that is dark with flowered slain,
Fragilely strewn
With patches of illuminated moon,
About my lonely head in flagged unlovely red.　　　　5

The frost has spake,
Frost secretive and thrilled in silent flake,
With unseen lips of blue
Glass in the glaze stars threw,
Only to my ears, has spake in visionary tears.　　　　10

The frost has known,
From scattered conclave by the few winds blown,
That the lone genius in my roots,
Bare down there in a jungle of fruits,
Has planted a green year, for praise, in the heart of my
　　upgrowing days.　　　　15

The frost has filled
My heart with longing that the night's sleeve spilled,
Frost of celestial vapour fraught,
Frost that the columns of unfallen snow have sought,
With desire for the fields of space hovering about my single
　　place.　　　　20

I know this vicious minute's hour

I know this vicious minute's hour;
It is a sour motion in the blood,
That, like a tree, has roots in you,
And buds in you.
Each silver moment chimes in steps of sound,　　　　5
And I, caught in mid-air perhaps,

Hear and am still the little bird.
You have offended, periodic heart;
You I shall drown unreasonably,
Leave you in me to be found
Darker than ever,
Too full with blood to let my love flow in.
Stop is unreal;
I want reality to hold within my palm,
Not, as a symbol, stone speaking or no,
But it, reality, whose voice I know
To be the circle not the stair of sound.
Go is my wish;
Then shall I go,
But in the light of going
Minutes are mine
I could devote to other things.
Stop has no minutes, but I go or die.

10

15

20

I, poor romantic, held her heel

I, poor romantic, held her heel
Upon the island of my palm,
And saw towards her tiny face
Going her glistening calves that minute.
There was a purpose in her pointed foot;
Her thighs and underclothes were sweet,
And drew my spiral breath
To circumambulate for decency
Their golden and their other colour.
The band was playing on the balcony.
One lady's hand was lifted,
But she did not cry, 'I see;
I see the man is mad with love.'
Her fan burst in a million lights
As that her heel was lifted,
Gone from my palm to leave it marked

5

10

15

With quite a kind of heart.
She is on dancing toes again,
Sparkling a twelve-legged body
And many arms to raise 20
Over her heel and me.
I, poor romantic, contemplate
The insect on this painted tree.
Which is the metal wing
And which the real? 25

How shall the animal

How shall the animal
Whose way I trace
Into the dark recesses
Be durable
Under such weight as bows me down, 5
The bitter certainty of waste,
The knowing that I hatch a thought
To see it crushed
Beneath your foot, my bantering Philistine?

I build a tower and I pull it down; 10
The flying bird's a feather,
Has no flesh or bone,
Carried by any wind to anywhere.

My senses see.
Speak then, o body, shout aloud, 15
And break my only mind from chains
To go where ploughing's ended.
The dancing women all lie down;
Their turning wheels are still as death;
No hope can make them glad, 20
Lifting their cheery bodies as before
In many shapes and signs,

A cross of legs
That Christ was never nailed upon,
A sea of breasts,   25
A thousand sailing thighs.

How shall the animal,
Dancer with lightest heel,
High bird
Who goes   30
Straight in a wingèd line
Beyond the air,
Horse in the meadow
With the plough for toiling,
A boy to call,   35
And all the shining ground to tread,
Woman and sloe,
Still dance, fly, labour, be,
When sense says stop?
Purpose is gone;   40
I try to hold, but can't,
Compress, inflate, grow old,
With all the tackle of my certain magic
Stone hard to lift.

To-day, this hour I breathe

To-day, this hour I breathe
In symbols, be they so light, of tongue and air,
The now I have space
And time that is already half
More than that I tell you in,   5
I have divided
Sense into sight and trust.
The certain is a fable.
Oh, iron bird, you are not credited
But fly, against joy, for that is not   10

If sea is rare
That does not imitate
Boy with the voice, or timpani,
The same, you likable machine.
As well, creature has no flesh   15
And does not try the sun with seeing,
But measures his own length on a wall,
And leaves his shell
A butterfly before the chrysalis,
A flying egg of inhibition.   20
My she loves me is easy prey
For moving down another shaft,
Up to the hilt in going-backs,
And here, upon a hand,
A hundred years are by me cut.   25

Rain cuts the place we tread

Rain cuts the place we tread,
A sparkling fountain for us
With no fountain boy but me
To balance on my palms
The water from a street of clouds.   5
We sail a boat upon the path,
Paddle with leaves
Down an ecstatic line of light,
Watching, not too aware
To make our senses take too much,   10
The unrolled waves
So starred with gravel,
The living vessels of the garden
Drifting in easy time;
And, as we watch, the rainbow's foot   15
Stamps on the ground,
A legendary horse with hoof and feather,
Impatient to be off.

He goes across the sky,
But, when he's out of sight, 20
The mark his flying tail has left
Branches a million shades,
A gay parabola
Above a boat of leaves and weeds.
We try to steer; 25
The stream's fantastically hard,
Too stiff to churn with leaves,
A sedge of broken stalks and shells.
This is a drain of iron plants,
For when we touch a flower with our oar 30
We strike but do not stir it.
Our boat is made to rise
By waves which grow again
Their own melodious height,
Into the rainbow's shy embrace. 35
We shiver uncomplainingly,
And taste upon our lips, this minute,
The emerald caress,
And breath on breath of indigo.

if the lady from the casino

if the lady from the casino
will stop the flacillating roof
de paris and many women from my thinking
over the running bannisters
who can tell I may be strong enough 5
to push the floor away with a great gesture
but for the navels and the chandelabra
mending my coloned head in hands
And are you parallel in thinking good with me
Of us beneath the shepherd's crook 10
Driving the wolves away
And walking the metallic fields

An inch's time away with every step
Who has no hope
I know him for he lives in me   15
lady gap
they're there I see them
on railings and on pots of ferns
seeking a sex in me
beneath the nose   20
Iif its no beginning in our love
wise woman true for heat
it's no end to us
or even interlude between the abstract
and the side or shell   25
hindering my knuckles or my knife
our modern formula
of death to sense and dissolution
where there is love there's agony
Ttheres sex where our mad hands rest   30
. . ..
Of ever watching your light
Come to a point with mine
Your pity left me high and dry
For appetites aren't fed with
can they for ever   35
stop their navels with their finger tops
or
. . . .Bbranch off straight to nonsense narrow . . . . .
Hope ah I know it
one naked hand upon the bracket   40
out of the pages
would I blind in puberty the phrases
grow and here's a castle
Hope I knew him out of Rreason
Faith messiah for what death   45
though they do not speak like that in France;
But while I'm deft and aphrodisiac
To her who her the nought for my loud nerves

Not to the incubator or the brain
A mass of words above the window   50
Chiming for room
One brings you allonal
Which bells grotesque parade
Of leg on breast
And vomit on a shining cheek   55
Of masks *two* can't take off
But in its true light devil naturally
And let there be an end to
evil
I have an explanation   60
And what is more an egg
So with my mind's catastrophe
And white and yellow anna
Three has no message in his sin
And *four* a skull for tympani   65
Choked up with wit
The *rest* shall wait for not engendering
And I along the skin
Think of my passionate alloy
I cool who's chastity   70
now nothing yes loud purity
With
bawdy
Eyes and with the nerves' unrest
shatter the french   75
to let Old Seduced crowd on
over the hurdle of the belly de
through mercy to paris
I'll in a moment but my version's sane
space is too small   80
hover along the saxophone
and tread the mandoline a navel's length
the women on the ground are dead
who her don't care for clothes
and I no longer itch at every trouble   85

Never to reach the oblivious dark

Never to reach the oblivious dark
And not to know
Any man's troubles nor your own—
Negatives impress negation,
Empty of light and find the darkness lit—   5
Never is nightmare,
Never flows out from the wound of sleep
Staining the broken brain
With knowledge that no use and nothing worth
Still's vain to argue after death;   10
No use to run your head against the wall
To find a sweet blankness in the blood and shell,
This pus runs deep.
There's poison in your red wine, drinker,
Which spreads down to the dregs   15
Leaving a corrupted vein of colour,
Sawdust beneath the skirts;
On every hand the evil's positive
For dead or live,
Froth or a moment's movement   20
All hold the sum, nothing to nothing,
Even the words are nothing
While the sun's turned to salt,
Can be but vanity, such an old cry,
Nothing never, nothing older   25
Though we're consumed by loves and doubts.
I love and doubt, it's vain, it's vain,
Loving and doubting like one who is to die
Planning what's good, though it's but winter,
When spring is come,   30
The jonquil and the trumpet.

Being but men, we walked into the trees

Being but men, we walked into the trees
Afraid, letting our syllables be soft
For fear of waking the rooks,
For fear of coming
Noiselessly into a world of wings and cries.   5

If we were children we might climb,
Catch the rooks sleeping, and break no twig,
And, after the soft ascent,
Thrust out our heads above the branches
To wonder at the unfailing stars.   10

Out of confusion, as the way is,
And the wonder that man knows,
Out of the chaos would come bliss.

That, then, is loveliness, we said,
Children in wonder watching the stars,   15
Is the aim and the end.

Being but men, we walked into the trees.

Out of the sighs

Out of the sighs a little comes,
But not of grief, for I have knocked down that
Before the agony; the spirit grows,
Forgets, and cries;
A little comes, is tasted and found good;   5
All could not disappoint;
There must, be praised, some certainty,
If not of loving well, then not,

And that is true after perpetual defeat.

After such fighting as the weakest know,   10
There's more than dying;
Lose the great pains or stuff the wound,
He'll ache too long
Through no regret of leaving woman waiting
For her soldier stained with spilt words   15
That spill such acrid blood.

Were that enough, enough to ease the pain,
Feeling regret when this is wasted
That made me happy in the sun,
And, sleeping, made me dream   20
How much was happy while it lasted,
Were vaguenesses enough and the sweet lies plenty,
The hollow words could bear all suffering
And cure me of ills.

Were that enough, bone, blood, and sinew,   25
The twisted brain, the fair-formed loin,
Groping for matter under the dog's plate,
Man should be cured of distemper.
For all there is to give I offer:
Crumbs, barn, and halter.   30

Before the gas fades

Before the gas fades with a harsh last bubble,
And the hunt in the hatstand discovers no coppers,
Before the last fag and the shirt sleeves and slippers,
The century's trap will have snapped round your middle,
Before the allotment is weeded and sown,   5
And the oakum is picked, and the spring trees have grown green,
And the state falls to bits,
And is fed to the cats,

Before civilization rises or rots
(It's a matter of guts,   10
Graft, poison, and bluff,
Sobstuff, mock reason,
The chameleon coats of the big bugs and shots),
The jaws will have shut, and life be switched out.
Before the arrival of angel or devil,   15
Before evil or good, light or dark,
Before white or black, the right or left sock,
Before good or bad luck.

Man's manmade sparetime lasts the four seasons,
Is empty in springtime, and no other time lessens   20
The bitter, the wicked, the longlying leisure,
Sleep punctured by waking, dreams
Broken by choking,
The hunger of living, the oven and gun
That turned on and lifted in anger   25
Make the hunger for living
When the purse is empty
And the belly is empty,
The harder to bear and the stronger.
The century's trap will have closed for good   30
About you, flesh will perish, and blood
Run down the world's gutters,
Before the world steadies, stops rocking, is steady,
Or rocks, swings and rocks, before the world totters.

Caught in the trap's machinery, lights out,   35
With sightless eyes and hearts that do not beat,
You will not see the steadying or falling,
Under the heavy layers of the night
Not black or white or left or right.

Was there a time

Was there a time when dancers with their fiddles
In children's circuses could stay their troubles?
There was a time they could cry over books,
But time has set its maggot on their track.

Under the arc of sky they are unsafe.
What's never known is safest in this life.
Under the skysigns they who have no arms
Have cleanest hands, and, as the heartless ghost
Alone's unhurt, so the blind man sees best.

'We who were young are old'

'We who were young are old. It is the oldest cry.
Age sours before youth's tasted in the mouth
And any sweetness that it hath
Is sucked away'.

We who are still young are old. It is a dead cry,
The squeal of the damned out of the old pit.
We have grown weak before we could grow strong,
For us there is no shooting and no riding,
The Western man has lost one lung
And cannot mount a clotheshorse without bleeding.

Until the whisper of the last trump louden
We shall play Chopin in our summer garden,
With half-averted heads, as if to listen,
Play Patience in the parlour after dark.
For us there is no riding and no shooting,
No frosty gallops through the winter park.

We who are young sit holding yellow hands
Before the fire, and hearken to the wind.

No faith to fix the teeth on carries
Men old before their time into dark valleys   20
Where death lies dead asleep, one bright eye open,
No faith to sharpen the old wits leaves us
Lost in the shades, no course, no use
To fight through the invisible weeds,
No faith to follow is the world's curse   25
That falls on chaos.

There is but one message for the earth,
Young men with fallen chests and old men's breath,
Women with cancer at their sides
And cancerous speaking dripping from their mouths,   30
And lovers turning on the gas,
Exsoldiers with horrors for a face,
A pig's snout for a nose,
The lost in doubt, the nearly mad, the young
Who, undeserving, have suffered the earth's wrong,   35
The living dead left over from the war,
The living after, the filled with fear,
The caught in the cage, the broken winged,
The flying loose, albino eyed, wing singed,
The white, the black, the yellow and mulatto   40
From Harlem, Bedlam, Babel, and the Ghetto,
The Piccadilly men, the back street drunks,
The grafters of cats' heads on chickens' trunks,
The whole, the crippled, the weak and strong,
The Western man with one lung gone—   45
Faith fixed beyond the spinning stars,
Fixed faith, believing and worshipping together
In god or gods, christ or his father,
Mary, virgin, or any other.
Faith. Faith. Firm faith in many or one,   50
Faith fixed like a star beyond the stars,

And the skysigns and the night lights,
And the shores of the last sun.

We who are young are old, and unbelieving,
Sit at our hearths from morning until evening,   55
Warming dry hands and listening to the air;
We have no faith to set between our teeth.
Believe, believe and be saved, we cry, who have no faith.

Out of a war of wits

Out of a war of wits, when folly of words
Was the world's to me, and syllables
Fell hard as whips on an old wound,
My brain came crying into the fresh light,
Called for confessor but there was none   5
To purge after the wits' fight,
And I was struck dumb by the sun.
Praise that my body be whole, I've limbs
Not stumps, after the hour of battle,
For the body's brittle and the skin's white.   10
Praise that only the wits are hurt after the wits' fight.
The sun shines strong, dispels
Where men are men men's smells.
Overwhelmed by the sun, with a torn brain
I stand beneath the clouds' confessional,   15
But the hot beams rob me of speech,
After the perils of fools' talk
Reach asking arms up to the milky sky,
After a volley of questions and replies
Lift wit-hurt head for sun to sympathize,   20
And the sun heals, closing sore eyes.
It is good that the sun shine,
And, after it has sunk, the sane moon,
For out of a house of matchboard and stone
Where men would argue till the stars be green,   25

It is good to step onto the earth, alone,
And be struck dumb, if only for a time.

In wasting one drop

In wasting one drop from the heart's honey cells,
One precious drop that, for the moment, quells
Desire's pain, eases love's itch and ills,
There's less remains, for only once love fills,
When love's mouth knows its greatest thirst.   5
That great love, in its passion, demands all
The honey that man had at first
Before, unthinkingly, he shared its gold
With one and all, being love's child.
In those far days he was not very old   10
In love, knew little of love's wrong.
Wrong love took much, and when love's great mouth
    called,
In earnest from a woman's face,
Little there was to moisten of the honey hoard.

Their faces shone under some radiance

Their faces shone under some radiance
Of mingled moonlight and lamplight
That turned the empty kisses into meaning,
The island of such penny love
Into a costly country, the graves   5
That neighboured them to wells of warmth
(And skeletons had sap). One minute
Their faces shone; the midnight rain
Hung pointed in the wind,
Before the moon shifted and the sap ran out,   10
She, in her summer frock, saying some cheap thing,
And he replying,

Not knowing radiance came and passed.
The suicides parade again, now ripe for dying.

I have longed to move away

I have longed to move away
From the hissing of the spent lie
And the old terrors' continual cry
Growing more terrible as the day
Goes over the hill into the deep sea;   5
I have longed to move away
From the repetition of salutes,
For there are ghosts in the air
And ghostly echoes on paper,
And the thunder of calls and notes.   10

I have longed to move away but am afraid;
Some life, yet unspent, might explode
Out of the old lie burning on the ground,
And, crackling into the air, leave me half-blind.
Neither by night's ancient fear,   15
The parting of hat from hair,
Pursed lips at the receiver,
Shall I fall to death's feather.
By these I would not care to die,
Half convention and half lie.   20

See, on gravel paths under the harpstrung trees

See, on gravel paths under the harpstrung trees,
He steps so near the water that a swan's wing
Might play upon his lank locks with its wind,
The lake's voice and the rolling of mock waves
Make discord with the voice within his ribs   5
That thunders as heart thunders, slows as heart slows.

Is not his heart imprisoned by the summer
Snaring the whistles of the birds
And fastening in its cage the flowers' colour?
No, he's a stranger, outside the season's humour,   10
Moves, among men caught by the sun,
With heart unlocked upon the gigantic earth.
He alone is free, and, free, moans to the sky.
He, too, could touch the season's lips and smile,
Under the hanging branches hear the winds' harps.   15
But he is left. Summer to him
Is the unbosoming of the sun.

So shall he step till summer loosens its hold
On the canvas sky, and all hot colours melt
Into the browns of autumn and the sharp whites of winter,   20
And so complain, in a vain voice, to the stars.

Even among his own kin he is lost,
Is love a shadow on the wall,
Among all living men he is a sad ghost.
He is not man's nor woman's man,   25
Leper among a clean people
Walks with the hills for company,
And has the mad trees' talk by heart.

You, too, know the exceeding joy
And the triumphant crow of laughter.   30
Out of a bird's wing writing on a cloud
You capture more than man or woman guesses;
Rarer delight shoots in the blood
At the deft movements of the irises
Growing in public places than man knows;   35
There in the sunset and sunrise
Joy lifts its head, wonderful with surprise.
A rarer wonder is than man supposes.

See, on gravel paths under the harpstrung trees,

Feeling the summer wind, hearing the swans,   40
Leaning from windows over a length of lawns,
On level hills admiring the sea
He is alone, alone complains to the stars.
Who are his friends? The wind is his friend,
The glow-worm lights his darkness, and   45
The snail tells of coming rain.

The ploughman's gone

The ploughman's gone, the hansom driver,
Left in the records of the living a not-to-be-broken picture,
In sun and rain working for good and gain,
Left only the voice in the old village choir
To remember, cast stricture on mechanics and man.   5
The windmills of the world stand still
With wooden arms revolving in the wind
Against the rusty sword and the old horse
Bony and spavined, rich with fleas.
But the horses are gone and the reins are green   10
As the hands that held them in my father's time.
The wireless snarls on the hearth.
Beneath a balcony the pianola plays
Black music to a Juliet in her stays
Who lights a fag-end at the flame of love.   15
No more toils over the fields
The rawboned horse to a man's voice
Telling it this, patting its black nose:
You shall go as the others have gone,
Lay your head on a hard bed of stone,   20
And have the raven for companion.
The ploughman's gone, the hansom driver,
With rain-beaten hands holding the whip,
Masters over unmastered nature,
Soil's stock, street's stock, of the moon lit, ill lit, field and town, 25
Lie cold, with their horses, for raven and kite.

Man toils now on an iron saddle, riding
In sun and rain over the dry shires,
Hearing the engines, and the wheat dying.
Sometimes at his ear the engine's voice   30
Revolves over and over again
The same tune as in my father's time:
You shall go as the others have gone,
Lay your head on a hard bed of stone,
And have the raven for companion.   35
It is the engine and not the raven.
Man who once drove is driven in sun and rain.
It is the engine for companion.
It is the engine under the unaltered sun.

And death shall have no dominion

And death shall have no dominion.
Dead men naked they shall be one
With the man in the wind and the west moon;
When their bones are picked clean and the clean bones gone,
They shall have stars at elbow and foot;   5
Though they go mad they shall be sane,
Though they sink through the sea they shall rise again;
Though lovers be lost love shall not;
And death shall have no dominion.

And death shall have no dominion.   10
Under the windings of the sea
They lying long shall not die windily;
Twisting on racks when sinews give way,
Strapped to a wheel, yet they shall not break;
Faith in their hands shall snap in two,   15
And the unicorn evils run them through;
Split all ends up they shan't crack;
And death shall have no dominion.

And death shall have no dominion.
No more may gulls cry at their ears   20
Or waves break loud on the seashores;
Where blew a flower may a flower no more
Lift its head to the blows of the rain;
Though they be mad and dead as nails,
Heads of the characters hammer through daisies;   25
Break in the sun till the sun breaks down,
And death shall have no dominion.

Within his head revolved a little world

Within his head revolved a little world
Where wheels, confusing music, confused doubts,
Rolled down all images into the pits
Where half dead vanities were sleeping curled
Like cats, and lusts lay half hot in the cold.   5

Within his head the engines made their hell,
The veins at either temple whipped him mad,
And, mad, he called his curses upon God,
Spied moon-mad beasts carousing on the hill,
Mad birds in trees, and mad fish in a pool.   10
Across the sun was spread a crazy smile.
The moon leered down the valley like a fool.

Now did the softest sound of foot or voice
Echo a hundred times, the flight of birds
Drum harshly on the air, the lightning swords   15
Tear with a great sound through the skies,
And there was thunder in an opening rose.

All reason broke, and horror walked the roads.
A smile let loose a devil, a bell struck.
He could hear women breathing in the dark,   20
See women's faces under living snoods,

With serpents' mouths and scolecophidian voids
Where eyes should be, and nostrils full of toads.

Taxis and lilies to tinned music stept
A measure on the lawn where cupids blew   25
Water through every hole, a Sanger's show
Paraded up the aisles and in the crypt
Of churches made from abstract and concrete.
Pole-sitting girls descended for a meal,
Stopped non-stop dancing to let hot feet cool,   30
Or all-in wrestling for torn limbs to heal,
The moon leered down the valley like a fool.

Where, what's my God among this crazy rattling
Of knives on forks, he cried, of nerve on nerve,
Man's ribs on woman's, straight line on a curve,   35
And hand to buttock, man to engine, battling,
Bruising, where's God's my Shepherd, God is Love?
No loving shepherd in this upside life.

So crying, he was dragged into the sewer,
Voles at his armpits, down the sad canal   40
Where floated a dead dog who made him ill,
Plunged in black waters, under hail and fire,
Knee-deep in vomit. I saw him there,
And thus I saw him searching for his soul.

And swimming down the gutters he looks up   45
At cotton worlds revolving on a hip,
Riding on girders of the air, looks down
On garages and clinics in the town.

Where, what's my God among this taxi stepping,
This lily crawling round the local pubs?   50
It was November there were whizzbangs hopping,
But now there are the butt-ends of spent squibs.

So crying, he was pushed into the Jordan.
He, too, has known the agony in the Garden,
And felt a skewer enter at his side.   55
He, too, has seen the world as bottom rotten,
Kicked, with a clatter, ash-bins marked verboten,
And heard the teeth of weasels drawing blood.

And thus I saw him. He was poised like this,
One hand at head, the other at a loss,   60
Between the street-lamps and the ill-lit sky,
And thus, between the seasons, heard him cry:

Where, what's my God? I have been mad, am mad,
Have searched for shells and signs on the sea shore,
Stuck straw and seven stars upon my hair,   65
And leant on stiles and on the golden bar,
I have ridden on gutter dung and cloud.
Under a hideous sea where coral men
Feed in the armpits of drowned girls. I've swum
And sunk; waved flags to every fife and drum;   70
Said all the usual things over and again;
Lain with parched things; loved dogs and women;
I have desired the circle of the sun.
Tested by fire, double thumb to nose,
I've mocked the moving of the universe.   75
Where, what? There was commotion in the skies,
But no god rose. I have seen bad and worse,
Gibed the coitus of the stars. No god
Comes from my evil or my good. Mad, mad,
Feeling the pinpricks of the blood, I've said   80
The novel things. But it has been no good.

Crying such words, he left the crying crowds,
Unshackled the weights of words from tired limbs,
And took to feeding birds with broken crumbs
Of old divinities, split bits of names.   85
Very alone, he ploughed the only way.

And thus I saw him in a square of fields,
Knocking off turnip tops, with trees for friends,
And thus, some time later, I heard him say:

Out of the building of the day I've stept   90
To hermits' huts, and talked to ancient men.
Out of the noise into quiet I ran.
My God's a shepherd, God's the love I hoped.
The moon peers down the valley like a saint.
Taxis and lilies, noise and no noise,   95
Pair off, make harmonies, harmonious chord,
For he has found his soul in loneliness,
Now he is one with many, one with all,
Fire and Jordan and the sad canal.
Now he has heard and read the happy word.   100
Still, in his hut, he broods among his birds.
I see him in the crowds, not shut
From you or me or wind or rat
Or this or that.

We lying by seasand

We lying by seasand, watching yellow
And the grave sea, mock who deride
Who follow the red rivers, hollow
Alcove of words out of cicada shade,
For in this yellow grave of sand and sea   5
A calling for colour calls with the wind
That's grave and gay as grave and sea
Sleeping on either hand.
The lunar silences, the silent tide
Lapping the still canals, the dry tide-master   10
Ribbed between desert and water storm,
Should cure our ills of the water
With a one-coloured calm;
The heavenly music over the sand

Sounds with the grains as they hurry
Hiding the golden mountains and mansions
Of the grave, gay, seaside land.
Bound by a sovereign strip, we lie,
Watch yellow, wish for wind to blow away
The strata of the shore and drown red rock;
But wishes breed not, neither
Can we fend off rock arrival,
Lie watching yellow until the golden weather
Breaks, O my heart's blood, like a heart and hill.

No man believes

No man believes who, when a star falls shot,
Cries not aloud blind as a bat,
Cries not in terror when a bird is drawn
Into the quicksand feathers down,
Who does not make a wound in faith   5
When any light goes out, and life is death.

No man believes who cries not, god is not,
Who feels not coldness in the heat,
In the breasted summer longs not for spring,
No breasted girl, no man who, young   10
And green, sneers not at the old sky.
No man believes who does not wonder why.

Believe and be saved. No man believes
Who curses not what makes and saves,
No man upon this cyst of earth   15
Believes who does not lance his faith,
No man, no man, no man.

And this is true, no man can live
Who does not bury god in a deep grave
And then raise up the skeleton again,   20
No man who does not break and make,
Who in the bones finds not new faith,
Lends not flesh to ribs and neck,
Who does not break and make his final faith.

Why east wind chills

Why east wind chills and south wind cools
Shall not be known till windwell dries
And west's no longer drowned
In winds that bring the fruit and rind
Of many a hundred falls;   5
Why silk is soft and the stone wounds
The child shall question all his days,
Why night-time rain and the breast's blood
Both quench his thirst he'll have a black reply.

When cometh Jack Frost? the children ask.   10
Shall they clasp a comet in their fists?
Not till, from high and low, their dust
Sprinkles in children's eyes a long-last sleep
And dusk is crowded with the children's ghosts,
Shall a white answer echo from the rooftops.   15

All things are known: the stars' advice
Calls some content to travel with the winds,
Though what the stars ask as they round
Time upon time the towers of the skies

Is heard but little till the stars go out. 20
I hear content, and 'Be content'
Ring like a handbell through the corridors,
And 'Know no answer', and I know
No answer to the children's cry
Of echo's answer and the man of frost 25
And ghostly comets over the raised fists.

Greek Play in a Garden

A woman wails her dead among the trees,
Under the green roof grieves the living;
The living sun laments the dying skies,
Lamenting falls. Pity Electra's loving

Of all Orestes' continent of pride 5
Dust in the little country of an urn,
Of Agamemnon and his kingly blood
That cries along her veins. No sun or moon

Shall lamp the raven darkness of her face,
And no Aegean wind cool her cracked heart; 10
There are no seacaves deeper than her eyes;
Day treads the trees and she the cavernous night.

Among the trees the language of the dead
Sounds, rich with life, out of a painted mask;
The queen is slain; Orestes' hands drip blood; 15
And women talk of horror to the dusk.

There can be few tears left: Electra wept
A country's tears and voiced a world's despair
At flesh that perishes and blood that's spilt
And love that goes down like a flower. 20

Pity the living who are lost, alone;
The dead in Hades have their host of friends,
The dead queen walketh with Mycenae's king
Through Hades' groves and the Eternal Lands.

Pity Electra loveless, she whose grief   25
Drowns and is drowned, who utters to the stars
Her syllables, and to the gods her love;
Pity the poor unpitied who are strange with tears.

Among the garden trees a pigeon calls,
And knows no woe that these sad players mouth   30
Of evil oracles and funeral ills;
A pigeon calls and women talk of death.

Praise to the architects

Praise to the architects;
Dramatic shadows in a tin box;
Nonstop; stoppress; vinegar from wisecracks;
Praise to the architects;
Radio's a building in the air;   5
The poster is today's text,
The message comes from negro mystics,
An old chatterbox, barenaveled at Nice,
Who steps on the gas;
Praise to the architects;   10
A pome's a building on a page;
Keatings is good for lice,
A pinch of Auden is the lion's feast;
Praise to the architects;
Empty, To Let, are signs on this new house;   15
To leave it empty lion's or louse's choice;
Lion or louse? Take your own advice;
Praise to the architects.

Here in this spring

Here in this spring, stars float along the void;
Here in this ornamental winter
Down pelts the naked weather;
This summer buries a spring bird.

Symbols are selected from the years'   5
Slow rounding of four seasons' coasts,
In autumn teach three seasons' fires
And four birds' notes.

I should tell summer from the trees, the worms
Tell, if at all, the winter's storms   10
Or the funeral of the sun;
I should learn spring by the cuckooing,
And the slug should teach me destruction.

A worm tells summer better than the clock,
The slug's a living calendar of days;   15
What shall it tell me if a timeless insect
Says the world wears away?

'Find meat on bones'

'Find meat on bones that soon have none,
And drink in the two milked crags,
The merriest marrow and the dregs
Before the ladies' breasts are hags
And the limbs are torn.   5
Disturb no winding-sheets, my son,
But when the ladies are cold as stone
Then hang a ram rose over the rags.

Rebel against the binding moon
And the parliament of sky,
The kingcrafts of the wicked sea,
Autocracy of night and day,
Dictatorship of sun.
Rebel against the flesh and bone,
The word of the blood, the wily skin,
And the maggot no man can slay.'

'The thirst is quenched, the hunger gone,
And my heart is cracked across;
My face is haggard in the glass,
My lips are withered with a kiss,
My breasts are thin.
A merry girl took me for man,
I laid her down and told her sin,
And put beside her a ram rose.

The maggot that no man can kill
And the man no rope can hang
Rebel against my father's dream
That out of a bower of red swine
Howls the foul fiend to heel.
I cannot murder, like a fool,
Season and sunshine, grace and girl,
Nor can I smother the sweet waking.

Black night still ministers the moon,
And the sky lays down her laws,
The sea speaks in a kingly voice,
Light and dark are no enemies
But one companion.
"War on the spider and the wren!
War on the destiny of man!
Doom on the sun!"
Before death takes you, O take back this.'

Ears in the turrets hear

Ears in the turrets hear
Hands grumble on the door,
Eyes in the gables see
The fingers at the locks.
Shall I unbolt or stay   5
Alone till the day I die
Unseen by stranger-eyes
In this white house?
Hands, hold you poison or grapes?

Beyond this island bound   10
By a thin sea of flesh
And a bone coast,
The land lies out of sound
And the hills out of mind.
No bird or flying fish   15
Disturbs this island's rest.

Ears in this island hear
The wind pass like a fire,
Eyes in this island see
Ships anchor off the bay.   20
Shall I run to the ships
With the wind in my hair,
Or stay till the day I die
And welcome no sailor?
Ships, hold you poison or grapes?   25

Hands grumble on the door,
Ships anchor off the bay,
Rain beats the sand and slates.
Shall I let in the stranger,

Shall I welcome the sailor,   30
Or stay till the day I die?

Hands of the stranger and holds of the ships,
Hold you poison or grapes?

That sanity be kept

That sanity be kept I sit at open windows,
Regard the sky, make unobtrusive comment on the moon,
Sit at open windows in my shirt,
And let the traffic pass, the signals shine,
The engines run, the brass bands keep in tune,   5
For sanity must be preserved.

Thinking of death, I sit and watch the park
Where children play in all their innocence,
And matrons, on the littered grass,
Absorb the daily sun.   10

The sweet suburban music from a hundred lawns
Comes softly to my ears. The English mowers mow and mow.

I mark the couples walking arm in arm,
Observe their smiles,
Sweet invitations and inventions,   15
See them lend love illustration
By gesture and grimace.
I watch them curiously, detect beneath the laughs
What stands for grief, a vague bewilderment
At things not turning right.   20

I sit at open windows in my shirt,
Observe, like some Jehovah of the west,
What passes by, that sanity be kept.

Shall gods be said

Shall gods be said to thump the clouds
When clouds are cursed by thunder,
Be said to weep when weather howls?
Shall rainbows be their tunics' colour?

When it is rain where are the gods?   5
Shall it be said they sprinkle water
From garden cans, or free the floods?

Shall it be said that, venuswise,
An old god's dugs are pressed and pricked,
The wet night scolds me like a nurse?   10

It shall be said that gods are stone.
Shall a dropped stone drum on the ground,
Flung gravel chime? Let the stones speak
With tongues that talk all tongues.

The hand that signed the paper

The hand that signed the paper felled a city;
Five sovereign fingers taxed the breath,
Doubled the globe of dead and halved a country;
These five kings did a king to death.

The mighty hand leads to a sloping shoulder,   5
The finger joints are cramped with chalk;
A goose's quill has put an end to murder
That put an end to talk.

The hand that signed the treaty bred a fever,
And famine grew, and locusts came; 10
Great is the hand that holds dominion over
Man by a scribbled name.

The five kings count the dead but do not soften
The crusted wound nor stroke the brow;
A hand rules pity as a hand rules heaven; 15
Hands have no tears to flow.

Let for one moment a faith statement

Let for one moment a faith statement
Rule the blank sheet of sleep,
The virgin line be mated with a circle.
A circle spins. Let each revolving spoke
Turn and churn nightseed till it curdle. 5

Let for one moment a faith statement
Strip the dreams' livery,
And gods be changed as often as the shift.
God is the same though he be praised as many,
Remains though gods be felled till none are left. 10

Let for one moment a faith statement
See the first living light,
And your maieutic slumber drag it forth.
The child tells, when the trembling cord is cut,
Gods shall be gods, and many deaths be death. 10

That the sum sanity

That the sum sanity might add to nought
And matrons ring the harebells on their lips,

Girls woo the weather through the Sabbath night
And rock twin floods upon their starry laps,
I would enforce the black apparelled flocks,
And raise a hallelujah to the Lamb,
Trace on my breast a covert crucifix;
I would be woven at the Sabbath loom.

I would be woven a religious shape;
That earth might reel upon its block of reason
I would resound the heavens with my homage,
I would make genuflexion with the sheep
That men might holla, when the dawn has risen,
At day burnt bright by one fanatic image.

Before I knocked

Before I knocked and flesh let enter,
With liquid hands tapped on the womb,
I who was shapeless as the water
That shaped the Jordan near my home
Was brother to Mnetha's daughter
And sister to the fathering worm.

I who was deaf to spring and summer,
Who knew not sun nor moon by name,
Felt thud beneath my flesh's armour,
As yet was in a molten form,
The leaden stars, the rainy hammer
Swung by my father from his dome.

I knew the message of the winter,
The darted hail, the childish snow,
And the wind was my sister suitor;
Wind in me leaped, the hellborn dew;
My veins flowed with the Eastern weather;
Ungotten I knew night and day.

As yet ungotten, I did suffer;
The rack of dreams my lily bones 20
Did twist into a living cipher,
And flesh was snipped to cross the lines
Of gallow crosses on the liver
And brambles in the wringing brains.

My throat knew thirst before the structure 25
Of skin and vein around the well
Where words and water make a mixture
Unfailing till the blood runs foul;
My heart knew love, my belly hunger;
I smelt the maggot in my stool. 30

And time cast forth my mortal creature
To drift or drown upon the seas
Acquainted with the salt adventure
Of tides that never touch the shores.
I who was rich was made the richer 35
By sipping at the vine of days.

I, born of flesh and ghost, was neither
A ghost nor man, but mortal ghost.
And I was struck down by death's feather.
I was mortal to the last 40
Long breath that carried to my father
The message of his dying christ.

You who bow down at cross and altar,
Remember me and pity Him
Who took my flesh and bone for armour 45
And doublecrossed my mother's womb.

We see rise the secret wind

We see rise the secret wind behind the brain,
The sphinx of light sit on the eyes,
The code of stars translate in heaven.
A secret night descends between
The skull, the cells, the cabined ears   5
Holding for ever the dead moon.

A shout went up to heaven like a rocket,
Woe from the rabble of the blind
Adorners of the city's forehead,
Gilders of streets, the rabble hand   10
Saluting the busy brotherhood
Of rod and wheel that wake the dead.

A city godhead, turbine moved, steel sculptured,
Glitters in the electric streets;
A city saviour, in the orchard   15
Of lamp-posts and high-volted fruits,
Speaks a steel gospel to the wretched
Wheel-winders and fixers of bolts.

We hear rise the secret wind behind the brain,
The secret voice cry in our ears,   20
The city gospel shout to heaven.
Over the electric godhead grows
One God, more mighty than the sun.
The cities have not robbed our eyes.

Not forever shall the lord of the red hail

Not forever shall the lord of the red hail
Hold in his velvet hand the can of blood;

He shall be wise and let his brimstone spill,
Free from their burning nests the arrows' brood.
And sweet shall fall contagion from his side,
And loud his anger stamp upon the hill.

As fire falls, two hemispheres divide,
The fields yet undivined behind the skull
Are made divine by every lightning rod,
And perish as the level lands of steel.
Both mind and matter at the golden word
Shall fall away, and leave one singing shell.

A hole in space shall keep the space of thought,
The line of earth, the curving of the heart,
And from this darkness spin the golden soul.
Intangible my world shall come to nought,
The solid world shall wither in the heat,
How soon, how soon, o lord of the red hail!

Before we mothernaked fall

Before we mothernaked fall
Upon the land of gold or oil
Between the raid and the response
    Of flesh and bones
Our claim is staked for once and all
Near to the quarry or the well
Before the promises fulfil
    And joys are pains.

Then take the gusher or the field
Where all the hidden stones are gold
We have no choice our choice was made
    Before our blood
And I will build my liquid world
And you, before the breath is cold

And doom is turned and veins are spilled,   15
    Your solid land.

My hero bares his nerves

My hero bares his nerves along my wrist
That rules from wrist to shoulder,
Unpacks the head that, like a sleepy ghost,
Leans on my mortal ruler,
The proud spine spurning turn and twist.   5

And these poor nerves so wired to the skull
Ache on the lovelorn paper
I hug to love with my unruly scrawl
That utters all love hunger
And tells the page the empty ill.   10

My hero bares my side and sees his heart
Tread, like a naked Venus,
The beach of flesh, and wind her bloodred plait;
Stripping my loin of promise,
He promises a secret heat.   15

He holds the wire from this box of nerves
Praising the mortal error
Of birth and death, the two sad knaves of thieves,
And the hunger's emperor;
He pulls the chain, the cistern moves.   20

Love me, not as the dreaming nurses

Love me, not as the dreaming nurses
My falling lungs, nor as the cypress
In his age the lass's clay.
Love me and lift your mask.

Love me, not as the girls of heaven   5
Their airy lovers, nor the mermaiden
Her salt lovers in the sea.
Love me and lift your mask.

Love me, not as the ruffling pigeon
The tops of trees, nor as the legion   10
Of the gulls the lip of waves.
Love me and lift your mask.

Love me, as loves the mole his darkness
And the timid deer the tigress:
Hate and fear be your twin loves.   15
Love me and lift your mask.

The force that through the green fuse

The force that through the green fuse drives the flower
Drives my green age; that blasts the roots of trees
Is my destroyer.
And I am dumb to tell the crooked rose
My youth is bent by the same wintry fever.   5

The force that drives the water through the rocks
Drives my red blood; that dries the mouthing streams
Turns mine to wax.
And I am dumb to mouth unto my veins
How at the mountain spring the same mouth sucks.   10

The hand that whirls the water in the pool
Stirs the quicksand; that ropes the blowing wind
Hauls my shroud sail.
And I am dumb to tell the hanging man
How of my clay is made the hangman's lime.   15

The lips of time leech to the fountain head;
Love drips and gathers, but the fallen blood
Shall calm her sores.
And I am dumb to tell a weather's wind
How time has ticked a heaven round the stars.   20

And I am dumb to tell the lover's tomb
How at my sheet goes the same crooked worm.

From love's first fever

From love's first fever to her plague, from the soft second
And to the hollow minute of the womb,
From the unfolding to the scissored caul,
The time for breast and the green apron age
When no mouth stirred about the hanging famine,   5
All world was one, one windy nothing,
My world was christened in a stream of milk.
And earth and sky were as one airy hill,
The sun and moon shed one white light.

From the first print of the unshodden foot, the lifting   10
Hand, the breaking of the hair,
And to the miracle of the first rounded word,
From the first secret of the heart, the warning ghost,
And to the first dumb wonder at the flesh,
The sun was red, the moon was grey,   15
The earth and sky were as two mountains meeting.

The body prospered, teeth in the marrowed gums,
The growing bones, the rumour of manseed
Within the hallowed gland, blood blessed the heart,
And the four winds, that had long blown as one,   20
Shone in my ears the light of sound,
Called in my eyes the sound of light.
And yellow was the multiplying sand,

Each golden grain spat life into its fellow,
Green was the singing house.   25

The plum my mother picked matured slowly,
The boy she dropped from darkness at her side
Into the sided lap of light grew strong,
Was muscled, matted, wise to the crying thigh
And to the voice that, like a voice of hunger,   30
Itched in the noise of wind and sun.

And from the first declension of the flesh
I learnt man's tongue, to twist the shapes of thoughts
Into the stony idiom of the brain,
To shade and knit anew the patch of words   35
Left by the dead who, in their moonless acre,
Need no word's warmth.
The root of tongues ends in a spentout cancer,
That but a name, where maggots have their X.

I learnt the verbs of will, and had my secret;   40
The code of night tapped on my tongue;
What had been one was many sounding minded.

One womb, one mind, spewed out the matter,
One breast gave suck the fever's issue;
From the divorcing sky I learnt the double,   45
The two-framed globe that spun into a score;
A million minds gave suck to such a bud
As forks my eye;
Youth did condense; the tears of spring
Dissolved in summer and the hundred seasons;   50
One sun, one manna, warmed and fed.

Light breaks where no sun shines

Light breaks where no sun shines;
Where no sea runs, the waters of the heart
Push in their tides;
And, broken ghosts with glow-worms in their heads,
The things of light   5
File through the flesh where no flesh decks the bones.

A candle in the thighs
Warms youth and seed and burns the seeds of age;
Where no seed stirs,
The fruit of man unwrinkles in the stars,   10
Bright as a fig;
Where no wax is, the candle shows its hairs.

Dawn breaks behind the eyes;
From poles of skull and toe the windy blood
Slides like a sea;   15
Nor fenced, nor staked, the gushers of the sky
Spout to the rod
Divining in a smile the oil of tears.

Night in the sockets rounds,
Like some pitch moon, the limit of the globes;   20
Day lights the bone;
Where no cold is, the skinning gales unpin
The winter's robes;
The film of spring is hanging from the lids.

Light breaks on secret lots,   25
On tips of thought where thoughts smell in the rain;
When logics die,
The secret of the soil grows through the eye,

And blood jumps in the sun;
Above the waste allotments the dawn halts.   30

See, says the lime

See, says the lime, my wicked milks
I put round ribs that packed their heart,
And elbowed veins that, nudging blood,
Roused it to fire;
Once in this clay fenced by the sticks   5
That starry fence the clay of light
The howling spirit shaped a god
Of death's undoer.

On these blue lips, the lime remarks,
The wind of kisses sealed a pact   10
That leaping veins threw to the wind
And brains turned sour;
The blood got up as red as wax
As kisses froze the waxing thought,
The spirit racked its muscles and   15
The loins cried murder.

The strings of fire choked his sex
And tied an iris in his throat
To burst into a hanging land
Where flesh's fever   20
Itched on the hangman's silks;
The brains of death undid the knot
Before the blood and flame were twined
In love's last collar.

See, says the lime, around these wrecks   25
Of growing bones the muscles slid;
I chalked upon the breastbone's slate

And ran a river
Up through the fingers' cracks;
The milk of death, I filled the hand   30
That drove my stuff through skin and gut;
Death's death's undoer.

A Letter to my Aunt, Discussing the Correct Approach to Modern Poetry

To you, my aunt, who would explore
The literary Chankley Bore,
The paths are hard for you are not
A literary Hottentot
But just a kind and cultured dame   5
Who knows not Eliot (to her shame).
Fie on you, aunt, that you should see
No genius in David G.,
No elemental form and sound
In T.S.E. and Ezra Pound.   10
Fie on you, aunt! I'll show you how
To elevate your middle brow,
And how to scale and see the sights
From modernist Parnassian heights.

First buy a hat, no Paris model   15
But one the Swiss wear when they yodel,
A bowler thing with one or two
Feathers to conceal the view.
And then in sandals walk the street
(All modern painters use their feet   20
For painting, on their canvas strips,
Their wives or mothers minus hips.)
Then sport an open skirt and blouse,
For every arty thing allows
Her wretchèd bosom to be loosed   25
For men to see who talk of Proust.

Remember this at every table
Talk as rudely as you're able,
And never pass the peas with less
Than *one* remark on sexiness.   30

Your wardrobe done, (forget the rest,
The little things like drawers and vest),
You next must learn the tricks of speech
(Here nothing rhymes but 'Chelsea Reach').
Learn to begin with words like these: 35
'Chiaroscuro', 'Bright's Disease',
'Timbre', 'soul', 'essential cheese',
'The social art', 'the rhomboid quip',
'The rhythmic works of Stink and Drip',
'The Joyce of Love', 'the D. H. 'Ell',   40
'The formal spheres of Little Nell'.
With such fine phrases on your tongue,
A knowledge of the old and Jung,
You can converse in any party
And keep the conversation arty.   45

Perhaps it would be best if you
Created something very new,
A dirty novel done in Erse
Or written backwards in Welsh verse,
Or paintings on the backs of vests,   50
Or Sanskrit psalms on lepers' chests.
But if this proved imposs-i-bel
Perhaps it would be just as well,
For you could then write what you please,
And modern verse is done with ease.   55

Do not forget that 'limpet' rhymes
With 'strumpet' in these troubled times,
And commas are the worst of crimes;
Few understand the works of Cummings,
And few James Joyce's mental slummings,   60

And few young Auden's coded chatter;
But then it is the few that matter.
Never be lucid, never state,
If you would be regarded great,
The simplest thought or sentiment,   65
(For thought, we know, is decadent);
Never omit such vital words
As belly, genitals, and — ,
 For these are things that play a part
(And what a part) in all good art.   70
Remember this: each rose is wormy,
And every lovely woman's germy;
Remember this: that love depends
On how the Gallic letter bends;
Remember, too, that life is hell   75
And even heaven has a smell
Of putrefying angels who
Make deadly whoopee in the blue.
These things remembered, what can stop
A poet going to the top?   80
A final word: before you start
The convolutions of your art,
Remove your brains, take out your heart;
Minus these curses, you can be
A genius like David G.   85

Take courage, aunt, and send your stuff
To Geoffrey Grigson with my luff,
And may I yet live to admire
How well your poems light the fire.

This bread I break

This bread I break was once the oat,
This wine upon a foreign tree
Plunged in its fruit;

Man in the day or wind at night
Laid the crops low, broke the grape's joy. 5

Once in this wine the summer blood
Knocked in the flesh that decked the vine,
Once in this bread
The oat was merry in the wind;
Man broke the sun, pulled the wind down. 10

This flesh you break, this blood you let
Make desolation in the vein,
Were oat and grape
Born of the sensual root and sap;
My wine you drink, my bread you snap. 15

A process in the weather of the heart

A process in the weather of the heart
Turns damp to dry; the golden shot
Storms in the freezing tomb.
A weather in the quarter of the veins
Turns night to day; blood in their suns 5
Lights up the living worm.

A process in the eye forewarns
The bones of blindness; and the womb
Drives in a death as life leaks out.

A darkness in the weather of the eye 10
Is half its light; the fathomed sea
Breaks on unangled land.
The seed that makes a forest of the loin
Forks half its fruit; and half drops down,
Slow in a sleeping wind. 15

A weather in the flesh and bone
Is damp and dry; the quick and dead
Move like two ghosts before the eye.

A process in the weather of the world
Turns ghost to ghost; each mothered child
Sits in their double shade.
A process blows the moon into the sun,
Pulls down the shabby curtains of the skin;
And the heart gives up its dead.

When once the twilight locks

When once the twilight locks no longer
Locked in the long worm of my finger
Nor dammed the sea that sped about my fist,
The mouth of time sucked, like a sponge,
The milky acid on each hinge,
And swallowed dry the waters of the breast.

When the galactic sea was sucked
And all the dry seabed unlocked,
I sent my creature scouting on the globe,
That globe itself of hair and bone
That, sewn to me by nerve and brain,
Had stringed my flask of matter to his rib.

My fuses timed to charge his heart,
He blew like powder to the light
And held a little sabbath with the sun,
But when the stars, assuming shape,
Drew in his eyes the straws of sleep,
He drowned his father's magics in a dream.

All issue armoured, of the grave,
The redhaired cancer still alive,

The cataracted eyes that filmed their cloth;
Some dead undid their bushy jaws,
And bags of blood let out their flies;
He had by heart the Christ-cross-row of death.

Sleep navigates the tides of time;   25
The dry Sargasso of the tomb
Gives up its dead to such a working sea;
And sleep rolls mute above the beds
Where fishes' food is fed the shades
Who periscope through flowers to the sky.   30

The hanged who lever from the limes
Ghostly propellers for their limbs,
The cypress lads who wither with the cock,
These, and the others in sleep's acres,
Of dreaming men make moony suckers,   35
And snipe the fools of vision in the back.

When once the twilight screws were turned,
And mother milk was stiff as sand,
I sent my own ambassador to light;
By trick or chance he fell asleep   40
And conjured up a carcase shape
To rob me of my fluids in his heart.

Awake, my sleeper, to the sun,
A worker in the morning town,
And leave the poppied pickthank where he lies;   45
The fences of the light are down,
All but the briskest riders thrown,
And worlds hang on the trees.

Our eunuch dreams

I

Our eunuch dreams, all seedless in the light,
Of light and love, the tempers of the heart,
Whack their boys' limbs,
And, winding-footed in their shawl and sheet,
Groom the dark brides, the widows of the night   5
Fold in their arms.

The shades of girls, all flavoured from their shrouds,
When sunlight goes are sundered from the worm,
The bones of men, the broken in their beds,
By midnight pulleys that unhouse the tomb.   10

II

In this our age the gunman and his moll,
Two one-dimensioned ghosts, love on a reel,
Strange to our solid eye,
And speak their midnight nothings as they swell;
When cameras shut they hurry to their hole   15
Down in the yard of day.

They dance between their arclamps and our skull,
Impose their shots, throwing the nights away;
We watch the show of shadows kiss or kill,
Flavoured of celluloid give love the lie.   20

III

Which is the world? Of our two sleepings, which
Shall fall awake when cures and their itch
Raise up this red-eyed earth?

Pack off the shapes of daylight and their starch,
The sunny gentlemen, the Welshing rich,   25
Or drive the night-geared forth.

The photograph is married to the eye,
Grafts on its bride one-sided skins of truth;
The dream has sucked the sleeper of his faith
That shrouded men might marrow as they fly.   30

IV

This is the world: the lying likeness of
Our strips of stuff that tatter as we move
Loving from rag to bone;
The dream that kicks the buried from their sack
And lets their trash be honoured as the quick.   35
Suffer this world to spin.

For we shall be a shouter like the cock,
Blowing the old dead back; our shots shall smack
The image from the plates;
And we shall be fit fellows for a life,   40
And who remain shall flower as they love,
Praise to our faring hearts.

Where once the waters of your face

Where once the waters of your face
Spun to my screws, your dry ghost blows,
The dead turns up its eye;
Where once the mermen through your ice
Pushed up their hair, the dry wind steers   5
Through salt and root and roe.

Where once your green knots sank their splice
Into the tided cord, there goes

The green unraveller,
His scissors oiled, his knife hung loose   10
To cut the channels at their source
And lay the wet fruits low.

Invisible, your clocking tides
Break on the lovebeds of the weeds;
The weed of love's left dry;   15
There round about your stones the shades
Of children go who, from their voids,
Cry to the dolphined sea.

Dry as a tomb, your coloured lids
Shall not be latched while magic glides   20
Sage on the earth and sky;
There shall be corals in your beds,
There shall be serpents in your tides,
Till all our sea-faiths die.

I see the boys of summer

I

I see the boys of summer in their ruin
Lay the gold tithings barren,
Setting no store by harvest, freeze the soils;
There in their heat the winter floods
Of frozen loves they fetch their girls,   5
And drown the cargoed apples in their tides.

These boys of light are curdlers in their folly,
Sour the boiling honey;
The jacks of frost they finger in the hives;
There in the sun the frigid threads   10
Of doubt and dark they feed their nerves;
The signal moon is zero in their voids.

I see the summer children in their mothers
Split up the brawned womb's weathers,
Divide the night and day with fairy thumbs;   15
There in the deep with quartered shades
Of sun and moon they paint their dams
As sunlight paints the shelling of their heads.

I see that from these boys shall men of nothing
Stature by seedy shifting,   20
Or lame the air with leaping from its heats;
There from their hearts the dogdayed pulse
Of love and light bursts in their throats.
O see the pulse of summer in the ice.

II

But seasons must be challenged or they totter   25
Into a chiming quarter
Where, punctual as death, we ring the stars;
There, in his night, the black-tongued bells
The sleepy man of winter pulls,
Nor blows back moon-and-midnight as she blows.   30

We are the dark deniers, let us summon
Death from a summer woman,
A muscling life from lovers in their cramp,
From the fair dead who flush the sea
The bright-eyed worm on Davy's lamp,   35
And from the planted womb the man of straw.

We summer boys in this four-winded spinning,
Green of the seaweeds' iron,
Hold up the noisy sea and drop her birds,
Pick the world's ball of wave and froth   40
To choke the deserts with her tides,
And comb the county gardens for a wreath.

In spring we cross our foreheads with the holly,
Heigh ho the blood and berry,
And nail the merry squires to the trees;   45
Here love's damp muscle dries and dies,
Here break a kiss in no love's quarry.
O see the poles of promise in the boys.

III

I see you boys of summer in your ruin.
Man in his maggot's barren.   50
And boys are full and foreign in the pouch.
I am the man your father was.
We are the sons of flint and pitch.
O see the poles are kissing as they cross.

In the beginning

In the beginning was the three-pointed star,
One smile of light across the empty face;
One bough of bone across the rooting air,
The substance forked that marrowed the first sun;
And, burning cyphers on the round of space,   5
Heaven and hell mixed as they spun.

In the beginning was the pale signature,
Three-syllabled and starry as the smile;
And after came the imprints on the water,
Stamp of the minted face upon the moon;   10
The blood that touched the crosstree and the grail
Touched the first cloud and left a sign.

In the beginning was the mounting fire
That set alight the weathers from a spark,
A three-eyed, red-eyed spark, blunt as a flower;   15
Life rose and spouted from the rolling seas,

Burst in the roots, pumped from the earth and rock
The secret oils that drive the grass.

In the beginning was the word, the word
That from the solid bases of the light   20
Abstracted all the letters of the void;
And from the cloudy bases of the breath
The word flowed up, translating to the heart
First characters of birth and death.

In the beginning was the secret brain.   25
The brain was celled and soldered in the thought
Before the pitch was forking to a sun;
Before the veins were shaking in their sieve,
Blood shot and scattered to the winds of light
The ribbed original of love.   30

If I were tickled by the rub of love

If I were tickled by the rub of love,
A rooking girl who stole me for her side,
Broke through her straws, breaking my bandaged string,
If the red tickle as the cattle calve
Still set to scratch a laughter from my lung,   5
I would not fear the apple nor the flood
Nor the bad blood of spring.

Shall it be male or female? say the cells,
And drop the plum like fire from the flesh.
If I were tickled by the hatching hair,   10
The winging bone that sprouted in the heels,
The itch of man upon the baby's thigh,
I would not fear the gallows nor the axe
Nor the crossed sticks of war.

Shall it be male or female? say the fingers   15
That chalk the walls with green girls and their men.
I would not fear the muscling-in of love
If I were tickled by the urchin hungers
Rehearsing heat upon a raw-edged nerve.
I would not fear the devil in the loin   20
Nor the outspoken grave.

If I were tickled by the lovers' rub
That wipes away not crow's-foot nor the lock
Of sick old manhood on the fallen jaws,
Time and the crabs and the sweethearting crib   25
Would leave me cold as butter for the flies,
The sea of scums could drown me as it broke
Dead on the sweethearts' toes.

This world is half the devil's and my own,
Daft with the drug that's smoking in a girl   30
And curling round the bud that forks her eye.
An old man's shank one-marrowed with my bone,
And all the herrings smelling in the sea,
I sit and watch the worm beneath my nail
Wearing the quick away.   35

And that's the rub, the only rub that tickles.
The knobbly ape that swings along his sex
From damp love-darkness and the nurse's twist
Can never raise the midnight of a chuckle,
Nor when he finds a beauty in the breast   40
Of lover, mother, lovers, or his six
Feet in the rubbing dust.

And what's the rub? Death's feather on the nerve?
Your mouth, my love, the thistle in the kiss?
My Jack of Christ born thorny on the tree?   45
The words of death are dryer than his stiff,

My wordy wounds are printed with your hair.
I would be tickled by the rub that is:
Man be my metaphor.

I dreamed my genesis

I dreamed my genesis in sweat of sleep, breaking
Through the rotating shell, strong
As motor muscle on the drill, driving
Through vision and the girdered nerve.

From limbs that had the measure of the worm, shuffled   5
Off from the creasing flesh, filed
Through all the irons in the grass, metal
Of suns in the man-melting night.

Heir to the scalding veins that hold love's drop, costly
A creature in my bones, I   10
Rounded my globe of heritage, journey
In bottom gear through night-geared man.

I dreamed my genesis and died again, shrapnel
Rammed in the marching heart, hole
In the stitched wound and clotted wind, muzzled   15
Death on the mouth that ate the gas.

Sharp in my second death I marked the hills, harvest
Of hemlock and the blades, rust
My blood upon the tempered dead, forcing
My second struggling from the grass.   20

And power was contagious in my birth, second
Rise of the skeleton and
Rerobing of the naked ghost. Manhood
Spat up from the resuffered pain.

I dreamed my genesis in sweat of death, fallen   25
Twice in the feeding sea, grown
Stale of Adam's brine until, vision
Of new man strength, I seek the sun.

I fellowed sleep

I fellowed sleep who kissed me in the brain,
Let fall the tear of time; the sleeper's eye,
Shifting to light, turned on me like a moon.
So, 'planing-heeled, I flew along my man
And dropped on dreaming and the upward sky.   5

I fled the earth and, naked, climbed the weather,
Reaching a second ground far from the stars;
And there we wept, I and a ghostly other,
My mothers-eyed, upon the tops of trees;
I fled that ground as lightly as a feather.   10

'My fathers' globe knocks on its nave and sings.'
'This that we tread was, too, your fathers' land.'
'But this we tread bears the angelic gangs,
Sweet are their fathered faces in their wings.'
'These are but dreaming men. Breathe, and they fade.'   15

Faded my elbow ghost, the mothers-eyed,
As, blowing on the angels, I was lost
On that cloud coast to each grave-gabbing shade;
I blew the dreaming fellows to their bed
Where still they sleep unknowing of their ghost.   20

Then all the matter of the living air
Raised up a voice, and, climbing on the words,
I spelt my vision with a hand and hair,
How light the sleeping on this soily star,
How deep the waking in the worlded clouds.   25

There grows the hours' ladder to the sun,
Each rung a love or losing to the last,
The inches monkeyed by the blood of man.
An old, mad man still climbing in his ghost,
My fathers' ghost is climbing in the rain.   30

All all and all

I

All all and all the dry worlds lever,
Stage of the ice, the solid ocean,
All from the oil, the pound of lava.
City of spring, the governed flower,
Turns in the earth that turns the ashen   5
Towns around on a wheel of fire.

How now my flesh, my naked fellow,
Dug of the sea, the glanded morrow,
Worm in the scalp, the staked and fallow.
All all and all, the corpse's lover,   10
Skinny as sin, the foaming marrow,
All of the flesh, the dry worlds lever.

II

Fear not the working world, my mortal,
Fear not the flat, synthetic blood,
Nor the heart in the ribbing metal.   15
Fear not the tread, the seeded milling,
The trigger and scythe, the bridal blade,
Nor the flint in the lover's mauling.

Man of my flesh, the jawbone riven,
Know now the flesh's lock and vice,   20
And the cage for the scythe-eyed raven.

Know, O my bone, the jointed lever,
Fear not the screws that turn the voice,
And the face to the driven lover.

III

All all and all the dry worlds couple,   25
Ghost with her ghost, contagious man
With the womb of his shapeless people.
All that shapes from the caul and suckle,
Stroke of mechanical flesh on mine,
Square in these worlds the mortal circle.   30

Flower, flower the people's fusion,
O light in zenith, the coupled bud,
And the flame in the flesh's vision.
Out of the sea, the drive of oil,
Socket and grave, the brassy blood,   35
Flower, flower, all all and all.

My world is pyramid

I

Half of the fellow father as he doubles
His sea-sucked Adam in the hollow hulk,
Half of the fellow mother as she dabbles
Tomorrow's diver in her horny milk,
Bisected shadows on the thunder's bone   5
Bolt for the salt unborn.

The fellow half was frozen as it bubbled
Corrosive spring out of the iceberg's crop,
The fellow seed and shadow as it babbled
The swing of milk was tufted in the pap,   10

For half of love was planted in the lost,
And the unplanted ghost.

The broken halves are fellowed in a cripple,
The crutch that marrow taps upon their sleep,
Limp in the street of sea, among the rabble   15
Of tide-tongued heads and bladders in the deep,
And stake the sleepers in the savage grave
That the vampire laugh.

The patchwork halves were cloven as they scudded
The wild pigs' wood, and slime upon the trees,   20
Sucking the dark, kissed on the cyanide,
And loosed the braiding adders from their hairs;
Rotating halves are horning as they drill
The arterial angel.

What colour is glory? death's feather? tremble   25
The halves that pierce the pin's point in the air,
And prick the thumb-stained heaven through the thimble.
The ghost is dumb that stammered in the straw,
The ghost that hatched his havoc as he flew
Blinds their cloud-tracking eye.   30

II

My world is pyramid. The padded mummer
Weeps on the desert ochre and the salt
Incising summer.
My Egypt's armour buckling in its sheet,
I scrape through resin to a starry bone   35
And a blood parhelion.

My world is cypress, and an English valley.
I piece my flesh that rattled on the yards
Red in an Austrian volley.

I hear, through dead men's drums, the riddled lads,   40
Strewing their bowels from a hill of bones,
Cry Eloi to the guns.

My grave is watered by the crossing Jordan.
The Arctic scut, and basin of the South,
Drip on my dead house garden.   45
Who seek me landward, marking in my mouth
The straws of Asia, lose me as I turn
Through the Atlantic corn.

The fellow halves that, cloven as they swivel
On casting tides, are tangled in the shells,   50
Bearding the unborn devil,
Bleed from my burning fork and smell my heels.
The tongues of heaven gossip as I glide
Binding my angel's hood.

Who blows death's feather? What glory is colour?   55
I blow the stammel feather in the vein.
The loin is glory in a working pallor.
My clay unsuckled and my salt unborn,
The secret child, I shift about the sea
Dry in the half-tracked thigh.   60

Foster the light

Foster the light nor veil the manshaped moon,
Nor weather winds that blow not down the bone,
But strip the twelve-winded marrow from his circle;
Master the night nor serve the snowman's brain
That shapes each bushy item of the air   5
Into a polestar pointed on an icicle.

Murmur of spring nor crush the cockerel's eggs,
Nor hammer back a season in the figs,

But graft these four-fruited ridings on your country;
Farmer in time of frost the burning leagues,   10
By red-eyed orchards sow the seeds of snow,
In your young years the vegetable century.

And father all nor fail the fly-lord's acre,
Nor sprout on owl-seed like a goblin-sucker,
But rail with your wizard's ribs the heart-shaped planet;   15
Of mortal voices to the ninnies' choir,
High lord esquire, speak up the singing cloud,
And pluck a mandrake music from the marrowroot.

Roll unmanly over this turning tuft,
O ring of seas, nor sorrow as I shift   20
From all my mortal lovers with a starboard smile;
Nor when my love lies in the cross-boned drift
Naked among the bow-and-arrow birds
Shall you turn cockwise on a tufted axle.

Who gave these seas their colour in a shape   25
Shaped my clayfellow, and the heaven's ark
In time at flood filled with his coloured doubles;
O who is glory in the shapeless maps,
Now make the world of me as I have made
A merry manshape of your walking circle.   30

Especially when the October wind

Especially when the October wind
With frosty fingers punishes my hair,
Caught by the crabbing sun I walk on fire
And cast a shadow crab upon the land,
By the sea's side, hearing the noise of birds,   5
Hearing the raven cough in winter sticks,
My busy heart who shudders as she talks
Sheds the syllabic blood and drains her words.

Shut, too, in a tower of words, I mark
On the horizon walking like the trees 10
The wordy shapes of women, and the rows
Of the star-gestured children in the park.
Some let me make you of the vowelled beeches,
Some of the oaken voices, from the roots
Of many a thorny shire tell you notes, 15
Some let me make you of the water's speeches.

Behind a pot of ferns the wagging clock
Tells me the hour's word, the neural meaning
Flies on the shafted disc, declaims the morning
And tells the windy weather in the cock. 20
Some let me make you of the meadow's signs;
The signal grass that tells me all I know
Breaks with the wormy winter through the eye.
Some let me tell you of the raven's sins.

Especially when the October wind 25
(Some let me make you of autumnal spells,
The spider-tongued, and the loud hill of Wales)
With fist of turnips punishes the land,
Some let me make you of the heartless words.
The heart is drained that, spelling in the scurry 30
Of chemic blood, warned of the coming fury.
By the sea's side hear the dark-vowelled birds.

When, like a running grave

When, like a running grave, time tracks you down,
Your calm and cuddled is a scythe of hairs,
Love in her gear is slowly through the house,
Up naked stairs, a turtle in a hearse,
Hauled to the dome, 5

Comes, like a scissors stalking, tailor age,
Deliver me who, timid in my tribe,
Of love am barer than Cadaver's trap
Robbed of the foxy tongue, his footed tape
Of the bone inch,   10

Deliver me, my masters, head and heart,
Heart of Cadaver's candle waxes thin,
When blood, spade-handed, and the logic time
Drive children up like bruises to the thumb,
From maid and head,   15

For, sunday faced, with dusters in my glove,
Chaste and the chaser, man with the cockshut eye,
I, that time's jacket or the coat of ice
May fail to fasten with a virgin o
In the straight grave,   20

Stride through Cadaver's country in my force,
My pickbrain masters morsing on the stone
Despair of blood, faith in the maiden's slime,
Halt among eunuchs, and the nitric stain
On fork and face.   25

Time is a foolish fancy, time and fool.
No, no, you lover skull, descending hammer
Descends, my masters, on the entered honour.
You hero skull, Cadaver in the hangar
Tells the stick 'fail'.   30

Joy is no knocking nation, sir and madam,
The cancer's fusion, or the summer feather
Lit on the cuddled tree, the cross of fever,
Nor city tar and subway bored to foster
Man through macadam.   35

I damp the waxlights in your tower dome.
Joy is the knock of dust, Cadaver's shoot
Of bud of Adam through his boxy shift,
Love's twilit nation and the skull of state,
Sir, is your doom. 40

Everything ends, the tower ending and,
(Have with the house of wind) the leaning scene,
Ball of the foot depending from the sun,
(Give, summer, over) the cemented skin,
The actions' end. 45

All, men my madmen, the unwholesome wind
With whistler's cough contages, time on track
Shapes in a cinder death; love for his trick,
Happy Cadaver's hunger as you take
The kissproof world. 50

Should lanterns shine

Should lanterns shine, the holy face,
Caught in an octagon of unaccustomed light,
Would wither up, and any boy of love
Look twice before he fell from grace.
The features in their private dark 5
Are formed of flesh, but let the false day come
And from her lips the added pigments fall,
The mummy cloths expose an ancient breast.

I have been taught to reason by the heart,
But heart, like head, leads helplessly; 10
I have been told to reason by the pulse,
And, when it quickens, alter the actions' pace
Till field and roof lie level and the same
So fast I move defying time, the quiet gentleman
Whose beard wags in Egyptian wind. 15

I have heard many years of telling,
And many years should see some change.

The ball I threw while playing in the park
Has not yet reached the ground.

I, in my intricate image

I

I, in my intricate image, stride on two levels,
Forged in man's minerals, the brassy orator
Laying my ghost in metal,
The scales of this twin world tread on the double,
My half ghost in armour hold hard in death's corridor,   5
To my man-iron sidle.

Beginning with doom in the bulb, the spring unravels,
Bright as her spinning-wheels, the colic season
Worked on a world of petals;
She threads off the sap and needles, blood and bubble   10
Casts to the pine roots, raising man like a mountain
Out of the naked entrail.

Beginning with doom in the ghost, and the springing marvels,
Image of images, my metal phantom
Forcing forth through the harebell,   15
My man of leaves and the bronze root, mortal, unmortal,
I, in my fusion of rose and male motion,
Create this twin miracle.

This is the fortune of manhood: the natural peril,
A steeplejack tower, bonerailed and masterless,   20
No death more natural;
Thus the shadowless man or ox, and the pictured devil,

In seizure of silence commit the dead nuisance:
The natural parallel.

My images stalk the trees and the slant sap's tunnel,   25
No tread more perilous, the green steps and spire
Mount on man's footfall,
I with the wooden insect in the tree of nettles,
In the glass bed of grapes with snail and flower,
Hearing the weather fall.   30

Intricate manhood of ending, the invalid rivals,
Voyaging clockwise off the symboled harbour,
Finding the water final,
On the consumptives' terrace taking their two farewells,
Sail on the level, the departing adventure,   35
To the sea-blown arrival.

II

They climb the country pinnacle,
Twelve winds encounter by the white host at pasture,
Corner the mounted meadows in the hill corral;
They see the squirrel stumble,   40
The haring snail go giddily round the flower,
A quarrel of weather and trees in the windy spiral.

As they dive, the dust settles,
The cadaverous gravels, falls thick and steadily,
The highroad of water where the seabear and mackerel   45
Turn the long sea arterial
Turning a petrol face blind to the enemy
Turning the riderless dead by the channel wall.

(Death instrumental,
Splitting the long eye open, and the spiral turnkey,   50
Your corkscrew grave centred in navel and nipple,
The neck of the nostril,

Under the mask and the ether, they making bloody
The tray of knives, the antiseptic funeral;

Bring out the black patrol,   55
Your monstrous officers and the decaying army,
The sexton sentinel, garrisoned under thistles,
A cock-on-a-dunghill
Crowing to Lazarus the morning is vanity,
Dust be your saviour under the conjured soil.)   60

As they drown, the chime travels,
Sweetly the diver's bell in the steeple of spindrift
Rings out the Dead Sea scale;
And, clapped in water till the triton dangles,
Strung by the flaxen whale-weed, from the hangman's raft,   65
Hear they the salt glass breakers and the tongues of burial.

(Turn the sea-spindle lateral,
The grooved land rotating, that the stylus of lightning
Dazzle this face of voices on the moon-turned table,
Let the wax disc babble   70
Shames and the damp dishonours, the relic scraping.
These are your years' recorders. The circular world stands still.)

III

They suffer the undead water where the turtle nibbles,
Come unto sea-stuck towers, at the fibre scaling,
The flight of the carnal skull   75
And the cell-stepped thimble;
Suffer, my topsy-turvies, that a double angel
Sprout from the stony lockers like a tree on Aran.

Be by your one ghost pierced, his pointed ferrule,
Brass and the bodiless image, on a stick of folly   80
Star-set at Jacob's angle,
Smoke hill and hophead's valley,

And the five-fathomed Hamlet on his father's coral,
Thrusting the tom-thumb vision up the iron mile.

Suffer the slash of vision by the fin-green stubble,   85
Be by the ships' sea broken at the manstring anchored
The stoved bones' voyage downward
In the shipwreck of muscle;
Give over, lovers, locking, and the seawax struggle,
Love like a mist or fire through the bed of eels.   90

And in the pincers of the boiling circle,
The sea and instrument, nicked in the locks of time,
My great blood's iron single
In the pouring town,
I, in a wind on fire, from green Adam's cradle,   95
No man more magical, clawed out the crocodile.

Man was the scales, the death birds on enamel,
Tail, Nile, and snout, a saddler of the rushes,
Time in the hourless houses
Shaking the sea-hatched skull,   100
And, as for oils and ointments on the flying grail,
All-hallowed man wept for his white apparel.

Man was Cadaver's masker, the harnessing mantle,
Windily master of man was the rotten fathom,
My ghost in his metal neptune   105
Forged in man's mineral.
This was the god of beginning in the intricate seawhirl,
And my images roared and rose on heaven's hill.

Hold hard, these ancient minutes

Hold hard, these ancient minutes in the cuckoo's month,
Under the lank, fourth folly on Glamorgan's hill,
As the green blooms ride upward, to the drive of time;

Time, in a folly's rider, like a county man
Over the vault of ridings with his hound at heel,   5
Drives forth my men, my children, from the hanging south.

Country, your sport is summer, and December's pools
By crane and water-tower by the seedy trees
Lie this fifth month unskated, and the birds have flown;
Hold hard, my country children in the world of tales,   10
The greenwood dying as the deer fall in their tracks,
This first and steepled season, to the summer's game.

And now the horns of England, in the sound of shape,
Summon your snowy horsemen, and the four-stringed hill,
Over the sea-gut loudening, sets a rock alive;   15
Hurdles and guns and railings, as the boulders heave,
Crack like a spring in a vice, bone breaking April,
Spill the lank folly's hunter and the hard-held hope.

Down fall four padding weathers on the scarlet lands,
Stalking my children's faces with a tail of blood,   20
Time, in a rider rising, from the harnessed valley;
Hold hard, my county darlings, for a hawk descends,
Golden Glamorgan straightens, to the falling birds.
Your sport is summer as the spring runs angrily.

Now

Now
Say nay,
Man dry man,
Dry lover mine
The deadrock base and blow the flowered anchor,   5
Should he, for centre sake, hop in the dust,
Forsake, the fool, the hardiness of anger.

Now
Say nay,
Sir no say,   10
Death to the yes,
The yes to death, the yesman and the answer,
Should he who split his children with a cure
Have brotherless his sister on the handsaw.

Now   15
Say nay,
No say sir
Yea the dead stir,
And this, nor this, is shade, the landed crow,
He lying low with ruin in his ear,   20
The cockerel's tide upcasting from the fire.

Now
Say nay,
So star fall,
So the ball fail,   25
So solve the mystic sun, the wife of light,
The sun that leaps on petals through a nought,
The come-a-cropper rider of the flower.

Now
Say nay   30
A fig for
The seal of fire,
Death hairy-heeled, and the tapped ghost in wood,
We make me mystic as the arm of air,
The two-a-vein, the foreskin, and the cloud.   35

How soon the servant sun

How soon the servant sun
(Sir morrow mark)

Can time unriddle, and the cupboard stone
(Fog has a bone
He'll trumpet into meat)   5
Unshelve that all my gristles have a gown
And the naked egg stand straight,

Sir morrow at his sponge,
(The wound records)
The nurse of giants by the cut sea basin,   10
(Fog by his spring
Soaks up the sewing tides)
Tells you and you, my masters, as his strange
Man morrow blows through food.

All nerves to serve the sun,   15
The rite of light,
A claw I question from the mouse's bone,
The long-tailed stone
Trap I with coil and sheet,
Let the soil squeal I am the biting man   20
And the velvet dead inch out.

How soon my level, lord,
(Sir morrow stamps
Two heels of water on the floor of seed)
Shall raise a lamp   25
Or spirit up a cloud,
Erect a walking centre in the shroud,
Invisible on the stump

A leg as long as trees,
This inward sir,   30
Mister and master, darkness for his eyes,
The womb-eyed, cries,
And all sweet hell, deaf as an hour's ear,
Blasts back the trumpet voice.

Do you not father me

Do you not father me, nor the erected arm
For my tall tower's sake cast in her stone?
Do you not mother me, nor, as I am,
The lovers' house, lie suffering my stain?
Do you not sister me, nor the erected crime   5
For my tall turrets carry as your sin?
Do you not brother me, nor, as you climb,
Adore my windows for their summer scene?

Am I not father, too, and the ascending boy,
The boy of woman and the wanton starer   10
Marking the flesh and summer in the bay?
Am I not sister, too, who is my saviour?
Am I not all of you by the directed sea
Where bird and shell are babbling in my tower?
Am I not you who front the tidy shore,   15
Nor roof of sand, nor yet the towering tiler?

You are all these, said she who gave me the long suck,
All these, he said who sacked the children's town,
Up rose the Abraham-man, mad for my sake,
They said, who hacked and humoured, they were mine.   20
I am, the tower told, felled by a timeless stroke,
Who razed my wooden folly stands aghast,
For man-begetters in the dry-as-paste,
The ringed-sea ghost, rise grimly from the wrack.

Do you not father me on the destroying sand?   25
You are your sisters' sire, said seaweedy,
The salt sucked dam and darlings of the land
Who play the proper gentleman and lady.
Shall I still be love's house on the widdershin earth,
Woe to the windy masons at my shelter?   30

Love's house, they answer, and the tower death
Lie all unknowing of the grave sin-eater.

Grief thief of time

Grief thief of time crawls off,
The moon-drawn grave, with the seafaring years,
The knave of pain steals off
The sea-halved faith that blew time to his knees,
The old forget the cries,   5
Lean time on tide and times the wind stood rough,
Call back the castaways
Riding the sea light on a sunken path,
The old forget the grief,
Hack of the cough, the hanging albatross,   10
Cast back the bone of youth
And salt-eyed stumble bedward where she lies
Who tossed the high tide in a time of stories
And timelessly lies loving with the thief.

Now Jack my fathers let the time-faced crook,   15
Death flashing from his sleeve,
With swag of bubbles in a seedy sack
Sneak down the stallion grave,
Bull's-eye the outlaw through a eunuch crack
And free the twin-boxed grief,   20
No silver whistles chase him down the weeks'
Dayed peaks to day to death,
These stolen bubbles have the bites of snakes
And the undead eye-teeth,
No third eye probe into a rainbow's sex   25
That bridged the human halves,
All shall remain and on the graveward gulf
Shape with my fathers' thieves.

Incarnate devil

Incarnate devil in a talking snake,
The central plains of Asia in his garden,
In shaping-time the circle stung awake,
In shapes of sin forked out the bearded apple,
And God walked there who was a fiddling warden   5
And played down pardon from the heavens' hill.

When we were strangers to the guided seas,
A handmade moon half holy in a cloud,
The wisemen tell me that the garden gods
Twined good and evil on an eastern tree;   10
And when the moon rose windily it was
Black as the beast and paler than the cross.

We in our Eden knew the secret guardian
In sacred waters that no frost could harden,
And in the mighty mornings of the earth;   15
Hell in a horn of sulphur and the cloven myth,
All heaven in a midnight of the sun,
A serpent fiddled in the shaping-time.

A grief ago

A grief ago,
She who was who I hold, the fats and flower,
Or, water-lammed, from the scythe-sided thorn,
Hell wind and sea,
A stem cementing, wrestled up the tower,   5
Rose maid and male,
Or, masted venus, through the paddler's bowl
Sailed up the sun;

Who is my grief,
A chrysalis unwrinkling on the iron,   10
Wrenched by my fingerman, the leaden bud
Shot through the leaf,
Was who was folded on the rod the aaron
Rose cast to plague,
The horn and ball of water on the frog   15
Housed in the side.

And she who lies,
Like exodus a chapter from the garden,
Brand of the lily's anger on her ring,
Tugged through the days   20
Her ropes of heritage, the wars of pardon,
On field and sand
The twelve triangles of the cherub wind
Engraving going.

Who then is she,   25
She holding me? The people's sea drives on her,
Drives out the father from the caesared camp;
The dens of shape
Shape all her whelps with the long voice of water,
That she I have,   30
The country-handed grave boxed into love,
Rise before dark.

The night is near,
A nitric shape that leaps her, time and acid;
I tell her this: before the suncock cast   35
Her bone to fire,
Let her inhale her dead, through seed and solid
Draw in their seas,
So cross her hand with their grave gipsy eyes,
And close her fist.   40

Altarwise by owl-light

I

Altarwise by owl-light in the halfway-house
The gentleman lay graveward with his furies;
Abaddon in the hang-nail cracked from Adam,
And, from his fork, a dog among the fairies,
The atlas-eater with a jaw for news,   5
Bit out the mandrake with tomorrow's scream.
Then, penny-eyed, that gentleman of wounds,
Old cock from nowheres and the heaven's egg,
With bones unbuttoned to the halfway winds,
Hatched from the windy salvage on one leg,   10
Scraped at my cradle in a walking word
That night of time under the Christward shelter,
I am the long world's gentleman, he said,
And share my bed with Capricorn and Cancer.

II

Death is all metaphors, shape in one history;
The child that sucketh long is shooting up,
The planet-ducted pelican of circles
Weans on an artery the gender's strip;
Child of the short spark in a shapeless country   5
Soon sets alight a long stick from the cradle;
The horizontal cross-bones of Abaddon,
You by the cavern over the black stairs,
Rung bone and blade, the verticals of Adam,
And, manned by midnight, Jacob to the stars;   10
Hairs of your head, then said the hollow agent,
Are but the roots of nettles and of feathers
Over these groundworks thrusting through a pavement
And hemlock-headed in the wood of weathers.

III

First there was the lamb on knocking knees
And three dead seasons on a climbing grave
That Adam's wether in a flock of horns,
Butt of the tree-tailed worm that mounted Eve,
Horned down with skullfoot and the skull of toes   5
On thunderous pavements in the garden time;
Rip of the vaults, I took my marrow-ladle
Out of the wrinkled undertaker's van,
And, Rip Van Winkle from a timeless cradle,
Dipped me breast-deep in the descended bone;   10
The black ram, shuffling of the year, old winter,
Alone alive among his mutton fold,
We rung our weathering changes on the ladder,
Said the antipodes, and twice spring chimed.

IV

What is the metre of the dictionary?
The size of genesis? the short spark's gender?
Shade without shape? the shape of Pharaoh's echo?
(My shape of age nagging the wounded whisper).
Which sixth of wind blew out the burning gentry?   5
(Questions are hunchbacks to the poker marrow).
What of a bamboo man among your acres?
Corset the boneyard for a crooked lad?
Button your bodice on a hump of splinters,
My camel's eye will needle through the shroud.   10
Love's a reflection of the mushroom features,
Stills snapped by night in the bread-sided field,
Once close-up smiling in the wall of pictures,
Ark-lamped thrown back upon the cutting flood.

V

And from the windy West came two-gunned Gabriel,
From Jesu's sleeve trumped up the king of spots,
The sheath-decked jacks, queen with a shuffled heart;
Said the fake gentleman in suit of spades,
Black-tongued and tipsy from salvation's bottle,   5
Rose my Byzantine Adam in the night;
For loss of blood I fell on Ishmael's plain,
Under the milky mushrooms slew my hunger,
A climbing sea from Asia had me down
And Jonah's Moby snatched me by the hair;   10
Cross-stroked salt Adam to the frozen angel
Pin-legged on pole-hills with a black medusa
By waste seas where the white bear quoted Virgil
And sirens singing from our lady's sea-straw.

VI

Cartoon of slashes on the tide-traced crater,
He in a book of water tallow-eyed
By lava's light split through the oyster vowels
And burned sea silence on a wick of words:
Pluck, cock, my sea eye, said medusa's scripture,   5
Lop, love, my fork tongue, said the pin-hilled nettle;
And love plucked out the stinging siren's eye,
Old cock from nowheres lopped the minstrel tongue
Till tallow I blew from the wax's tower
The fats of midnight when the salt was singing;   10
Adam, time's joker, on a witch of cardboard
Spelt out the seven seas, an evil index,
The bagpipe-breasted ladies in the deadweed
Blew out the blood gauze through the wound of manwax.

VII

Now stamp the Lord's Prayer on a grain of rice,
A Bible-leaved of all the written woods
Strip to this tree: a rocking alphabet,
Genesis in the root, the scarecrow word,
And one light's language in the book of trees;   5
Doom on deniers at the wind-turned statement.
Time's tune my ladies with the teats of music,
The scaled sea-sawers, fix in a naked sponge
Who sucks the bell-voiced Adam out of magic,
Time, milk, and magic, from the world beginning.   10
Time is the tune my ladies lend their heartbreak,
From bald pavilions and the house of bread
Time tracks the sound of shape on man and cloud,
On rose and icicle the ringing handprint.

VIII

This was the crucifixion on the mountain,
Time's nerve in vinegar, the gallow grave
As tarred with blood as the bright thorns I wept;
The world's my wound, God's Mary in her grief,
Bent like three trees and bird-papped through her shift,   5
With pins for teardrops is the long wound's woman.
This was the sky, Jack Christ, each minstrel angle
Drove in the heaven-driven of the nails
Till the three-coloured rainbow from my nipples
From pole to pole leapt round the snail-waked world.   10
I by the tree of thieves, all glory's sawbones
Unsex the skeleton this mountain minute,
And by this blowclock witness of the sun
Suffer the heaven's children through my heartbeat.

IX

From the oracular archives and the parchment,
Prophets and fibre kings in oil and letter,
The lamped calligrapher, the queen in splints,
Buckle to lint and cloth their natron footsteps,
Draw on the glove of prints, dead Cairo's henna   5
Pour like a halo on the caps and serpents.
This was the resurrection in the desert,
Death from a bandage, rants the mask of scholars
Gold on such features, and the linen spirit
Weds my long gentleman to dusts and furies;   10
With priests and pharaoh bed my gentle wound,
World in the sand, on the triangle landscape,
With stones of odyssey for ash and garland
And rivers of the dead around my neck.

X

Let the tale's sailor from a Christian voyage
Atlaswise hold halfway off the dummy bay
Time's ship-racked gospel on the globe I balance:
So shall winged harbours through the rockbirds' eyes
Spot the blown word, and on the seas I image   5
December's thorn screwed in a brow of holly.
Let the first Peter from a rainbow's quayrail
Ask the tall fish swept from the bible east,
What rhubarb man peeled in her foam-blue channel
Has sown a flying garden round that sea-ghost?   10
Green as beginning, let the garden diving
Soar, with its two bark towers, to that Day
When the worm builds with the gold straws of venom
My nest of mercies in the rude, red tree.

The seed-at-zero

The seed-at-zero shall not storm
That town of ghosts, the trodden womb
With her rampart to his tapping,
No god-in-hero tumble down
Like a tower on the town   5
Dumbly and divinely stumbling
Over the manwaging line.

That seed-at-zero shall not storm
That town of ghosts, the manwaged womb
With her rampart to his tapping,   10
No god-in-hero tumble down
Like a tower on the town
Dumbly and divinely leaping
Over the warbearing line.

Through the rampart of the sky   15
Shall the star-flanked seed be riddled,
Manna for the rumbling ground,
Quickening for the riddled sea;
Settled on a virgin stronghold
He shall grapple with the guard   20
And the keeper of the key.

Through the rampart of the sky
Shall the star-flanked seed be riddled,
Manna for the guarded ground,
Quickening for the virgin sea;   25
Settling on a riddled stronghold
He shall grapple with the guard
And the loser of the key.

May a humble village labour
And a continent deny?   30
A hemisphere may scold him
And a green inch be his bearer;
Let the hero seed find harbour,
Seaports by a drunken shore
Have their thirsty sailors hide him.   35

May a humble planet labour
And a continent deny?
A village green may scold him
And a high sphere be his bearer;
Let the hero seed find harbour,   40
Seaports by a thirsty shore
Have their drunken sailors hide him.

Man-in-seed, in seed-at-zero,
From the foreign fields of space,
Shall not thunder on the town   45
With a star-flanked garrison,
Nor the cannons of his kingdom
Shall the hero-in-tomorrow
Range on the sky-scraping place.

Man-in-seed, in seed-at-zero,   50
From the star-flanked fields of space,
Thunders on the foreign town
With a sand-bagged garrison,
Nor the cannons of his kingdom
Shall the hero-in-tomorrow   55
Range from the grave-groping place.

To-day, this insect

To-day, this insect, and the world I breathe,
Now that my symbols have outelbowed space,

Time at the city spectacles, and half
The dear, daft time I take to nudge the sentence,
In trust and tale have I divided sense,   5
Slapped down the guillotine, the blood-red double
Of head and tail made witnesses to this
Murder of Eden and green genesis.

The insect certain is the plague of fables.

This story's monster has a serpent caul,   10
Blind in the coil scrams round the blazing outline,
Measures his own length on the garden wall
And breaks his shell in the last shocked beginning;
A crocodile before the chrysalis,
Before the fall from love the flying heartbone,   15
Winged like a sabbath ass this children's piece
Uncredited blows Jericho on Eden.

The insect fable is the certain promise.

Death: death of Hamlet and the nightmare madmen,
An air-drawn windmill on a wooden horse,   20
John's beast, Job's patience, and the fibs of vision,
Greek in the Irish sea the ageless voice:
'Adam I love, my madmen's love is endless,
No tell-tale lover has an end more certain,
All legends' sweethearts on a tree of stories,   25
My cross of tales behind the fabulous curtain.'

Then was my neophyte

Then was my neophyte,
Child in white blood bent on its knees
Under the bell of rocks,
Ducked in the twelve, disciple seas
The winder of the water-clocks   5

Calls a green day and night.
My sea hermaphrodite,
Snail of man in His ship of fires
That burn the bitten decks,
Knew all His horrible desires   10
The climber of the water sex
Calls the green rock of light.

Who in these labyrinths,
This tidethread and the lane of scales,
Twine in a moon-blown shell,   15
Escapes to the flat cities' sails
Furled on the fishes' house and hell,
Nor falls to His green myths?
Stretch the salt photographs,
The landscape grief, love in His oils   20
Mirror from man to whale
That the green child see like a grail
Through veil and fin and fire and coil
Time on the canvas paths.

He films my vanity.   25
Shot in the wind, by tilted arcs,
Over the water come
Children from homes and children's parks
Who speak on a finger and thumb,
And the masked, headless boy.   30
His reels and mystery
The winder of the clockwise scene
Wound like a ball of lakes
Then threw on that tide-hoisted screen
Love's image till my heartbone breaks   35
By a dramatic sea.

Who kills my history?
The year-hedged row is lame with flint,
Blunt scythe and water blade.

'Who could snap off the shapeless print   40
From your tomorrow-treading shade
With oracle for eye?'
Time kills me terribly.
'Time shall not murder you', He said,
'Nor the green nought be hurt;   45
Who could hack out your unsucked heart,
O green and unborn and undead?'
I saw time murder me.

It is the sinners' dust-tongued bell

It is the sinners' dust-tongued bell claps me to churches
When, with his torch and hourglass, like a sulphur priest,
His beast heel cleft in a sandal,
Time marks a black aisle kindle from the brand of ashes,
Grief with dishevelled hands tear out the altar ghost   5
And a firewind kill the candle.

Over the choir minute I hear the hour chant:
Time's coral saint and the salt grief drown a foul sepulchre
And a whirlpool drives the prayerwheel;
Moonfall and sailing emperor, pale as their tideprint,   10
Hear by death's accident the clocked and dashed-down spire
Strike the sea hour through bellmetal.

There is loud and dark directly under the dumb flame,
Storm, snow, and fountain in the weather of fireworks,
Cathedral calm in the pulled house;   15
Grief with drenched book and candle christens the cherub time
From the emerald, still bell; and from the pacing weathercock
The voice of bird on coral prays.

Forever it is a white child in the dark-skinned summer
Out of the font of bone and plants at that stone tocsin   20
Scales the blue wall of spirits;

From blank and leaking winter sails the child in colour,
Shakes, in crabbed burial shawl, by sorcerer's insect woken,
Ding dong from the mute turrets.

I mean by time the cast and curfew rascal of our marriage,   25
At nightbreak born in the fat side, from an animal bed
In a holy room in a wave;
And all love's sinners in sweet cloth kneel to a hyleg image,
Nutmeg, civet, and sea-parsley serve the plagued groom and bride
Who have brought forth the urchin grief.   30

Two limericks

i.
There was an old bugger called God
    Who put a young virgin in pod:
        This amazing behaviour
    Produced Christ our saviour,
Who died on a cross, poor old sod.   5

ii.
The last time I slept with the Queen,
 I repeatedly muttered, 'Ich Dien':
        She called me a shite
        And said, 'Put out the light.
A Queen should be served but not seen.'   5

From the Veronica Sibthorpe papers

i. Three verses

a) Welsh lazy

Oh oh there's lazy I
Am
Damn
It all I am, aye.

b) Poem to Veronica

Wherever there's honey there's bees & bears there
And I'm a bad bee & you're a good bear.

c) Shouldn't

All I know about death
Can be said in one breath:
It's tall and it's short
And it shouldn't ought.

ii. For as long as forever is

For as long as forever is
And the fast sky quakes in the web, as the fox in the wave,
With heels of birds and the plumed eyes,
Shakes in its stride the partridge fence and the sea-duck rows,
And a flame in a wheel jumps the nave,   5
As a dozen winds drop the dark by the one moonrise,
And the stag through a trap grave,
Forever the hunted world at a snail's gallop goes.

Over the packed nests now, the snare and the she-bear's floes,
Through the cat's mountain and the cave   10
By the market and a feather street near the townspires,
Narrowly time's slow riders shave.

I make this in a warring absence

I make this in a warring absence when
Each ancient, stone-necked minute of love's season
Harbours my anchored tongue, slips the quaystone,
When, praise is blessed, her pride in mast and fountain
Sailed and set dazzling by the handshaped ocean,   5

In that proud sailing tree with branches driven
Through the last vault and vegetable groyne,
And this weak house to marrow-columned heaven,

Is corner-cast, breath's rag, scrawled weed, a vain
And opium head, crow stalk, puffed, cut, and blown,   10
Or like the tide-looped breastknot reefed again
Or rent ancestrally the roped sea-hymen,
And, pride is last, is like a child alone
By magnet winds to her blind mother drawn,
Bread and milk mansion in a toothless town.   15

She makes for me a nettle's innocence
And a silk pigeon's guilt in her proud absence,
In the molested rocks the shell of virgins,
The frank, closed pearl, the sea-girls' lineaments
Glint in the staved and siren-printed caverns,   20
Is maiden in the shameful oak, omens
Whalebed and bulldance, the gold bush of lions
Proud as a sucked stone and huge as sandgrains.

These are her contraries: the beast who follows
With priest's grave foot and hand of five assassins   25
Her molten flight up cinder-nesting columns,
Calls the starved fire herd, is cast in ice,
Lost in a limp-treed and uneating silence,
Who scales a hailing hill in her cold flintsteps
Falls on a ring of summers and locked noons.   30

I make a weapon of an ass's skeleton
And walk the warring sands by the dead town,
Cudgel great air, wreck east, and topple sundown,
Storm her sped heart, hang with beheaded veins
Its wringing shell, and let her eyelids fasten.   35
Destruction, picked by birds, brays through the jawbone,
And, for that murder's sake, dark with contagion
Like an approaching wave I sprawl to ruin.

Ruin, the room of errors, one rood dropped
Down the stacked sea and water-pillared shade,   40
Weighed in rock shroud, is my proud pyramid;
Where, wound in emerald linen and sharp wind,
The hero's head lies scraped of every legend,
Comes love's anatomist with sun-gloved hand
Who picks the live heart on a diamond.   45

'His mother's womb had a tongue that lapped up mud',
Cried the topless, inchtaped lips from hank and hood
In that bright anchorground where I lay linened,
'A lizard darting with black venom's thread
Doubled, to fork him back, through the lockjaw bed   50
And the breath-white, curtained mouth of seed'.
'See', drummed the taut masks, 'how the dead ascend;
In the groin's endless coil a man is tangled.'

These once-blind eyes have breathed a wind of visions,
The cauldron's root through this once-rindless hand   55
Fumed like a tree, and tossed a burning bird;
With loud, torn tooth and tail and cobweb drum
The crumpled packs fled past this ghost in bloom,
And, mild as pardon from a cloud of pride,
The terrible world my brother bares his skin.   60

Now in the cloud's big breast lie quiet countries,
Delivered seas my love from her proud place
Walks with no wound, nor lightning in her face,
A calm wind blows that raised the trees like hair
Once where the soft snow's blood was turned to ice.   65
And though my love pulls the pale, nippled air,
Prides of tomorrow suckling in her eyes,
Yet this I make in a forgiving presence.

In the Direction of the Beginning

In the light tent in the swinging field in the great spring evening, near the sea and the shingled boat with a mast of cedar-wood, the hinderwood decked with beaks and shells, a folded, salmon sail, and two finned oars; with gulls in one flight high over, stork, pelican, and sparrow, flying to the ocean's end and the first grain of a time- 5 less land that spins on the head of a sand glass, a hoop of feathers down the dark of the spring in a topsy-turvy year; as the rocks in history, by every feature and scrawled limb, eye of a needle, shadow of a nerve, cut in the heart, by rifted fibre and clay thread, recorded for the rant of odyssey the dropping of the bay-leaf toppling of the 10 oak-tree splintering of the moonstone against assassin avatar undead and numbered waves, a man was born in the direction of the begin- ning. And out of sleep, where the moon had raised him through the mountains in her eyes and by the strong, eyed arms that fall behind her, full of tides and fingers, to the blown sea, he wrestled over the 15 edge of the evening, took to the beginning as a goose to the sky, and called his furies by their names from the wind-drawn index of the grave and waters. Who was this stranger who came like a hailstone, cut in ice, a snow-leafed seabush for her hair, and taller than a cedar- mast, the north white rain descending and the whale-driven sea cast 20 up to the caves of the eye, from a fisherman's city on the floating island? She was salt and white and travelling as the field, on one blade, swung with its birds around her, evening centred in the never- still heart, he heard her hands among the treetops—a feather dived, her fingers flowed over the voices—and the world went drowning 25 down through a siren stranger's vision of grass and waterbeasts and snow. The world was sucked to the last lake's drop; the cataract of the last particle worried in a lather to the ground, as if the rain from heaven had let its clouds fall turtle-turning like a manna made of the soft-bellied seasons, and the hard hail, falling, spread and flus- 30 tered in a cloud half flower half ash or the comb-footed scavenger's wind through a pyramid raised high with mud or the soft slow drift of mingling steam and leaves. In the exact centre of enchantment he was a shoreman in deep sea, lashed by his hair to the eye in the cyclop breast, with his swept thighs strung among her voice; white bears swam and sailors drowned to the music she scaled and drew with hands and fables from his upright hair; she plucked his terror by the ears, and bore him singing into light through the forest of the serpent-haired and the stone-turning voice. Revelation stared back over its transfixed shoulder. Which was her genesis, the last spark of judgement or the first whale's spout from the waterland? The conflagration at the end, a burial fire jumping, a spent rocket hot on its tail, or, where the first spring and its folly climbed the sea barriers and the garden locks were bruised, capped and douting water over the mountain candle-head? Whose was the image in the wind, the print on the cliff, the echo knocking to be answered? She was orioled and serpent-haired. She moved in the swallowing, salty field, the chronicle and the rocks, the dark anatomies, the anchored sea itself. She raged in the mule's womb. She faltered in the galloping dynasty. She was loud in the old grave, kept a still, quick tongue in the sun. He marked her outcast image, mapped with a nightmare's foot in poison and framed against the wind, print of her thumb that buckled on its hand with a webbed shadow, interrogation of the familiar echo: which is my genesis, the granite fountain extinguishing where the first flame is cast in the sculptured world, or the bonfire maned like a lion in the threshold of the last vault? One voice then in that evening travelled the light and water waves, one lineament took on the sliding moods, from where the gold green sea cantharis dyes the trail of the octopus one venom crawled through foam, and from the four map corners one cherub in an island shape puffed the clouds to sea.

He fed on the fattened terror of death ['Epitaph']

He fed on the fattened terror of death, and died.
(And his mother's womb had a tongue that lapped up mud).
The terrible grave was lesson for the suicide:
He slit his throat in the coffin and shed dried blood.

O make me a mask

O make me a mask and a wall to shut from your spies
Of the sharp, enamelled eyes and the spectacled claws
Rape and rebellion in the nurseries of my face,
Gag of a dumbstruck tree to block from bare enemies
The bayonet tongue in this undefended prayerpiece,   5
The present mouth, and the sweetly blown trumpet of lies,
Shaped in old armour and oak the countenance of a dunce
To shield the glistening brain and blunt the examiners,
And a tear-stained widower grief drooped from the lashes
To veil belladonna and let the dry eyes perceive   10
Others betray the lamenting lies of their losses
By the curve of the nude mouth or the laugh up the sleeve.

The spire cranes

The spire cranes. Its statue is an aviary.
From the stone nest it does not let the feathery
Carved birds blunt their striking throats on the salt gravel,
Pierce the spilt sky with diving wing in weed and heel
An inch in froth. Chimes cheat the prison spire, pelter   5
In time like outlaw rains on that priest, water,
Time for swimmers' hands, music for silver lock
And mouth. Both note and plume plunge from the spire's hook.
Those craning birds are choice for you, songs that jump back
To the built voice, or fly with winter to the bells,   10
But do not travel down dumb wind like prodigals.

When all my five and country senses

When all my five and country senses see,
The fingers will forget green thumbs and mark

How, through the halfmoon's vegetable eye,
Husk of young stars and handfull zodiac,
Love in the frost is pared and wintered by,   5
The whispering ears will watch love drummed away
Down breeze and shell to a discordant beach,
And, lashed to syllables, the lynx tongue cry
That her fond wounds are mended bitterly.
My nostrils see her breath burn like a bush.   10

My one and noble heart has witnesses
In all love's countries, that will grope awake;
And when blind sleep drops on the spying senses,
The heart is sensual, though five eyes break.

Not from this anger

Not from this anger, anticlimax after
Refusal struck her loin and the lame flower
Bent like a beast to lap the singular floods
In a land strapped by hunger
Shall she receive a bellyful of weeds   5
And bear those tendril hands I touch across .
The agonized, two seas.

Behind my head a square of sky sags over
The circular smile tossed from lover to lover
And the golden ball spins out of the skies;   10
Not from this anger after
Refusal struck like a bell under water
Shall her smile breed that mouth, behind the mirror,
That burns along my eyes.

How shall my animal

How shall my animal
Whose wizard shape I trace in the cavernous skull,
Vessel of abscesses and exultation's shell,
Endure burial under the spelling wall,
The invoked, shrouding veil at the cap of the face,   5
Who should be furious,
Drunk as a vineyard snail, flailed like an octopus,
Roaring, crawling, quarrel
With the outside weathers,
The natural circle of the discovered skies   10
Draw down to its weird eyes?

How shall it magnetize,
Towards the studded male in a bent, midnight blaze
That melts the lionhead's heel and horseshoe of the heart,
A brute land in the cool top of the country days   15
To trot with a loud mate the haybeds of a mile,
Love and labour and kill
In quick, sweet, cruel light till the locked ground sprout out,
The black, burst sea rejoice,
The bowels turn turtle,   20
Claw of the crabbed veins squeeze from each red particle
The parched and raging voice?

Fishermen of mermen
Creep and harp on the tide, sinking their charmed, bent pin
With bridebait of gold bread, I with a living skein,   25
Tongue and ear in the thread, angle the temple-bound
Curl-locked and animal cavepools of spells and bone,
Trace out a tentacle,
Nailed with an open eye, in the bowl of wounds and weed
To clasp my fury on ground   30
And clap its great blood down;

Never shall beast be born to atlas the few seas
Or poise the day on a horn.

Sigh long, clay cold, lie shorn,
Cast high, stunned on gilled stone; sly scissors ground in frost   35
Clack through the thicket of strength, love hewn in pillars drops
With carved bird, saint, and sun, the wrackspiked maiden mouth
Lops, as a bush plumed with flames, the rant of the fierce eye,
Clips short the gesture of breath.
Die in red feathers when the flying heaven's cut,   40
And roll with the knocked earth:
Lie dry, rest robbed, my beast.
You have kicked from a dark den, leaped up the whinnying light,
And dug your grave in my breast.

After the funeral
(In memory of Ann Jones)

After the funeral, mule praises, brays,
Windshake of sailshaped ears, muffle-toed tap
Tap happily of one peg in the thick
Grave's foot, blinds down the lids, the teeth in black,
The spittled eyes, the salt ponds in the sleeves,   5
Morning smack of the spade that wakes up sleep,
Shakes a desolate boy who slits his throat
In the dark of the coffin and sheds dry leaves,
That breaks one bone to light with a judgement clout,
After the feast of tear-stuffed time and thistles   10
In a room with a stuffed fox and a stale fern,
I stand, for this memorial's sake, alone
In the snivelling hours with dead, humped Ann
Whose hooded, fountain heart once fell in puddles
Round the parched worlds of Wales and drowned each sun   15
(Though this for her is a monstrous image blindly
Magnified out of praise; her death was a still drop;
She would not have me sinking in the holy

Flood of her heart's fame; she would lie dumb and deep
And need no druid of her broken body).   20
But I, Ann's bard on a raised hearth, call all
The seas to service that her wood-tongued virtue
Babble like a bellbuoy over the hymning heads,
Bow down the walls of the ferned and foxy woods
That her love sing and swing through a brown chapel,   25
Bless her bent spirit with four, crossing birds.
Her flesh was meek as milk, but this skyward statue
With the wild breast and blessed and giant skull
Is carved from her in a room with a wet window
In a fiercely mourning house in a crooked year.   30
I know her scrubbed and sour humble hands
Lie with religion in their cramp, her threadbare
Whisper in a damp word, her wits drilled hollow,
Her fist of a face died clenched on a round pain;
And sculptured Ann is seventy years of stone.   35
These cloud-sopped, marble hands, this monumental
Argument of the hewn voice, gesture and psalm
Storm me forever over her grave until
The stuffed lung of the fox twitch and cry Love
And the strutting fern lay seeds on the black sill.   40

O Chatterton and others in the attic

O Chatterton and others in the attic
Linked in one gas bracket
Taking Jeyes' fluid as narcotic;
Drink from the earth's teats,
Life neat's a better poison than in bottle,   5
A better venom seethes in spittle
Than one could probe out of a serpent's guts;
Each new sensation emits
A new vinegar;
Be a regular   10
Fellow with saw at the jugular.

On giddy nights when slap on the moon's mask
A madman with a brush has slapped a face
I pick a stick of celery from the valley
I find a tripper's knicker in the gully 15
And take another nibble at my flask.
What meaning, voices, in the straight-ruled grass,
Meaning in hot sock soil? A little cuss
Can't read sense in the rain that willy nilly
Soaks to the vest old dominies and drunks. 20
Dissect that statement, voices, on the slabs.
Love's a decision of 3 nerves
And Up or Down love's questions ask;
On giddy nights I slap a few drunk curves
Slap on the drunk moon's mask. 25
Rape gulp and be merry, he also serves
Who only drinks his profits
And would a-wooing go around the graves.
Celibate I sit and see
Women figures round my cell, 30
Women figures on the wall
Point their little breasts at me;
I must wait for a woman's smile
Not in the sun but in the dark;
The two words stallion and sterile 35
Stand in a question mark.
The smiling woman is a mad story,
Wipe it away, wipe a crumb
From the preacher's table.
I offer you women, not woman, 40
A home and a dowry:
3 little lusts shall your dowry be,
And your home in a centaur's stable.

On no work of words

On no work of words now for three lean months in the bloody
Belly of the rich year and the big purse of my body
I bitterly take to task my poverty and craft:

To take to give is all, return what is hungrily given
Puffing the pounds of manna up through the dew to heaven,   5
The lovely gift of the gab bangs back on a blind shaft.

To lift to leave from the treasures of man is pleasing death
That will rake at last all currencies of the marked breath
And count the taken, forsaken mysteries in a bad dark.

To surrender now is to pay the expensive ogre twice.   10
Ancient woods of my blood, dash down to the nut of the seas
If I take to burn or return this world which is each man's work.

I, the first named

I, the first named, am the ghost of this sir and Christian friend
Who writes these words I write in a still room in a spellsoaked
    house:
I am the ghost in this house that is filled with tongues and eyes
Of a lack-a-head ghost I fear to the anonymous end.

The tombstone told

The tombstone told when she died.
Her two surnames stopped me still.
A virgin married at rest.
She married in this pouring place,

That I struck one day by luck, 5
Before I heard in my mother's side
Or saw in the looking-glass shell
The rain through her cold heart speak
And the sun killed in her face.
More the thick stone cannot tell. 10

Before she lay on a stranger's bed
With a hand plunged through her hair,
Or that rainy tongue beat back
Through the devilish years and innocent deaths
To the room of a secret child, 15
Among men later I heard it said
She cried her white-dressed limbs were bare
And her red lips were kissed black,
She wept in her pain and made mouths,
Talked and tore though her eyes smiled. 20

I who saw in a hurried film
Death and this mad heroine
Meet once on a mortal wall
Heard her speak through the chipped beak
Of the stone bird guarding her: 25
I died before bedtime came
But my womb was bellowing
And I felt with my bare fall
A blazing red harsh head tear up
And the dear floods of his hair. 30

A saint about to fall

A saint about to fall,
The stained flats of heaven hit and razed
To the kissed kite hems of his shawl,
On the last street wave praised
The unwinding, song by rock, 5

Of the woven wall
Of his father's house in the sands,
The vanishing of the musical ship-work and the chucked bells,
The wound-down cough of the blood-counting clock
Behind a face of hands, 10
On the angelic etna of the last whirring featherlands,
Wind-heeled foot in the hole of a fireball,
Hymned his shrivelling flock,
On the last rick's tip by spilled wine-wells
Sang heaven hungry and the quick 15
Cut Christbread spitting vinegar and all
The mazes of his praise and envious tongue were worked in flames
     and shells.

Glory cracked like a flea.
The sun-leaved holy candlewoods
Drivelled down to one singeing tree 20
With a stub of black buds,
The sweet, fish-gilled boats bringing blood
Lurched through a scuttled sea
With a hold of leeches and straws,
Heaven fell with his fall and one crocked bell beat the left air. 25
O wake in me in my house in the mud
Of the crotch of the squawking shores,
Flicked from the carbolic city puzzle in a bed of sores
The scudding base of the familiar sky,
The lofty roots of the clouds. 30
From an odd room in a split house stare,
Milk in your mouth, at the sour floods
That bury the sweet street slowly, see
The skull of the earth is barbed with a war of burning brains and
     hair.

Strike in the time-bomb town, 35
Raise the live rafters of the eardrum,
Throw your fear a parcel of stone
Through the dark asylum,

Lapped among herods wail
As their blade marches in   40
That the eyes are already murdered,
The stocked heart is forced, and agony has another mouth to feed.
O wake to see, after a noble fall,
The old mud hatch again, the horrid
Woe drip from the dishrag hands and the pressed sponge of the
    forehead,   45
The breath draw back like a bolt through white oil
And a stranger enter like iron.
Cry joy that this witchlike midwife second
Bullies into rough seas you so gentle
And makes with a flick of the thumb and sun   50
A thundering bullring of your silent and girl-circled island.

Twenty-four years

Twenty-four years remind the tears of my eyes.
(Bury the dead for fear that they walk to the grave in labour.)
In the groin of the natural doorway I crouched like a tailor
Sewing a shroud for a journey
By the light of the meat-eating sun.   5
Dressed to die, the sensual strut begun,
With my red veins full of money,
In the final direction of the elementary town
I advance for as long as forever is.

Once it was the colour of saying

Once it was the colour of saying
Soaked my table the uglier side of a hill
With a capsized field where a school sat still
And a black and white patch of girls grew playing;
The gentle seaslides of saying I must undo   5
That all the charmingly drowned arise to cockcrow and kill.

When I whistled with mitching boys through a reservoir park
Where at night we stoned the cold and cuckoo
Lovers in the dirt of their leafy beds,
The shade of their trees was a word of many shades   10
And a lamp of lightning for the poor in the dark;
Now my saying shall be my undoing,
And every stone I wind off like a reel.

Because the pleasure-bird whistles

Because the pleasure-bird whistles after the hot wires,
Shall the blind horse sing sweeter?
Convenient bird and beast lie lodged to suffer
The supper and knives of a mood.
In the sniffed and poured snow on the tip of the tongue of the
    year   5
That clouts the spittle like bubbles with broken rooms,
An enamoured man alone by the twigs of his eyes, two fires,
Camped in the drug-white shower of nerves and food,
Savours the lick of the times through a deadly wood of hair
In a wind that plucked a goose,   10
Nor ever, as the wild tongue breaks its tombs,
Rounds to look at the red, wagged root.
Because there stands, one story out of the bum city,
That frozen wife whose juices drift like a fixed sea
Secretly in statuary,   15
Shall I, struck on the hot and rocking street,
Not spin to stare at an old year
Toppling and burning in the muddle of towers and galleries
Like the mauled pictures of boys?
The salt person and blasted place   20
I furnish with the meat of a fable;
If the dead starve, their stomachs turn to tumble
An upright man in the antipodes
Or spray-based and rock-chested sea:
Over the past table I repeat this present grace.   25

'If my head hurt a hair's foot'

'If my head hurt a hair's foot
Pack back the downed bone. If the unpricked ball of my breath
Bump on a spout let the bubbles jump out.
Sooner drop with the worm of the ropes round my throat
Than bully ill love in the clouted scene.   5

All game phrases fit your ring of a cockfight:
I'll comb the snared woods with a glove on a lamp,
Peck, sprint, dance on fountains and duck time
Before I rush in a crouch the ghost with a hammer, air,
Strike light, and bloody a loud room.   10

If my bunched, monkey coming is cruel
Rage me back to the making house. My hand unravel
When you sew the deep door. The bed is a cross place.
Bend, if my journey ache, direction like an arc or make
A limp and riderless shape to leap nine thinning months.'   15

'No. Not for Christ's dazzling bed
Of nacreous sleep among soft particles and charms
My dear would I change my tears or your iron head.
Thrust, my daughter or son, to escape, there is none, none, none,
Nor when all ponderous heaven's host of waters breaks.   20

Now to awake husked of gestures and my joy like a cave
To the anguish and carrion, to the infant forever unfree,
O my lost love bounced from a good home;
The grain that hurries this way from the rim of the grave
Has a voice and a house, and there and here you must couch and
    cry.   25

Rest beyond choice in the dust-appointed grain,
At the breast stored with seas. No return

Through the waves of the fat streets nor the skeleton's thin ways.
The grave and my calm body are shut to your coming as stone,
And the endless beginning of prodigies suffers open.'   30

Poem
(To Caitlin)

Unluckily for a death
Waiting with phoenix under a stone
And long fidelity grown grey in her lop-briared
And thigh-describing wreath
Intact among the passionate dead and gone   5
In the burial holes of enticement
Though the brawl of the kiss has not occurred,
On the wanting mouth,
On the split, exhibiting forehead,
That binds her constant,   10
Nor the naked, original, lyrical
Aggression of love in a bridal broth
Or a continent-sheeted bed with animal rails
And a tucked crust of fossils,

Loving on a sea-banged shelf   15
My lucky burly body
Holy happy and greedy under the managed storm,
Luckily my sore ghost
In this collapsing day, the dark our pity,
Cut in this mustard moment, soothed of fever   20
By your kind health that keeps the west wrongs calm,
Fireworks at your breast,
And weeps on the inflammable gulf,
Myself will never
Arch that turkey's neck of a far-gone woman   25
To sing underground like a married thrush
Or shoo up the light that extinct, sparkling bird to heaven:
The dust-drenched two must wait my wish.

I see the tigron in tears
In the androgynous dark   30
To escape from the hot, brown caves and ramming columns
Of his half families
That stripe the forests with want, and the duck-
Billed platypus broody in the sexless bush.
There from a red and white clot of women   35
Juan runs like the waters.
In an imagining of tumbled mantime
Suddenly cold as fish,
I see through briar and stone, the black our business,
That patient love below and almost mistress,   40
Through masterless ground all loaded events of her flesh,
Great crotch, and giant continence.

Love, my fate got luckily,
May teach me now with no telling
That every drop of water is both kind and cruel,   45
With articulate eyes
Tell me the money-coloured sun sees poorly,
Teach that the child who sucks on innocence
Is spinning fast and loose on a fiery wheel,
All that we do, cruelly, kindly,   50
Will kiss in a huddle:
In the teeth of that black-and-white wedding
I chuck my armed happiness.
Though the puffed phoenix stir in the rocks
And lucklessly fair or sycorax the widow wait,   55
We abide with our pride, the unalterable light,
On this turning lump of mistakes.

To Others than You

Friend by enemy I call you out.

You with a bad coin in your socket,
You my friend there with a winning air
Who palmed the lie on me when you looked
Brassily at my shyest secret,   5
Enticed with twinkling bits of the eye
Till the sweet tooth of my love bit dry,
Rasped at last, and I stumbled and sucked,
Whom now I conjure to stand as thief
In the memory worked by mirrors,   10
With unforgettably smiling act,
Quickness of hand in the velvet glove
And my whole heart under your hammer,
Were once such a creature, so gay and frank
A desireless familiar   15
I never thought to utter or think
While you displaced a truth in the air,

That though I loved them for their faults
As much as for their good,
My friends were enemies on stilts   20
With their heads in a cunning cloud.

When I woke

When I woke, the town spoke.
Birds and clocks and cross bells
Dinned aside the coiling crowd,
The reptile profligates in a flame,
Spoilers and pokers of sleep,   5
The next-door sea dispelled

Frogs and satans and woman-luck,
While a man outside with a billhook,
Up to his head in his blood,
Cutting the morning off, 10
The warm-veined double of Time
And his scarving beard from a book,
Slashed down the last snake as though
It were a wand or subtle bough,
Its tongue peeled in the wrap of a leaf. 15

Every morning I make,
God in bed, good and bad,
After a water-face walk,
The death-stagged scatter-breath
Mammoth and sparrowfall 20
Everybody's earth.
Where birds ride like leaves and boats like ducks
I heard, this morning, waking,
Crossly out of the town noises
A voice in the erected air, 25
No prophet-progeny of mine,
Cry my sea town was breaking.
No Time, spoke the clocks, no God, rang the bells,
I drew the white sheet over the islands
And the coins on my eyelids sang like shells. 30

Paper and sticks

Paper and sticks and shovel and match
Why won't the news of the old world catch
And the fire in a temper start

Once I had a rich boy for myself
I loved his body and his navy blue wealth 5
And I lived in his purse and his heart

When in our bed I was tossing and turning
All I could see were his brown eyes burning
By the green of a one pound note

I talk to him as I clean the grate   10
O my dear it's never too late
To take me away as you whispered and wrote

I had a handsome and well-off boy
I'll share my money and we'll run for joy
With a bouncing and silver spooned kid   15

Sharp and shrill my silly tongue scratches
Words on the air as the fire catches
You never did and *he* never did.

Once below a time

I

Once below a time,
When my pinned-around-the-spirit
Cut-to-measure flesh bit,
Suit for a serial sum
On the first of each hardship,   5
My paid-for slaved-for own too late
In love torn breeches and blistered jacket
On the snapping rims of the ashpit,
In grottoes I worked with birds,
Spiked with a mastiff collar,   10
Tasselled in cellar and snipping shop
Or decked on a cloud swallower,

Then swift from a bursting sea with bottlecork boats
And out-of-perspective sailors,
In common clay clothes disguised as scales,   15

As a he-god's paddling water skirts,
I astounded the sitting tailors,
I set back the clock faced tailors,

Then, bushily swanked in bear wig and tails,
Hopping hot leaved and feathered   20
From the kangaroo foot of the earth,
From the chill, silent centre
Trailing the frost bitten cloth,
Up through the lubber crust of Wales
I rocketed to astonish   25
The flashing needle rock of squatters,
The criers of Shabby and Shorten,
The famous stitch droppers.

II

My silly suit, hardly yet suffered for,
Around some coffin carrying   30
Birdman or told ghost I hung.
And the owl hood, the heel hider,
Claw fold and hole for the rotten
Head, deceived, I believed, my maker,

The cloud perched tailors' master with nerves for cotton.   35
On the old seas from stories, thrashing my wings,
Combing with antlers, Columbus on fire,
I was pierced by the idol tailor's eyes,
Glared through shark mask and navigating head,
Cold Nansen's beak on a boat full of gongs,   40

To the boy of common thread,
The bright pretender, the ridiculous sea dandy
With dry flesh and earth for adorning and bed.
It was sweet to drown in the readymade handy water
With my cherry capped dangler green as seaweed   45
Summoning a child's voice from a webfoot stone,

Never never oh never to regret the bugle I wore
On my cleaving arm as I blasted in a wave.

Now shown and mostly bare I would lie down,
Lie down, lie down and live   50
As quiet as a bone.

There was a Saviour

        There was a saviour
        Rarer than radium,
    Commoner than water, crueller than truth;
        Children kept from the sun
        Assembled at his tongue   5
    To hear the golden note turn in a groove,
Prisoners of wishes locked their eyes
In the jails and studies of his keyless smiles.

        The voice of children says
        From a lost wilderness   10
    There was calm to be done in his safe unrest,
        When hindering man hurt
        Man, animal, or bird
    We hid our fears in that murdering breath,
Silence, silence to do, when earth grew loud,   15
In lairs and asylums of the tremendous shout.

        There was glory to hear
        In the churches of his tears,
    Under his downy arm you sighed as he struck,
        O you who could not cry   20
        On to the ground when a man died
    Put a tear for joy in the unearthly flood
And laid your cheek against a cloud-formed shell:
Now in the dark there is only yourself and myself.

Two proud, blacked brothers cry,   25
    Winter-locked side by side,
To this inhospitable hollow year,
    O we who could not stir
    One lean sigh when we heard
    Greed on man beating near and fire neighbour   30
But wailed and nested in the sky-blue wall
Now break a giant tear for the little known fall,

    For the drooping of homes
    That did not nurse our bones,
Brave deaths of only ones but never found,   35
    Now see, alone in us,
    Our own true strangers' dust
    Ride through the doors of our unentered house.
Exiled in us we arouse the soft,
Unclenched, armless, silk and rough love that breaks all rocks.   40

The Countryman's Return

Embracing low-falutin
London (said the odd man in
A country pot, his hutch in
The fields, by a motherlike henrun)
With my fishtail hands and gently   5
Manuring popeye or
Swelling in flea-specked linen
The rankest of the city
I spent my unwasteable
Time among walking pintables   10
With sprung and padded shoulders,
Tomorrow's drunk club majors
Growing their wounds already,
The last war's professional
Unclaimed dead, girls from good homes   15
Studying the testicle

In communal crab flats
With Sunflowers laid on,
Old paint-stained tumblers riding
On stools to a one man show down,   20
Gasketted and sirensuited
Bored and viciously waiting
Nightingales of the casualty stations
In the afternoon wasters
White feathering the living.   25

London's arches are falling
In, in Pedro's or Wendy's
With a silverfox farmer
Trying his hand at failing
Again, a collected poet   30
And some dismantled women,
Razor man and belly king,
I propped humanity's weight
Against the fruit machine,
Opened my breast and into   35
The spongebag let them all melt.
Zip once more for a traveller
With his goods under his eyes,
Another with hers under her belt,
The black man bleached to his tide   40
Mark, trumpet lipped and blackhead
Eyed, while the tears drag on the tail,
The weighing-scales, of my hand.
Then into blind streets I swam
Alone with my bouncing bag,   45
Too full to bow to the dim
Moon with a relation's face
Or lift my hat to unseen
Brothers dodging through the fog
The affectionate pickpocket   50
And childish, snivelling queen.

Beggars, robbers, inveiglers,
Voices from manholes and drains,
Maternal short time pieces,
Octopuses in doorways,   55
Dark inviters to keyholes
And evenings with great danes,
Bedsitting girls on the beat
With nothing for the metre,
Others whose single beds hold two   60
Only to make two ends meet,
All the hypnotised city's
Insidious procession
Hawking for money and pity
Among the hardly possessed.   65
And I in the wanting sway
Caught among never enough
Conjured me to resemble
A singing Walt from the mower
And jerrystone trim villas   70
Of the upper of the lower half,
Beardlessly wagging in Dean Street,
Blessing and counting the bustling
Twolegged handbagged sparrows,
Flogging into the porches   75
My cavernous, featherbed self.

Cut. Cut the crushed streets, leaving
A hole of errands and shades;
Plug the paper-blowing tubes;
Emasculate the seedy clocks;   80
Rub off the scrawl of prints on
Body and air and building;
Branch and leaf the birdless roofs;
Faces of melting visions,
Magdalene prostitution,   85
Glamour of the bloodily bowed,
Exaltation of the blind,

That sin-embracing dripper of fun
Sweep away like a cream cloud;
Bury all rubbish and love signs 90
Of my week in the dirtbox
In this anachronistic scene
Where sitting in clean linen
In a hutch in a cowpatched glen
Now delight, I suppose, in 95
The countryman's return
And count by birds' eggs and leaves
The rusticating minutes,
The wasteful hushes among trees.
An O to cut the green field, leaving 100
One rich street with hunger in it.

Into her lying down head

I

Into her lying down head
His enemies entered bed,
Under the encumbered eyelid,
Through the rippled drum of the hair-buried ear;
And Noah's rekindled now unkind dove 5
Flew man-bearing there.
Last night in a raping wave
Whales unreined from the green grave
In fountains of origin gave up their love,
Along her innocence glided 10
Juan aflame and savagely young King Lear,
Queen Catherine howling bare
And Samson drowned in his hair,
The colossal intimacies of silent
Once seen strangers or shades on a stair; 15
There the dark blade and wanton sighing her down
To a haycock couch and the scythes of his arms

Rode and whistled a hundred times
Before the crowing morning climbed;
Man was the burning England she was sleep-walking, and the
enamouring island   20
Made her limbs blind by luminous charms,
Sleep to a newborn sleep in a swaddling loin-leaf stroked and sang
And his runaway beloved childlike laid in the acorned sand.

II

There where a numberless tongue
Wound their room with a male moan,   25
His faith around her flew undone
And darkness hung the walls with baskets of snakes,
A furnace-nostrilled column-membered
Super-or-near man
Resembling to her dulled sense   30
The thief of adolescence
Early imaginary half remembered
Oceanic lover alone
Jealousy cannot forget for all her sakes,
Made his bad bed in her good   35
Night, and enjoyed as he would.
Crying, white-gowned, from the middle moonlit stages
Out to the tiered and hearing tide,
Close and far she announced the theft of the heart
In the taken body at many ages,   40
Trespasser and broken bride
Celebrating at her side
All blood-signed assailings and vanished marriages in which he
had no lovely part
Nor could share, for his pride, to the least
Mutter and foul wingbeat of the solemnizing nightpriest   45
Her holy unholy hours with the always anonymous beast.

Two sand grains together in bed,
Head to heaven-circling head,
Singly lie with the whole wide shore,
The covering sea their nightfall with no names; 50
And out of every domed and soil-based shell
One voice in chains declaims
The female, deadly, and male
Libidinous betrayal,
Golden dissolving under the water veil. 55
A she bird sleeping brittle by
Her lover's wings that fold tomorrow's flight,
Within the nested treefork
Sings to the treading hawk
Carrion, paradise, chirrup my bright yolk. 60
A blade of grass longs with the meadow,
A stone lies lost and locked in the lark-high hill.
Open as to the air to the naked shadow
O she lies alone and still,
Innocent between two wars, 65
With the incestuous secret brother in the seconds to perpetuate the
stars,
A man torn up mourns in the sole night.
And the second comers, the severers, the enemies from the deep
Forgotten dark, rest their pulse and bury their dead in her faithless
sleep.

Deaths and Entrances

On almost the incendiary eve
Of several near deaths,
When one at the great least of your best loved
And always known must leave
Lions and fires of his flying breath, 5
Of your immortal friends

Who'd raise the organs of the counted dust
    To shoot and sing your praise,
One who called deepest down shall hold his peace
    That cannot sink or cease   10
    Endlessly to his wound
In many married London's estranging grief.

On almost the incendiary eve
    When at your lips and keys,
Locking, unlocking, the murdered strangers weave,   15
    One who is most unknown,
Your polestar neighbour, sun of another street,
    Will dive up to his tears.
He'll bathe his raining blood in the male sea
    Who strode for your own dead   20
And wind his globe out of your water thread
    And load the throats of shells
    With every cry since light
Flashed first across his thunderclapping eyes.

On almost the incendiary eve   25
    Of deaths and entrances,
When near and strange wounded on London's waves
    Have sought your single grave,
One enemy, of many, who knows well
    Your heart is luminous   30
In the watched dark, quivering through locks and caves,
    Will pull the thunderbolts
To shut the sun, plunge, mount your darkened keys
    And sear just riders back,
    Until that one loved least   35
Looms the last Samson of your zodiac.

On a Wedding Anniversary

The sky is torn across
This ragged anniversary of two
Who moved for three years in tune
Down the long walks of their vows.

Now their love lies a loss   5
And Love and his patients roar on a chain:
From every true or crater
Carrying cloud, Death strikes their house.

Too late in the wrong rain
They come together whom their love parted: 10
The windows pour into their heart
And the doors burn in their brain.

Parodies from *The Death of the King's Canary*

Lamentable Ode
by Albert Ponting

I, I, my own gauze phantom am,
My head frothing under my arm,
The buttocks of Venus for my huge davenport.
I orgillous turn, burn, churn,
As his rubbery bosom curds my perspiring arm—   5
The gust of my ghost, I mean—
And he wears no woman-sick, puce, and oriflammed a brow
That, yes, yes, my hair screamed aloud
Louder than death's orchestra or sirocco.
The urge of the purge of the womb of the worm   10
I renege in the flail-like failing of
The detumescent sun.

This my crepuscular palimpsest is:
I am so greatly him that lazarhouses and such
Lascivious lodges of the unloved   15
Peel like pomegranates at my nasal touch
And Balham faints in a scalecophidian void.
To him who broods in the nest of my arches,
Fallen or Charing Cross's, like a big bumbling bird,
Before the metropolitan horde   20
Funicling darkly lairward
I lay the most holy gifts of my spilt flesh:
Far beyond comprehension of golden asinine error
I raise to the mirror the maggots and lumps of my terror.

Brothers Beneath the Skin
by Wyndham Nils Snowden

Preached the archbishop from his high gothic pulpit
After the choirboys' shrilling and the canons' Oxford roar;
    'England Home and Beauty
    Are for those who do their Duty,
Respect the King, respect the Cloth, give honour to the Law.'   5

The communist made answer from his back room in Bloomsbury,
Marx and Lenin open by the Woodbines on the floor:
    'You may preach of Kingdom Come
    But in factory and slum
Is brewing such a trouble as was never seen before.'   10

Then cried the tired mechanic with the good bones mechanically,
'O I am fine and dandy and the master of my soul.
    My granddad was a peasant
    And it wasn't very pleasant
Without cinemas and birth-control and unions and the dole.'   15

Arrogant in answer spoke the massive humming turbines
Turning in the powerhouse like the grinding mills of God:
    'Little man in your manhole
    You may stand at the control
But you're no more our master than a peasant with a hod.'   20

Cool in his clinic chimed the sexless psychoanalyst:
'You may flap your little flags and build Empires overseas
    But there's something lies behind
    In the bad rooms of your mind
Made of father-hates, castration-fears, and such-like things
    as these.   25

Hotly they answered from their battleships and compounds,
Plethoric, bristling, turning red and white and blue:
    'You nasty little cad,
    We've clean bodies; and, by Gad,
We'd rather have a dirty mind than be a filthy Jew.'   30

Thus said the poet in the prep room with his pretty ones,
Calling pukka sahibs and the soakers on verandahs:
    'Lo! The true-blue day has scrammed
    When you Did and Iffed and Damned,
And all the jellybellies are as soft as baby pandas.'   35

Lightning-quick as Larwood cried the silly, silly cricketers:
'Dirty little highbrow with your black and bitten nails,
    We knew the Empire backwards
    When you were learning sex words
And the lesser breeds of scribbler were hanging by their tails.'   40

Straight-mouthed the master, eternally quadrangular:
'Oh purple men at tiffin with your horse-faced better halves,
    Did you never stop to think
    As you downed the sun in drink
That the bums you bruise and beat will have the last and longer
    laughs?'   45

'Look what we have given them: God, and guns and discipline,
Syphilis and alcohol, and missionaries and whips.'
    Came the cry beyond the waves
    Of emancipated slaves:
'We were doing very nicely till the white lord came in ships.'   50

'You have stole my chanty metre', called Kipling from the clouds,
'And what you've written in it ain't no bleedin' earthly good;
    You're a lily-livered pup
    What should be delivered up
To do packdrill with the Horse Marines and Foot, which same are
    rude.'   55

Look, dead man, at this Empire, at this Eastscape of suffering,
Monocled glaucoma over India's coral strand.
    They can hear in twilight Ealing
    The forts fall in Darjeeling
As the last White Hope is snuffed out in that dark-skinned
    No-Man's-Land.   60

Parachutist
by Christopher Garvin

I shall never forget his blue eye,
Bright as a bird's but larger,
Imprinting on my own
Tear-wounded but merciless iris
The eternal letters   5
Of his blond incomprehension.

He came down lightly by the lilypool
Where a bird was washing,
But he did not frighten her:
A touselled boy from the skies   10
Petrol should not have signed
Shamefully to his surprised dishonour;

His uniform like an obscene shroud
Fretted his hands that should have held in peace
A girl's two kind ones in a public park,   15
Handled a boat or fashioned simple things,
Flutes, clogs, and little wooden bears,
Or in beer gardens by the ribboning Rhine
Mirthfully gestured under linden trees.

Now these once loving-kindly hands   20
Cherished, like an adder picked up on a walk,
A tommy-gun, cold threat to love in steel:
Icarus he stands; his silken clouds of glory
Trailing behind him—a bird's broken wing—
Still trembling from his fallen angel's flight   25
Down the sky weeping death.

His wide amazed gaze like the child Mozart's
Straight would have stripped like an X-ray
Each last layer of my inmost heart
Had he but seen his enemy standing there   30
By the desk heaped high with betrayals and public faces
Of private friends false as a walking tour.

Suddenly splintered like glass the brittle dome
Enfolding our silence; an unjust bullet
Destroyed the delicate whorl on whorl of his brain.   35
Under the rosebush his trigger finger trembled.

O young man; O my might-have-been; understander.
We could have watched the dawn rise over München
Or gathered chestnuts under Hanniker Hill.
I who have known you only in unknowing   40
May now, alone, know you never at all,
O enemy not of my choice.

Request to Leda (Homage to William Empson)

Not your winged lust but his must now change suit
The harp-waked Casanova wakes no change
The worm is (pinpoint) rational in the fruit.

Not girl for bird (gourd being man) breaks root.
Taking no plume for index in love's change   5
Not your winged lust but his must now change suit.

Desire is phosphorous: the chemic bruit
Lust bears like volts, who'll amplify, and strange
The worm is (pinpoint) rational in the fruit.

Ballad of the Long-legged Bait

The bows glided down, and the coast
Blackened with birds took a last look
At his thrashing hair and whale-blue eye;
The trodden town rang its cobbles for luck.

Then goodbye to the fishermanned   5
Boat with its anchor free and fast
As a bird hooking over the sea,
High and dry by the top of the mast,

Whispered the affectionate sand
And the bulwarks of the dazzled quay.   10
For my sake sail, and never look back,
Said the looking land.

Sails drank the wind, and white as milk
He spread into the drinking dark;
The sun shipwrecked west on a pearl   15
And the moon swam out of its hulk.

Funnels and masts went by in a whirl.
Goodbye to the man on the sea-legged deck
To the gold gut that sings on his reel
To the bait that stalked out of the sack,   20

For we saw him throw to the swift flood
A girl alive with his hooks through her lips;
All the fishes were rayed in blood,
Said the dwindling ships.

Goodbye to chimneys and funnels,   25
Old wives that spin in the smoke,
He was blind to the eyes of candles
In the praying windows of waves

But heard his bait buck in the wake
And tussle in a shoal of loves.   30
Now cast down your rod, for the whole
Of the sea is hilly with whales,

She longs among horses and angels,
The rainbow-fish bend in her joys,
Floated the lost cathedral   35
Chimes of the rocked buoys.

Where the anchor rode like a gull
Miles over the moonstruck boat
A squall of birds bellowed and fell,
A cloud blew the rain from its throat;   40

He saw the storm smoke out to kill
With fuming bows and ram of ice,
Fire on starlight, rake Jesu's stream;
And nothing shone on the water's face

But the oil and bubble of the moon, 45
Plunging and piercing in his course
The lured fish under the foam
Witnessed with a kiss.

Whales in the wake like capes and Alps
Quaked the sick sea and snouted deep, 50
Deep the great bushed bait with raining lips
Slipped the fins of those humpbacked tons

And fled their love in a weaving dip.
Oh, Jericho was falling in their lungs!
She nipped and dived in the nick of love, 55
Spun on a spout like a long-legged ball

Till every beast blared down in a swerve
Till every turtle crushed from his shell
Till every bone in the rushing grave
Rose and crowed and fell! 60

Good luck to the hand on the rod,
There is thunder under its thumbs;
Gold gut is a lightning thread,
His fiery reel sings off its flames,

The whirled boat in the burn of his blood 65
Is crying from nets to knives,
Oh the shearwater birds and their boatsized brood
Oh the bulls of Biscay and their calves

Are making under the green, laid veil
The long-legged beautiful bait their wives.   70
Break the black news and paint on a sail
Huge weddings in the waves,

Over the wakeward-flashing spray
Over the gardens of the floor
Clash out the mounting dolphin's day,   75
My mast is a bell-spire,

Strike and smoothe, for my decks are drums,
Sing through the water-spoken prow
The octopus walking into her limbs
The polar eagle with his tread of snow.   80

From salt-lipped beak to the kick of the stern
Sing how the seal has kissed her dead!
The long, laid minute's bride drifts on
Old in her cruel bed.

Over the graveyard in the water   85
Mountains and galleries beneath
Nightingale and hyena
Rejoicing for that drifting death

Sing and howl through sand and anemone
Valley and sahara in a shell,   90
Oh all the wanting flesh his enemy
Thrown to the sea in the shell of a girl

Is old as water and plain as an eel;
Always goodbye to the long-legged bread
Scattered in the paths of his heels   95
For the salty birds fluttered and fed

And the tall grains foamed in their bills;
Always goodbye to the fires of the face,
For the crab-backed dead on the sea-bed rose
And scuttled over her eyes,   100

The blind, clawed stare is cold as sleet.
The tempter under the eyelid
Who shows to the selves asleep
Mast-high moon-white women naked

Walking in wishes and lovely for shame   105
Is dumb and gone with his flame of brides.
Susanna's drowned in the bearded stream
And no-one stirs at Sheba's side

But the hungry kings of the tides;
Sin who had a woman's shape   110
Sleeps till Silence blows on a cloud
And all the lifted waters walk and leap.

Lucifer that bird's dropping
Out of the sides of the north
Has melted away and is lost   115
Is always lost in her vaulted breath,

Venus lies star-struck in her wound
And the sensual ruins make
Seasons over the liquid world,
White springs in the dark.   120

Always goodbye, cried the voices through the shell,
Goodbye always for the flesh is cast
And the fisherman winds his reel
With no more desire than a ghost.

Always good luck, praised the finned in the feather 125
Bird after dark and the laughing fish
As the sails drank up the hail of thunder
And the long-tailed lightning lit his catch.

The boat swims into the six-year weather,
A wind throws a shadow and it freezes fast. 130
See what the gold gut drags from under
Mountains and galleries to the crest!

See what clings to hair and skull
As the boat skims on with drinking wings!
The statues of great rain stand still, 135
And the flakes fall like hills.

Sing and strike his heavy haul
Toppling up the boatside in a snow of light!
His decks are drenched with miracles.
Oh miracle of fishes! The long dead bite! 140

Out of the urn the size of a man
Out of the room the weight of his trouble
Out of the house that holds a town
In the continent of a fossil

One by one in dust and shawl, 145
Dry as echoes and insect-faced,
His fathers cling to the hand of the girl
And the dead hand leads the past,

Leads them as children and as air
On to the blindly tossing tops; 150
The centuries throw back their hair
And the old men sing from newborn lips:

Time is bearing another son.
Kill Time! She turns in her pain!
The oak is felled in the acorn   155
And the hawk in the egg kills the wren.

He who blew the great fire in
And died on a hiss of flames
Or walked the earth in the evening
Counting the denials of the grains   160

Clings to her drifting hair, and climbs;
And he who taught their lips to sing
Weeps like the risen sun among
The liquid choirs of his tribes.

The rod bends low, divining land,   165
And through the sundered water crawls
A garden holding to her hand
With birds and animals

With men and women and waterfalls
Trees cool and dry in the whirlpool of ships   170
And stunned and still on the green, laid veil
Sand with legends in its virgin laps

And prophets loud on the burned dunes;
Insects and valleys hold her thighs hard,
Time and places grip her breast bone,   175
She is breaking with seasons and clouds;

Round her trailed wrist fresh water weaves,
With moving fish and rounded stones
Up and down the greater waves
A separate river breathes and runs;   180

Strike and sing his catch of fields
For the surge is sown with barley,
The cattle graze on the covered foam,
The hills have footed the waves away,

With wild sea fillies and soaking bridles   185
With salty colts and gales in their limbs
All the horses of his haul of miracles
Gallop through the arched, green farms,

Trot and gallop with gulls upon them
And thunderbolts in their manes.   190
O Rome and Sodom Tomorrow and London
The country tide is cobbled with towns,

And steeples pierce the cloud on her shoulder
And the streets that the fisherman combed
When his long-legged flesh was a wind on fire   195
And his loin was a hunting flame

Coil from the thoroughfares of her hair
And terribly lead him home alive
Lead her prodigal home to his terror,
The furious ox-killing house of love.   200

Down, down, down, under the ground,
Under the floating villages,
Turns the moon-chained and water-wound
Metropolis of fishes,

There is nothing left of the sea but its sound,   205
Under the earth the loud sea walks,
In deathbeds of orchards the boat dies down
And the bait is drowned among hayricks,

Land, land, land, nothing remains
Of the pacing, famous sea but its speech,   210
And into its talkative seven tombs
The anchor dives through the floors of a church.

Goodbye, good luck, struck the sun and the moon,
To the fisherman lost on the land.
He stands alone at the door of his home,   215
With his long-legged heart in his hand.

Love in the Asylum

        A stranger has come
To share my room in the house not right in the head,
        A girl mad as birds

Bolting the night of the door with her arm her plume.
        Strait in the mazed bed   5
She deludes the heaven-proof house with entering clouds

Yet she deludes with walking the nightmarish room,
        At large as the dead,
Or rides the imagined oceans of the male wards.

        She has come possessed   10
Who admits the delusive light through the bouncing wall,
        Possessed by the skies

She sleeps in the narrow trough yet she walks the dust
        Yet raves at her will
On the madhouse boards worn thin by my walking tears.   15

And taken by light in her arms at long and dear last
        I may without fail
Suffer the first vision that set fire to the stars.

On the Marriage of a Virgin

Waking alone in a multitude of loves when morning's light
Surprised in the opening of her nightlong eyes
His golden yesterday asleep upon the iris
And this day's sun leapt up the sky out of her thighs
Was miraculous virginity old as loaves and fishes,   5
Though the moment of a miracle is unending lightning
And the shipyards of Galilee's footprints hide a navy of doves.

No longer will the vibrations of the sun desire on
Her deepsea pillow where once she married alone,
Her heart all ears and eyes, lips catching the avalanche   10
Of the golden ghost who ringed with his streams her mercury
    bone,
Who under the lids of her windows hoisted his golden luggage,
For a man sleeps where fire leapt down and she learns through
    his arm
That other sun, the jealous coursing of the unrivalled blood.

The hunchback in the park

The hunchback in the park
A solitary mister
Propped between trees and water
From the opening of the garden lock
That lets the trees and water enter   5
Until the Sunday sombre bell at dark

Eating bread from a newspaper
Drinking water from the chained cup
That the children filled with gravel
In the fountain basin where I sailed my ship   10
Slept at night in a dog kennel
But nobody chained him up.

Like the park birds he came early
Like the water he sat down
And Mister they called Hey mister   15
The truant boys from the town
Running when he had heard them clearly
On out of sound

Past lake and rockery
Laughing when he shook his paper   20
Hunchbacked in mockery
Through the loud zoo of the willow groves
Dodging the park keeper
With his stick that picked up leaves.

And the old dog sleeper   25
Alone between nurses and swans
While the boys among willows
Made the tigers jump out of their eyes
To roar on the rockery stones
And the groves were blue with sailors   30

Made all day until bell time
A woman figure without fault
Straight as a young elm
Straight and tall from his crooked bones
That she might stand in the night   35
After the locks and chains

All night in the unmade park
After the railings and shrubberies
The birds the grass the trees the lake
And the wild boys innocent as strawberries   40
Had followed the hunchback
To his kennel in the dark.

Among those Killed in the Dawn Raid was a Man Aged a Hundred

When the morning was waking over the war
He put on his clothes and stepped out and he died,
The locks yawned loose and a blast blew them wide,
He dropped where he loved on the burst pavement stone
And the funeral grains of the slaughtered floor.   5
Tell his street on its back he stopped a sun
And the craters of his eyes grew springshoots and fire
When all the keys shot from the locks, and rang.
Dig no more for the chains of his grey-haired heart.
The heavenly ambulance drawn by a wound   10
Assembling waits for the spade's ring on the cage.
O keep his bones away from that common cart,
The morning is flying on the wings of his age
And a hundred storks perch on the sun's right hand.

On-and-on General Bock is driving a wedge among pincers

On-and-on General Bock is driving a wedge among pincers,
Timothy Jenkins feints on the flank and the rouged Duke is
    wan,
The war is sweet with the summer breath of the panzers
And the dehydrated choirs of day welcome the dawn.

As I tossed off this morning over Talsarn Bridge to the fishes,   5
At war myself with the Celtic gnats under a spitfire sun,
Reading that twenty poems makes fifteen cartridge cases,
Commandos are trained to be cannibals and bombs weigh a hun-
    dred ton,
Poison is dropped from the sky in the shape of hipflasks and
    cheque-books,
Pigs can be taught to firewatch and hens to lay handgrenades: 10

O the summer grew suddenly lovely as the woodland rose
   in a phalanx
And the planted privates I thought were bushes moved in their
  Nash parades.

When next shall we stumble to the stutter . . .?

When next shall we stumble to the stutter of our lewis-gun carols
From bombazine-bosomed bar to a bliss of barrels,
Two period percies frescoed with ladders and banting,
Two spoonered swiss pillars, tumble falsetting and ranting?

O when, marcel-bound, shall we ruth our swine's way
   to the many-johned   5
Penny-fond antelope's cavern from the royal back-bar of beyond,
Or, sinister self-mabuses ripe for the phelan of the withy,
Peggy-legged limping in bottle-dress be hooved from the Wardour-
  street smithy?

Lie still, sleep becalmed

Lie still, sleep becalmed, sufferer with the wound
In the throat, burning and turning. All night afloat
On the silent sea we have heard the sound
That came from the wound wrapped in the salt sheet.

Under the mile off moon we trembled listening   5
To the sea sound flowing like blood from the loud wound
And when the salt sheet broke in a storm of singing
The voices of all the drowned swam on the wind.

Open a pathway through the slow sad sail,
Throw wide to the wind the gates of the wandering boat   10
For my voyage to begin to the end of my wound,
We heard the sea sound sing, we saw the salt sheet tell.

Lie still, sleep becalmed, hide the mouth in the throat,
Or we shall obey, and ride with you through the drowned.

From Wales – Green Mountain, Black Mountain *(film script)*

Remember the procession of the old-young men
From dole queue to corner and back again,
From the pinched, packed streets to the peak of slag
In the bite of the winters with shovel and bag,
With a drooping fag and a turned-up collar,   5
Stamping for the cold at the ill lit corner
Dragging through the squalor with their hearts like lead
Staring at the hunger and the shut pit-head
Nothing in their pockets, nothing home to eat.
Lagging from the slag heap to the pinched, packed street.   10
Remember the procession of the old-young men.
It shall never happen again.

Ceremony After a Fire Raid

I

Myselves
The grievers
Grieve
Among the street burned to tireless death
A child of a few hours   5
With its kneading mouth
Charred on the black breast of the grave
The mother dug, and its arms full of fires.

Begin
With singing   10
Sing

Darkness kindled back into beginning
When the caught tongue nodded blind,
A star was broken
Into the centuries of the child   15
Myselves grieve now, and miracles cannot atone.

Forgive
Us forgive
Give
Us your death that myselves the believers   20
May hold it in a great flood
Till the blood shall spurt,
And the dust shall sing like a bird
As the grains blow, as your death grows, through our heart.

Crying   25
Your dying
Cry,
Child beyond cockcrow, by the fire-dwarfed
Street we chant the flying sea
In the body bereft.   30
Love is the last light spoken. Oh
Seed of sons in the loin of the black husk left.

II

I know not whether
Adam or Eve, the adorned holy bullock
Or the white ewe lamb   35
Or the chosen virgin
Laid in her snow
On the altar of London,
Was the first to die
In the cinder of the little skull,   40
O bride and bride groom
O Adam and Eve together
Lying in the lull

Under the sad breast of the head stone
White as the skeleton   45
Of the garden of Eden.

I know the legend
Of Adam and Eve is never for a second
Silent in my service
Over the dead infants   50
Over the one
Child who was priest and servants,
Word, singers, and tongue
In the cinder of the little skull,
Who was the serpent's   55
Night fall and the fruit like a sun,
Man and woman undone,
Beginning crumbled back to darkness
Bare as the nurseries
Of the garden of wilderness.   60

III

Into the organpipes and steeples
Of the luminous cathedrals,
Into the weathercocks' molten mouths
Rippling in twelve-winded circles,
Into the dead clock burning the hour   65
Over the urn of sabbaths
Over the whirling ditch of daybreak
Over the sun's hovel and the slum of fire
And the golden pavements laid in requiems,
Into the cauldrons of the statuary,   70
Into the bread in a wheatfield of flames,
Into the wine burning like brandy,
The masses of the sea
The masses of the sea under
The masses of the infant-bearing sea   75
Erupt, fountain, and enter to utter for ever

Glory glory glory
The sundering ultimate kingdom of genesis' thunder.

Our Country *(film script)*

GLASGOW

To begin with
a city
a fair grey day
a day as lively and noisy as a close gossip of sparrows
as terribly impersonal as a sea cavern full of machines   5
when morning is driving down from the roofs of buildings
into stone labyrinths and traffic webs
when each man is alone forever in the midst of the masses of men

LONDON

and all the separate movements of the morning crowds
are lost together in the heartbeat of the clocks   [Big Ben] 10
a day when the long noise of the sea is forgotten
street-drowned in another memory
of the sound itself of smoke and sailing dust
trumpets of traffic signs and hoardings and posters
                                        [Piccadilly Circus]
rasp of the red and green signal lights   15
and scraped string voices of overhead wires
and the owl sound of the dry wind in the Tube tunnels
and blare and ragged drumroll of the armies of pavements and
    chimneys
and crossings and street walls
the riding choirs of the wheels   20
the always to be remembered even through continual sea music
music of the towers and bridges and spires and domes
of the island city.

There is peace under one roof.   [St Paul's Cathedral]

And then birds flying   25
suddenly easily as though from another country.

And all the stones remember and sing   [Blitzed streets]
the cathedral of each blitzed dead body that lay or lies
in the bomber-and-dove-flown-over cemeteries
of the dumb heroic streets.   30

And the eyes of St Paul's move over London: [Waterloo Station]

To the crowds of the shunting flagged and whistling cluttered
    cave-hollow other world under glass and steam
the loudspeaking terminus.

Going home now   35
going home now to a quiet country
going to war now
going to that strange country
going away
coming back to the ten million-headed city   40
or going away never to come back.

Going out
out over the racing rails in a grumble of London-leaving thunder
over the maze track of metal
through a wink and a spin of towns and signals and fields   45
out
to the edges of the explosive the moon-moved man-indifferent cap-
    sizing sea.

DOVER CLIFFS

The shape of another country lies so near
the wind on Dover cliffs could touch it with its finger

and from this island end white faced over the shifting sea-dyes   50
a man may hear his country's body talking
and be caught in the weathers of her eyes
and striding inland be plunged again in the armoured floods.

THE HARVEST

Nothing under the sun can change the smiling of sun on harvest

[Apple picking]
the ripeness the sun dust.   55

War hangs heavy over the apple-dangled acres
shadowing the small round hills of the heavy hanging fruit.
Only the fruit-loving birds flew once over these treetops.

Summer is flying along plants and flowers   [Hop picking]
through harvest corridors   60
swiftly over the short country days of women and children from
    city smoke.

They come like a holiday every year
they come to work in the fields
and catch again the flying open Summer in their hands and eyes.

In the airless courts and alleys at home   65
it must last them a long Winter
and a leafless dark Spring.

A man may see on the roads he rides   [The Fens and Midlands]
Summer and war on all four fair sides.
A man may hear on every hand   70
the voice of the rejoicing land
sounding together with the shout of the guns
and the swooping tons of the 'planes.

Outside the kitchens and music   [Harvest]
the laughing the loving the midnight talking the resting the
   sleeping   75
in all the blind houses
outside
the searchlighted night is at war with another darkness
and men who were late at harvest stand cold and calm and armed
on hilltops under the punishing rush of 'planes.   80

THE ROADS

All night long the lorries have roared the long roads.
Now it is dawn.

All night through villages asleep
they grumbled past pond and school and green
oast house or windmill   85
the weathercocked church and the unseen wind-swung inn sign.

By orchard and cottage cluster
the drinking trough in the market square
and the lovers' lanes
they thundered through a hundred   90
all over the country's strangely singing names

Black Motley White Motley Paddon Hollow
Mintern Magna and Much Marcle
Finchingfield Corfe Sturminster Marshall
Shipbourne and Bredon   95
Walton in Gordano.

THE MARKETS

The journeying man from the sea may find some peace
and be at home again in the country towns
among coops and hutches and stalls and pens   [Hereford]

listening to the noises of farmers and horses and hens   100
breathing the smell of cattle and leather and straw
on the clucking quacking whinnying mooing market day
and going into the farmers' pubs
that once were all haggling and cider
and once a week news of the slow countryside.   105

WALES

And a man may journey still within the island gates
through valleys and troules over hills slag-black or grey as slates
                                                  [Aberdare]
or through fat lovely fields all lying green under their flower folds
to where Wales waits

with hymns and coal and castles and tinplate   [Rhondda Valley] 110
pithead and ploughland and ricketty streets
grit wind in the mine mounds
snow over the rough mountain hair
meadow and chapel and huge bitten sea coast
humpbacked irontracked bricked over smoked out spreadeagled 115
bundle of valleys:
the valley's voice.

The voice of the pick in the hand hewn seam
the hunger born pit boy and blind pony
denial of defeat   120
the grief-fed country's furnace
the fire in men:
the valley's voice.

THE BUS RIDE

Take any direction any road up or down
the island alters round every village corner   125
at every turn of a town.

Take to the woods
or the slow lanes drenched with quietness and leaves
or to the climbing roads above the valleys
where the bright plaits of the rivers weave: 130
the weaving island leads all ways
calls a man down from the windblown sky-touching island height
to the towns in the bowls of smoke
the clamorous galleries and metalscapes of mechanised night.

[Sheffield]

THE GIRL'S STORY

Night after night, night after night, walking back from the factory 135
all alone, all alone, and then the warning going, and looking up at the
sky just like someone looking up to see if it's going to rain to-night,
quite calm you'd think from looking at me but running home all the
same because you never knew you never knew if there wouldn't be a
whine and a scream and a noise like the whole town blowing up and 140
then suddenly all the houses falling down on you and everybody you
knew lying all dead in the street. And suddenly the lights would be
out, and then, this is the end of the world I would say to myself, in
case the others heard, though they were thinking it too in the dark.
This is the end of the world. And you were dead as well.   145

And then we'd grow alive again, slowly, just like blind people
creeping out of a cave into the light at the very beginning of the
world. And you were alive. And when the morning came it was like
Spring in the middle of the Winter.

Oh, walking through the streets in the morning would make 150
you nearly want to sing, though there were people dead under the
stones, or people not dead, sing because the world was alive again
in the daytime, and I was alive, and you were alive.

THE TRAIN JOURNEY

The train is racing the trees to Scotland   [Berwick]
racing the towns that fly by like snowflakes   155

racing the rest of the world to the Highlands
sunrise and sunset over the rainy lakes.

TIMBER FELLING   [Highlands]

Here near at one island end, the north fringe,
walk deep through the forbidding timber temples
count the Samson pillars fall   160
the thwacks of the wood-and-wind-splintering axe
crack of the trunk-shorn boughs
shuffle of leaves
the suddenly homeless birds' tree-call.

Forget for a second the beckoning sea   165
that lies at the end of the journey,
commanding your coming back
behind each fated tree.

ABERDEEN

To end with
a quayside   170
a fair grey day
with the long noise of the sea flowing back
as though never in factory or harvestfield
market or timber temple street or hill
it could have been forgotten   175
for a moment in the tidal movement of man's time
with the call of ships
the monotonous sea voice of the beautiful scavenging gull
the salt smell strong as sunlight
grease on the deck   180
the facing of the sea.

The end with
the faces of fishermen.

Last night I dived my beggar arm

Last night I dived my beggar arm
Days deep in her breast that wore no heart
For me alone but only a rocked drum
Telling the heart I broke of a good habit

That her loving, unfriendly limbs   5
Would plunge my betrayal from sheet to sky
So the betrayed might learn in the sun beams
Of the death in a bed in another country.

Your breath was shed

Your breath was shed
Invisible to make
About the soiled undead
Night for my sake,

A raining trail   5
Invisible to them
With biter's tooth and tail
And cobweb drum,

A dark as deep
My love as a round wave   10
To hide the wolves of sleep
And mask the grave.

Vision and Prayer

I

Who
Are you
Who is born
In the next room
So loud to my own
That I can hear the womb
Opening and the dark run
Over the ghost and the dropped son
Behind the wall thin as a wren's bone?
In the birth bloody room unknown
To the burn and turn of time
And the heart print of man
Bows no baptism
But dark alone
Blessing on
The wild
Child.

I

Must lie
Still as stone
By the wren bone
Wall hearing the moan
Of the mother hidden
And the shadowed head of pain
Casting tomorrow like a thorn
And the midwives of miracle sing
Until the turbulent new born
Burns me his name and his flame
And the winged wall is torn
By his torrid crown
And the dark thrown
From his loin
To bright
Light.

When
The wren
Bone writhes down
And the first dawn
Furied by his stream
Swarms on the kingdom come
Of the dazzler of heaven
And the splashed mothering maiden
Who bore him with a bonfire in
His mouth and rocked him like a storm
I shall run lost in sudden
Terror and shining from
The once hooded room
Crying in vain
In the cauldron
Of his
Kiss

In
The spin
Of the sun
In the spuming
Cyclone of his wing
For I was lost who am
Crying at the man drenched throne
In the first fury of his stream
And the lightnings of adoration
Back to black silence melt and mourn
For I was lost who have come
To dumbfounding haven
And the finding one
And the high noon
Of his wound
Blinds my
Cry.

There
Crouched bare
In   the   shrine
Of   his   blazing
Breast I shall waken
To the judge blown bedlam
Of the uncaged sea bottom
The cloud climb of the exhaling tomb
And the bidden dust upsailing
With his flame in every grain.
O spiral of ascension
From the vultured urn
Of the morning
Of man when
The land
And

The
Born sea
Praised the sun
The finding one
And   upright   Adam
Sang   upon   origin!
O the wings of the children!
The woundward flight of the ancient
Young from the canyons of oblivion!
The sky stride of the always slain
In   battle!   The   happening
Of saints to their vision!
The world winding home!
And the whole pain
Flows open
And I
Die.

II

In the name of the lost who glory in
The swinish plains of carrion
Under the burial song
Of the birds of burden
Heavy with the drowned
And the green dust
And bearing
The ghost
From
The ground
Like pollen
On the black plume
And the beak of slime
I pray though I belong
Not wholly to that lamenting
Brethren for joy has moved within
The inmost marrow of my heart bone

That he who learns now the sun and moon
Of his mother's milk may return
Before the lips blaze and bloom
To the birth bloody room
Behind the wall's wren
Bone and be dumb
And the womb
That bore
For
All men
The adored
Infant light or
The dazzling prison
Yawn to his upcoming.
In the name of the wanton
Lost on the unchristened mountain
In the centre of dark I pray him

That he let the dead lie though they moan
For his briared hands to hoist them
To the shrine of his world's wound
And the blood drop's garden
Endure   the   stone   140
Blind host to sleep
In the dark
And deep
Rock
Awake   145
No heart bone
But let it break
On the mountain crown
Unbidden   by   the   sun
And the beating dust be blown   150
Down to the river rooting plain
Under   the   night   forever   falling.

Forever falling night is a known
Star and country to the legion
Of sleepers whose tongue I toll   155
To   mourn   his   deluging
Light through sea and soil
And we have come
To know all
P l a c e s   160
Ways
M a z e s
P a s s a g e s
Quarters and graves
Of the endless fall.   165
Now   common   lazarus
Of the charting sleepers prays
Never   to   awake   and   arise
For the country of death is the heart's size

And the star of the lost the shape of the eyes.   170
In the name of the fatherless
In the name of the unborn
And the undesirers
Of midwiving morning's
Hands or instruments   175
O in the name
Of no one
Now or
No
One to   180
Be I pray
May the crimson
Sun spin a grave grey
And the colour of clay
Stream upon his martyrdom   185
In the interpreted evening
And the known dark of the earth amen.

I turn the corner of prayer and burn
In a blessing of the sudden
Sun. In the name of the damned   190
I would turn back and run
To the hidden land
But the loud sun
Christens down
The sky.   195
I
Am found.
O let him
Scald me and drown
Me in his world's wound.   200
His lightning answers my
Cry. My voice burns in his hand.
Now I am lost in the blinding
One. The sun roars at the prayer's end.

Poem in October

It was my thirtieth year to heaven
Woke to my hearing from harbour and neighbour wood
   And the mussel pooled and the heron
         Priested shore
      The morning beckon
With water praying and call of seagull and rook
And the knock of sailing boats on the net webbed wall
      Myself to set foot
        That second
In the still sleeping town and set forth.

My birthday began with the water-
Birds and the birds of the winged trees flying my name
   Above the farms and the white horses
        And I rose
      In rainy autumn
And walked abroad in a shower of all my days.
High tide and the heron dived when I took the road
      Over the border
        And the gates
Of the town closed as the town awoke.

A springful of larks in a rolling
Cloud and the roadside bushes brimming with whistling
   Blackbirds and the sun of October
        Summery
      On the hill's shoulder,
Here were fond climates and sweet singers suddenly
Come in the morning where I wandered and listened
      To the rain wringing
        Wind blow cold
In the wood faraway under me.

Pale rain over the dwindling harbour
And over the sea wet church the size of a snail
  With its horns through mist and the castle
        Brown as owls
     But all the gardens   35
Of spring and summer were blooming in the tall tales
Beyond the border and under the lark full cloud.
     There could I marvel
       My birthday
Away but the weather turned around.   40

  It turned away from the blithe country
And down the other air and the blue altered sky
  Streamed again a wonder of summer
        With apples
     Pears and red currants   45
And I saw in the turning so clearly a child's
Forgotten mornings when he walked with his mother
     Through the parables
       Of sun light
And the legends of the green chapels   50

  And the twice told fields of infancy
That his tears burned my cheeks and his heart moved in mine.
  These were the woods the river and sea
        Where a boy
     In the listening   55
Summertime of the dead whispered the truth of his joy
To the trees and the stones and the fish in the tide.
     And the mystery
       Sang alive
Still in the water and singingbirds.   60

  And there could I marvel my birthday
Away but the weather turned around. And the true
  Joy of the long dead child sang burning

In the sun.
It was my thirtieth   65
Year to heaven stood there then in the summer noon
Though the town below lay leaved with October blood.
O may my heart's truth
Still be sung
On this high hill in a year's turning.   70

So much Meux has flowed under the bridges

So much Meux has flowed under the bridges
You could drown London town, which would be just,
Since we met in the spring and drank religious.
If we don't meet again I shall throw away my trust.
And bitter's gone up and bombs have come down   5
Since Pera and pal like a pair of mouse
Squeaked in the liquorish wainscots of the town
And thumbed their whiskers at Philmayicity House.
It's a long way from London, as the fly bombs,
And nothing of Donald's guile can lug me   10
Away from this Wales where I sit in my combs
As safe and snug as a bugger in Rugby.
We've got a new house and it's called Majoda.
Majoda, Cards, on the Welsh-speaking sea.
And we'll stay in this wood-and-asbestos pagoda   15
Till the blackout's raised on London and on me.
But meet we must before the dove of peace
Drops in my eye his vain and priggish turd,
And England's full of cultural police,
(For you, at once, a sentence of three months Heard,   20
For me a year on bread and de Polnay, Peter),
And verse inspectors kick up a mingy din
Demanding, at pistol point, to read your metre,
And oh the significant form troops mincing in!
How shall we meet, then, since countries lie between   25

The Rimbaud of Ockham and Swansea's Villon?
O fly the miles in Stephenson's machine
And spend a month with

                  Yours ever,
                      Dylan.

Dear Tommy, please, from far, sciatic Kingsley

Dear Tommy, please, from far, sciatic Kingsley
Borrow my eyes. The darkening sea flings Lee
And Perrins on the cockled tablecloth
Of mud and sand. And, like a sable moth,
A cloud against the glassy sun flutters his   5
Wings. It would be better if the shutter is
Shut. Sinister dark over Cardigan
Bay. No-good is abroad. I unhardy can
Hardly bear the din of No-good wracked dry on
The pebbles. It is time for the Black Lion   10
But there is only Buckley's unfrisky
Mild. Turned again, Worthington. Never whisky.
I sit at the open window, observing
The salty scene and my Playered gob curving
Down to the wild, umbrella'd, and French lettered   15
Beach, hearing rise slimy from the Welsh lechered
Caves the cries of parchs and their flocks. I
Hear their laughter sly as gonococchi . . .
There slinks a snoop in black. I'm thinking it
Is Mr. Jones the Cake, that winking-bit,   20
That hymning gooseberry, that Bethel-worm
At whose ball-prying even death'll squirm
And button up. He minces among knickers,
That prince of pimps, that doyen of dung-lickers.
Over a rump on the clerical-grey seashore,   25
See how he stumbles. Hallelujah hee-haw!,
His head's in a nest where no bird lays her egg.

He cuts himself on an elder's razor leg.
Sniff, here is sin! Now must he grapple, rise:
He snuggles deep among the chapel thighs,   30
And when the moist collection plate is passed
Puts in his penny, generous at last.

On Saturday Augustus comes, bearded
Like Cardy's bard, and howling as Lear did.
A short stay only but oh, how nice. No   35
One more welcome than the oaktrunked maestro—
No-one but you who'll never come unless
I send the million-miscarriaged Welsh Express,
A train of thought run on wheels within wheels.
But on October 1 I show my heels   40
To New Quay, Cards, and then shall brave V.2.
And come to London. Remember me to
May. Is there a chance of one I never see
Coming up, also? Write me: Ever,
                                   D.

Back in the bosom, repentant and bloodshot

Back in the bosom, repentant and bloodshot,
Under the draper-sly skies,
I try to forget my week in the mudpot
And cottonwool it in lies:

'I do not, my dear, pretend that I mastered   5
Altogether the intemperate vice.
I may in the Gargoyle have fallen down plastered,
But I did see my publishers—twice.

You wouldn't believe me were I to aver
That I never went out "on the bust".   10
You'll pardon the phrase? Ah, thank you, my dear,
And I did see an editor—just.

Now let us be frank. I behaved, I'm afraid,
Like a squalid and tiddly dunce.
But I really was brave in that *terrible* raid,   15
And I did make some money—once.'

Holy Spring

O
Out of a bed of love
When that immortal hospital made one more move to soothe
The cureless counted body,
And ruin and his causes   5
Over the barbed and shooting sea assumed an army
And swept into our wounds and houses,
I climb to greet the war in which I have no heart but only
That one dark I owe my light,
Call for confessor and wiser mirror but there is none   10
To glow after the god stoning night
And I am struck as lonely as a holy maker by the sun.

No
Praise that the spring time is all
Gabriel and radiant shrubbery as the morning grows joyful   15
Out of the woebegone pyre
And the multitude's sultry tear turns cool on the weeping wall,
My arising prodigal
Sun the father his quiver full of the infants of pure fire,
But blessed be hail and upheaval   20
That uncalm still it is sure alone to stand and sing
Alone in the husk of man's home
And the mother and toppling house of the holy spring,
If only for a last time.

Verses from Quite Early One Morning

I am Miss May Hughes 'The Cosy', a lonely lady,
Waiting in her house by the nasty sea,
Waiting for her husband and pretty baby
To come home at last from wherever they may be.

I am Captain Tiny Evans, my ship was the *Kidwelly*   5
And Mrs Tiny Evans has been dead for many a year.
'Poor Captain Tiny all alone', the neighbours whisper,
But I like it all alone and I hated her.

Clara Tawe Jenkins, 'Madame' they call me,
An old contralto with her dressing-gown on,   10
And I sit at the window and I sing to the sea,
For the sea doesn't notice that my voice has gone.

Parchedig Thomas Evans making morning tea,
Very weak tea too, you mustn't waste a leaf.
Every morning making tea in my house by the sea   15
I am troubled by one thing only, and that's Belief.

Open the curtains, light the fire, what are servants for?
I am Mrs Ogmore-Pritchard and I want another snooze.
Dust the china, feed the canary, sweep the drawing-room floor;
And before you let the sun in, mind he wipes his shoes.   20

I am only Mr Griffiths, very short-sighted, B.A., Aber.
As soon as I finish my egg I must shuffle off to school.
O patron saint of teachers, teach me to keep order,
And forget those words on the blackboard—'Griffiths Bat is a fool.'

Do you hear that whistling?—It's me, I am Phoebe,   25
The maid at the King's Head and I'm whistling like a bird.
Someone spilt a tin of pepper in the tea.
There's twenty for breakfast and I'm not going to say a word.

I can see the Atlantic from my bed where I always lie,
Night and day, night and day, eating my bread and slops.   30
The quiet cripple staring at the sea and the sky.
I shall lie here till the sky goes out and the sea stops.

A Winter's Tale

It is a winter's tale
That the snow blind twilight ferries over the lakes
And floating fields from the farm in the cup of the vales,
Gliding windless through the hand folded flakes,
The pale breath of cattle at the stealthy sail,   5

And the stars falling cold,
And the smell of hay in the snow, and the far owl
Warning among the folds, and the frozen hold
Flocked with the sheep white smoke of the farm house cowl
In the river wended vales where the tale was told.   10

Once when the world turned old
On a star of faith pure as the drifting bread,
As the food and flames of the snow, a man unrolled
The scrolls of fire that burned in his heart and head,
Torn and alone in a farm house in a fold   15

Of fields. And burning then
In his firelit island ringed by the winged snow
And the dung hills white as wool and the hen
Roosts sleeping chill till the flame of the cock crow
Combs through the mantled yards and the morning men   20

Stumble out with their spades,
The cattle stirring, the mousing cat stepping shy,
The puffed birds hopping and hunting, the milk maids
Gentle in their clogs over the fallen sky,
And all the woken farm at its white trades,   25

He knelt, he wept, he prayed,
By the spit and the black pot in the log bright light
And the cup and the cut bread in the dancing shade,
In the muffled house, in the quick of night,
At the point of love, forsaken and afraid.   30

He knelt on the cold stones,
He wept from the crest of grief, he prayed to the veiled sky
May his hunger go howling on bare white bones
Past the statues of the stables and the sky roofed sties
And the duck pond glass and the blinding byres alone   35

Into the home of prayers
And fires where he should prowl down the cloud
Of his snow blind love and rush in the white lairs.
His naked need struck him howling and bowed
Though no sound flowed down the hand folded air   40

But only the wind strung
Hunger of birds in the fields of the bread of water, tossed
In high corn and the harvest melting on their tongues.
And his nameless need bound him burning and lost
When cold as snow he should run the wended vales among   45

The rivers mouthed in night,
And drown in the drifts of his need, and lie curled caught
In the always desiring centre of the white
Inhuman cradle and the bride bed forever sought
By the believer lost and the hurled outcast of light.   50

Deliver him, he cried,
By losing him all in love, and cast his need
Alone and naked in the engulfing bride,
Never to flourish in the fields of the white seed
Or flower under the time dying flesh astride.   55

Listen. The minstrels sing
In the departed villages. The nightingale,
Dust in the buried wood, flies on the grains of her wings
And spells on the winds of the dead his winter's tale.
The voice of the dust of water from the withered spring   60

      Is telling. The wizened
Stream with bells and baying water bounds. The dew rings
On the gristed leaves and the long gone glistening
Parish of snow. The carved mouths in the rock are wind swept
    strings.
Time sings through the intricately dead snow drop. Listen.   65

      It was a hand or sound
In the long ago land that glided the dark door wide
And there outside on the bread of the ground
A she bird rose and rayed like a burning bride.
A she bird dawned, and her breast with snow and scarlet
    downed.   70

      Look. And the dancers move
On the departed, snow bushed green, wanton in moon light
As a dust of pigeons. Exulting, the grave hooved
Horses, centaur dead, turn and tread the drenched white
Paddocks in the farms of birds. The dead oak walks for love.   75

      The carved limbs in the rock
Leap, as to trumpets. Calligraphy of the old
Leaves is dancing. Lines of age on the stones weave in a flock.
And the harp shaped voice of the water's dust plucks in a fold
Of fields. For love, the long ago she bird rises. Look.   80

      And the wild wings were raised
Above her folded head, and the soft feathered voice
Was flying through the house as though the she bird praised
And all the elements of the slow fall rejoiced
That a man knelt alone in the cup of the vales,   85

In the mantle and calm,
By the spit and the black pot in the log bright light.
And the sky of birds in the plumed voice charmed
Him up and he ran like a wind after the kindling flight
Past the blind barns and byres of the windless farm.   90

        In the poles of the year
When black birds died like priests in the cloaked hedge row
And over the cloth of counties the far hills rode near,
Under the one leaved trees ran a scarecrow of snow
And fast through the drifts of the thickets antlered like deer,   95

        Rags and prayers down the knee-
Deep hillocks and loud on the numbed lakes,
All night lost and long wading in the wake of the she-
Bird through the times and lands and tribes of the slow flakes.
Listen and look where she sails the goose plucked sea,   100

        The sky, the bird, the bride,
The cloud, the need, the planted stars, the joy beyond
The fields of seed and the time dying flesh astride,
The heavens, the heaven, the grave, the burning font.
In the far ago land the door of his death glided wide,   105

        And the bird descended.
On a bread white hill over the cupped farm
And the lakes and floating fields and the river wended
Vales where he prayed to come to the last harm
And the home of prayers and fires, the tale ended.   110

        The dancing perishes
On the white, no longer growing green, and, minstrel dead,
The singing breaks in the snow shoed villages of wishes
That once cut the figures of birds on the deep bread
And over the glazed lakes skated the shapes of fishes   115

Flying. The rite is shorn
Of nightingale and centaur dead horse. The springs wither
Back. Lines of age sleep on the stones till trumpeting dawn.
Exultation lies down. Time buries the spring weather
That belled and bounded with the fossil and the dew reborn.   120

          For the bird lay bedded
In a choir of wings, as though she slept or died,
And the wings glided wide and he was hymned and wedded,
And through the thighs of the engulfing bride,
The woman breasted and the heaven headed   125

          Bird, he was brought low,
Burning in the bride bed of love, in the whirl-
Pool at the wanting centre, in the folds
Of paradise, in the spun bud of the world.
And she rose with him flowering in her melting snow.   130

The conversation of prayers

The conversation of prayers about to be said
By the child going to bed and the man on the stairs
Who climbs to his dying love in her high room,
The one not caring to whom in his sleep he will move
And the other full of tears that she will be dead,   5

Turns in the dark on the sound they know will arise
Into the answering skies from the green ground,
From the man on the stairs and the child by his bed.
The sound about to be said in the two prayers
For the sleep in a safe land and the love who dies   10

Will be the same grief flying. Whom shall they calm?
Shall the child sleep unharmed or the man be crying?
The conversation of prayers about to be said
Turns on the quick and the dead, and the man on the stairs
Tonight shall find no dying but alive and warm   15

In the fire of his care his love in the high room.
And the child not caring to whom he climbs his prayer
Shall drown in a grief as deep as his true grave,
And mark the dark eyed wave, through the eyes of sleep,
Dragging him up the stairs to one who lies dead.   20

A Refusal to Mourn the Death, by Fire, of a Child in London

Never until the mankind making
Bird beast and flower
Fathering and all humbling darkness
Tells with silence the last light breaking
And the still hour   5
Is come of the sea tumbling in harness

And I must enter again the round
Zion of the water bead
And the synagogue of the ear of corn
Shall I let pray the shadow of a sound   10
Or sow my salt seed
In the least valley of sackcloth to mourn

The majesty and burning of the child's death.
I shall not murder
The mankind of her going with a grave truth   15
Nor blaspheme down the stations of the breath
With any further
Elegy of innocence and youth.

Deep with the first dead lies London's daughter,
Robed in the long friends,
The grains beyond age, the dark veins of her mother,
Secret by the unmourning water
Of the riding Thames.
After the first death, there is no other.

This side of the truth
(for Llewelyn)

This side of the truth,
You may not see, my son,
King of your blue eyes
In the blinding country of youth,
That all is undone,
Under the unminding skies,
Of innocence and guilt
Before you move to make
One gesture of the heart or head,
Is gathered and spilt
Into the winding dark
Like the dust of the dead.

Good and bad, two ways
Of moving about your death
By the grinding sea,
King of your heart in the blind days,
Blow away like breath,
Go crying through you and me
And the souls of all men
Into the innocent
Dark, and the guilty dark, and good
Death, and bad death, and then
In the last element
Fly like the stars' blood,

Like the sun's tears, 25
Like the moon's seed, rubbish
And fire, the flying rant
Of the sky, king of your six years.
And the wicked wish,
Down the beginning of plants 30
And animals and birds,
Water and light, the earth and sky,
Is cast before you move,
And all your deeds and words,
Each truth, each lie, 35
Die in unjudging love.

Sooner than you can water milk, or cry Amen

Sooner than you can water milk, or cry Amen,
Darkness comes, psalming, over Cards again;
Some lights go on; some men go out; some men slip in;
Some girls lie down, calling the beer-brown bulls to sin
And boom among their fishy fields; some elders stand 5
With thermoses and telescopes and spy the sand
Where farmers plough by night and sailors rock and rise,
Tattooed with texts, between the atlantic thighs
Of Mrs Rosser Tea and little Nell the Knock:
One pulls out Pam in Paris from his money-sock; 10
One, in the bible black of his back, mothy house,
Drinks paraffin and vinegar, and blinds a mouse;
One reads his cheque book in the dark, & eats fish-heads;
One creeps into the Lion Inn to foul the beds;
One, in the rubbered hedges, rolls with a bald liz 15
Who's old enough to be his mother (and she is);
The grocer lies in ambush in his smelling shop,
Praying for land-girls, and the preacher lies on top;
In snug and public, hunched by the gob-green logs,
The customers are telling what they do to dogs; 20

The chemist is performing an unnatural act
In the organ loft; and the lavatory is packed.

Unluckily for a death

Unluckily for a death
Waiting with phoenix under
The pyre yet to be lighted of my sins and days,
And for the woman in shades
Saint carved and sensual among the scudding   5
Dead and gone, dedicate forever to my self
Though the brawl of the kiss has not occurred,
On the clay cold mouth, on the fire
Branded forehead, that could bind
Her constant, nor the winds of love broken wide   10
To the wind the choir and cloister
Of the wintry nunnery of the order of lust
Beneath my life, that sighs for the seducer's coming
In the sun strokes of summer,

Loving on this sea banged guilt   15
My holy lucky body
Under the cloud against love is caught and held and kissed
In the mill of the midst
Of the descending day, the dark our folly,
Cut to the still star in the order of the quick   20
But blessed by such heroic hosts in your every
Inch and glance that the wound
Is certain god, and the ceremony of souls
Is celebrated there, and communion between suns.
Never shall my self chant   25
About the saint in shades while the endless breviary
Turns of your prayed flesh, nor shall I shoo the bird below me:
The death biding two lie lonely.

I see the tigron in tears
In the androgynous dark,   30
His striped and noon maned tribe striding to holocaust,
The she mules bear their minotaurs,
The duck-billed platypus broody in a milk of birds.
I see the wanting nun saint carved in a garb
Of shades, symbol of desire beyond my hours   35
And guilts, great crotch and giant
Continence. I see the unfired phoenix, herald
And heaven crier, arrow now of aspiring
And the renouncing of islands.
All love but for the full assemblage in flower   40
Of the living flesh is monstrous or immortal,
And the grave its daughters.

Love, my fate got luckily,
Teaches with no telling
That the phoenix' bid for heaven and the desire after   45
Death in the carved nunnery
Both shall fail if I bow not to your blessing
Nor walk in the cool of your mortal garden
With immortality at my side like Christ the sky.
This I know from the native   50
Tongue of your translating eyes. The young stars told me,
Hurling into beginning like Christ the child.
Lucklessly she must lie patient
And the vaulting bird be still. O my true love, hold me.
In your every inch and glance is the globe of genesis spun, 55
And the living earth your sons.

In my craft or sullen art

In my craft or sullen art
Exercised in the still night
When only the moon rages
And the lovers lie abed

With all their griefs in their arms,   5
I labour by singing light
Not for ambition or bread
Or the strut and trade of charms
On the ivory stages
But for the common wages   10
Of their most secret heart.

Not for the proud man apart
From the raging moon I write
On these spindrift pages
Nor for the towering dead   15
With their nightingales and psalms
But for the lovers, their arms
Round the griefs of the ages,
Who pay no praise or wages
Nor heed my craft or art.   20

Fern Hill

Now as I was young and easy under the apple boughs
About the lilting house and happy as the grass was green,
    The night above the dingle starry,
      Time let me hail and climb
      Golden in the heydays of his eyes,   5
And honoured among wagons I was prince of the apple towns
And once below a time I lordly had the trees and leaves
      Trail with daisies and barley
    Down the rivers of the windfall light.

And as I was green and carefree, famous among the barns   10
About the happy yard and singing as the farm was home,
    In the sun that is young once only,
      Time let me play and be
      Golden in the mercy of his means,
And green and golden I was huntsman and herdsman, the calves 15

Sang to my horn, the foxes on the hills barked clear and cold,
     And the sabbath rang slowly
    In the pebbles of the holy streams.

All the sun long it was running, it was lovely, the hay
Fields high as the house, the tunes from the chimneys, it was air   20
     And playing, lovely and watery
      And fire green as grass.
     And nightly under the simple stars
As I rode to sleep the owls were bearing the farm away,
All the moon long I heard, blessed among stables, the nightjars   25
      Flying with the ricks, and the horses
       Flashing into the dark.

And then to awake, and the farm, like a wanderer white
With the dew, come back, the cock on his shoulder: it was all
      Shining, it was Adam and maiden,   30
       The sky gathered again
      And the sun grew round that very day.
So it must have been after the birth of the simple light
In the first, spinning place, the spellbound horses walking warm
      Out of the whinnying green stable   35
       On to the fields of praise.

And honoured among foxes and pheasants by the gay house
Under the new made clouds and happy as the heart was long,
     In the sun born over and over,
      I ran my heedless ways,   40
     My wishes raced through the house high hay
And nothing I cared, at my sky blue trades, that time allows
In all his tuneful turning so few and such morning songs
     Before the children green and golden
      Follow him out of grace,   45

Nothing I cared, in the lamb white days, that time would take me
Up to the swallow thronged loft by the shadow of my hand,
     In the moon that is always rising,

Nor that riding to sleep
I should hear him fly with the high fields   50
And wake to the farm forever fled from the childless land.
Oh as I was young and easy in the mercy of his means,
Time held me green and dying
Though I sang in my chains like the sea.

In Country Heaven [fragment]

Always, when he, in Country Heaven,
(Whom my heart hears),
Crosses the breast of the praising East, and kneels,
Humble in all his planets,
And weeps on the abasing hill,   5

Then in the delight and groves of beasts and birds
And the canonized valley
Where the dewfall stars sing grazing still
And the angels whirr like pheasants
Through aisles of leaves,   10

Light and his tears glide down together
(O hand in hand)
From the country eyes, salt and sun, star and woe
Down the cheek bones and whinnying
Downs into the low browsing dark.   15

Doused in hamlets of heaven swing the loft lamps,
In the black buried spinneys
Bushes and owls blow out like a spark,
And the seraphic fields of shepherds
Fade with their rose-   20

White, Gods' bright, flocks, the belled lambs leaping,
(His gentle kind);
The shooting-star hawk locked blind in a lame cloud

Over the blackamoor shires
Hears the belfries and the cobbles   25

Of the twelve apostles' towns ring in his night;
And the long fox like fire
Prowls flaming among the cockerels
In the plunged farms of Heaven's keeping,
But they sleep sound.   30

For the fifth element is pity,
(Pity for death);
No fowl or field mouse that night of his kneeling
Lies in the fox's fires
Or twice dies in the screech-owl's eyes;   35

All the canterbury tales in the wild hedge-
Row of the small, brown friars,
The lithe reeve and the rustling wife
Blithe in the tall telling of his pitch
Time go sleeping   40

Under the switchback glide of his tears,
(And the salt light).

Young Aesop fabling by the coracled Towy.

In Country Sleep

I

Never and never, my girl riding far and near
In the land of the hearthstone tales, and spelled asleep,
Fear or believe that the wolf in a sheepwhite hood
Loping and bleating roughly and blithely shall leap,
My dear, my dear,   5
Out of a lair in the flocked leaves in the dew dipped year
To eat your heart in the house in the rosy wood.

Sleep, good, for ever, slow and deep, spelled rare and wise,
My girl ranging the night in the rose and shire
Of the hobnail tales: no gooseherd or swine will turn   10
Into a homestall king or hamlet of fire
                    And prince of ice
To court the honeyed heart from your side before sunrise
In a spinney of ringed boys and ganders, spike and burn,

Nor the innocent lie in the rooting dingle wooed   15
And staved, and riven among plumes my rider weep.
From the broomed witch's spume you are shielded by fern
And flower of country sleep and the greenwood keep.
                    Lie fast and soothed,
Safe be and smooth from the bellows of the rushy brood.   20
Never, my girl, until tolled to sleep by the stern

Bell believe or fear that the rustic shade or spell
Shall harrow and snow the blood while you ride wide and near,
For who unmanningly haunts the mountain ravened eaves
Or skulks in the dell moon but moonshine echoing clear   25
                    From the starred well?
A hill touches an angel. Out of a saint's cell
The nightbird lauds through nunneries and domes of leaves

Her robin breasted tree, three Marys in the rays.
Sanctum sanctorum the animal eye of the wood   30
In the rain telling its beads, and the gravest ghost
The owl at its knelling. Fox and holt kneel before blood.
                    Now the tales praise
The star rise at pasture and nightlong the fables graze
On the lord's table of the bowing grass. Fear most   35

For ever of all not the wolf in his baaing hood
Nor the tusked prince, in the ruttish farm, at the rind
And mire of love, but the Thief as meek as the dew.
The country is holy: O bide in that country kind,
                    Know the green good,   40

Under the prayer wheeling moon in the rosy wood
Be shielded by chant and flower and gay may you

Lie in grace. Sleep spelled at rest in the lowly house
In the squirrel nimble grove, under linen and thatch
And star: held and blessed, though you scour the high four   45
Winds, from the dousing shade and the roarer at the latch,
                    Cool in your vows.
Yet out of the beaked, web dark and the pouncing boughs
Be you sure the Thief will seek a way sly and sure

And sly as snow and meek as dew blown to the thorn,   50
This night and each vast night until the stern bell talks
In the tower and tolls to sleep over the stalls
Of the hearthstone tales my own, last love; and the soul walks
                    The waters shorn.
This night and each night since the falling star you were born,   55
Ever and ever he finds a way, as the snow falls,

As the rain falls, hail on the fleece, as the vale mist rides
Through the haygold stalls, as the dew falls on the wind-
Milled dust of the apple tree and the pounded islands
Of the morning leaves, as the star falls, as the winged   60
                    Apple seed glides,
And falls, and flowers in the yawning wound at our sides,
As the world falls, silent as the cyclone of silence.

II

Night and the reindeer on the clouds above the haycocks
And the wings of the great roc ribboned for the fair!   65
The leaping saga of prayer! And high, there, on the hare-
                    Heeled winds the rooks
Cawing from their black bethels soaring, the holy books
Of birds! Among the cocks like fire the red fox

Burning! Night and the vein of birds in the winged, sloe wrist   70
Of the wood! Pastoral beat of blood through the laced leaves!
The stream from the priest black wristed spinney and sleeves
     Of thistling frost
Of the nightingale's din and tale! The upgiven ghost
Of the dingle torn to singing and the surpliced   75

Hill of cypresses! The din and tale in the skimmed
Yard of the buttermilk rain on the pail! The sermon
Of blood! The bird loud vein! The saga from mermen
     To seraphim
Leaping! The gospel rooks! All tell, this night, of him 80
Who comes as red as the fox and sly as the heeled wind.

Illumination of music! The lulled black backed
Gull, on the wave with sand in its eyes! And the foal moves
Through the shaken greensward lake, silent, on moonshod hooves,
     In the winds' wakes. 85
Music of elements, that a miracle makes!
Earth, air, water, fire, singing into the white act,

The haygold haired, my love asleep, and the rift blue
Eyed, in the haloed house, in her rareness and hilly
High riding, held and blessed and true, and so stilly 90
     Lying the sky
Might cross its planets, the bell weep, night gather her eyes,
The Thief fall on the dead like the willynilly dew,

Only for the turning of the earth in her holy
Heart! Slyly, slowly, hearing the wound in her side go 95
Round the sun, he comes to my love like the designed snow,
     And truly he
Flows to the strand of flowers like the dew's ruly sea,
And surely he sails like the ship shape clouds. Oh he

Comes designed to my love to steal not her tide raking
Wound, nor her riding high, nor her eyes, nor kindled hair,
But her faith that each vast night and the saga of prayer
                         He comes to take
Her faith that this last night for his unsacred sake
He comes to leave her in the lawless sun awaking   105

Naked and forsaken to grieve he will not come.
Ever and ever by all your vows believe and fear
My dear this night he comes and night without end my dear
                         Since you were born:
And you shall wake, from country sleep, this dawn and each first
    dawn,   110
Your faith as deathless as the outcry of the ruled sun.

Over Sir John's hill

Over Sir John's hill,
The hawk on fire hangs still;
In a hoisted cloud, at drop of dusk, he pulls to his claws
And gallows, up the rays of his eyes the small birds of the bay
And the shrill child's play   5
Wars
Of the sparrows and such who swansing, dusk, in wrangling
    hedges.
And blithely they squawk
To fiery tyburn over the wrestle of elms until
The flash the noosed hawk   10
Crashes, and slowly the fishing holy stalking heron
In the river Towy below bows his tilted headstone.

Flash, and the plumes crack,
And a black cap of jack-
Daws Sir John's just hill dons, and again the gulled birds hare   15
To the hawk on fire, the halter height, over Towy's fins,
In a whack of wind.

There
Where the elegiac fisherbird stabs and paddles
In the pebbly dab filled   20
Shallow and sedge, and 'dilly dilly', calls the loft hawk,
'Come and be killed',
I open the leaves of the water at a passage
Of psalms and shadows among the pincered sandcrabs prancing

And read, in a shell,   25
Death clear as a buoy's bell:
All praise of the hawk on fire in hawk-eyed dusk be sung,
When his viperish fuse hangs looped with flames under the brand
Wing, and blest shall
Young   30
Green chickens of the bay and bushes cluck, 'dilly dilly,
Come let us die.'
We grieve as the blithe birds, never again, leave shingle and elm,
The heron and I,
I young Aesop fabling to the near night by the dingle   35
Of eels, saint heron hymning in the shell-hung distant

Crystal harbour vale
Where the sea cobbles sail,
And wharves of water where the walls dance and the white cranes
    stilt.
It is the heron and I, under judging Sir John's elmed   40
Hill, tell-tale the knelled
Guilt
Of the led-astray birds whom God, for their breast of whistles,
Have mercy on,
God in his whirlwind silence save, who marks the sparrows hail, 45
For their souls' song.
Now the heron grieves in the weeded verge. Through windows
Of dusk and water I see the tilting whispering

Heron, mirrored, go,
As the snapt feathers snow,   50
Fishing in the tear of the Towy. Only a hoot owl
Hollows, a grassblade blown in cupped hands, in the looted elms,
And no green cocks or hens
Shout
Now on Sir John's hill. The heron, ankling the scaly   55
Lowlands of the waves,
Makes all the music; and I who hear the tune of the slow,
Wear-willow river, grave,
Before the lunge of the night, the notes on this time-shaken
Stone for the sake of the souls of the slain birds sailing.   60

Verse letter to Loren McIver and Lloyd Frankenberg

Now 15 odd months have come to live in your dome
sweet dome for the pleasure of dying with loren
          (hullo!) and long (thank you!) lloyd,
since in that titan's canoe I hiccupped for home
(I mean the queen e. where the limeys spoke foreign,   5
          to bowery me, as freud)
and shared my cabin with a minikin moron
who'd fifteen suits and was always milking his gnome
          with hairy cries in a com
          a, and a haggis embroid   10
ering dominie who'd not behave as in rome
the romans behave but who thought me gomorrhan
          and (how the hell dare he!) hom
osexual too, an unsoberly fairy nom
an of probity'd deign to touch with his sporran.   15

And, cooped in that mastadon's sloop, I for the frank
enberg eyrie yearned for nearly a week and wept
          in deed for the scrapered shores;
and the pettylike pretties, twotitted and swank
en, went esquired, and never their beds were slept   20

in at all (at all!) by whores
truck me, though little I thought of but bribing cept
in god on the braided bridge for a chance to dank
        their doors with the rank
        and file of their downers of drawers   25
and the borers off of their bras, or alone and drank
en or sober to enter and probe a much leapt
        in tallulah, be she a lank
un or buttered with goosefat on breast, flank, bank
and brae. And never one word (the vicar's except   30

in) was asked but of gables, brown derbies, jane russell
's fables, minxes and sables, high balls (how heaver
        ly!), b. grable's pylons,
is m. west a lesbian, does bette d. hustle
in parties out there do the stars wear dishever   35
        ly? Did ever poor dȳlan's
onslaught on silence throughout his so clever
ly agented odyssey raise any bustle
        in this cockles and mussel
s town? No, not on your nylons!   40
'Tell us', they cried, 'of the boulevard tussle,
the bumdance of sunset, the strumpetting rever
        ly, hug, fug, and guzzle
in the chromium homes on the hills of bever
ly, hashish, hot splashes, nipple nibble and nuzzle.   45

Did you paint yale and harvard o'hara scarlet?
have a bash at the deans? did you maestro their broad
        s with a flash of cold mutton?
were holyoke girls all t. bara harlet
s? did you cry, "come into the garden brynmawr maud   50
        s and act like betty manhutton"?
did you pluck the g strings (how your plectrum pawed!)
of vassar's trig chippies and tiara'd starlet
        s and put in their belly button
        holes whole bowls and pink bord   55

ers of gypsy lee roses? did a harvard charlet
an, sweeny erect, dance on those tse-tse-flied swards?
and did loopy chicago aquinasses rut on
poor sinused st thomas like capricorn hebawd

s?' Just as a blind man's nose gives a wriggle and twitch   60
as he passes a fish shop, he bowing and leery
   with, 'how d'you do, ladies?',
so some snobs' noses, that hang by their snot to the rich—
for the rich are of heaven, hail croesus and meary!—
   writhe with some kind of sádis   65
tic joy at the name of some lionised, dreary
and serialised trilogist stuck in his saintly niche.
'Tell me, who did you meet?'—oh, the rabbity snitch
   es wiggle like nymphs with the itch—
   'not mere ritas and hedies'   70
(as though they wouldn't piss blood to meet either bitch)
'but someone, really, you know, I mean seri
   ous'. Prigs, fakes, and afraidies,
writers, backbiters, and, frothing, I ponder which,
till at last: 'well I met oscar williams, dearie.'   75

The inhaling bunion halfway between peepers
and chops does not wobble or whipcrack a bristle
   as this treasured name is struck—
(though down in derwood forest something stirs the creepers,
not robin hood, surely, and all his merry gristle,   80
   and it *can't* be friar tuck)—
no, from the cultural schnozzle not one wet whistle!
I skim through a scum of vogues for a deep as
   charles morgan betrophied cuck
   old to buck these snout sleepers,   85
grope through the open fannies of flairs for a thistle
of fame but can find only vaselined weepers,
then, ah! not oscar but tennessee williams, this'll
st vitus 'em! and indeed the pig vents sizzle!
'Didn't he write . . .?' He did, he did. A truck called fuck.   90

In this pretty as a stricture town by the eel
y, oily, licking sea full of fish that taste like feet
      and feet that taste like fur,
under a bathwater sky where angels fly like teal
eaves, gritty I sit me down greeting on my fat seat,   95
      o faraway madam and sir,
and hear the goitred, scraggy swans deathsing like gigl
i, and the cow pouncing owls sneer in the groinpit heat.
      Here a whiskey whiskered seal
      wet barking virgin with spur   100
s on her teats gives birth to a mole in the main street.
Today we hunt babies (d'you ken your little john peel
      s right down to his marrow meat?)
Tomorrow's the day for the circumcision of bir
ds. And on cannibal sunday let's hope the vicar's sweet.   105

Nine hundred gabies; two chapels soprano with rat
s; five catafalque pubs licensed to sell embalming gin
      and aconite tobacc
o: such is my home, and welcome is botched on the mat
of the excrementitious townhall with blood and spin   110
      ach, this rack a jack crack
a jill bug brained ball bearing year in the bloody vat.
And how long here shall my red market ration of skin
      and bone wait for the knack
      er yard? shall I champ the slack   115
bit of these verses, this adjective gravied lack
a bone hunk of monkey beef skewered with winkle pin
      s and tureened with a comic hat,
until crabs strut straight and statesmen are sardined in
sacks, the moon beams black, and generals scream in the bin?   120

Must I stand in this public uranium ('please
adjust your bomb before leaving') until the back room
      boys find a ray to gamma
themselves alone? must I (to hell with my pis
an q's!) pound out these cuntos on candystuck keys   125

until orchidaceous, ama
rous oscar w. (a very watered street bloom)
discovers, at last, if women's elbows and knees—
        (to william blake I owe these
        sacred bedpanorama   130
s)—are only glued together (as rare bits to cheese)?
must I strain out this mousecrap until damndom boom,
        until theodore reothke's seize
d with the king kong's evil and, searching his pomes for fleas,
snarls out, 'shit!' as he tarzans his way to the tomb?   135

Must I dree this wierd that is drier than moth's wee
wee till miracles happen as often as rape?
        till stephen the seaman
's bender bullbellows and belches with me big chi
chi chief wigwam hamingway, stiff as a stewed ape?   140
        till sick of laying shemen
john lehman the leman beds and bigbellies a fi
fi or mimi and grows a casanova shape?
        till peter lyrical tap
        ir tongued toryballed screamen   145
viereck turns russian red as a lobster? and e.
e. eimi gorblimey joyfarmer cummings goes pap
ist and shirty as trappissed merton and t.
        t. too and writes in the then
dormouse room of respectable mountains?—(though gee   150
gee jesus defend us from canter! emen!)

But let rancour, like chancres, b off! penic
illin them both! rhymes of cantankerous malice
        and an epileptic beat,
no more, on my septic oath, shall spout their menace   155
into the idylls and oils of perry palace,
        like a sewer on heat—
(O sixty one! o beer in a bishop's chalice!)
Please, nice penicillin, drip down! a nasty den is
        today my once tennys   160

onian house, and excret
a whirls through the window, turdy as venice.
Blow away, naughty thoughts, like a mummy's phallus—
      (and isn't mummy complete!)
This mummery's over. The paunched, maudlin villain   165
in cloaca and dagger, bows. And says,
                    Love,
                       Dylan.

Lament

When I was a windy boy and a bit
And the black spit of the chapel fold,
(Sighed the old ram rod, dying of women),
I tiptoed shy in the gooseberry wood,
The rude owl cried like a telltale tit,   5
I skipped in a blush as the big girls rolled
Ninepin down on the donkeys' common,
And on seesaw sunday nights I wooed
Whoever I would with my wicked eyes,
The whole of the moon I could love and leave   10
All the green leaved little weddings' wives
In the coal black bush and let them grieve.

When I was a gusty man and a half
And the black beast of the beetles' pews,
(Sighed the old ram rod, dying of bitches),   15
Not a boy and a bit in the wick-
Dipping moon and drunk as a new dropped calf,
I whistled all night in the twisted flues,
Midwives grew in the midnight ditches,
And the sizzling beds of the town cried, Quick!—   20
Whenever I dove in a breast high shoal,
Wherever I ramped in the clover quilts,
Whatsoever I did in the coal-
Black night, I left my quivering prints.

When I was a man you could call a man   25
And the black cross of the holy house,
(Sighed the old ram rod, dying of welcome),
Brandy and ripe in my bright, bass prime,
No springtailed tom in the red hot town
With every simmering woman his mouse   30
But a hillocky bull in the swelter
Of summer come in his great good time
To the sultry, biding herds, I said,
Oh, time enough when the blood creeps cold,
And I lie down but to sleep in bed,   35
For my sulking, skulking, coal black soul!

When I was a half of the man I was
And serve me right as the preachers warn,
(Sighed the old ram rod, dying of downfall),
No flailing calf or cat in a flame   40
Or hickory bull in milky grass
But a black sheep with a crumpled horn,
At last the soul from its foul mousehole
Slunk pouting out when the limp time came;
And I gave my soul a blind, slashed eye,   45
Gristle and rind, and a roarer's life,
And I shoved it into the coal black sky
To find a woman's soul for a wife.

Now I am a man no more no more
And a black reward for a roaring life,   50
(Sighed the old ram rod, dying of strangers),
Tidy and cursed in my dove cooed room
I lie down thin and hear the good bells jaw—
For, oh, my soul found a sunday wife
In the coal black sky and she bore angels!   55
Harpies around me out of her womb!
Chastity prays for me, piety sings,
Innocence sweetens my last black breath,

Modesty hides my thighs in her wings,
And all the deadly virtues plague my death!   60

Do not go gentle into that good night

Do not go gentle into that good night,
Old age should burn and rave at close of day;
Rage, rage against the dying of the light.

Though wise men at their end know dark is right,
Because their words had forked no lightning they   5
Do not go gentle into that good night.

Good men, the last wave by, crying how bright
Their frail deeds might have danced in a green bay,
Rage, rage against the dying of the light.

Wild men who caught and sang the sun in flight,   10
And learn, too late, they grieved it on its way,
Do not go gentle into that good night.

Grave men, near death, who see with blinding sight
Blind eyes could blaze like meteors and be gay,
Rage, rage against the dying of the light.   15

And you, my father, there on the sad height,
Curse, bless, me now with your fierce tears, I pray.
Do not go gentle into that good night.
Rage, rage against the dying of the light.

Song

When Mr Watts-Ewers
(Licensed to sell
Beer wine & spirits

And tobacco as well),
Advertised in the papers
He would open that night
His brand new hotel,
The town had a fright—

Mr Alf Measure
Who kept the Bull's Head
Wept like a baby
And took to his bed—

Mrs Lil Jenkins
Of the old Pig & Swill
Sacked all the barmaids
And was sick in the till—

In every saloon
And public too
There was such a commotion
As nobody knew—

For Mr Watts-Ewers
(Licensed for all
Drinking and Smoking
By men small & tall)
Had decided to call
His hotel the Liberty
Flipperty gibbetty
Liberty Hall—Hotel!

Oh, all drinks were free
(And cigarettes as well)
In Mr Watts-Ewers'
Brand-new hotel—

There were no set hours
There were no decrees
And nobody shouted   35
Time gentlemen Please,

For in Mr Watts-Ewers'
Splendiferous place
No gentleman ever
Disgraced our fair race—   40

There was nothing to pay
And nothing to lose
In Mr Watts-Ewers'
Buckingham Palace of booze.

In the White Giant's Thigh

Through throats where many rivers meet, the curlews cry,
Under the conceiving moon, on the high chalk hill,
And there this night I walk in the white giant's thigh
Where barren as boulders women lie longing still

To labour and love though they lay down long ago.   5

Through throats where many rivers meet, the women pray,
Pleading in the waded bay for the seed to flow
Though the names on their weed grown stones are rained away,

And alone in the night's eternal, curving act
They yearn with tongues of curlews for the unconceived   10
And immemorial sons of the cudgelling, hacked

Hill. Who once in gooseskin winter loved all ice leaved

In the courters' lanes, or twined in the ox roasting sun
In the wains tonned so high that the wisps of the hay
Clung to the pitching clouds, or gay with any one   15
Young as they in the after milking moonlight lay

Under the lighted shapes of faith and their moonshade
Petticoats galed high, or shy with the rough riding boys,
Now clasp me to their grains in the gigantic glade,

Who once, green countries since, were a hedgerow of joys.   20

Time by, their dust was flesh the swineherd rooted sly,
Flared in the reek of the wiving sty with the rush
Light of his thighs, spreadeagle to the dunghill sky,
Or with their orchard man in the core of the sun's bush
Rough as cows' tongues and thrashed with brambles their
      buttermilk   25
Manes, under his quenchless summer barbed gold to the bone,

Or rippling soft in the spinney moon as the silk
And ducked and draked white lake that harps to a hail stone.

Who once were a bloom of wayside brides in the hawed house
And heard the lewd, wooed field flow to the coming frost,   30
The scurrying, furred small friars squeal, in the dowse
Of day, in the thistle aisles, till the white owl crossed

Their breast, the vaulting does roister, the horned bucks climb
Quick in the wood at love, where a torch of foxes foams,
All birds and beasts of the linked night uproar and chime   35

And the mole snout blunt under his pilgrimage of domes,

Or, butter fat goosegirls, bounced in a gambo bed,
Their breasts full of honey, under their gander king
Trounced by his wings in the hissing shippen, long dead
And gone that barley dark where their clogs danced in the spring, 40

And their firefly hairpins flew, and the ricks ran round—

(But nothing bore, no mouthing babe to the veined hives
Hugged, and barren and bare on Mother Goose's ground
They with their simple Jacks were a boulder of wives)—

Now curlew cry me down to kiss the mouths of their dust.   45

The dust of their kettles and clocks swings to and fro
Where the hay rides now or the bracken kitchens rust
As the arc of the billhooks that flashed the hedges low
And cut the birds' boughs that the minstrel sap ran red.
They from houses where the harvest kneels, hold me hard,   50
Who heard the tall bell sail down the Sundays of the dead
And the rain wring out its tongues on the faded yard,
Teach me the love that is evergreen after the fall leaved
Grave, after Beloved on the grass gulfed cross is scrubbed
Off by the sun and Daughters no longer grieved   55
Save by their long desirers in the fox cubbed
Streets or hungering in the crumbled wood: to these
Hale dead and deathless do the women of the hill
Love forever meridian through the courters' trees

And the daughters of darkness flame like Fawkes fires still.   60

Poem on his Birthday

In the mustardseed sun,
By full tilt river and switchback sea
    Where the cormorants scud,
In his house on stilts high among beaks
    And palavers of birds   5
This sandgrain day in the bent bay's grave
    He celebrates and spurns
His driftwood thirty-fifth wind turned age;
    Herons spire and spear.

Under and round him go   10
Flounders, gulls, on their cold, dying trails,
    Doing what they are told,
Curlews aloud in the congered waves
    Work at their ways to death,
And the rhymer in the long tongued room,   15
    Who tolls his birthday bell,
Toils towards the ambush of his wounds;
    Herons, steeple stemmed, bless.

    In the thistledown fall,
He sings towards anguish; finches fly   20
    In the claw tracks of hawks
On a seizing sky; small fishes glide
    Through the wynds and shells of drowned
Ship towns to pastures of otters. He
    In his slant, racking house   25
And the hewn coils of his trade perceives
    Herons walk in their shroud,

    The livelong river's robe
Of minnows wreathing around their prayer;
    And far at sea he knows,   30
Who slaves to his crouched, eternal end
    Under a serpent cloud,
Dolphins dive in their turnturtle dust,
    The rippled seals streak down
To kill and their own tide daubing blood   35
    Slides good in the sleek mouth.

    In a cavernous, swung
Wave's silence, wept white angelus knells.
    Thirty-five bells sing struck
On skull and scar where his loves lie wrecked,   40
    Steered by the falling stars.
And tomorrow weeps in a blind cage

Terror will rage apart
Before chains break to a hammer flame
    And love unbolts the dark 45

    And freely he goes lost
In the unknown, famous light of great
    And fabulous, dear God.
Dark is a way and light is a place,
    Heaven that never was 50
Nor will be ever is always true,
    And, in that brambled void,
Plenty as blackberries in the woods
    The dead grow for His joy.

    There he might wander bare 55
With the spirits of the horseshoe bay
    Or the stars' seashore dead,
Marrow of eagles, the roots of whales
    And wishbones of wild geese,
With blessed, unborn God and His Ghost, 60
    And every soul His priest,
Gulled and chanter in young Heaven's fold
    Be at cloud quaking peace,

    But dark is a long way.
He, on the earth of the night, alone 65
    With all the living, prays,
Who knows the rocketing wind will blow
    The bones out of the hills,
And the scythed boulders bleed, and the last
    Rage shattered waters kick 70
Masts and fishes to the still quick stars,
    Faithlessly unto Him

    Who is the light of old
And air shaped Heaven where souls grow wild
    As horses in the foam: 75

Oh, let me midlife mourn by the shrined
   And druid herons' vows
The voyage to ruin I must run,
   Dawn ships clouted aground,
Yet, though I cry with tumbledown tongue,   80
   Count my blessings aloud:

   Four elements and five
Senses, and man a spirit in love
   Tangling through this spun slime
To his nimbus bell cool kingdom come   85
   And the lost, moonshine domes,
And the sea that hides his secret selves
   Deep in its black, base bones,
Lulling of spheres in the seashell flesh,
   And this last blessing most,   90

   That the closer I move
To death, one man through his sundered hulks,
   The louder the sun blooms
And the tusked, ramshackling sea exults;
   And every wave of the way   95
And gale I tackle, the whole world then
   With more triumphant faith
Than ever was since the world was said
   Spins its morning of praise,

   I hear the bouncing hills   100
Grow larked and greener at berry brown
   Fall and the dew larks sing
Taller this thunderclap spring, and how
   More spanned with angels ride
The mansouled fiery islands! Oh,   105
   Holier then their eyes,
And my shining men no more alone
   As I sail out to die.

Prologue to Collected Poems 1934–1952

This day winding down now
At God speeded summer's end
In the torrent salmon sun,
In my seashaken house
On a breakneck of rocks   5
Tangled with chirrup and fruit,
Froth, flute, fin and quill
At a wood's dancing hoof,
By scummed, starfish sands
With their fishwife cross   10
Gulls, pipers, cockles, and sails,
Out there, crow black, men
Tackled with clouds, who kneel
To the sunset nets,
Geese nearly in heaven, boys   15
Stabbing, and herons, and shells
That speak seven seas,
Eternal waters away
From the cities of nine
Days' night whose towers will catch   20
In the religious wind
Like stalks of tall, dry straw,
At poor peace I sing
To you, strangers (though song
Is a burning and crested act,   25
The fire of birds in
The world's turning wood,
For my sawn, splay sounds),
Out of these seathumbed leaves
That will fly and fall   30
Like leaves of trees and as soon
Crumble and undie
Into the dogdayed night.

Seaward the salmon, sucked sun slips,
And the dumb swans drub blue   35
My dabbled bay's dusk, as I hack
This rumpus of shapes
For you to know
How I, a spinning man,
Glory also this star, bird   40
Roared, sea born, man torn, blood blest.
Hark: I trumpet the place,
From fish to jumping hill! Look:
I build my bellowing ark
To the best of my love   45
As the flood begins,
Out of the fountainhead
Of fear, rage red, manalive,
Molten and mountainous to stream
Over the wound asleep   50
Sheep white hollow farms

To Wales in my arms.
Hoo, there, in castle keep,
You king singsong owls, who moonbeam
The flickering runs and dive   55
The dingle furred deer dead!
Huloo, on plumbed bryns,
O my ruffled ring dove
In the hooting, nearly dark
With Welsh and reverent rook,   60
Coo rooing the woods' praise,
Who moons her blue notes from her nest
Down to the curlew herd!
Ho, hullaballoing clan
Agape, with woe   65
In your beaks, on the gabbing capes!
Heigh, on horseback hill, jack
Whisking hare! who
Hears, there, this fox light, my flood ship's

Clangour as I hew and smite 70
(A clash of anvils for my
Hubbub and fiddle, this tune
On a tongued puffball)
But animals thick as thieves
On God's rough tumbling grounds 75
(Hail to His beasthood!).
Beasts who sleep good and thin,
Hist, in hogsback woods! The haystacked
Hollow farms in a throng
Of waters cluck and cling, 80
And barnroofs cockcrow war!
O kingdom of neighbours, finned
Felled and quilled, flash to my patch
Work ark and the moonshine
Drinking Noah of the bay, 85
With pelt, and scale, and fleece:
Only the drowned deep bells
Of sheep and churches noise
Poor peace as the sun sets
And dark shoals every holy field. 90
We shall ride out alone, and then,
Under the stars of Wales,
Cry, Multitudes of arks! Across
The water lidded lands,
Manned with their loves they'll move, 95
Like wooden islands, hill to hill.
Huloo, my prowed dove with a flute!
Ahoy, old sea-legged fox,
Tom tit and Dai mouse!
My ark sings in the sun 100
At God speeded summer's end
And the flood flowers now.

Two Epigrams of Fealty

(i) Upon King Julian's Return From Stebbing

From fourteen Great Danes he came to me.
To be, small, local Hamlet? O, not to be!

(ii) King Juan Advocates King Felipe

She'll do this, she'll do that:
People sigh in the local vat;
But Shiel *is* this, and Shiel *is* that
Cries the vocal King with his golden hat.

Galsworthy & Gawsworth

Galsworthy's verse I find unworthy. 'Fust is'
My verdict on his verse: skinned game, by justice.

Gawsworth, on the other hand,
Is worthy, unjust, skinned, not grand;
May he continue just as long
As frogs are in the throat of song.

Verses and songs from Under Milk Wood

i. Morning hymn of the Reverend Eli Jenkins

Dear Gwalia! I know there are
Towns lovelier than ours,
And fairer hills and loftier far,
And groves more full of flowers,

And boskier woods more blithe with spring   5
And bright with birds' adorning,
And sweeter bards than I to sing
Their praise this beauteous morning.

By Cader Idris, tempest-torn,
Or Moel y Wyddfa's glory,   10
Carnedd Llewelyn beauty born,
Plinlimmon old in story,

By mountains where King Arthur dreams,
By Penmaen Mawr defiant,
Llareggub Hill a molehill seems,   15
A pygmy to a giant.

By Sawdde, Senni, Dovey, Dee,
Edw, Eden, Aled, all
Taff and Towy broad and free,
Llyfnant with its waterfall,   20

Claerwen, Cleddau, Dulas, Daw,
Ely, Gwili, Ogwr, Nedd,
Small is our *River Dewi*, Lord,
A baby on a rushy bed.

By Carreg Cennen, King of time,   25
Our *Heron Head* is only
A bit of stone with seaweed spread
Where gulls come to be lonely.

A tiny dingle is *Milk Wood*
By Golden Grove 'neath Grongar,   30
But let me choose and oh! I should
Love all my life and longer

To stroll among our trees and stray
In Goosegog Lane, on Donkey Down,
And hear the Dewi sing all day,   35
And never, never, leave the town.

ii. School children's song

Johnnie Crack and Flossie Snail
Kept their baby in a milking pail
Flossie Snail and Johnnie Crack
One would pull it out and one would put it back
O it's my turn now said Flossie Snail   5
To take the baby from the milking pail
And it's my turn now said Johnnie Crack
To smack it on the head and put it back

Johnnie Crack and Flossie Snail
Kept their baby in a milking pail   10
One would put it back and one would pull it out
And all it had to drink was ale and stout
For Johnnie Crack and Flossie Snail
Always used to say that stout and ale
Was *good* for a baby in a milking pail.   5

iii. Polly Garter's song

I loved a man whose name was Tom
He was strong as a bear and two yards long
I loved a man whose name was Dick
He was big as a barrel and three feet thick
And I loved a man whose name was Harry   5
Six feet tall and sweet as a cherry
But the one I loved best awake or asleep
Was little Willie Wee and he's six feet deep.

Oh Tom Dick and Harry were three fine men
And I'll never have such loving again   10
But little Willie Wee who took me on his knee
Little Willie Weazel is the man for me.

Now men from every parish round
Run after me and roll me on the ground
But whenever I love another man back   15
Johnnie from the Hill or Sailing Jack
I always think as they do what they please
Of Tom Dick and Harry who were tall as trees
And most I think when I'm by their side
Of little Willie Wee who downed and died.   20

Oh Tom Dick and Harry were three fine men
And I'll never have such loving again
But little Willie Wee who took me on his knee
Little Willie Weazel is the man for me.

Now when farmers' boys on the first fair day   25
Come down from the hills to drink and be gay,
Before the sun sinks I'll lie there in their arms—
For they're *good* bad boys from the lonely farms,
But I always think as we tumble into bed
Of little Willie Wee who is dead, dead, dead . . .   30

iv. Captain Cat remembers Rosie Probert

ROSIE PROBERT [Softly]
What seas did you see,
Tom Cat, Tom Cat,
In your sailoring days
Long long ago?
What sea beasts were   5
In the wavery green
When you were my master?

CAPTAIN CAT
I'll tell you the truth.
Seas barking like seals,
Blue seas and green,
Seas covered with eels
And mermen and whales.

ROSIE PROBERT
What seas did you sail
Old whaler when
On the blubbery waves
Between Frisco and Wales
You were my bosun?

CAPTAIN CAT
As true as I'm here dear
You Tom Cat's tart
You landlubber Rosie
You cosy love
My easy as easy
My true sweetheart,
Seas green as a bean
Seas gliding with swans
In the seal-barking moon.

ROSIE PROBERT
What seas were rocking
My little deck hand
My favourite husband
In your seaboots and hunger
My duck my whaler
My honey my daddy
My pretty sugar sailor
With my name on your belly
When you were a boy
Long long ago?

CAPTAIN CAT
I'll tell you no lies.
The only sea I saw
Was the seasaw sea
With you riding on it.   40
Lie down, lie easy.
Let me shipwreck in your thighs.

ROSIE PROBERT
Knock twice, Jack,
At the door of my grave
And ask for Rosie.   45

CAPTAIN CAT
Rosie Probert.

ROSIE PROBERT
Remember her.
She is forgetting.
The earth which filled her mouth
Is vanishing from her.   50
Remember me.
I have forgotten you.
I am going into the darkness of the darkness for ever.
I have forgotten that I was ever born.

v. Evening hymn of the Reverend Eli Jenkins

Every morning when I wake,
Dear Lord, a little prayer I make,
O please to keep Thy lovely eye
On all poor creatures born to die.

And every evening at sun-down   5
I ask a blessing on the town,
For whether we last the night or no
I'm sure is always touch-and-go.

We are not wholly bad or good
Who live our lives under Milk Wood,   10
And Thou, I know, wilt be the first,
To see our best side, not our worst.

O let us see another day!
Bless us this holy night, I pray,
And to the sun we all will bow   15
And say goodbye—but just for now!

vi. Mr Waldo's song

In Pembroke City when I was young
I lived by the Castle Keep
Sixpence a week was my wages
For working for the chimbley sweep.

Six cold pennies he gave me   5
Not a farthing more or less
And all the fare I could afford
Was parsnip gin and watercress.

I did not need a knife and fork
Or a bib up to my chin   10
To dine on a dish of watercress
And a jug of parsnip gin.

Did you ever hear a growing boy
To live so cruel cheap
On grub that has no flesh and bones   15
And liquor that makes you weep?

Sweep sweep chimbley sweep
I wept through Pembroke City
Poor and barefoot in the snow
Till a kind young woman took pity.   20

Poor little chimbley sweep she said
Black as the ace of spades
Oh nobody's swept my chimbley
Since my husband went his ways.

Come and sweep my chimbley   25
Come and sweep my chimbley
She sighed to me with a blush
Come and sweep my chimbley
Come and sweep my chimbley
Bring along your chimbley brush!   30

Elegy [unfinished]

Too proud to die, broken and blind he died
The darkest way, and did not turn away,
A cold, kind man brave in his burning pride

On that darkest day. Oh, forever may
He live lightly, at last, on the last, crossed   5
Hill, and there grow young, under the grass, in love,

Among the long flocks, and never lie lost
Or still all the days of his death, though above
All he longed all dark for his mother's breast

Which was rest and dust, and in the kind ground   10
The darkest justice of death, blind and unblessed.
Let him find no rest but be fathered and found,

I prayed in the crouching room, by his blind bed,
In the muted house, one minute before
Noon, and night, and light. The rivers of the dead   15

Moved in his poor hand I held, and I saw
Through his faded eyes to the roots of the sea.
Go calm to your crucifixed hill, I told

The air that drew away from him.

Appendices

Appendix 1: *Extracts from letters to Pamela Hansford Johnson 1933–34*

I am in the path of Blake, but so far behind him that only the wings on his heels are in sight. I have been writing since I was a very little boy, and have always been struggling with the same things, with the idea of poetry as a thing entirely removed from such accomplishments as 'word-painting', and the setting down of delicate but usual emotions in a few wellchosen words. There must be no compromise; there is always only the right word: use it, despite its foul or merely ludicrous associations; I used 'double-crossed' [in 'Before I knocked'] because it was what I meant . . . Poetry finds its own form; form should never be superimposed; the structure should rise out of the words and the expression of them.

EARLY NOVEMBER 1933

What you call ugly in my poetry is, in reality, nothing but the strong stressing of the physical. Nearly all my images, coming as they do, from my solid and fluid world of flesh and blood, are set out in terms of their progenitors. To contrast a superficial beauty with a superficial ugliness, I do not contrast a tree with a pylon . . . but rather the human limbs with the human tripes. Deeply, of course, all these contrasting things are equally beautiful and equally ugly. Only by association is the refuse of the body more to be abhorred than the body itself. . . . It is polite to be seen at one's dining table, and impolite to be seen in one's lavatory. It might well have been decided . . . that celebrations should be held in the w.c., and that the mere mention of 'eating and drinking' would be the height of impropriety. . . . I fail to see how the emphasising of the body can, in any way, be regarded as hideous. The body, its appearance, death, and diseases, is a fact, sure as the fact of a tree. It has its roots in the same earth as the tree. The greatest description I know of our own 'earthiness' is to be found in John Donne's

Devotions, where he describes man as the earth of the earth, his body earth, his hair a wild shrub growing out of the land. All thoughts and actions emanate from the body. Therefore the description of a thought or action – however abstruse it may be – can be translated in terms of the body, its flesh, skin, blood, sinews, veins, glands, organs, cells, or senses.

Through my small, bonebound island I have learnt all I know, experienced all, and sensed all. All I write is inseparable from the island. As much as possible, therefore, I employ the scenery of the island to describe the scenery of my thoughts, the earthquakes of the body to describe the earthquakes of the heart.

25 DECEMBER 1933

[Y]ou confessed that you were one with the 'sparrow', and then, as a natural conclusion, went on to say that you were one with the 'arrow', too. If it comes to that, you can say you are one with the barrow as well. For you are, my dear, you are. I'm not trying to be flippant; I'm merely trying to show you . . . how *essentially* false such writing is.

> I am one with the wind and one with the breezes,
> And one with the torrent that drowns the plain,
> I am one with the streams and one with the seas-es,
> And one with the maggot that snores in the grain.

. . . there's too much 'Uncle Tom Collie [sic] & all' about that. Primarily, you see, the reader refuses to believe that *you* believe that you are one with all these things; you have to prove it to him, and you most certainly won't by cataloguing a number of other things to which you *say* you are related. By the magic of words and images you must make it clear to him that the relationships are real. And only in 'My blood is drawn from the veins of the roses', do you provide any proof. . . . Though you talk all through of the relationship of yourself to other things, there is no relationship at all in the poem between the things you example. If you are one with the swallow & one with the rose, then the rose is one with the swallow. Link together these things you talk of; show, in your words & images, how *your* flesh covers the tree & the tree's flesh covers you. I see what you have done, of course – 'I am one with the opposites', you say. You are, I know, but you must prove it to me by linking yourself to the opposites and by linking the opposites together. . . .

2 MAY 1934

Have I ever told you of the theory of how all writers either work towards or away from words? Even if I have I'll tell you again because it's true. Any poet or novelist you like to think of – he either works *out of* words or in the *direction of* them. The realistic novelist – Bennett, for instance – sees things, hears things, imagines things, (& all things of the material world or the materially cerebral world), & then goes towards words as the most suitable medium through which to express those experiences. A romanticist like Shelley, on the other hand, is his medium first, & expresses out of his medium what he sees, hears, thinks, & imagines.

Appendix 2: *Extracts from letters to Henry Treece*

23 MARCH 1938

... You mention Cameron and Madge. Cameron's verse has no greater admirer than myself, and I respect Madge's verse though with complete lack of affection. But when you say that I have not Cameron's or Madge's 'concentric movement round a central image', you are not accounting for the fact that it is consciously not my method to move concentrically round a central image. A poem by Cameron *needs* no more than one image; it moves around one idea, from one logical point to another, making a full circle. A poem by myself *needs* a host of images, because its centre is a host of images. I make one image, – although 'make' is not the word, I let, perhaps, an image be 'made' emotionally in me and then apply to it what intellectual & critical forces I possess – let it breed another, let that image contradict the first, make, of the third image bred out of the other two together, a fourth and contradictory image, and let them all, within my imposed formal limits, conflict. Each image holds within it the seed of its own destruction, and my dialectical method, as I understand it, is a constant building up and breaking down of the images that come out of the central seed, which is itself destructive and constructive at the same time.

Reading back over that, I agree it looks preciously like nonsense. To say that I 'let' my images breed and conflict is to deny my critical part in the business. But what I want to try to explain – and it's necessarily vague to me – is that the life in any poem of mine cannot move concentrically round a central image; the life must come out of the centre; an image must be born and die in another; and any sequence of my images must be a sequence of creations, recreations, destructions, contradictions. I cannot, either – as Cameron does, and as others do, and this primarily explains his and their writing round the central image – make a poem out of a single, motivating experience; I believe in the single thread of action through a poem, but that is an intellectual thing aimed at lucidity through narrative. My object is, as you say, conventionally to 'get things straight'. Out of the inevitable conflict of images – inevitable, because of the creative, recreative, destructive, and contradictory nature of the motivating centre, the womb of war – I try to make that momentary peace which is a poem. I do not want a poem of mine to be, nor can it be, a circular piece of experience placed neatly outside the living stream of time from which it came; a poem of mine is, or should be, a watertight section of the stream that is flowing all ways; all warring images within it should be reconciled for that small stop of time. I agree that each of my earlier poems might appear to constitute a section from one long poem; that is because I was not successful in making a momentary peace with my images at the correct moment; images were left dangling over the formal limits, and dragged the poem into another; the warring stream ran on over the insecure barriers, the fullstop armistice was pulled & twisted raggedly on into a conflicting series of dots and dashes.

16 MAY 1938

Very much of my poetry is, I know, an enquiry and a terror of fearful expectation, a discovery and facing of fear. I hold a beast, an angel, and a madman in me, and my enquiry is as to their working, and my problem is their subjugation and victory, downthrow & upheaval, and my effort is their self-expression. The new poem I enclose, 'How Shall My Animal', is a detailed enquiry; and the poem too is the result of the enquiry, and is the furthest I can, at present, reach or hope for. The poem is, as all poems are, its own question and answer, its own contradiction, its own agreement. I ask only that my poetry be taken literally. The aim of the poem is the mark that the poem itself makes; it's the bullet and the bullseye; the knife, the growth, and the patient. A poem moves only towards its own end, which is the last line. Anything further than that is the problematical stuff of poetry, not of the poem. That's my one critical argument, if it can be called that; the rest is a poetical argument, and can only be worked out in poems. . . . Stephen Spender, by the way, said in a review of the year's poetry some time ago . . . 'Thomas's poetry is turned on like a tap; it is just poetic stuff with no beginning nor end, shape or intelligent and intelligible control'. . . . [but] Spender's remark is really the exact opposite of what is true. My poems *are* formed, they are not turned on like a tap at all, they are 'watertight compartments'. Much of the obscurity is due to rigorous compression; the last thing they do is to flow; they are much rather hewn. Now Spender himself has no idea of form; his poetry is so much like poetry, & so remote from poems, that I think most of his work will become almost as unreadable as the worst of the Georgians – and very soon.

6 OR 7 JULY 1938

I was interested in what you said about my lack, except in that little finger-poem ['The hand that signed the paper'], of any social aware-ness. I suppose I am, broadly, (as opposed to regimented thinkers and poets in uniform) antisocial, but I am extremely sociable. But, surely it is evasive to say that my poetry has no social awareness – no evidence of contact with society – while quite a good number of my images come from the cinema & the gramophone and the newspaper, while I use contemporary slang, cliché, and pun. You meant, I know, that my poetry isn't concerned with politics (supposedly the science of achiev-ing and 'administrating' human happiness) but with poetry (which is unsentimental revelation, and to which happiness is no more impor-tant – or any other word – than misery): – (I'll elaborate that if you'd like me to. Not that it's obscure, but it may, in some way, be helpful to add it.) But the idea you gave me was that you actually consider me unaware of my surroundings, out-of-contact with the society from which I am necessarily outlaw. You are right when you suggest that I think a squirrel stumbling at least of equal importance as Hitler's invasions, murder in Spain, the Garbo-Stokowski romance, royalty, Horlicks, lynchlaw, pit disasters, Joe Louis, wicked capitalists, saintly communists, democracy, the Ashes, the Church of England, birth-control, Yeats' voice, the machines of the world I tick and revolve in, pub-baby-weather-government-football-youthandage-speed-lipstick, all small tyrannies, means tests, the fascist anger, the daily, momentary lightnings, eruptions, farts, dampsquibs, barrelorgans, tinwhistles, howitzers, tiny death-rattles, volcanic whimpers of the world I eat, drink, love, work, hate and delight in – but I *am* aware of these things as well.

Appendix 3: *'Poetry Programme', broadcast for BBC Radio's Third Programme, 25 September 1950*

These three poems ['Over Sir John's hill', 'In Country Sleep' and 'In the White Giant's Thigh'] will, one day, form separate parts of a long poem which is in preparation . . . What can I say about this long poem-to-be except that the plan of it is grand and simple and that the grandeur will seem, to many, to be purple and grandiose and the simplicity crude and sentimental? The poem is to be called 'In Country Heaven'. The godhead, the author, the milky-way farmer, the first cause, architect, lamplighter, quintessence, the beginning Word, the anthropomorphic bawler-out and blackballer, the stuff of all men, scapegoat, martyr, maker, woe-bearer — He, on top of a hill in Heaven, weeps whenever, outside that state of being called his country, one of his worlds drops dead, vanishes screaming, shrivels, explodes, murders itself. And, when he weeps, Light and His tears glide down together, hand in hand. So, at the beginning of the projected poem, he weeps, and Country Heaven is suddenly dark. Bushes and owls blow out like sparks. And the countrymen of heaven crouch all together under the hedges and, among themselves in the tear-salt darkness, surmise which world, which star, which of their late, turning homes, in the skies has gone for ever. And this time, spreads the heavenly hedgerow rumour, it is the Earth. The Earth has killed itself. It is black, petrified, wizened, poisoned, burst; insanity has blown it rotten; and no creatures at all, joyful, despairing, cruel, kind, dumb, afire, loving, dull, shortly and brutishly hunt their days down like enemies on that corrupted face. And, one by one, these heavenly hedgerow-men, who once were of the Earth, tell one another, through the long night, Light and His tears falling, what they remember, what they sense in the submerged wilderness and on the exposed hair's breadth of the mind, what they feel on the trembling on the nerves of a nerve, what they know in their Edenic hearts, of that self-killed place. They remember places, fears, loves, exultation, misery, animal joy, ignorance and mysteries, all *we* know and do not know.

The poem is made of these tellings. And the poem becomes, at last, an affirmation of the beautiful and terrible worth of the Earth. It grows into a praise of what is and what could be on this lump in the skies. It is a poem about happiness.

I do not expect that a first hearing of the three separate poems I am going to read can give any idea of how and where they will, eventually, take their places in that lofty, pretentious, down-to-earth-and-into-the-secrets, optimistic, ludicrous, knock-me-down moony scheme. I do not yet know myself their relevance to the whole, hypothetical structure. But I do know they belong to it.

The remembered tellings, which are the components of the poem, are not all told as they are remembered; the poem will not be a series of poems in the present tense. The memory, in all tenses, can look towards the future, can caution and admonish. The rememberer may live himself back into active participation in the remembered scene, adventure, or spiritual condition.

The first poem is 'Over Sir John's Hill'. Sir John's Hill is a real hill overlooking an estuary in West Wales. [Reads 'Over Sir John's hill']

The next poem, 'In Country Sleep', is divided into two parts. [Reads 'In Country Sleep']

And here, lastly, is the first part of a poem – a poem within the poem-to-be – called 'In the White Giant's Thigh'. This, just written, will, no doubt, have many small details altered before it is printed, but the general feel and sound of it will remain the same even when I have cleared up some of its more obviously overlush, arch and exuberant, mauve gauche moments.

Appendix 4: *Answers to questionnaires*

a) 'Answers to an Enquiry', published in New Verse, *11 October 1934*

1. Do you intend your poetry to be useful to yourself or others?

To both. Poetry is the rhythmic, inevitably narrative, movement from
an overclothed blindness to a naked vision that depends, in its intensi-
ty, on the strength of the labour put into the creation of the poetry. My
poetry is, or should be, useful to me for one reason: it is the record of
my individual struggle from darkness towards some measure of light,
and what of the individual struggle is still to come benefits by the sight
and knowledge of the faults and fewer merits in that concrete record.
My poetry is, or should be, useful to others for its individual recording
of that same struggle with which they are necessarily acquainted.

2. Do you think there can now be a use for narrative poetry?

Yes. Narrative is essential. Much of the flat, abstract poetry of the
present has no narrative movement, no movement at all, and is
consequently dead. There must be a progressive line, or theme, of
movement in every poem. The more subjective a poem, the clearer
the narrative line. Narrative, in its widest sense, satisfies what Eliot,
talking of 'meaning', calls 'one habit of the reader'. Let the narrative
take that one logical habit of the reader along with its movement, and
the essence of the poem will do its work on him.

*3. Do you wait for a spontaneous impulse before writing a poem; if so, is
   this impulse verbal or visual?*

No. The writing of a poem is, for me, the physical and mental task
of constructing a formally watertight compartment of words, prefer-
ably with a main moving column (i.e. narrative) to hold a little of the
real causes and forces of the creative brain and body. The causes and
forces are always there, and they always need a concrete expression.
To me, the poetical 'impulse' or 'inspiration' is only the sudden, and
generally physical, coming of energy to the constructional, craftsman

ability. The laziest workman receives the fewest impulses. And vice versa.

4. *Have you been influenced by Freud and how do you regard him?*

Yes. Whatever is hidden should be made naked. To be stripped of darkness is to be clean, to strip of darkness is to make clean. Poetry, recording the stripping of the individual darkness, must inevitably cast light upon what has been hidden for too long, and, by so doing, make clean the naked exposure. Freud cast light on a little of the darkness he had exposed. Benefiting by the sight of the light and the knowledge of the hidden nakedness, poetry must drag further into the clean nakedness of light more even of hidden causes than Freud could realise.

5. *Do you take your stand with any political or politico-economic party or creed?*

I take my stand with any revolutionary body that asserts it to be the right of all men to share, equally and impartially, every production of man from man and from the forces of production at man's disposal, for only through such an essentially revolutionary body can there be the possibility of a communal art.

6. *As a poet what distinguishes you, do you think, from an ordinary man?*

Only the use of the medium of poetry to express the causes and forces which are the same in all men.

b) Replies to questions by student at the University of Texas in 1950, known as 'Poetic Manifesto', published in Texas Quarterly *in 1961.*

You want to know why and how I first began to write poetry, and which kinds of poets or kind of poetry I was first moved and influenced by.

To answer the first part of this question, I should say I wanted to write poetry in the beginning because I had fallen in love with words. The first poems I knew were nursery rhymes, and before I could read them for myself I had come to love just the words of them, the words alone. What the words stood for, symbolized, or meant, was of very secondary importance. What mattered was the *sound* of them as I heard them for the first time on the lips of those remote and incomprehensible grown-ups who seemed, for some reason, to be living in my world. And these words were, to me, as the notes of bells, the sounds of musical instruments, the noises of wind, sea, and rain, the rattle of milkcarts, the clopping of hooves on cobbles, the fingering of branches on a window pane, might be to someone, deaf from birth, who has miraculously found his hearing. I did not care what the words said, overmuch, nor what happened to Jack & Jill & the Mother Goose rest of them; I cared for the shapes of sound that their names, and the words describing their actions, made in my ears; I cared for the colours the words cast on my eyes. I realise that I may be, as I think back all that way, romanticising my reactions to the simple and beautiful words of those pure poems; but that is all I can honestly remember, however much time might have falsified my memory. I fell in love – that is the only expression I can think of – at once, and am still at the mercy of words, though sometimes now, knowing a little of their behaviour very well, I think I can influence them slightly and have even learnt to beat them now and then, which they appear to enjoy. I tumbled for words at once. And, when I began to read the nursery rhymes for myself, and, later, to read other verses and ballads, I knew that I had discovered the most important things, to me, that could be ever. There they were, seemingly lifeless, made only of black and white, but out of them, out of their own being, came love and terror and pity and pain and wonder and all the other vague abstractions that make our ephemeral lives dangerous, great, and bearable. Out of them came the gusts and grunts and hiccups and heehaws of the common fun of the earth; and though what the words meant was, in its own way, often deliciously funny enough, so much funnier seemed to me, at that almost forgotten time, the shape and shade and size and noise of the words as they hummed, strummed, jigged and galloped along. That was the time of innocence; words burst upon me, unencumbered by trivial or portentous association; words were their spring-like selves, fresh with Eden's dew, as they flew out of the air. They made their own original associations as they sprang and shone. The words, 'Ride a cock-horse to Banbury Cross', were as haunting to me, who did not know then what a cock-horse was nor cared a damn where Banbury Cross might be, as, much later, were such lines as John Donne's, 'Go and catch a falling star, Get with child a mandrake root', which also I could not understand when I first read them. And as I read more and more, and it was not all verse, by any means, my love for the real life of words increased until I knew that I must live *with* them and *in* them, always. I knew, in fact, that I must be a writer of words, and nothing else. The first thing was to feel and know their sound and substance; what I was going to do with those words, what use I was going to make of them, what I was going to *say* through them, would come later. I knew I had to know them most intimately in all their forms and moods, their ups and downs, their chops and changes, their needs and demands. (Here, I am afraid, I am beginning to talk too vaguely. I do not like writing *about* words, because then I often use bad and wrong and stale and woolly words. What I like to do is to treat words as a craftsman does his wood or stone or what-have-you, to hew, carve, mould, coil, polish and plane them into patterns, sequences, sculptures, fugues of sound expressing some lyrical impulse, some spiritual doubt or conviction, some dimly-realised truth I must try to reach and realise.) It was when I was very young, and just at school, that, in my father's study, before homework that was never done, I began to know one kind of writing from another, one kind of goodness, one kind of badness. . . .

You ask me, next, if it is true that three of the dominant influences on my published prose and poetry are Joyce, the Bible, and Freud. (I purposely say my 'published' prose and poetry as, in the preceding pages, I have been talking about the primary influences upon my very first and forever unpublishable juvenilia.) I cannot say that I have been 'influenced' by Joyce, whom I enormously admire, and whose *Ulysses* and earlier stories I have read a great deal. . . . I do not think that Joyce has had any hand at all in my writing; certainly his *Ulysses* has not. On the other hand, I cannot deny that the shaping of some of my *Portrait* stories might owe something to Joyce's stories in the volume, *Dubliners*. But then *Dubliners* was a pioneering work in the world of the short story and no good storywriter since can have failed, in some way, however little, to have benefited by it.

The Bible, I have referred to . . . Its great stories of Noah, Jonah, Lot, Moses, Jacob, David, Solomon and a thousand more, I had, of course, known from very early youth; the great rhythms had rolled over me from the Welsh pulpits; and I read, for myself, from Job and Ecclesiastes; and the story of the New Testament is part of my life. But I have never sat down and studied the Bible, never consciously echoed its language, and am, in reality, as ignorant of it as most brought-up Christians. All of the Bible that I use in my work is remembered from childhood, and is the common property of all who were brought up in English-speaking communities. Nowhere, indeed, in all my writing, do I use any knowledge which is not commonplace to any literate person. I *have* used a few difficult words in early poems, but they are easily looked-up and were, in any case, thrown into the poems in a kind of adolescent showing-off which I hope I have now discarded.

And that leads me to the third 'dominant influence': Sigmund Freud. My only acquaintance with the theories and discoveries of Dr Freud has been through the work of novelists who have been excited by his case-book histories, of popular newspaper scientific-potboilers who have, I imagine, vulgarized his work beyond recognition, and of a few modern poets, including Auden, who have attempted to use psychoanalytical phraseology and theory in some of their poems. I have read only one book of Freud's, *The Interpretation of Dreams*, and do not recall having been influenced by it in any way. Again, no honest writer today can possibly avoid being influenced by Freud through his pioneering work into the Unconscious and by the influence of those discoveries on the scientific, philosophic, and artistic work of his contemporaries: but not, by any means, necessarily through Freud's own writing.

To your third question – Do I deliberately utilise devices of rhyme, rhythm, and word-formation in my writing – I must, of course, answer with an immediate, Yes. I am a painstaking, conscientious, involved and devious craftsman in words, however unsuccessful the result so often appears, and to whatever wrong uses I may apply my technical paraphernalia, I use everything and anything to make my poems work and move them in the directions I want to: old tricks, new tricks, puns, portmanteau-words, paradox, allusion, paronomasia, paragram, catachresis, slang, assonantal rhymes, vowel rhymes, sprung rhythm. Every device there is in language is there to be used if you will. Poets have got to enjoy themselves sometimes, and the twistings and convolutions of words, the inventions and contrivances, are all part of the joy that is part of the painful, voluntary work . . .

And question five is, God help us, what is my definition of Poetry?

I, myself, do not read poetry for anything but pleasure. I read only the poems I like. This means, of course, that I have to read a lot of poems I don't like before I find the ones I *do*, but, when I do find the ones I do, then all I can say is, 'Here they are', and read them to myself for pleasure.

Read the poems you like reading. Don't bother whether they're 'important', or if they'll live. What does it matter what poetry is, after all? If you want a definition of poetry, say: 'Poetry *is* what makes me laugh or cry or yawn, what makes my toenails twinkle, what makes me want to do this or that or nothing', and let it go at that. All that matters about poetry is the enjoyment of it, however tragic it may be. All that matters is the eternal movement behind it, the vast undercurrent of human grief, folly, pretension, exaltation, or ignorance, however unlofty the intention of the poem.

You can tear a poem apart to see what makes it technically tick, and say to yourself, when the works are laid out before you, the vowels, the consonants, the rhymes or rhythms, 'Yes, this is *it*. This is why the poem moves me so. It is because of the craftsmanship.' But you're back again where you began.

You're back with the mystery of having been moved by words. The best craftsmanship always leaves holes and gaps in the works of the poem so that something that is *not* in the poem can creep, crawl, flash, or thunder in.

The joy and function of poetry is, and was, the celebration of man, which is also the celebration of God.

Appendix 5: *'Note' to* Collected Poems 1934–1952

The prologue in verse, written for this collected edition of my poems, is intended as an address to my readers, the strangers.

This book contains most of the poems I have written, and all, up to the present year, that I wish to preserve. Some of them I have revised a little, but if I went on revising everything that I now do not like in this book I should be so busy that I would have no time to try to write new poems.

I read somewhere of a shepherd who, when asked why he made, from within fairy rings, ritual observances to the moon to protect his flocks, replied: 'I'd be a damn' fool if I didn't!' These poems, with all their crudities, doubts, and confusions, are written for the love of Man and in praise of God, and I'd be a damn' fool if they weren't.

November 1952

Appendix 6: *Contents of volumes*

18 Poems (1934)

I see the boys of summer; When once the twilight locks; A process in the weather of the heart; Before I knocked; The force that through the green fuse; My hero bares his nerves; Where once the waters of your face; If I were tickled by the rub of love; Our eunuch dreams; Especially when the October wind; When, like a running grave; From love's first fever; In the beginning; Light breaks where no sun shines; I fellowed sleep; I dreamed my genesis; My world is pyramid; All all and all.

Twenty-five Poems (1936)

I, in my intricate image; This bread I break; Incarnate devil; To-day, this insect; The seed-at-zero; Shall gods be said; Here in this spring; Do you not father me; Out of the sighs; Hold hard, these ancient minutes; Was there a time; Now; Why east wind chills; A grief ago; How soon the servant sun; Ears in the turrets hear; Foster the light; The hand that signed the paper; Should lanterns shine; I have longed to move away; 'Find meat on bones'; Grief thief of time; And death shall have no dominion; Then was my neophyte; Altarwise by owl-light.

The Map of Love (1939)

Poems: Because the pleasure-bird whistles; I make this in a warring absence; When all my five and country senses; We lying by seasand; It is the sinners' dust-tongued bell; O make me a mask; The spire cranes; After the funeral; Once it was the colour of saying; Not from this anger; How shall my animal; The tombstone told; On no work of words; A saint about to fall; 'If my head hurt a hair's foot'; Twenty-four years. Stories: 'The Visitor', 'The Enemies', 'The Tree', 'The Map of Love', 'The Mouse and the Woman', 'The Dress', 'The Orchards'.

Deaths and Entrances (1946)

The conversation of prayers; A Refusal to Mourn the Death, by Fire, of a Child in London; Poem in October; This side of the truth; To Others than You; Love in the Asylum; Unluckily for a death; The hunchback in the park; Into her lying down head; Paper and sticks; Deaths and Entrances; A Winter's Tale; On a Wedding Anniversary; There was a saviour; On the Marriage of a Virgin; In my craft or sullen art; Ceremony After a Fire Raid; When I woke; Among those Killed in the Dawn Raid was a Man Aged a Hundred; Lie still, sleep becalmed; Vision and Prayer; Ballad of the Long-legged Bait; Holy Spring; Fern Hill.

In Country Sleep (1952)

Over Sir John's hill; Poem on his Birthday; Do not go gentle into that good night; Lament; In the White Giant's Thigh; In Country Sleep.

Collected Poems 1934–1952 (1952)

Thomas opted to simply run together all five previous volumes, dropping 'Paper and sticks'; its place, after 'Into her lying down head', was taken by 'Do not go gentle'. He also inserted 'Once below a time', which had been dropped from *Deaths and Entrances*, after 'Ceremony After a Fire Raid'. The preface took the form of a short 'Note' (Appendix 5), followed by 'Prologue' (titled 'Author's Prologue' by Dent). In post-1956 editions, a version of 'Elegy' by Vernon Watkins closed the volume.

The Notebooks of Dylan Thomas / Poet in the Making (1967, 1968)

The US and UK editions of the four surviving poetry notebooks from the period 1930–34, now held in the Margaret Lockwood Library Special Poetry Collection at the State University of New York at Buffalo. The first notebook (B432F7) covers 27 April 1930–9 December 1930; the second (B432F6) December 1930–1 July 1932; the third (B432F5) 1 February 1933–16 August 1933; the fourth (B432F4) 17 August 1933–30 April 1934. Both editions contain an Introduction, full textual apparatus and exhaustive notes; *Poet in the Making* includes eleven examples of juvenilia and eight poems conjectured to be from a lost notebook of July 1932–February 1933. The 1989 *The Notebook Poems 1930–1934* contained three juvenilia items, all 'lost notebook' pieces, and fifteen other poems, among them other juvenilia, poems from the *Swansea Grammar School Magazine*, poems deleted from the first notebook, and the poems from the short story 'The Fight'.

The Poems (1971)

To the ninety-one poems of the post-1956 *Collected Poems*, Daniel Jones added fifty-six notebook poems, 'A Letter to My Aunt', the revised 'That the sum sanity', 'O Chatterton', 'I, the first named', 'The Molls', 'Paper and sticks', 'The Countryman's Return', 'Request to Leda', 'Youth Calls to Age', 'Last night I dived my beggar arm', 'Your breath was shed' and 'New Quay'. He added seven poems from the British Library ms 48217 of autumn 1932, two from the other poems collateral with the notebooks (but not 'That sanity be kept'), the 1947 version of 'In Country Heaven' and thirty-six poems 'written before the poet's sixteenth birthday' (but not the lyrics from 'The Fight'), giving a total of 201 poems.

Collected Poems 1934–1953 (1988)

Walford Davies and Ralph Maud returned to the contents of the *Collected Poems* of 1952, adding 'Once below a time', restoring 'Paper and sticks', and returning 'Do not go gentle' to its place in the *In Country Sleep* section. A version of Thomas's 'Elegy' assembled by Vernon Watkins from Thomas's notes and included in the *Collected Poems* after 1956 was dropped in favour of the seventeen-line fragment as Thomas had left it, with two lines which seem its likeliest continuation. A sixteen-line version of 'In Country Heaven', conjectured to be the latest version, was added in an appendix.

Abbreviations

Publications may also be cited by name and date (e.g. Davies [1993]); items cited in this form but not contained in the following list will be found in the Bibliography.

Libraries

Austin   Harry Ransom Center Library, University of Austin at Texas, USA.

BL   Department of Manuscripts of the British Library, St Pancras, London.

Buffalo Special Poetry Collection, Margaret Lockwood Memorial Library, SUNY (State University of New York) at Buffalo, USA.

NLW   National Library of Wales, Aberystwyth.

Books

18P   *18 Poems, Sunday Referee* / Parton Books, London, 1934.

25P   *Twenty-five Poems*, Dent, London, 1936.

CL   *The Collected Letters*, ed. Paul Ferris, Dent, London, 2000.

CP52   *Collected Poems 1934–1952*, Dent, London, 1952.

CP88   *Collected Poems 1934–1953*, intro. and ed. Walford Davies and Ralph Maud, Dent, London, 1988.

CS   *Collected Stories*, ed. Walford Davies and intro. Leslie Norris, Dent, London, 1983.

CSP   *The Complete Screenplays*, ed. John Ackerman, Applause Books, New York, 1995.

DE   *Deaths and Entrances*, Dent, London, 1946.

EPW   *Early Prose Writings*, ed. and intro. Walford Davies, Dent, London, 1971.

ICS	*In Country Sleep*, New Directions Books, New York, 1952.
LVW	*Letters to Vernon Watkins*, ed. Vernon Watkins, Dent/Faber, London, 1957.
N1	Notebook 1 (1930)
N2	Notebook 2 (1930–32)
N3	Notebook 3 (February 1933–August 1933)
N4	Notebook 4 (August 1933–April 1934)
NP	*The Notebook Poems 1930–1934*, ed. and intro. Ralph Maud, Dent, London, 1989.
PITM	*Poet in the Making: The Notebooks of Dylan Thomas*, ed. and intro. Ralph Maud, Dent, London, 1968; repr. *The Notebooks of Dylan Thomas*, New Directions, New York, 1967.
PM	'Poetic Manifesto', *Texas Quarterly*, 4 (Winter 1961), pp. 45–53 (Appendix 4).
Portrait	*Portrait of the Artist as a Young Dog*, Dent, London, 1940 repr. 1990.
QEOM	*Quite Early One Morning*, New Directions, New York, 1960.
SP1	*Selected Poems*, ed. and intro. Walford Davies, Dent, London, 1993.
SP2	*Selected Poems*, ed. and intro. Walford Davies, Dent, London, 2000.
TB	*The Broadcasts*, ed. Ralph Maud, Dent, London, 1991.
TP71	*The Poems*, ed. and intro. Daniel Jones, Dent, London; New Directions, New York, 1971.
TML	*The Map of Love*, Dent, London, 1939.
UMW	*Under Milk Wood*, ed. Ralph Maud and Walford Davies, intro. Walford Davies, Dent, London, 1995.

Notes to the Poems

All *N1*, *N2*, *N3* and *N4* poems were first published in Ralph Maud's *PITM* (1968) and *NP* (1989). *NP* also includes eight typescript poems (held in the BL) which Maud judges to originate in a notebook, now lost, covering the second half of 1932 and early 1933 (*N2* ends June 1932, while *N3* begins February 1933). In addition, *NP* includes nine 'collateral poems', stylistically resembling *N1* and *N2* poems, and later pieces which may derive from pages torn from *N3* and *N4*, and/or are intermediate between the notebook and published versions. If poems (e.g. from the letters) were first published in book form in Daniel Jones's *TP71*, this is noted.

Poems from 'The Fight' (p. 3)

These lyrics appear in the short story 'The Fight' (1938), a fictionalised account of Thomas's first meeting with Daniel Jones, which was published in *Portrait*. They were first published as a group of poems in *TP71*.

The Thomas character in the story gives his age as fourteen and three-quarters, which dates the poems to summer 1929, before *N1* was started in April 1930. Their foreshadowing of Thomas's cosmic themes and formal tautness suggests that they may have been polished before their use in the story.

I know this vicious minute's hour (p. 4)

N1 '30', dated 3 November 1930.

Set in an imaginary dance hall, or nightclub, with (very probably) an equally imaginary female addressee.

I, poor romantic, held her heel (p. 5)

N1 '37', dated 22 November 1930.

19–25 Sparkling a twelve-legged body ... which the real? = the 'lady' with whom the speaker is in love is changed into an insect, and this in turn raises the question of appearance and reality.

How shall the animal (p. 6)

N1 '42', the final poem in the first notebook, dated 9 December 1930.
Completely rewritten as 'How shall my animal' in 1938 (see below).

10 I build a tower and I pull it down = anticipates the imagery of towers, and of language as a tower. With 'tower' revised to 'flying tower', this line was used to

illustrate 'creative destruction, destructive creation' in a letter of 21 March 1938 to Vernon Watkins.

14 My senses see = an early example of Thomas's interest in synaesthesia.

23–26 A cross of legs . . . sailing thighs = for Thomas's fascination with Christ as a sexual being see 'Altarwise by owl-light'.

To-day, this hour I breathe (p. 7)

N2 'II', dated 18 December 1930.
      Completely rewritten in early 1936 as 'To-day, this insect'.

Rain cuts the place we tread (p. 8)

N2 'VII', dated 2 January 1931.
      An early exploration of the differences between kinds of poetic language and poem (static vs. fluid, carved vs. spontaneous; cf. 'The spire cranes').

if the lady from the casino (p. 9)

N2 'XXIV', dated 16 June 1931.
      The closest Thomas ever came to automatic writing, possibly reflecting an encounter with surrealism. The primary subject, however, is adolescent fascination with, and fear of, the opposite sex.

52 allonal = drug with various sedative, hypnotic and analgesic applications.

63 anna = Indian currency (one-hundredth of a rupee).

Never to reach the oblivious dark (p. 12)

N2 'XLVIX', dated 26 October 1931.
      Marks a shift to gloomier subject matter, perhaps because Thomas had recently begun work at the *South Wales Evening Post* and had encountered some of the more sordid aspects of Swansea life as a result. Just as striking is his use of Jacobean soliloquy and iambic pentameter to deal with the darker, more sexual material.

1–7 Never . . . Negatives impress negation . . . Never . . . Never = the use of 'never' as a noun, and reference to 'negation', anticipates the later use of the double negative to produce qualified positives.

Being but men, we walked into the trees (p. 13)

N2 'LVVIV', dated 7 May 1932.
      Followed in the notebook by the first version of 'The hunchback in the park';

both poems reflect the proximity of Cwmdonkin Park to Thomas's home.

Out of the sighs (p. 13)

The first two stanzas of this poem are *N2* 'LVVVI', dated 7 June 1932. These were amalgamated, barely changed, with 'Were that enough', the unnumbered final poem in *N2*, dated 1 July 1932; first published in *25P*.

Like 'Never to reach the oblivious dark', this poem finds Thomas adapting the soliloquy for the purposes of moody self-dramatisation. The subject is disappointment in love, but the elliptical syntax and abstraction make it an existential, stoic response to life's defeats, and a good example of his growing ability to deal with adolescent angst objectively.

1–6   Out of the sighs . . . not disappoint = a pre-emptive rejection of a tragic view of life ('grief', 'agony') as too painful; the speaker is resigned to putting up with diminished rewards. Cf. Emily Dickinson, 'After great pain, a formal feeling comes'.

7–9   There must . . . perpetual defeat = if he cannot be sure of 'loving well', then at least 'not loving well' is a certainty, which is a kind of consolation.

10–11   After such fighting . . . dying = cf. Shakespeare, *Julius Caesar*: 'Cowards die many times before their deaths'.

12–16   Lose the great pains . . . such acrid blood = even if you could ease the pangs of parting (with a lover), they would be prolonged by your sense that regret so easily overcome was not really regret in the first place.

17–24   Were that enough . . . cure me of ills = furthermore, if simply feeling regret after lost happiness could completely 'ease the pain' and make me able to accept that I was happy while it (love) lasted, and this verbal consolation ('sweet lies') was sufficient, then I would willingly let hypocritical 'hollow words' lighten my load ('suffering').

25–28   Were that enough . . . cured of distemper = if the remedies outlined were effective, man would be little more than a dog; 'distemper' puns on the dog's disease and 'dis-temper', being out of sorts.

29–30   For all there is . . . halter = ironic recognition and acceptance; since this is all there is, I 'offer' it back, accept it; the dog's life of 'crumbs' from the table, 'barn' for housing animals, 'halter' a lead (or noose).

Before the gas fades (p. 14)

N3 'Four', dated 6 February 1933.

Reflects the influence of John Lehmann's *New Signatures* anthology of April 1932, and the politically left poetry of W. H. Auden and his followers.

4, 28 The century's trap = an apt characterisation of the historical moment for a poem written just a week after Hitler's swearing-in as German Chancellor, on 30 January 1933.

5 allotment = a characteristic signifier of suburban life in 1930s poetry; cf. 'Light breaks where no sun shines'.

13 big bugs and shots = US slang for the rich and powerful.

19 Man's manmade sparetime = unemployment.

24 the oven and gun = means for committing suicide (cf. 'Their faces shone', 'Now', 'O Chatterton', and letter to Trevor Hughes of 8 February 1933: 'I continue writing in the most futile manner, looking at the gas-oven . . . with a wistful eye').

39 Nor black or white or left or right = civilisational chaos (i.e. the next war) will blur all distinctions, and the speaker will not live to see the new order which emerges from it.

Was there a time (p. 16)

N3 'Five', dated 8 February, revised for publication in 25P.
   Stanza 1 questions the ability of art ('fiddles' and 'books') to affect personal circumstances, and foregrounds the second stanza's bleak paradox – that, in order to preserve 'hope' or 'trust', it must 'never see the light', and that art therefore may as well not exist. Hence the bitter final lines, which mockingly hail ignorance as bliss.

'We who were young are old' (p. 16)

N3 'Seven', dated 16 February 1933, continued as N3 'Nine', dated 17 February.
   Like 'Before the gas fades', but with an intensified mood of civilisational decline, this poem addresses a prematurely aged generation which has never had the chance to 'grow strong', and now faces a new world war.

42 Piccadilly men = frequenters of London's nightclub district.

43 The grafters of cats' heads on chickens' trunks = cf. the story 'The Lemon' (1936): 'Early one morning, under the arc of a lamp, carefully, silently, in smock and rubber gloves, the doctor grafted a cat's head on to a chicken's trunk.'

Out of a war of wits (p. 18)

N3 'Ten', dated 22 February 1933.
   The 'war' refers to the regular evenings of debate and literary discussion Thomas enjoyed with friends such as Bert Trick before he left Swansea for

London. The story 'Where Tawe Flows', in *Portrait*, gives a comic version of such occasions.

In wasting one drop (p. 19)

N3 'Eleven', dated 23 February 1933.

A poem about prematurely giving one's love and having little left to give when a true love appears. The imagery of honey, drops, easing the pain of desire and love's 'itch', etc., is also masturbatory, revealing the speaker's fear that auto-eroticism will exhaust the ability to respond. Like *N3* 'Thirteen' (below), at fourteen lines long, and with irregular rhyme, this is a sonnet of sorts.

Their faces shone under some radiance (p. 19)

N3 'Thirteen', undated, but positioned between poems dated at the end of February and 1 March 1933, with the provisional title 'Hyde Park'.

Suicide is alluded to in several other poems of the period (cf. 'Before the gas fades').

I have longed to move away (p. 20)

N3 'Fourteen', dated 1 March 1933; published in *New Verse* in December 1935; revised 1936 and collected in *25P*.

Revision eliminated much of the social context of the original, giving the satire of moribund behavioural codes a more menacing, existential edge.

2 hissing of the spent lie = suggests the serpent in Eden as well as a firework.

7 salutes = conventional greetings; but also punning on military salutes (see l.10).

8–9 ghosts in the air . . . ghostly echoes on paper = Walford Davies (1993) glosses this as 'conventional superstition . . . is also dictating the attitudes of his poetry'.

10 calls and notes = military (and religious) trumpet calls and musical notes; also telephone calls and visiting cards and notes.

12 Some life = by granting this positive quality to the firework-like 'old lie', Thomas emphasises that to 'move away' may not solve the problem of arrest; the word 'life' contains 'lie'.

13 old lie = cf. Wilfred Owen's 'Dulce et decorum est': 'The old lie: dulce et decorum est / Pro patria mori'. One of the 'terrors' is the threat of another world war.

15–18 Neither by . . . death's feather = ironic; we don't die from superstitions and outworn conventions, despite fearfully obeying them, but from death; death's feather = a complex image, used in various forms in the early poetry. Sources include: *a* John Donne's *Devotions*: 'There is scarce anything that hath not killed some body; a hair, a feather hath done it'; *b* the practice of placing of a feather on someone's lips to determine if they were still alive; *c* proverbial 'You could have knocked me down with a feather', expressive of incredulity; *d* Ancient Egyptian belief that after death the *ka* (life-spirit) was weighed by the god Anubis against the feather of Ma'at, the feather of truth and harmony. If the *ka* balanced the feather, it was admitted into bliss; if not, it was eaten by Ammit, the Devourer of Souls – a crocodile-headed god with a lion's trunk and forelegs, and the hind legs of a hippopotamus – and ceased to exist; *e* WWI practice of women giving out white feathers to young men not in uniform in an attempt to shame them into joining up.

16 parting of hat from hair = hair standing on end, out of fright; another convention, a gentleman lifting his hat to ladies.

17 receiver = telephone receiver.

19–20 By these . . . half lie = 'would not care to' can mean 'wouldn't mind' and 'wouldn't like to'; hence *a* bogus deaths are not to be feared, and *b* the speaker rejects them because he wants a real sense of death, and of life.

See, on gravel paths under the harpstrung trees (p. 20)

N3 'Seventeen', dated 31 March 1933. An edited version (with 28 lines deleted) was published in the *Herald of Wales*, 8 June 1935, with the title 'Poet: 1935'; the version given here is based on the *NP* version and also incorporates smaller deletions made by Thomas to the *N3* text.

The BBC broadcast 'Reminiscences of Childhood' (1943) quotes the notebook version of the last lines of this poem, substituting 'I' for 'he'. It appears in the context of an account of Cwmdonkin Park, where, Thomas notes, 'I endured, with pleasure . . . the first slow boiling in the belly of a bad poem, the strutting raven-locked self-dramatization of . . . *incurable* adolescence', and fibs in describing this poem as 'never to be published'. However, the ironising of the younger self is already present in the poem.

1 harpstrung trees = cf. Psalm 137, 1–2: 'By the rivers of Babylon, there we sat down, yea, we wept, when we remembered Zion: We hanged our harps upon the willows in the midst thereof.'

The ploughman's gone (p. 22)

N3 'Twenty', dated 28 March 1933.

An example of Thomas's concern at technological progress, with a fatalistic twist. Humanity today is ruled by its creation, the 'engine', which speaks to it as it once spoke to horses, telling them of death as part of the cycle of nature. By trying to be 'Masters over unmastered nature', humans have deadened themselves in a creaturely sense, and are now merely an extension of the machine.

1   ploughman's ... hansom = hansom carriages were two-wheeled, horse-drawn precursors to today's taxis; the line establishes that both country and town have been subjected to the 'engine', ruling out Romantic idealisation of the former.

And death shall have no dominion (p. 23)

N3 'Twenty Three', dated 'April 1933', located between poems of 2 and 16 April. Published in *New English Weekly*, 18 May 1933, Thomas's first appearance in a national journal. Revised, apparently at Vernon Watkins' instigation, for *25P*, the revision is copied opposite 'Twenty Three' in *N3* and dated 'Feb 1936'; collected *25P*.

In this breakthrough poem, Thomas achieved for the first time a fusion of a pantheistic, apocalyptic vision and regular stanza form, rhyme, refrain and metre. It is flanked in *N3* by poems that refer to WWI, and the image of the naked dead body exposed on open ground or a battlefield became a staple. In the *N3* version of the poem, the doctrinal message of bodily resurrection overrides the less comforting pantheistic one that after death we simply rejoin the natural cycle. The 1936 revision reverses this relationship by removing 'soul' in Stanza 1 and dropping the fourth stanza of *N3* and *New English Weekly* versions, in which the speaker declares he has 'no doubt' about the biblical promise of the refrain. The poem now contained the rhetoric of faith, but the substance of non-belief, and seems to simultaneously endorse two mutually incompatible messages. This opened the way for a poetry of paradoxical states, and is the origin of what James Keery (2002) calls Thomas's 'mode of visionary modernism . . . in particular on the theme of (im)mortality'.

1   And death shall have no dominion = from St Paul's Epistle to the Romans 6:8–9: 'Now if we be dead with Christ, we believe that we shall also live with him: Knowing that Christ being raised from the dead dieth no more; death hath no more dominion over him.'

2–3   one / With the man in the wind and the west moon = merging into the universe is enacted by the transposition of epithets (from 'the man in the moon' and 'west wind').

4   When their bones are picked clean and the clean bones gone = originally 'With the harmonious thunder of the sun', followed by the current l.4 as l.5.

7–11   Though they sink through the sea . . . Under the windings of the sea = alludes to Revelation 20:13: 'And the sea gave up the dead which were in it', a favourite text (cf. 'A process in the weather of the heart').

12   windily = slang for cowardly; perhaps from play on 'windings' in l.11.

14   Strapped to a wheel = in WWi, 'Field Punishment No. 1' for a soldier guilty of indiscipline specified the fastening of the offender to a fixed object for a specified time. The object was usually the wheel of a wagon or gun-carriage. A spiked wheel was also the instrument on which St Catherine was tortured.

22–23   blew . . . blows = as with 'windings' / 'windily', this wordplay was added in the February 1936 revision; blows of the rain = a Welsh phrase for 'raining' is *bwrw glaw* ('blows of the rain').

24   dead as nails = from proverbial 'dead as a doornail'.

24   Heads of the characters hammer through daisies = the dead have heads, like nails, and may, therefore, be 'hammered' back into the world above, as 'daisies', by the life force; cf. proverbial euphemism for being dead, 'pushing up the daisies'. Cf. Wilfred Owen, 'À Terre': 'The dullest Tommy hugs that fancy now. / "Pushing up the daisies" is their creed, you know.' 'Characters' has the Greek sense of 'forms', as well as personalities.

25   Break in the sun till the sun breaks down = as James A. Davies (1998) notes: 'The dead possess a continuing and strangely violent power . . . in direct contrast to the helplessness of the living and the dying.'

Within his head revolved a little world (p. 24)

N3 'Twenty Four', dated 16–20 April 1933. Published in *New English Weekly*, 25 January 1934, as 'Out of the Pit'.

8–12   mad . . . The moon leered down the valley like a fool = a large and highly visible asylum, Cefn Coed, was built on a hill overlooking Swansea in 1931; Thomas refers to it in several poems and letters of the time.

22   scolecophidian = belonging to the genus of worms.

26 Sanger's = a travelling circus.

29   Pole-sitting girls descended for a meal = flagpole-sitting marathons were a craze in the 1920s and early 1930s.

51   whizzbangs = WWI slang for a high-explosive shell.

57   verboten = forbidden (German).

98 Now he is one with many, one with all = the interconnectedness of the self with the universe, and hence the ability to imagine it, is the basic premise of Thomas's process poetic; however, the extreme form of dissolution of the self into the object world may lead to madness, as suggested here.

We lying by seasand (p. 27)

N3 'Twenty Nine', dated 16 May 1933; revised and published in *Poetry* (Chicago), January 1937; collected *TML*.

The poem has been linked to the landscape of Rhossili and the Worm's Head, at the end of the Gower peninsula. However, it is primarily a symbolist narrative about the 'calling for colour', as reflected in its complex synaesthesia and verbal music. Yellow and red, associated with stasis and activity, fertility and sterility, are established as the antinomies which underlie the poem, but their meanings, like those of other symbols, are not fixed. Thus, the 'tide-master' promises 'cure', but is 'dry', and 'one-coloured calm' has an entropic ring; and while 'red' is associated with sterility, it is also the colour of 'my heart's blood': the watchers may fear the arrival of vigorous life. The general sense is that, while 'bound' to yellow, and wishing for the red rock's disappearance, 'we' cannot fend off its 'arrival'.

1 yellow = adverb and noun. Thomas wrote to Pamela Hansford Johnson of the 'yellow coldness' of Rhossili beach and a 'table of rock on the Worm's back ... covered with long yellow grass'. Cf. Ariel's song 'Come unto these yellow sands', in *The Tempest*.

4 cicada shade = cf. the cicadas in Part V of *The Waste Land*.

14–15 sand ... grains = sand grains in Thomas fuse his seaside locale and the visionary image of the opening line of Blake's 'Auguries of Innocence': 'To see the world in a grain of sand'.

18 sovereign strip = beach on which the watchers lie.

24 Breaks, O my heart's blood = echoes Tennyson's 'Break, break, break / On thy cold grey stones, O Sea!' (mocked in the short story 'The Fight').

No man believes (p. 28)

N3 'Thirty Three', dated 23 May; published in *Adelphi* (September 1933).

An early example of Thomas's belief that true faith was confirmed to the degree to which one feared for its loss, allowed it to be tested and threatened, or even denied it. This is closely linked to the use of double negatives to make tentative statements of poems such as 'And death shall have no dominion' and 'In country sleep'.

Why east wind chills (p. 29)

N3 'Thirty Seven', dated 1 July 1933; revised and published in the *New English Weekly* on 16 July 1936; collected *25P*.

In a similar vein to 'No man believes', the subject is the ultimate unknowability of the universe; the poem draws on Donne and reflects a turn towards Metaphysical models. The repeated 'Why' reflects a probing of the limits of ratiocinative thought. The general sense is that new discoveries about the cosmos and the self mean that the universe has become irreducibly mysterious; some things will simply never be known until we dissolve into the flux of process after death.

1 Why east wind chills = cf. Donne's 'Of the Progress of the Soul': 'Why grass is green, or why our blood is red, / Are mysteries which none have reached unto'. Such questions were a commonplace of seventeenth-century enquiry into the nature of the universe. Thomas alters the question from one answered by science to one concerning the relativity of subjective perception.

2 windwell = like Aeolus's cave of winds in classical mythology.

11 clasp a comet in their fists? = Walford Davies (2000) notes: 'An image for a metaphysical answer coming down into man's hands, echoing John Donne's poem "Go, catch a falling star", a similar attack on a futile need to know.'

20 till the stars go out = cf. Donne's 'A Funeral Elegy': 'they doubt, / Argue, and agree not, till those stars go out'.

21–23 I hear content . . . And 'Know no answer' = 'handbell' and 'corridors' suggest Thomas is thinking of a school.

26 raised fists = reaching futilely for the comets; but also recalling the left-wing clenched-fist salute.

Greek Play in a Garden (p. 30)

N3 'Forty', dated 7 July 1933, with the subtitle 'After the performance of Sophocles' Electra in a garden. Written for a local paper'. Published in *The Herald of Wales*, 15 July 1933, as 'Greek Play in a Garden'; collected *TP71*.

The play was produced by Thomas Taig, an acquaintance of Thomas's who worked at the University of Wales, Swansea, with music by Daniel Jones, and was performed on 5/6 July 1933 in a garden in the suburb of Sketty, near the Uplands, where Thomas lived. He refers to it in his radio feature 'Return Journey' and the story 'The Mouse and the Woman' (1936).

9 lamp = illuminate.

Praise to the architects (p. 31)

N3 'Forty One', dated 7 July 1933; collected *TP71*.

The last example in the notebooks of plain-style poetry of social commentary, and a dismissal of it as resembling advertising; the title is ironic.

11   pome = Daniel Jones's note in *TP71* reads: 'It was a jocular version of the word "poem" often used by Dylan Thomas and his friends, sometimes satirically, as here, but more often with a kind of affectionate informality. "Poems" were, of course, written by "potes" and bound into wafer-thin volumes of "potry".'

12   Keatings = a brand of all-purpose insecticide powder.

13   Auden = quoting Auden's 'Sir, no man's enemy' in a letter of January 1934 to Trevor Hughes, Thomas asked: 'Does one need "New styles of architecture, a change of heart"? Does one not need a new consciousness of the old universal architecture and a tearing away from the old heart of the things that have clogged it up?'

Here in this spring (p. 32)

N3 'Forty Two', dated 9 July 1933. A slightly revised version on the facing page in *N3* is dated January 1936; collected in *25P*.

In philosophical terms, this anticipates the process poetry of later 1933. Symbols are given for the seasons, but in Stanza 3 the speaker berates himself for not grasping the process of growth and destruction – above all the passing of time – more directly from his observation of the natural world (trees, worms, cuckoo, slug). The final question, concerning the significance of the signs of worldly decay and the responsibility such knowledge brings, is rhetorical; nature's message, if we attend to it, is that we die too.

2   ornamental winter = winter weather which ornaments a scene with snow (like a snow-globe ornament, shaken to produce a snowstorm).

3   Down pelts the naked weather = snow falls swiftly (pelts down); *down* (fur) *pelts* (covers like an animal skin) the earth; downy snow clothes the (paradoxically) naked weather.

7   In autumn = the last of the seasons to have a symbol 'selected' for it, possibly because, as the season of Thomas's birthday, it is viewed as crowning the others. The implication is that while autumn suggests 'three seasons' (spring, summer, autumn), autumnal decay reminds us that it takes winter to complete the seasonal cycle.

9, 10, 14, 16   tell = used variously in the senses of 'think', 'read from' and 'speak to, address'.

11 funeral of the sun = winter; more apocalyptically, the end of the solar system.

16 timeless insect = because unheeding of time; without time (insects having a proverbially brief lifespan); beyond or before time (because they pre-date humanity); associated with immortality (like the Egyptian scarab).

'Find meat on bones' (p. 32)

N3 'Forty Six', dated 15 July 1933; revised interlinearly in late January 1936; published in *Purpose* (April–June 1936); collected *25P*.

Another breakthrough poem, exemplifying Blake's maxim that 'without contraries is no progression', and with a dialogic structure that anticipates 'I see the boys of summer'. Stanzas 1 and 2 are spoken by a father who advocates a rapaciously *carpe diem* stance – sexual opportunism and opposition to the laws of nature. Stanza 3 is in the voice of his son, who has taken his advice and regrets it. In Stanza 4 we learn that his contrition is based on the opposition of nature itself to his 'father's dream', and on a rejection of that dream's antagonistic view of the relationship between the universe and humanity. The poem inclines towards the son's position, but its dramatisation of conflicting aspects of Thomas himself – rage against time and death, and recognition of ubiquity of process – is what gives it its force.

1–16 'Find meat on bones . . . maggot no man can slay' = the father's diatribe has distinct overtones of Lear's lascivious imaginings in his mad scenes.

8 ram rose = a symbol of sexual conquest and deflowering.

25 maggot = fly larva; thought, curious notion, obsession (cf. 'I see the boys of summer').

26–29 And the man . . . foul fiend to heel = 'man' is individual mortal man on its first appearance, but a general principle of humanity, or spirit, on the second. The over-reaching of the father is associated with hyper-rationality, 'reason's wrong'. His belief that he can control the forces of evil released by unleashing the animal in man ('red swine') is contradicted by the symbols ('maggot' and 'man') of process, the real order of the universe.

38–40 The son quotes his father.

40 Doom on the sun! = an ultimate blasphemy against the natural world; also, the working title of a novel, based on the early Jarvis Valley stories, which Thomas was planning at this time.

Ears in the turrets hear (p. 34)

N3 'Forty Seven', dated 17 July 1933; published without current Stanza 2 in *John O'London's Weekly* (5 May 1934), with the title 'Dare I?'; collected in *25P*.

Writing to Pamela Hansford Johnson on 9 May 1934, Thomas dismissed this poem as 'a terribly weak, watery little thing'. However, it very effectively dramatises his ambivalence about the isolation necessary for writing. On the one hand it resists Donne's claim that 'no man is an Island entire of it self', reflecting a comment of November 1933: 'Through my small, bonebound island I have learnt all I know, experienced all, and sensed all. All I write is inseparable from this island. As much as possible, therefore, I employ the scenery of the island to describe the scenery of my thoughts, the earthquakes of the body to describe the earthquakes of the heart.' But Thomas also worried about solipsism, and what he described to Trevor Hughes as 'my islandic egoism', and this tension finds subtle expression in the oscillation between nine- and seven-line stanzas, irregular end-rhyme and delicate verbal music.

1, 8, 10   turrets . . . house . . . island = common images for the isolated self in Thomas: cf. 'Especially when the October wind'.

9   poison or grapes = sickbed images; is the patient convalescing or about to be put out of his misery? Thomas told Johnson on 21 December 1933 that 'a born writer is born scrofulous; his career is an accident dictated by physical or circumstantial disabilities'.

That sanity be kept (p. 35)

No autograph ms exists for this poem, but Ralph Maud (1989) plausibly conjectures that it is the missing 'Forty Nine', torn out of *N3*, one of the 'collateral poems' in *NP*; this would date it to late July or early August 1933; published in the *Sunday Referee*, 3 September 1933.

As does 'Within his head', this piece contrasts a smoothly functioning external world with an inner reality concerned with madness, sexual frustration, lack of faith and fear of death. Like that poem, this one also assembles the raw materials of the process poetic, but presents them inertly. Thomas seems to have felt this himself; to Pamela Hansford Johnson, who wrote to congratulate him in mid-September 1933, he noted: 'The more I think of my Referee poem the less I like it. The idea of myself, sitting in the open window, in my shirt, and imagining myself as some Jehovah of the West, is really odd. If I were some Apollo it would be different.'

1   That sanity be kept I sit at open windows = ironic; in fact, sanity is the lie of social convention, and the speaker's relation to it is amusedly disbelieving, one in which he pretends to be responsible for 'letting' things happen around him.

12   The English mowers mow and mow = the Audenesque poets, making hay while the sun shines, while the isolated Thomas can only look on and imitate them.

21 in my shirt = cf. T.S. Eliot's 'The Love Song of J. Alfred Prufrock': 'lonely men in shirt-sleeves, leaning out of windows'.

Shall gods be said (p. 36)

N3 'Fifty Two', dated 'August'; published, with revisions, in 25P.

What could have developed into a critique of natural religion – the bathetic 'garden [watering] can' and 'old gods' dugs' – endorses a supernatural explanation of natural phenomena (thunder, rainbows, sun, stars) along with others ('all tongues'). The answer to the rhetorical questions is 'yes', as the bald declaration of l.11 makes clear.

The hand that signed the paper (p. 36)

N4 'One', dated 17 August 1933; published after the deletion of a fifth stanza in New Verse (December 1935); collected 25P.

The dedication in N4 – to 'To A.E.T.', Bert Trick, Thomas's Labour Party friend and a socialist activist – gives the context for his most overtly political poem. The 'hand', as a metonym for power, is developed through hand/arm imagery, but this may also be a more literal play on 'arms'; letters of this period to Johnson argue the case for a socialist transformation of society and blame arms manufacturers, among others, for having dragged WWI out so bloodily.

1 The hand that signed the paper = cf. 'The hand that sign'd the mortgage paid the shot', in 'Elegy on Mr Demar, the Famous Rich Man', by Jonathan Swift.

2 taxed the breath = by causing a war which 'Doubled the globe of dead'. 'Taxed' is derived from a pun on 'sovereigns' as coins as well as rulers/fingers.

4 five kings = the 'five sovereign fingers' of l.2.

5–6 sloping shoulder . . . cramped with chalk = total power is exercised despite bodily decrepitude.

7–8 put an end to murder / That put an end to talk = seems benign, but in context it is simply another example of the cold and bloodless exercise of supreme power.

Let for one moment a faith statement (p. 37)

N4 'Two', dated and place of composition noted as 'August 20, 33. Rayner's Lane'; it was dedicated to Trevor Hughes after visiting him in Harrow (see 'Foster the light' and 'Now', below).

5 nightseed = dreams; a nocturnal seminal emission.

6–10 Let . . . gods be changed as often as the shift . . . till none are left = this religious relativism, and the idea of negative theology, is central to understanding Thomas's use of double negative and his representation of Christian faith.

13   maieutic = obstetric; sleep is regarded as the midwife of faith.

That the sum sanity (p. 37)

N4 'Four', dated 24 August 1933; revised, probably March/April 1934, and referred to in a letter to Pamela Hansford Johnson of 2 May. Published in the *Swansea and West Wales Guardian* on 8 June 1934 as 'Twelve', from its number in a typed-up sequence of poems. This second version (not given here) was considered, but not chosen, for *18P*.

In this sonnet, Thomas imagines himself as a preacher, ironically adopting the stance of the churches (denouncing sexual desires, preaching pie-in-the-sky to the oppressed) in order to expose their hypocrisy and bring about a revolt against their teachings. The first version seems to me the most successful, and is the one given here.

1   That the sum sanity = sanity, associated with social convention, repression and hypocrisy, is imagined as a sum which the speaker wishes to make add *down* rather than up.

2   matrons ring the harebells on their lips = wordplay involving the splitting of hare-lip, a play on hair/hare and on flower 'bells' being rung. 'On their lips' can also mean 'about to be spoken'. The main sense seems to be that the 'matrons' should overcome disfiguring inhibition and 'ring' out their desires.

3–4   Girls woo . . . laps = like the matrons, the girls should 'woo' despite Sabbath prohibitions; starry laps = sexual activity and conception is linked to the cosmic order and vice versa.

10   reel upon its block of reason = doubt its enforcement of 'sanity', the status quo and a hypocritical social order.

11–14   I would resound the heavens . . . one fanatic image = He would pay such fulsome and unfelt tribute to religion that he would expose its falsity and make men cry out with revelation (ironically, becoming a 'fanatic' himself to achieve this).

Before I knocked (p. 38)

N4 'Seven', dated 6 September 1933. Thomas described it as 'the Jesus poem', enclosing it in his first extant letter to Pamela Hansford Johnson, on 15 September 1933. Revising it for *18P*, he cut a fifth stanza and one of two concluding quatrains.

The poem's speaker, as Thomas's description suggests, is a fusion of himself, everyman and Christ, in both his mortal and divine natures. The speaker recalls his existence from before the time he was conceived, and tells of the pangs of conception, gestation and birth. The tension between the different forms of Christ is brought to a head in the final lines, in which the mortal Christ asks Christians to 'remember' him and 'pity' his divine self, as if lamenting the fact that the latter was cheated of human life by his sacred mission. More than simply reimagining individual and divine incarnations, it expresses the existential unease we all suffer in a deterministic universe in which not only human existence but that of God is a kind of cosmic black joke.

1 knocked = was conceived (with sexual connotation 'knocked up'); the foetus knocking on the womb-wall. Echoes the 'knocking time' of God's summons in Henry Vaughan's 'The Night', quoted in Thomas's 1946 radio broadcast 'Welsh Poets'.

2–3 With liquid hands . . . shapeless as the water = as sperm, undifferentiated energy; 'tapped' is 'knocked upon' and 'insert a tap [umbilical cord] into'.

4 Jordan = the biblical River Jordan; slang for a chamber pot.

5–6 brother to Mnetha's daughter . . . sister to the fathering worm = cf. Job, 17:14: 'I have said to corruption, Thou *art* my father: to the worm, *Thou art* my mother, and my sister.' Mnetha is from Blake's *Tiriel*; she personifies intelligence and is mother to Har, who personifies poetry, and his sister Heva, who personifies painting and who shares kinship with all things.

9 Felt thud beneath my flesh's armour = the rhythm of orgasm, of the creating father's penis at the doors of the womb; the speaker is still in 'molten form'.

11 leaden stars = suggests the divinity of the father but also its antithesis; rainy hammer = another antithesis, of liquid and solid, symbolising the mysterious union of body and soul within the womb; a phallic image alluding to the form Jupiter took as a rainstorm, Jupiter Pluvius.

12 dome = the head, directing sexual activity; 'dome' of heaven, home of God the Father and Christ; a mortal father's balding pate.

17 Eastern weather = hints at the divine aspect of the narrator.

18 Ungotten = unbegotten. Cf. Shakespeare, *Henry V*, I, ii, 228, has 'some as yet ungotten and unborn'; but the main allusion is to John 3:16: 'For God so loved the world, that he gave his only begotten Son'; the poem challenges this claim for an all-loving God the Father.

20 lily bones = conflates Christ's growing bones with the lilies traditionally borne by the archangel Gabriel at the annunciation.

22–24 flesh was snipped to cross the lines . . . brambles in the wringing brains = suggestive of the crucifixion and WWI trench warfare.

39 death's feather = see note to 'I have longed to move away'.

42 The lower-case 'christ' is Christ as everyman.

46 doublecrossed my mother's womb = literally, the threshold of Mary's womb was 'crossed' twice by God entering it (as the Holy Ghost) and exiting it (as Jesus); figuratively it was 'cheated' – *a* the crucifixion ('cross') cheated Mary of her mortal son; *b* she suffered twice, in giving birth and in witnessing the crucifixion; *c* she was cheated of pleasure in the conception of Jesus because it was sexless. *N4* 'Seven' has '*his* mother's womb', and the change to 'my' may suggest *a* that *every* birth is an Incarnation, and *b* that the precedent of Christ's (spiritual) birth cheats every later, merely secular (physical) birth. The same idea occurs in *N4* 'Twelve': 'A mother in labour pays twice her pain, / Once for the Virgin's child, once for her own.'

We see rise the secret wind (p. 40)

N4 'Eight', dated 8 September 1933.
    A fascinatingly futuristic poem; cf. Thomas's letter of Armistice Day 1933 to Pamela Hansford Johnson. This declares that contemporary poets 'are wrong because their vision is not a vision but a squint; they look at our world, and yet their eyes are staring back along the roads of past centuries, never into the huge, electric promise of the future.'

Not forever shall the lord of the red hail (p. 40)

N4 'Ten', date and place of composition noted as 'September 15. '33 Llangain Carms'. Dedicated to 'B.C.', who has not been identified. Thomas intended to revise it for inclusion in *18P*, but did not do so.
    God in his apocalyptic aspect unleashes destruction on the world in Stanza 1; but in Stanza 2 this becomes a fusion of microcosm and macrocosm ('hemispheres' as globe and brain). Ultimately, 'both mind and matter' leave a 'singing shell', while in Stanza 3 a void ('shell' in a negative sense) preserves the abstract 'shape of thought', world and heart. From its 'darkness' the void will 'spin the golden soul' analogous to the 'golden word'. The poem combines a destruction-creation trope with the common modernist goal of radical purification.

Before we mothernaked fall (p. 41)

N4 'Eleven', dated 16 September 1933. Probably revised early 1936 and published in *New English Weekly*, 30 July 1936.
    A good example of Thomas's taste for playing opposites off against each

other as part of a debate between determinism and free will, or aspiration. The poem describes a time before loss of innocence, or birth, before 'joys are pains'. Its location is womb-like, a place where potential was positive and 'all the hidden stones are gold'. This is grounds for encouraging the addressee to overcome determinism in the present. The poem both acknowledges determinism and resists it, although it could be understood to state that our nature is determined before birth. Its account of conception, from a male point of view, as a 'raid', links it to 'The seed-at-zero'.

3 raid and the response = a WWI image.

6 quarry or the well = like 'gusher or the field' these properties are vaguely sexual (phallic-ejaculatory, womb-like).

13 build = originally 'plumb'; 'build' is less specific to 'liquid world', but Thomas presumably needed a word that could cover both it and the addressee's 'solid land'. It also gives an internal rhyme with 'spilled'.

15 doom is turned = [the corner to] doom is turned; however, 'turned' can mean evaded or overthrew, in an ambiguity which encapsulates that of the poem generally.

My hero bares his nerves (p. 42)

N4 'Thirteen', date and place of composition noted as 'September 17 33 Llangain'; published in *18P.*

When Thomas revised *N4* 'Five', 'Grief thief of time', in summer 1935, he took lines cut from 'Thirteen' as the basis of the second stanza of the new poem (see below).

'My hero' appears to find the poet-'hero' coordinating wrist, shoulder and head in the act of writing. However, a series of double entendres ('head', 'ruler', 'secret heat', etc.) show that he is also the penis, the 'unruly scrawl' that of ejaculated semen, and the 'lovelorn paper' a tissue placed to catch it, as well as the site of writing. The parallel narratives of writing and masturbation collide in the final line, where the romantic rhetoric of Stanza 3 is deflated in the bathos of 'chain' and 'cistern'. The speaker's anxieties concerning poetic and sexual empowerment are analogous; indeed, the 'pen/is' pun may be said to underlie the poem.

Several other poems of the period explore auto-eroticism, but this is the most subtle consideration of the entrapment of both sex and writing in a circle of incomplete, auto-erotic identity formation; like 'Grief thief of time', it ironises Thomas's attempts at fathering his own authority. There is honesty not only in its frankness, but also in its understanding that both writing and auto-eroticism promise a fulfilment which is always deferred by the 'lovelorn page'.

1, 6, 16   nerves = associated with masturbation, via Ezra Pound's 'Fratres Minores', quoted in a letter to Trevor Hughes of January 1934: 'Still our minds are hovering too much about our testicles, complaining ". . . In delicate and exhausted metres / That the twitching of three abdominal nerves / Is incapable of producing a lasting Nirvana."' Cf. 'O Chatterton'.

3   Unpacks the head = composes poetry; pulls the foreskin back from the glans.

4   mortal ruler = will (to write); penis.

5   turn and twist = the subject of the verbs is 'nerves'.

6, 16   wired . . . wire = play on the idiom 'to pull your wire' (masturbate).

7   lovelorn paper = on which a love poem is being written; to catch semen.

8   unruly scrawl = untidy handwriting; ejaculated semen.

9–10   love-hunger . . . empty ill = desire (literary and sexual) is discharged, but what it expresses is literary derivativeness and auto-erotic isolation.

12–13   naked Venus . . . her bloodred plait = Botticelli's painting 'The Birth of Venus', depicting a naked red-haired Venus, was a Thomas favourite; the shape of Venus's hair and plaits resembles the heart and its blood vessels.

16   box of nerves = brain; penis.

18–19   two sad knaves . . . hunger's emperor = the penis hanging between the two testicles is likened to Christ on the Cross, flanked by the two thieves.

20   He pulls the chain, the cistern moves = he flushes the lavatory.

Love me, not as the dreaming nurses (p. 42)

N4 'Sixteen', dated 18 September 1933; published in the *Sunday Referee*, 7 January 1934.
      Referred to by Pamela Hansford Johnson as 'that love poem' in a letter of 25 December 1933, it may have been written for her.

The force that through the green fuse (p. 43)

N4 'Twenty Three', and dedicated there 'To E.P.' (perhaps Evelyn 'Titch' Phillips, an Uplands friend and member of Thomas's social circle), dated 12 October 1933. The final form of the poem had not been settled when Thomas began copying it into *N4*; after the first three lines there is a different, crossed-out attempt at Stanza 1. Published in the *Sunday Referee* on 29 October 1933 and winner of its best annual poem prize; collected in *18P*.
      'The force' is one of Thomas's most famous poems, discussed by almost all critics. William Empson, one of the earliest and best, described it as 'comparing

the blood-stream . . . to the sea-cloud-river cycle by which water moves round this planet . . . [Thomas] is united with the planet, also personally guilty of murder whenever a murderer is hanged, and so forth. The mining term "vein" for a line of ore was naturally a crucial pun for the early Dylan, because of his central desire to identify events inside his own skin with the two main things outside it, the entire physical world and also his relations with other men.'

Using the conceit of the microcosm, and taking the (dis)unity of nature and human beings as his theme, Thomas develops a series of antithetical contrasts, varying the position of human and natural elements to suggest their increasing inter-involvement, until in Stanza 4 the forward momentum is slowed by an end-stopped opening line. The 'fallen blood' of birth and death calms the 'sores' of 'love', and the focus on the 'force' of process is broken by a larger considera- tion of time. The final couplet, with its sardonic, brilliant multiple puns, fashions a powerful and appropriate close.

Discussion has concentrated on Stanza 4 and the meaning of the refrain 'And I am dumb'. 'Dumb' seems to denote the speaker's paradoxical inability to com- municate his insight that process makes him one with nature itself; the human dilemma is to exist within nature but to be separated from it by self-conscious- ness and foreknowledge of death. Language, the key to human mastery over nature, cannot communicate with it, and 'dumb' is thus a self-critique, with its US slang sense of 'foolish'. But, less passively, 'dumb' also signifies a refusal of repressive totalities; it does not just confess inability, but actively refuses to grasp conceptually (and hence reduce) the singularity of the world, expressing a pleasure in inarticulacy, and an unwillingness to speak in conventionally logical terms. By undercutting pantheism in this way, Thomas avoids the usual traps of nature poetry, in which the natural image often endorses a falsely comforting solution to the contradictions of existence.

1   The force = the creative-destructive energy that powers the universe; fuse = archaic for a plant stem; detonation device; electrical circuit-breaker; flower = a two-syllabled word, after a string of monosyllabic ones, which mimics the energy of the plant forcing a passage through the stem to explode from its tip.

2   green age = youth; simultaneity of age and youth; naive youth; blasts = blows up; blights.

4   dumb = physically unable to tell of unity with nature; foolish to attempt to; crooked rose = like Blake's 'The Sick Rose', this one is diseased.

5   fever = continues imagery of disease established in 'blast' as 'blight'.

6–10   water through the rocks . . . streams . . . mountain spring = microcosmic identification of blood circulation with the water cycle of the planet; mouthing streams = streams at the estuary, or mouth, sucking the whole length of the stream into the sea. This initiates a series of forms of 'mouth', as participle, infinitive and noun, culminating in 'lips of time' and 'leech'; play on 'mountain'.

7 Drives . . . dries = loss of 'v' enacts the 'drying'.

8 wax = primarily a noun, synonymous in Thomas with dead flesh, yet also with its sense of 'to grow larger', describing the simultaneity of life and death.

9 veins = microcosmically, both veins of ore and blood vessels. Cf. Donne, Elegy 11, 'The Bracelet': 'As streams, like veins, run through th'earth's every part', and note to 'I fellowed sleep who kissed me in the brain'.

11 hand = the agent of 'the force', now tending towards personification.

12 quicksand = engulfing sands; sand running through an hourglass, an emblem of mortality; living sand, through pun on 'quick'; 'quick' also completes 'lime' in l.15 as 'quicklime'; ropes the blowing wind = ropes attached to a sail; the governing image is of the voyage of life.

13 shroud sail = the sail for the voyage of one's life is the shroud we are wrapped in at death (technically, 'shrouds' are ropes and belong to the rigging).

14 hanging man = cf. the 'Hanged Man' card missing from Madame Sosostris's Tarot pack in T. S. Eliot's *The Waste Land* (associated with the Hanged God whose sacrifice guarantees the land's fertility).

15 hangman's lime = quicklime, used to dissolve the bodies of executed criminals; cf. 'See, says the lime'.

16 The lips of time leech to the fountain head = *a* an infant mouth at the breast; *b* sipping water from a drinking-fountain; *c* a personified time drawing new life from the womb; *d* the natural cycle renewing itself; *e* time feeding the embryo through the umbilicus or sucking it from the aquatic womb.

17–18 Love drips . . . calm her sores = love leaks and withers (flesh 'gathers' like cloth), but creates children ('fallen blood') which 'calm' the anguish of mortality.

19–20 I am dumb . . . round the stars = *N4* has: 'And I am dumb to tell the timeless sun / How time is all'. The *Sunday Referee* has 'tell the timeless clouds / That time is all'. All versions emphasise that even vast natural cycles succumb to time, but in the last the daunting expanses of cosmological time lead to man's invention of 'heaven' and eternity; ticked = clock-like (the cosmos as a clock face); like a bloodsucking tick (cf. echoing 'leech'), undercutting the romantic associations of 'heaven' and 'stars'.

21–22 And I am dumb to tell . . . goes the same crooked worm = alludes to *Romeo and Juliet*'s 'lover's tomb', punningly fusing the poem's themes: 'sheet' is lovers' bedsheet, shroud and sheet of paper on which the poem is written; 'worm' is penis, grave-worm and the crooked writing finger.

From love's first fever (p. 44)

N4 'Twenty Four', dated 14 October 1933, ending at the present l.31 with the reminder '(Incomplete)'; completed as *N4* 'Twenty Six', dated 17 October 1933. Published in *The Criterion* (October 1934); collected, with minor revisions, in *18P*.

The progress of the child is traced from the parental 'fever' of conception, to birth, weaning, walking and speech acquisition. Pre-linguistic unity with the maternal body is followed by movement into the world beyond it, and into language, but there is no traumatic break or 'fall' involved. The child develops by self-division: 'one' is the primal unity of the neonate, 'two' shows self-consciousness dawning, 'four' is adolescence, and adulthood is 'many sounding minded'. In keeping with Thomas's process poetic, the different states all hint at the others. Throughout, language's miraculous potential is stressed, and division and multiplication evoke not loss, but delight in its proliferation of an ever more complex and differentiated world.

1 plague = conception, as commonly in early Thomas. Cf. 'A grief ago'.

3 caul = a rarely occurring cartilaginous plate protecting the head of the embryo.

4–5 green apron age . . . hanging famine = i.e. the period after suckling, contrasting with the 'time for breast'.

6 one windy nothing = pre-linguistic ('windy' is 'wordy').

11 breaking of the hair = originally 'hatching', defended by Thomas to Pamela Hansford Johnson: 'Leave me my "hatching of the hair". It's verminous, I know, but isn't it lovely? And what is more refreshing than the smell of vermin? Hardy loved to sit beside a rotten sheep and see the flies make a banquet of it. A dark thought, but good and lively. One of the hardest and most beneficial kicks of life comes from the decaying foot of death.'

15–16 The sun was red . . . as two mountains meeting = the child's development and differentiation and awareness of the body and the world lead to 'wonder'.

20–25 the four winds . . . Green was the singing house = language does not imprison the self, but awakens it, stimulating pleasure by building a relationship between it and its surroundings, as reflected in the synaesthesia of ll.21–22.

23 the multiplying sand = an image of promiscuity (cf. 'Into her lying down head').

32–35 And from the first . . . the patch of words = the syntax of l.33 makes learning language, and turning thoughts into language, simultaneous events, and our power to reconfigure 'stony' inherited language is optimistically emphasised; first declension of the flesh = bodily development in linguistic terms, suggesting the way body and language are one and the same in Thomas; stony idiom of the brain = ambiguous as to whether the 'idiom' is language or thought.

38 The root of tongues ends in a spentout cancer = alludes to D. J. Thomas's treatment for cancer; he was readmitted to hospital on 17 October 1933, the day the final section of this poem was copied into *N4*.

41 The code of night = sexual fantasy; dream; religion; awareness of mortality.

43–51 One womb . . . double . . . score . . . A million minds . . . the hundred seasons . . . One sun = recapitulates the earlier numerical progression to emphasise the new unity achieved in maturity.

47–48 such a bud / As forks my eye = evolutionary development and intellectual and cultural inheritance have nurtured the speaker's multiple vision ('forks' my 'I'); cf. 'the bud that forks her eye' in 'If I were tickled', where 'bud' is sexual.

49–50 the tears of spring / Dissolved in summer = the bitterness of adolescent tribulations disappeared with the multiple possibilities of adult vision.

Light breaks where no sun shines (p. 46)

N4 'Thirty', dated 20 November 1933; published in *The Listener*, 14 March 1934; collected in *18P*.

'Light breaks' is the most perfect lyric in Thomas's early biomorphic style, and its appearance marked a further step in his recognition. Although less explosive than 'The force that through the green fuse', the extent to which it identifies body and universe, microcosmically conflating them and making it almost impossible to distinguish the different aspects of process, mean that this poem surpasses even 'The force' in elementalising the body and personalising the cosmos. A letter of early January 1934 to Trevor Hughes, which probably accompanied it, justifies the physiological emphases: 'They are, I admit, unpretty things, with their imagery almost totally anatomical. But I defend the diction, the perhaps wearisome succession of blood and bones, the never ending similes of the streams of veins and the lights in the eyes, by saying that, for the time at least, I realise that it is impossible for me to raise myself to the altitude of the stars, and that I am forced, therefore, to bring down the stars to my own level and to incorporate them into my own physical universe.'

Accordingly, the poem presents the simultaneity of the forces of growth and decay in a richly inter-involved fashion. Life and death occur not only alternately and inextricably, but in terms of each other. Thus, Stanzas 1, 2 and 5 can each be read as divided into a first part concerned with the living body and a second concerned with death, with Stanza 3 wholly concerned with life, Stanza 4 wholly with death. But these schemas are fluid; l.6 of 1 could refer to embryos as readily as to decayed bodies, for example. Stanza 2 contrasts youth (virility) and age (impotence), thoughts sublimated with age to 'unwrinkle in the stars' as religion – but 'fig' is decidedly sexual. Stanza 3 seems more unambiguously to present consciousness dawning in the embryo/infant, but 'skull' is ominous; and if Stanza 4 seems to slip clearly from sleep to death, in Stanza 5 the ambiguity returns – a new consciousness seems to emerge after bodily dissolution, but 'halts' may seem more final than just the end of one kind of consciousness, or 'dawn'.

Form: five six-line stanzas with a syllable count of 6-10-4-10-4-10, broken in the poem's penultimate line.

1–3   Light breaks . . . Push in their tides = as the foetus forms in the womb's darkness, the light of consciousness dawns and the tide-like circulation of the blood begins; light breaks on the dead body.

1, 2, 9, 22   where no sun shines . . . Where no sea runs . . . Where no seed stirs . . . Where no cold is = suggests variations on Wilfred Owen's 'Foreheads of men have bled *where no wounds were*' ('Strange Meeting').

4–6   And, broken ghosts . . . where no flesh decks the bones = at conception, spermatozoa create the embryo; after death, grave-worms move through the earth into which the dead flesh has merged.

7–8   A candle in the thighs . . . burns the seeds of age = sexual desire, surreally figured as a candle-phallus, 'waxes' in youth, with sperm created and destroyed.

9–11   Where no seed stirs . . . Bright as a fig = after death, man's progeny multiplies like stars in the sky (a biblical image for multiplication), with emphasis on the sexual aspect ('fig').

12   Where no wax is, the candle shows its hairs = after death ('wax' is verb and noun, signifying dead flesh), the penis-candle is stripped (to the 'hair' of its wick).

13–15   Dawn breaks . . . Slides like a sea = consciousness dawns in the (foetal) body and the blood-tides move within it (but with the sense of 'cowardly' in 'windy', and suggestion of dissolution in 'slides').

16–18   Nor fenced, nor staked . . . the oil of tears = a metaphysical conceit in which tears and rain are likened to each other has a real basis in process; however, process differs in insisting on the impossibility of ultimately distinguishing between positive and negative terms. The idea is presented using images drawn from the oil industry. Thomas joked to Johnson that the BBC had 'banned my poetry' because *Listener* readers complained about these three lines: 'The little smut-hounds thought I was writing a copulatory anthem. In reality, of course, it was a metaphysical image of rain & grief. . . . Jesus, what are we up against, Pam?'

19–21 Night in the sockets rounds . . . Day lights the bone = 'rounds' is a verb; night and day expose the limits of sight (but 'globes' is planetary too), rendering the unseeing eyes in the darkness no more use than 'sockets', a reminder of the skull that holds them; while day's brightness is a reminder of the bones' whiteness beneath the flesh.

22–24 Where no cold is . . . hanging from the lids = after death, when cold is not felt, the 'skinning gales' of decomposition remove the 'winter's robes' of old flesh from the body, leaving a mere 'film' of matter. This is either blocking the vision of new life, but 'hanging' and hence about to fall, or will be the source of regeneration in spring, or both; skinning = removing skin *and* renewing it; film = invisible layer on the eyeball, sign of death, but also a film (or movie) of coming spring – hence of future growth from decay.

25–28 Light breaks . . . blood jumps in the sun = after-death consciousness dawns as a new kind of physical perception through, and as part of, the natural world; lots = plots (graves), spaces; fates; tips of thought . . . smell in the rain = abstract thought now seems putrid ('tips' suggests vegetable shoots *and* coal-spoil) under the reviving rain of spring; logics die = (hyper-)rationalism is superseded; The secret of the soil grows through the eye = a new knowledge appears as growth pushing through the eye, or, punning on 'I', out of the old ego.

30 waste allotments = graves; vegetable-growing plots; bleak fates ('allotted span'); dawn halts = the old consciousness ends with death, and a new consciousness awaits as one re-enters the organic round – dawn is arrested, briefly, before continuing in different form.

See, says the lime (p. 47)

N4 'Thirty Two', dated 13 December 1933.
   In early December 1933 Thomas sent this poem to Johnson, with an explanation of his procedures reminiscent of *Frankenstein*, reflecting his interest in horror films:

I suppose it's my usual stuff again, and even a little more death-struck. But don't be put off by my anatomical imagery, which I explained months ago. Because I so often write in terms of the body, of the death, disease, and breaking of the body, it doesn't necessarily mean that my Muse (*not* one of my favourite words) is a sadist. For the time at least, I believe in the writing of poetry from the flesh, and generally from the dead flesh. So many modern poets take the *living* flesh as their object, and, by their clever dissecting, turn it into a carcase. I prefer to take the *dead* flesh, and, by any positivity of faith and belief that is in me, to build up a *living* flesh from it.

On 25 December, he told her it was '*not* very good, and I'm glad you attacked it', but added 'the images are *not* mixed; they are severely physical all through; what gave you the impression of "mixedness" was the conscious rapidity with which I changed the angles of the images. Yes, the "iris" is a little bit too facile. But the poem . . . is . . . on one level and one note, with one idea and one image, changed and transfigured as that image may be.' He confessed, 'one day I hope to write something altogether out of the hangman's sphere, something larger, wider, more comprehensible, and less selfcentred'. A clue to the 'one idea' is given by a margin note reading 'See 28' – *N4* 'Twenty Eight', a poem which also has 'milk of death'. Thomas develops that image further here, by making the quicklime, source of the corpse-dissolving 'milk', the poem's narrator.

1 lime = quicklime, used to speed up the decomposition of corpses, especially of executed criminals; cf. 'The force that through the green fuse'; wicked milks = as quicklime is slaked by liquid, such as that within a body, it forms a corrosive white alkaline liquid.

6 starry = adverbial, qualifying 'fence' ('starrily').

32 Death's death's undoer = a basic principle behind all the early process poetry.

A letter to my Aunt, Discussing the Correct Approach to Modern Poetry (p. 48)

Contained in a letter to Pamela Hansford Johnson, dated c. 21 December 1933; first published in *TP71*.

 Thomas's letters often express solidarity with Johnson's strivings as a beginning writer by mocking the attitudes of London bohemians, particularly those gathered around the *Sunday Referee*. Daniel Jones claimed that these verses drew on a report of his own meeting in summer 1933 with Johnson, Runia Tharp and Victor Neuberg, the editor of the *Referee*'s 'Poet's Corner'. The mockery is light hearted, and satirises Thomas's own half-rhymes, preciosity and morbidity.

2 Chankley Bore = something remote and exotic; the intrepid subjects of Edward Lear's poem 'The Jumblies' visit 'the Hills of the Chankley Bore'.

4 Hottentot = Dutch colonists' name for the Khoikhoi people of Namibia, related to the Bushmen; racialist ethnography designated them the most 'backward' of human types. Cf. Edith Sitwell's 'Hornpipe', *Façade* (1922): 'hot as any hottentot and not the goods for me!'

8, 85 David G. = David Gascoyne, leading British surrealist poet.

10   T.S.E. = T. S. Eliot.

16   But one the Swiss wear when they yodel = a margin note reads: 'what a line!'

34   (Here ... 'Chelsea Reach') = a margin note reads: 'sorry!' Johnson's first poem in the *Sunday Referee* (13 April 1933) had been 'Chelsea Reach'.

40   'the D. H. 'Ell' = D. H. Lawrence.

51   Sanskrit psalms = cf. 'What the Thunder Said', Section V of *The Waste Land*.

74   Gallic letter = i.e. French letter (condom).

87   Geoffrey Grigson = poet, critic and editor of *New Verse*; initially Thomas's friend, he became an enemy from around 1936 (cf. 'To Others than You').

This bread I break (p. 50)

N4 'Thirty Three', dated 24 December 1933. Published *New English Weekly*, 16 July 1936; collected in *25P*.

On the opposite page in *N4* is a draft variant, titled 'Breakfast Before Execution', identical except for the final line, which reads: 'God's bread you break, you drain His cup'. As a Christmas poem structured by Eucharistic symbolism, this lyric turns on the paradox that the life-giving symbolism of Christ's giving of his body at the Last Supper (the 'breakfast') involved the 'desolation' of the body of nature, as crops of oats are 'laid low' and the 'joy' of the grape is 'broken' in making bread and wine. The poem, which some read as spoken by Christ, may be interpreted as an expression of the belief that from suffering ('man broke the sun/son') came salvation. However, by minimising explicit Christian references, Thomas opposes to this sense the more process-based, 'sensual' one of the simultaneity and inseparability of life and death, and casts ironic light on the reduction of the natural world to supernatural symbolism.

1   This bread I break = at one level the poem may be thought of as a play on the single-letter difference between 'break' and 'bread'.

2   foreign tree = vine, but also the Cross.

5   grape's joy = inverts 'Joy's grape' from Keats's 'Ode on Melancholy'.

11   This flesh you break = the 'you' is not only the reader but death, which puts us back in the universal round of the processes of mortality, even as it lays waste and devours us.

12   desolation in the vein = cf. the story 'The Enemies': 'desolation in his vein'.

A process in the weather of the heart (p. 51)

N4 'Thirty Five', dated 2 February 1934, with a variant titled 'DRAFT' on op-
posite pages. Published in the *Sunday Referee*, 11 February 1934, and collected
in *18P*.

The paradigmatic process poem, and the only one to actually use the word.
Like others, it draws analogies between the body's internal processes and those
in the external world, using verbs ('forks', 'weather') and nouns ('quarter',
'worm', 'forest') which inter-involve inner and outer, darkness and light, 'damp
and dry': Thomas told Glyn Jones in March 1934 that his obscurity stemmed
from a 'preconceived symbolism derived . . . from the cosmic significance of
the human anatomy', and the symbolism operates here in a pared-back, almost
diagrammatic way.

1 weather = an exemplary 'process' word.

2 golden shot = the ejaculate.

3 tomb = the womb as bearer of life which is always already dying; so, a tomb.

6 living worm = penis; grave-worm, maggot.

9 Drives in a death as life leaks out = the contrast between the forceful verb
for death, and the weak, passive one for life, gives 'drive' a negative emphasis.

11 fathomed sea = measured; the point seems to be that if the sea has been meas-
ured the land in the next line has not.

12 unangled = by contrast with the 'fathomed sea', with sense of unfished; pun-
ning allusion to the fact that Wales has never been wholly *angl*icized.

13 seed . . . forest of the loin = a gland (testicle, ovary) which triggers the
growth of pubic hair, although 'forest' is metaphorical too.

17–21 the quick and dead / Move like two ghosts . . . Turns ghost to ghost . . .
double shade = the living and dead are wraith-like in that they participate in
each other's condition (dead matter stirring with new life, living flesh always
dying). Every human, 'mothered child' is overshadowed by this duality from
birth. Cf. Donne, *Fifty Sermons* (1649), Sermon XIV: '[W]hen I consider what
I am now . . . an aged childe, a gray-headed Infant, and but the ghost of mine
own youth'.

24 the heart gives up its dead = the body at death is imagined as the stripping
of a house (e.g. of curtains) after its owner has died, with the heart disclosing its
secrets; in his vision of the Day of Judgement, St John claims 'the sea gave up
the dead which were in it' (Revelation 20:13).

When once the twilight locks (p. 52)

N4 'Twenty nine', dated 11 November 1933; revised March 1934, published in *New Verse*, June 1934; collected in *18P*, and in *CP52* without Stanza 6 (restored in *CP88*).

Post-natal and adolescent states of self-discovery seem to be conflated; the child's induction into the perilous antinomies of the world blurs into teenage negotiation of morbidity and sexual fantasy. The birth of Stanza 1 is therefore an image of the need for a symbolic birth from adolescence into adulthood, with the speaker sending off his 'creature', or physical self, to explore the microcosmic and actual world of 'hair and bone' after he had been weaned. But after a brief celebration of the light of day and reason, it drowns its 'father's magics' in a morbid dream-world of disease and death; Stanzas 4–6 form its report on this world. Sleep and dream are, of course, necessary to the adult confrontation with sex and mortality; however, the unconscious, where this occurs, accessed in dream, is also the dark zone of the neonate's nightmares and adolescent morbidity. Here dream- and death-realms overlap, and to succumb to the former is to be threatened by the latter. The sexual subtext of (wet) dreams as spiritual wastage and death is apparent in 'the hanged' of Stanza 6 (hanging associated with involuntary erection) and the punning, detumescent sense of 'cypress lads who wither with the cock'; 'these' and 'others' lie in wait in 'sleep's acres' (cf. the idiom 'death's acre' for graveyard), ready to 'snipe' the unwary dreamer. Stanza 7 sums up the narrative, and Stanza 8 is a Hamlet-like self-exhortation to engage with the everyday world, where 'worlds' of opportunity await it.

1 twilight locks = noun, as 'locks' of the womb (birth canal); verb, with 'twilight' as its subject, leading to wordplay in 'locked' and 'unlocked'.

2 long worm of my finger = the embryo's finger, like the worm-like umbilical cord and the long worm screw by which sluices in canal locks are opened.

3 dammed = *a* the 'locked in' amniotic sea; *b* in animal husbandry a 'dam' is a mother (cf. 'I see the boys of summer'); *c* 'damned'.

4 The mouth of time sucked = cf. Stanza 4 of 'The force'.

7 galactic sea = the universe (in which the galaxies swim), but also – punning on 'lactic' – milky, the maternal breast at which the newborn child sucks.

9 scouting = begins a series of mixed archaic and modern military terms.

12 his rib = of the 'creature' which is a 'globe itself'. Cf. Donne's 'Holy Sonnets': 'I am a little world made cunningly / Of Elements'.

15 sun = play on 'sabbath' as '*Sun*day'; pun on 'son' (see l.18).

17   Drew . . . the straws of sleep = to draw straws is to draw lots; hence, the chanciness of what comes in sleep/dreams (see l.18).

18   He drowned his father's magics in a dream = paternal Prospero-like power and enchantment – sexual and poetic – are let down by his son's 'creature' and its morbid, auto-erotic self-indulgence.

19   All issue armoured = syntactically ambiguous; 'issue' can be noun or verb; 'armour' is usually the flesh; 'grave' is also the womb. As noun, 'issue' may be pus (womb/tomb as suppurating wound), offspring and army equipment. The allusion is to Hamlet's father's ghost, both 'armoured' and 'of the grave', often used in the early poems to mediate Thomas's relationship with his own father.

24   Christ-cross-row = archaic alphabet-teaching device, the name of which came from the figure of the Cross (+) prefixed to the list of letters; 'of death' evokes the lines of crosses in the WWI war cemeteries in Flanders.

26   Sargasso = the Sargasso Sea is an area of the Atlantic synonymous with stasis (sailing ships were often becalmed there).

30   periscope through flowers = periscopes were used in the trenches in WWI; here the dead are imagined viewing the world through flowers growing from their graves.

32   Ghostly propellers = develops flower-as-periscope; the 'hanged' dead find new life in lime trees ('limes'), whose seeds are propeller-shaped.

35   moony suckers = the dead – 'the hanged', 'cypress lads' and 'others' – mock the 'moony' 'dreaming men' and 'fools of vision'.

37   twilight screws = in the canal-lock sense of the 'worm' of l.2; given 'stiff' in l.38, and the general context, also sexual (cf. 'Where once the waters of your face').

41–42   carcase shape . . . fluids in his heart = morbid and masturbatory urges generated sexual fantasy, leading to ejaculation and loss of vital fluid. Cf. 'In wasting one drop', 'Our eunuch dreams'.

45   pickthank = in Shakespeare, Bunyan and Blake, one who curries favour, especially by acting as an informer; 'a flatterer, sycophant, tale-bearer, tell-tale' (*OED*).

46   The fences of the light are down = the imagery is of a morning hunt, which the speaker exhorts his spirit-self to join (cf. 'Hold hard, these ancient minutes').

48   And worlds hang on the trees = are ripe for gathering; from *N4* 'Thirty One', 'I fellowed sleep who kissed between the brain'.

Our eunuch dreams (p. 54)

N4 'Thirty Seven', dated March 1934. Revised and published in *New Verse* April 1934; Stanza 2 of Part I was rewritten, and other lesser changes were made, before collection in *18P*.

Thomas told Edith Sitwell in January 1936 that this was a 'silly' 'Welsh-starch-itch-trash poem'. However, it succeeds very well in fusing his fascination with film with concerns about sex and sexual fantasy, and he defended it against Pamela Hansford Johnson's charges of 'pylon poetry' in March 1934: 'There is no reason at all why I should not write of gunmen, cinemas & pylons if what I have to say necessitates it. Those words & images were essential.' It has more to do with sexual repression and social revolution than modernity, however. Thus, in December 1933, Thomas inveighed, in a letter to Johnson, against 'the medieval laws of this corrupted hemisphere', which 'have dictated a more or less compulsory virginity during the period of life when virginity should be regarded as a crime against the dictates of the body', and stigmatised sex as 'unclean' in order to protect the institution of marriage: 'the physical expression of sex must be caged up for six or more years until . . . opportunity is presented with all the ceremony of a phallic religion'. The result, he informed her, was that 'so often the opportunity [for sex] comes too late; the seed has soured; love has turned to lust, and lust to sadism; the mind has become . . . choked by the weeds of inhibition; and the union of two starved creatures . . . is doomed from the start.'

Such thinking was influenced by D. H. Lawrence and Blake; one likely source was Blake's *The Visions of the Daughters of Albion*, and its critique of sexual fantasy is updated to cover film's glamorous but 'one-sided' version of it, exploring 'projection' in its filmic, Freudian and political senses. In Part I the 'light and love' of the 'eunuch dreams' by day are distorted by internal repression into fantasy, leading to morbid, masturbatory sex. In Part II, glamorous yet equally barren fantasies are offered by film. Part III wonders which of these two sterile, 'eunuch' projections will survive the 'cure' of a revolution; sexual freedom and social transformation are predicated upon each other. In the meantime, however, the ideological forms, film and fantasy, uphold the belief that it is impossible to escape their 'one-sided', emptied-out reality. Part IV begins by recapitulating this message, comes close to resignation, then pulls back, in the final stanza, to another form of (revolutionary) projection.

1–2 Our eunuch dreams = the sense is completed by 'of light and love'; tempers of the heart = an appositive clause that can qualify more than one predecessor. 'Tempers' sounds like 'tempters', and 'whack' has a masturbatory sense.

4 winding-footed = the sexual 'eunuch dreams' wind about the boy during daylight hours; 'winding' also applies to 'sheet' (and 'shawl') to make them grave-clothes, and anticipates winding film reels, a different ensnarement, in Part II.

5 Groom = become bridegrooms to the 'dark brides'; as of an animal.

8 sundered = applies retrospectively, as main verb, to 'shades of girls', and forward to 'bones of men'; agency is supplied by the 'midnight pulleys'. Auto-erotic sex is viewed as necrophilic because the images it relies on are not, strictly speaking, alive.

11 the gunman and his moll = allusion to contemporary US gangster movies such as *Scarface* (1932).

12 one-dimensioned ghosts = film-screen images; love on a reel = (make) love (verb) on a film(-reel); play on 'unreal'.

14 swell = tumescence; screen images growing larger than life; show off.

18 shots = filmic shots; gunshots by the 'gunman'.

21 Which is the world? = an analogy between waking/sleep and faith/doubt.

23 red-eyed earth = the bleary-eyed film-watcher, but also the red (social-ist)-eyed bedrock of the working classes, particularly miners, who can be said to literally 'raise up' from the 'earth'.

24–26 Pack off . . . forth = drive away the 'real world', a capitalist one domi-nated by the 'rich', or the two 'night-geared' worlds of fantasy or film (which complement and reinforce it). The next four lines insist just how difficult this will be; starch = as in starched shirts, metonymic of upper-class proprieties; Welshing rich = 'to welsh' is 'to swindle (a person) out of money laid as a bet' (*OED*), to fail to pay a debt of honour and keep one's word, or promise.

29 The dream has sucked the sleeper of his faith = evokes 'succubus'; dream robs the victim of 'faith' that he can break the cycle of morbid auto-erotic fantasy.

30 marrow = to marry, make equal to, multiply one's essence; echoes 'married' (l.27), but expands its scope.

31 This is the world = answers 'Which is the world' (l.21) with fatalism: is the 'lying likeness' the true reality?

33 Loving from rag to bone = read 'Loving and being loth' in previous pub-lished versions (see l.36 below). Thomas altered it to give an end-rhyme for 'spin'.

36 Suffer this world to spin = 'This is the world. Have faith' in previous ver-sions. In a PS to his late March letter to Grigson, Thomas offered a revision of this stanza: 'I have been reading over again . . . "Our eunuch dreams . . ." and am struck more forcibly than before by what might seem to be the jarring op-timism of the first six lines of the fourth part. I suggest that this revised stanza

sounds far less false.' Grigson did not agree; I do, because Thomas was right to try to have the abrupt mood-shift occur within the final stanza, not in the last line of the penultimate one.

37–38 cock / Blowing the old dead back = cock-crow, announcing day (metaphorically a revolutionary dawn), is said to send ghosts back to the grave; with 'cock' as penis, this might read: 'a healthy sexual life will dispel the projections of fantasy and film'.

38 shots = of sperm; fired in revolutionary uprising.

39 plates = photographic plates.

40–42 fit fellows ... flower ... faring = alliteration gives an upbeat conclusion, with Thomas's characteristic visionary, sexual-political emphasis (cf. 'All all and all').

Where once the waters of your face (p. 55)

N4 'Thirty Eight', dated 18 March 1934; published in the *Sunday Referee*, 25 March 1934, collected in *18P*.

The narrator appears to lament the passing of childlike delight, and then to assert its renewal. *CP88* cites a letter to Trevor Hughes of January 1934: 'This new year has brought back to my mind the sense of magic that was lost – irretrievably I thought – so long ago. I am conscious, if not of the probability of the impossible, then at least its possibility.' More specifically, the lyric could address the speaker's mother, recalling antenatal existence ('screws' as turnings in the womb), a lover, past or present, a dried sea-channel, or the speaker himself. Certainly, erotic desire and embryonic bliss seem to be evoked in imagery which is both umbilical-amniotic and genital. Enumerating what has been lost, the poem ambiguously but vividly evokes it, and the figure of the 'green unraveller' combines undoing and release. In each interpretation, the 'waters of your face' takes on a different meaning, while remaining a common denominator of forms of creation, procreation and recreation. Nor are the different possibilities mutually exclusive; this is Thomas as what Stewart Crehan (1990) calls a 'Freudian exemplar', playing the roles of lover, child, elegist and prophet.

1 waters of your face = reverses 'And the Spirit of God moved upon the face of the waters', Genesis 1:2. Olson (1954) notes: 'the reader tends naturally to take "waters" as metaphorical and "face" as literal, whereas the opposite is the case'. Lear's double entendre may lurk in 'face': 'Behold yon simp'ring dame / Whose face between her forks presageth snow' (*King Lear*, 4:4, 120–21).

2 Spun to my screws = 'did as I desired' (cf. 'the screws that turn the voice' in 'All all and all'). 'Screws' are also the propellers of ships on the 'waters'; its sexual sense cannot be discounted either.

3 turns up its eye = the eye of the 'face' of l.1, now subject to the 'dead'; alters the idiom 'turn up one's nose'.

16–18 the shades / Of children . . . Cry to the dolphined sea = lost (or yet-to-be) children yearning for a visionary perception (of the world or the womb).

19–24 Dry as a tomb . . . Till all our sea-faiths die = the 'invisible' former sea which will never be relinquished while 'magic' – poetry – retains its 'sage' power to keep 'sea-faiths' alive and the 'coloured lids' of the (Egyptian sarcophagus-style) 'tomb' 'unlatched'; serpents = possible allusion to the Gower tidal island, Worm's Head, with its 'clocking' tidal causeway, and name from the Old Norse for 'serpent'.

I see the boys of summer (p. 56)

N4 'Thirty Nine', dated 'April '34', written late March/early April 1934; published in *New Verse* (June 1934); collected in *18P*.

Thomas opened *18P* with 'I see the boys of summer', considering it and 'When, like a running grave' the two best poems in the book, and it is undoubtedly a high point of his new style, brilliantly exemplifying its sonorous music, concrete imagery, mythic resonance and sardonic, oracular wit. The tripartite structure embodies the contrary terms by which the poem proceeds at a local level and frames the debate between the boys' denouncer (Part I) and the boys themselves (Part II) before a stark and cathartic conjunction of opposites yields a powerful but paradoxical closure (Part III).

The poem progresses via the generation of oppositional images of 'ruin' and those of 'summer' and vice versa; its subject is the boys' repression of natural and adult sexual instinct, and their condemnation of even the unborn to lives of 'seedy shifting'. Part I's blend of linguistic inventiveness and archetypal force gives the visionary critique of religious prohibition, political-economic crisis and Freudian repression a universal resonance. In Part II the boys accept these charges, but turn them back on their attacker by asserting the necessity of challenging the 'seasons' of growth and harvest, celebrating denial, waste and death-in-life with a nihilistic energy. The areas of ambiguity in both parts are brought to a kind of resolution in Part III, which seems to be uttered by accuser and boys, and possibly a third voice, and the poem concludes with an excruciatingly conflicted image of the 'kissing' poles, uniting opposites but also forming an instrument of torture, the Cross.

Taken together, the boys and their accuser personify the simultaneous growth and decay energies of process, with a particular emphasis on Depression-era waste and the kinds of frustration and anxiety explored in poems such as 'Our eunuch dreams'. Yet the boys also embody the fact that the best way to serve tradition is by rebellion, since unchallenged systems oppress and enslave;

countering this, the poem moves in the direction of myth and ritual, 'crossing' Easter and Christmas, and hinting at pagan sacrifice towards its close.

Form: nine stanzas of 11-7-10-8-8-10 syllables pararhyming *aabcbc* (with minor variants).

I

1 boys of summer in their ruin = cf. W. H. Auden's *The Orators*: 'They gave the prizes to the ruined boys' (a summer prize-giving scene, where 'ruined' has masturbatory undertones).

2 Lay . . . barren = ripe corn flattened, hence wasted sexual potential (paradoxically reinforced by pun on 'lay'); tithings = a 'tithe' was the percentage of one's annual produce claimed by the feudal Church; the noun is given verbal energy. Stan Smith (2001) detects an echo of Auden's 'Hearing of harvests rotting in the valleys'.

3 Setting no store = failing to store the harvest; not caring about it.

4–6 There . . . their . . . their . . . their = the slippage between these homophones hints at the difficulty readers will have in keeping track of the identities of the poem's speakers; heat = readiness for sexual activity; winter floods = the boys deliberately chill the ardour of 'their girls'.

6 And drown the cargoed apples in their tides = symbolic stifling of fecundity.

9 jacks of frost = play on Jack Frost; icicle-like penises and the sterility of those who 'finger' them, suggesting the slang 'jack off', for masturbate; hives = wombs.

13–18 The stifling of natural sexuality affects even 'boys' yet to be born.

14 Split up = as in mitosis (with suggestion that the foetus is in conflict with its mother's usual 'weathers'); brawned = muscled.

15 fairy thumbs = delicate, diminutive; magical, fairy-like dividing of night and day; hermaphrodite, like the indeterminately gendered foetus; homosexual.

16–17 quartered shades = measurements of time – the stanza has progressed from 1 ('I') to 2 ('split') and 4 ('quartered'), like the developing foetus; also the quarters of the year ('sun'); and of the month ('moon'); accommodated ghosts (the foetuses in the womb).

17 they paint their dams = the unborn children paint the seasons on their mothers, make them aware of their mortality.

18 the shelling of their heads = the sun creates the egg-shell-like head; after birth it will reveal a world careering towards war, and explosive 'shelling'.

20 seedy = full of seed, in one's sexual prime; degenerate, down-at-heel; shift-ing = changing, hinting at 'shifty'.

22 dogdayed = dog days, named after the dog star, Sirius, are the hottest of the year; they fall between early July to mid-August, and are synonymous with lethargy.

23 bursts in their throats = metaphorically, 'breaks into song'; literally, bursts the carotid artery. 'Love and light' are conventional terms, and depending on how one takes the speaker's attitude to these, the bursting could be rupture, rapture or both.

24 O see the pulse of summer in the ice = each section ends with an appeal to 'see' a symbol which ambiguously sums it up; here the heat of summer trapped in (or with the potential to melt) icy frigidity.

II

25–26 But seasons . . . a chiming quarter = the boys oppose attempts to arrest time.

27 ring the stars = anticipates the analogy drawn between stars and bells in the next two lines (for the association of stars and inexorable time, cf. 'The force').

28 the black-tongued bells = of death.

30 Nor blows back . . . as she blows = the 'man of winter' – perhaps the speaker of Part I – cannot arrest the passing of time (signified by 'moon-and-midnight'); 'there she blows' was the cry of the lookout on a whaler on sighting a whale.

31 deniers = those who deny.

35 bright-eyed worm = an object of 'summon', this is the wick in a lamp, or its possessor, a miner (eyes bright in a blackened face, 'worm'-like underground), or a marine creature; Davy's lamp = combines 'Davy Jones's locker', a term for the seabed (from Davy Jones, an evil sea-spirit), and the Davy safety lamp used by miners.

36 planted womb = *plant* is Welsh for 'child'; the man of straw = proverbial for someone weak; straw effigies used in the May Day ritual of carrying out Death, or 'wicker men'.

37 four-winded spinning = periphrasis for the (revolving) earth.

43 we cross our foreheads with the holly = allusion to the Cross and crown of thorns; but this is also a misplaced vegetation rite (holly is used in winter to symbolise future rebirth). The 'squires' suggest the hanged god, the human sacrifices which are his surrogates, phalluses and the 'boys'.

45 nail the merry squires to the trees = crucify their own sexual desires.

46 dries and dies = cf. l.7 of 'The force'.

47 break a kiss in no love's quarry = rocks were broken up in quarries by pris-
oners condemned to hard labour.

48 O see the poles . . . the boys = summarising the boys' self-defence, perhaps
stressing their positive potential.

III

The identity and order of the speakers can be read as: *a* alternate lines by the
speakers of Part I and Part II (121212); *b* these followed (twice) by a third, per-
haps the poet (123123); *c* speakers (121), a fourth line spoken by either 1 or 2,
reinforcing the idea of complementary roles, a fifth which moves from 'I' to
'we', creating a duet on the theme of opposites meeting (Don McKay, 1985/86).

50 Man in his maggot's barren = *a* man is merely food for worms; *b* man's
sexual activity ('maggot' as penis/worm) is ultimately futile; *c* man is fruitlessly
concerned with himself ('maggot' in the archaic sense of whim, obsession).

51 full and foreign in the pouch = pouch is the scrotal sac; like 'seedy', the
image is of simultaneous sexual plenitude and alienation from it.

54 O see the poles are kissing as they cross = the warring phallic polarities
of life and anti-life seem briefly reconciled; the Cross reconciles God to man,
but the echo of 'kissing the rod' and 'cross's' sense of 'angry', or of thwarting
someone, prevents an easy resolution of polarities. Cf. the story 'A Prospect of
the Sea': 'the two poles [of the globe] kissed behind his shoulder', and Herbert's
'The Search': 'Thy will such a strange distance is, / As that to it / East and West
touch, the poles do kisse, / And parallels meet'.

In the beginning (p. 58)

N4 'Fifteen', dated 'September 18 '33 Llangain', rewritten as *N4* 'Forty', dated
'April '34'; published in *18P*.
   The source is John's Gospel, 1:1, which rewrites Genesis: 'In the beginning
was the Word, and the Word was with God, and the Word was God'. Echoing
an echo, Thomas develops the conceit that the creation of the world resembles
the conception of the embryo. In line with Thomas's poetic, this entails a myth
of simultaneous origin for language, the body and the universe, and some crea-
tive blasphemy. Stanza 1 of 'Fifteen' described hell as 'A burning stick across the
bum', and Stanza 3 began: 'In the beginning was the three-eyed prick'. Its last
stanza is a symbolist translation of thought into language and light, however,
from which Thomas took his cue in the revision. For all this, the finished poem

still powerfully suggests the identity of the Creation and sexual activity, and the poet as demiurge.

1, 19 In the beginning = St John's Gospel was a favourite Thomas text; three-pointed star = the trinity of Father, Son and Holy Ghost; but also of the penis and testicles (cf. 'My hero bares his nerves').

2 face = sexual as well as physiognomic.

3 bough of bone . . . rooting air = images of vegetable growth, but with sexual undertones.

11 crosstree = the Cross; junction of spar and mast on a sailing ship; grail = the Holy Grail.

13 mounting = rising, including in a sexual sense.

25–26 secret brain . . . in the thought = 'brain' is chosen rather than 'mind' in order to emphasise the inseparability of spirit and matter.

30 The ribbed original of love = Adam, who was 'ribbed' to produce Eve, but also as the butt of the cosmic joke played on him by Eve and Satan (cf. 'Altarwise', III).

If I were tickled by the rub of love (p. 59)

'Forty One', the final poem in N4, dated 'April 30 '34'; slightly revised for publication in *New Verse*, August 1934; collected in *18P*.

Thomas sent this poem to Pamela Hansford Johnson on 2 May 1934: '[It] is, I think, the best I've written – I've said that to you about a lot of mine, including all sorts of wormy beasts.' Like others of the period, it has Hamlet's morbid indecision as an intertext, signalled by the punning use of 'rub' from his 'To be or not to be' soliloquy. There it signifies 'a physical obstacle or impediment to movement' (*OED*); Thomas riffs on its other senses, primarily that of (sexual) friction, but also 'to erase' and 'an advantage' (as in 'to get the rub of the green' in bowls).

Stanzas 1–4 consider four life-stages (embryo, baby, adolescent and old man). If the speaker were tickled (sexually 'aroused', 'amused' but also 'emotionally touched') by the 'rub' of these life-phases, he would not fear: Stanza 1, biblical prohibitions or adolescent turmoil; Stanza 2, death in war or at the hands of the law; Stanza 3, the punishments threatened for masturbation; or – Stanza 4 – ageing or venereal disease. But in fact, as Stanza 6 admits, 'the only rub that tickles' is the morbid fascination with death admitted to in Stanza 5; neither sex nor beauty can arouse his interest. Stanza 7 recapitulates this; the ultimate 'rub' is that everything understood to make one feel most intensely – death, religion and romantic love – is subordinated to his 'words of death'. This is a final qualification in a threatening scenario similar to that of 'Especially when the October wind', leading to a desire to escape it. The concluding exhortation is more ambiguous than it might seem, however; the tone is ironic rather than ringingly humanistic, and the poem more generally undoes bravado, particularly in Stanza 4, where love is not efficacious against 'sick old manhood'. Thomas's own reading brings this out, replete as it is with sardonic, stage-villain relish.

Form: seven seven-line stanzas, consisting of six iambic pentameters and final six-syllable trimeter; pararhyming *abcacbc*, irregular in Stanzas 2 and 7.

2 rooking = thieving; girl who stole me for her side = as sexual partner; but the wording confuses this with a mother 'stealing' the speaker for her 'side' (womb).

3 breaking my bandaged string = freeing me from the metaphorical umbilicus, or apron strings, attaching me to my mother; actually cutting it, as my mother did. Cf. Donne's 'Death's Duell': 'when the *wombe* hath discharg'd us, yet we are bound to it by *cordes of flesh* by such a *string*, as that wee cannot goe thence, nor stay there'.

4 red tickle = the mating urge of spring.

5 Still = as in the past; always.

6–7 the apple . . . the flood . . . the bad blood of spring = symbols developed throughout the rest of the poem.

8, 15 Shall it be male or female? say the cells . . . fingers = the difference between the sexes, a matter of genetic lottery in the womb, is later signalled in the crude drawings of genitals made by adolescents on toilet walls.

11 winging bone . . . in the heels = like Hermes, the trickster and messenger of Roman mythology.

14 the crossed sticks of war = cf. 'the poles are kissing as they cross' in 'I see the boys of summer'; pun on Styx, which the dead 'cross' to reach Hades.

23–28 lock . . . jaws . . . butter . . . flies . . . sea . . . Dead = usually linked words, which have been separated ('lockjaw' is diphtheria).

25 sweethearting crib = as an old man he would be indifferent to the predictable ('crib' as 'rote learning device') endearments of youthful sweethearts; 'crib' is also cradle, for babies produced by the activity which can begin with such endearments.

31 curling round the bud that forks her eye = 'bud' is the object of the 'drug'; 'forks' as a pitchfork develops 'devil' and 'smoking', leading to an image of horticulture – an 'eye', or undeveloped bud, is removed from the stock of a plant, and replaced ('forked') by one from the scion to be grafted on to it. But the image is also powerfully sexual, with the hormonal 'drug' drawing attention

to 'bud' as the 'eye'-like pudenda and 'forks' (homophonic with 'fucks') as the groin.

33 herrings smelling = active and passive: herring search for food ('smell out'), as scavenging bottom feeders, and smell when they are dead.

35 quick = living tissue under the fingernails; life itself.

40–41 the breast / Of lover, mother, lovers = a Freudian slippage through a series of love objects; the list suggests that desire can never be earthed or grounded.

42 rubbing dust = which 'rubs out', or erases, bodies buried in it.

43 Death's feather = see note to 'I have longed to move away'.

45 Born thorny on the tree = Christmas (birth) and Easter (death and resurrection) fuse.

46 The words of death = so word-centred is the speaker that *words* about death outdo the deathly aspect of the dead Christ; stiff = dead body; erect penis.

47 My wordy wounds . . . your hair = the reality of the living woman is subservient to the speaker's poem, or 'wordy wounds'; to Johnson, c. 21 May 1934, Thomas wrote: 'I wonder whether I love your word, the word of your hair – . . . the word of your voice, the word of your flesh, & the word of your presence.'

49 Man be my metaphor = not liberal humanist, but following Blake's belief that man is the only way to understand the universe.

I dreamed my genesis (p. 61)

Derived from *N3* 'Two', rewritten between late April and late May 1934; published in *18P*.

Writing to Pamela Hansford Johnson in May 1934, Thomas cited 'the opening of my new poem', 'I dreamed the genesis of mildew John', a self-parody resembling a draft poem held in Austin which shows him turning it into this poem. Adjoining the draft is a letter to Hamish Miles of Cape, attempting to interest him in publishing *18P*. It reads: 'I'm enclosing three poems . . . The one beginning "I dreamed my genesis" is more or less based on Welsh rhythms, & may seem, rhythmically, a bit strange at first.' The claim has led to much conjecture about the extent of Thomas's knowledge of *cynghanedd*, the intricate metrical and musical techniques of classical Welsh poetry. It is generally agreed that he had some sense of these, and devised English equivalents to replicate their effects. In this case the stanzas of twelve-, seven-, ten- and eight-syllable lines do follow a discernible Welsh pattern, and the break preceding the last word in the first line of each stanza, and strong enjambement, also mimics the effect of the *englyn*, in which a final, grammatically separate word or phrase, is attached to a line.

The poem presents two dreams: one of the narrator's conception and birth in the first three stanzas, and one of death, resurrection, erection and emission in the next three, with a final stanza of optimistic rebirth. However, cycles of various deaths, as birth pangs, sexual acts and extinction, are intertwined with each other, and often figured in violent WWI imagery.

2–3 rotating shell . . . the drill = mother (womb) and father (penis) respectively.

3–4 muscle on the drill . . . girdered nerve = examples of Thomas's cybernetic-surreal conjunctions of organic and inorganic (cf. 'All all and all', etc.).

5–6 shuffled / Off = cf. *Hamlet*: 'shuffle off this mortal coil'; creasing = wrinkling, hence ageing.

6 filed = progressed in single file; the action of using the tool, leading to 'irons' and 'metal' in l.7. (cf. 'Light breaks').

7–8 irons in the grass, metal / Of suns = we are made of metals (e.g. the iron in haemoglobin) created in dying stars, and grass will grow from our bodies; with puns on 'mettle' and 'sons'.

10–12 I / Rounded . . . night-geared man = as in 'When once the twilight', the speaker's 'creature' undergoes the universal round of death and renewal, passing through the unconscious or dreaming mind 'in bottom gear' because in the nethermost depths of the sleeping, 'night-geared', mind.

13–16 shrapnel . . . marching . . . stitched wound . . . ate the gas = WWI imagery.

17, 21–23, 25–26 my second death . . . second / Rise of the skeleton . . . fallen / Twice in the feeding sea = a second sexual 'little death' of orgasm after the first death of birth.

23–24 Manhood / Spat up = ejaculation.

27 Adam's brine = sperm or the amniotic sea of his genesis which the exhausted narrator no longer needs.

I fellowed sleep (p. 62)

Probably written April 1934; published in *18P*.

On 2 May 1934 Thomas wrote to Pamela Hansford Johnson concerning *N4* 'Twenty Two', the earlier version of this poem: 'I have rewritten "The Eye of Sleep" almost entirely, and it is now a little better, though still shaky on its rhythms and very woolly as to its intention (if any).' In rewriting it, he gave it a new first line, adapted from the opening of *N4* 'Thirty One' of 27 November 1933.

'Twenty Two' is overtly religious, but the rewriting dramatises a tussle between maternal (religious-spiritual) and paternal (atheistic-materialist) aspects of the self in Stanzas 2–4. In the last stanza, we seem to see the cost of rejecting the 'mothers-eyed' to ascend the patriarchal 'ladder to the sun', imaged in the pitiable 'old, mad man', both singular father and the collective ghost of all fathers who remain 'in the rain'.

1 I fellowed sleep = partnered; play on 'felloe', the rim of a wheel.

4 'planing-heeled = 'aeroplaning', and so like Hermes, with wings on his heels (cf. 'If I were tickled'); flew along my man = internal or projected self.

6–7 climbed . . . far from the stars = that is, ascended to the 'upward sky' (l.5) of the 'tops of trees' (l.9) and clouds (ll.18, 25); but this conventional 'heaven' is 'far from' a truly visionary vantage point, symbolised by the stars.

8–9 a ghostly other, / My mothers-eyed = Thomas's mother was an assiduous chapel-goer, in contrast to her husband.

10 I fled that ground as lightly as a feather = as in l.6; not a further 'fleeing'.

11 'My fathers' globe knocks on its nave and sings' = 'globe' is a wheel; the technical term for the hub of a wheel is the 'nave', which is also the main space in a church, hence 'sings'.

24–25 How light the sleeping . . . in the worlded clouds = the sense is of the equality between the two worlds, waking as a form of sleeping, sleep (dreaming) as a form of waking; cf. letter to Johnson of 25 December 1933: 'I want to sleep and wake, and look upon my sleeping as only another waking.'

28 monkeyed = allusion to Darwin's *The Ascent of Man*; the ladder of (a) life is 'monkeyed', insofar as it includes the 'rungs' of human evolutionary development, these being both species-biological and individual.

30 My fathers' ghost is climbing in the rain = reading makes clear the plural possessive, as at l.11, giving 'ghost' a species aspect; however, if heard it would be taken as a singular possessive (referring to D. J. Thomas).

All all and all (p. 63)

Probably written May–July 1934, and first referred to in a letter to Pamela Hansford Johnson of 20 July; published in *18P*.

The opening refrain has a summatory, even totalising, ring appropriate to the poem's position at the end of *18P*. Yet this is less authoritative than it seems; if the 'dry worlds' are human bodies, then either they or 'all' can be the subject of 'lever' (which has the quality of a noun too). Parts I and II record an attempt to overcome adolescent anxiety at an adult 'working world', but even more at biological determinism and a machine-like universe, which seems to run itself with complete disregard for its inhabitants. Trying to bypass the tyrannies of biological and cosmic determinism, but avoid religious doctrine, Thomas affirms the unity of creation in the hope that, if we can live in harmony with the machinery, the spirit may be able to imbue our elemental impulses with creative purpose and make life meaningful. This poem has the highest density of organic/inorganic compounds of any by Thomas, as summed up by 'mechanical flesh'; true harmony involves merging the human and machine – a confusion of metal and flesh, using cyborg symbolism. This is hinted at in the letter to Johnson: '"Flower", by the way, in my "All all and all" (Bradall, Nuttall, & Bugger-all) is a two-syllabled word.' A bradawl is a tool for boring holes, and the bracketed phrase sounds like the name of an engineering firm. Part III's 'coupling' promises to give meaning to the eternal round, in a sexual-socialist 'fusion' of 'flesh's vision' and the 'people'.

1 All all and all = cf. Fulke Greville's 'When all this *All* doth pass from age to age', also about epochal and personal change.

2 Stage = links back to the opening to recall *As You Like It*: 'All the world's a stage'.

3 pound of lava = an antithetical (inorganic) equivalent of *The Merchant of Venice*'s 'pound of flesh'.

4 governed flower = governed by natural (deterministic) law.

6 wheel of fire = cf. *King Lear*, 4:5, 49–51: 'I am bound / Upon a wheel of fire'.

8 Dug = breast; glanded morrow = the imagery of contemporary 'gland-grafting' treatments is used to present the prospect of a re-energised future.

24 driven = because 'love' is an epiphenomenon of the sexual urge, governed, like the flower of Part I, by hormonal, physio-chemical imperatives.

25 In response to Henry Treece's study of the sources of his poetry, Thomas wrote on 16 May 1938: 'Sometimes, I think, the influence of Swinburne is more obvious than that of Hopkins in a couple of quotations . . . that you use. "All all and all the dry worlds couple", for example. This is rhythmically true, at least.'

30 Square . . . the mortal circle = to come to terms with the constraints on human existence; politically, the 'working world' of capitalism is brought into accord with the world of natural desire and human fulfilment through revolution.

My world is pyramid (p. 64)

Probably written July 1934; published in *New Verse* (December 1934) as 'Half of the fellow father as he doubles', collected in *18P*.

'My world is pyramid' offers a complex identification of conception with mortality, in the form of a debate between parts of the self. Part I is a Gothic-grotesque account of sexual congress, a joining of parental genetic materials, and the compound creature that results. From its start, the 'salt unborn' is shadowed by its dire inheritance, with its parents themselves halved in creating a 'bisect-ed', vampiric 'cripple'. The embryo is 'cloven' into angelic and devilish aspects, or 'ghosts', with Stanza 2's 'unplanted ghost' likely to be the 'havoc'-creating 'ghost' of Stanza 5. In Stanza 5, the 'arterial angel' is quizzed about the mysteries of existence, perhaps by its parents, but is unable to answer; the other (devilish) ghost seems to blind their 'cloud-tracking [heaven-fixated] eye'.

The 'I' of Part II, now the 'unborn devil' and 'secret child' of Stanzas 4 and 5, tells of a death-possessed womb-tomb world, in which it finds itself bloodily pieced together from Europe's recent history. In Stanza 8 this acquires global scope, and the 'I' is hunted as well as haunted; the scenario resembles the search for Satan in *Paradise Lost*. This may not be wholly negative; references to 'straw' and 'corn' link the figure to a dying god, or harvest deity, and it has a trickster-like aspect, evading heaven's spies and repressive 'gossip' disguised in an 'angel's hood'. Stanza 10 may be a kind of self-justification: stubbornly restating/inverting the questions the 'angel' embryo could not answer, it offers its own by insisting: I am responsible for living, red blood, and I celebrate sexuality. This is why, as the downbeat ending hints, the parental 'halves' ignore their 'secret child' – a euphe-mism for a bastard – even though death has no meaning, life no 'colour', unless it is acknowledged.

1 doubles = in size (applies to the engorged 'Adam' of l.2).

2 sea-sucked Adam = the penis, drawn to the sea of the womb in sex; hollow hulk = euphemism for the womb (the penis seen as a diver descending to a shipwreck).

4 Tomorrow's diver = the child who will eventually 'dive' from the womb into the future; horny milk = hormones and/or amniotic fluid; the image is a Freudian blend of procreative, sexual and maternal instincts.

5 Bisected = pun on the Latin root of 'bisect', from *sectare*, meaning sex, so 'bi-sexed', as the embryo potentially is; thunder's bone = penis or pubis.

6 Bolt = dash towards; fix together.

7 fellow half = male half ('fellow' as slang for male friend).

9 The fellow seed = female half ('fellow' as one of a pair).

10 tufted in the pap = like 'horny milk', runs different developmental phases together ('pap' as baby food and mother's breast, 'tufted' suggesting pubic hair).

11–12 planted . . . unplanted ghost = the main image is of the egg attaching itself, or not, to the womb wall, and the chief concern is the 'planting' of an identity in the embryo. But there is a 'ghostly other', a mixture of alter ego and twin, who fails to gestate in the womb.

13–17 The broken halves . . . stake = the subject is passive with regard to the description of the embryo, active with regard to the sleepers; they stake, or kill off, the other identities the embryo could have had, through their sexual activity.

13 cripple = the newly created embryo.

14 marrow = semen.

15 street of sea = the womb.

16 tide-tongued = play on 'tongue-tied'; heads and bladders = perhaps the other sperm (and eggs) which could have joined to make the child, now discarded.

16, 17 the deep . . . savage grave = the womb

18 That the vampire laugh = (in order) that the vampire (child, drawing substance from its parents) can laugh.

20 The wild pigs' wood = sexual activity of mother and father: 'wood' can mean 'madness'.

23 drill = create through sexual intercourse; coach.

24 arterial angel = regenerated man.

25 What colour is glory? = a typical riddle, drawing attention to the strangeness of existence, and the limited power of instrumental reason to explain it (cf. 'Why east wind chills'). 'Glory' may also have the sense of orgasm, as in 'A saint about to fall' and elsewhere; death's feather = cf. 'I have longed to move away'.

26–27 pin's point . . . thimble = recalls the classic instance of medieval scholastic disputatiousness – 'How many angels can dance on the point of a needle?' – and hence to critique the kind of questions being asked by the parental 'halves'.

28–29 The ghost . . . ghost = the 'broken halves' of Stanza 3. 'Ghost' is often embryo or child; cf. 'A process'.

29 havoc = violent destruction; a hawk.

31 pyramid . . . padded mummer = on 6 July 1934, Thomas wrote in the *Swansea and West Wales Guardian*: 'Our symbol of faith must be a naked life, not a pale cross of death done up in a mummy blanket and surrounded by the Pyramid walls of an established stupidity.'

34–35 My Egypt's armour . . . starry bone = continues the Egyptian resurrection theme. In the very early poems, Egyptian motifs are simply exotic; by this point they are complex images for the afterlife, death, stasis, repression and rebirth.

36 blood parhelion = 'A spot on a solar halo at which the light is intensified . . . formerly supposed to be a reflected image of the sun; a mock sun' (*OED*).

37 My world is cypress = cypress is a natural counterpart to the pyramid: triangular, associated with death, but also (as evergreen) with death's defeat, offering refuge and hope for a new life (its wood was used to build the Ark).

39 Red in an Austrian volley = the Social Democratic working class of Vienna had been bloodily suppressed in February 1934 by the Dollfuss government. In December 1934 Thomas had negatively reviewed Stephen Spender's *Vienna*, and wrote his own poem on the subject; this stanza is the only part of it to survive.

40 riddled = pierced; questioned; sieved.

41 hill of bones = the Western Front; Golgotha, 'the place of the skull'.

42 Cry Eloi to the guns = the despair of WWI soldiers; cf. Mark, 15:34: 'And at the ninth hour Jesus cried with a loud voice, saying, Eloi, Eloi, lama sabachthani? which is, being interpreted, My God, my God, why hast thou forsaken me?'

43 Jordan = river the Israelites cross to reach the Promised Land and in which Jesus was baptised; slang for a chamber pot (cf. 'Before I knocked').

44 The Arctic scut = the Arctic hare.

56 stammel = archaic word for red; life-giving antithesis of the death-associated white feather elsewhere in the early poems.

57 The loin is glory in a working pallor = that is: 'I stand for the red-blooded glory of sexuality in a world where pallid men and women are trapped in their life-denying work routines.'

59 The secret child = probably 'the lost, / . . . unplanted ghost' of ll.11–12. Thomas used the same term self-referentially in 'The tombstone told'. Cf. William Blake's *Europe*: 'The deep of winter came, / What time the secret child / Descended thro the orient gates of the eternal day', alluding to Christ's birth.

Foster the light (p. 66)

N4 'Thirty-Six', dated 23 February 1934; published in the *Sunday Referee* on 28 October 1934; revised and republished in Desmond Hawkins' *Purpose* in 1935; and yet again for *Contemporary Poetry and Prose*, May 1936; collected in *25P*.

In a letter to Trevor Hughes of January 1935, Thomas discussed their struggles as writers, gave news of his father's cancer, and claimed that he escaped the depression Hughes suffered from because of his 'islandic egoism'. Hughes's reply concluded: 'How shall a man die if he has never lived, or seen the beauty of the stars through the lenses of his own darkness? For so many God has never lived, the faint glimmer within them the glimmer of their own mean ego. This dies upon them, and they must die in darkness; die in the night and move to eternal fields of darkness. Foster the light, and God be with you.'

Thomas seems to have taken issue with Hughes's final phrase in this poem, perhaps feeling that no God could eradicate the darker aspects of experience so neatly, and that there was no clear choice between darkness and light. The injunction to 'foster' is therefore qualified by 'nor', which means 'yet do not', and invokes 'neither' as an omitted precedent: '*Neither* foster the light, nor yet . . .'. Thomas draws on his process poetic, using ideas in the letter which Hughes had misconstrued; chiefly, that his 'egoism' was a considered belief that 'the flesh that covers me is the flesh that covers the sun'. Typically, the level of sympathy is hard to determine because a hortatory tone coexists with an advocacy of nuance and ambiguity.

1 manshaped moon = religion; the point is neither to 'foster' nor cut off the light it offers, but rather to rely more on the cosmic creative forces within the self.

4–6 the snowman's brain . . . on an icicle = alludes to Wallace Stevens' 'The Snow Man'; Thomas opposes its endorsement of the snowman's 'mind of winter', which sees the outside world as completely other.

7 Murmur of spring = restatement of Stanza 1 in horticultural and seasonal terms; don't rely on a single season for creativity, certainly not the obvious one; cockerel's eggs = archaic term for a yolkless egg, commonly supposed to be laid by a cockerel; possibly an image for (male) creativity.

9 graft these four-fruited ridings . . . country = make your inner energy bear sexual-creative fruit.

12 vegetable century = governed by 'farmer' and 'sow'; attend in your youth to your oneness with the cosmos. Cf. 'vegetable love', Marvell's 'To His Coy Mistress'.

13 fly-lord's acre = the domain of Beelzebub, 'Lord of flies', death; the sense is: use awareness of death to spur your creativity and 'father all' – that is, to breed like flies.

14 owl-seed = nocturnal emissions; goblin-sucker = incubus who draws out 'owl-seed'.

15 But rail . . . the heart-shaped planet = man must understand that his 'wizard' (magical) ribs enclose love (Venus), instead of dwelling on negativity.

16–18 Of mortal voices . . . marrowroot = the subject is 'High lord esquire', the object the 'mortal voices' he is being urged to 'speak up' to the immortal ones in order to fashion literary 'music'; ninnies' choir = satirical; 'don't be too bothered about reproduction, but let love into your heart and sing your own song, however jarring or strange it may seem'.

19 Roll = *neither* roll; turning tuft = periphrasis for earth; euphemism for pubic hair (cf. 'tufted in the pap', in 'My world is pyramid').

20 ring of seas = the earth's oceans and the womb. The creative process becomes more explicitly sexual in this stanza.

20–21 nor sorrow . . . a starboard smile = do not mourn.

23 bow-and-arrow birds = cupids; cf. the nursery rhyme 'Who Killed Cock Robin?' ('"I" said the sparrow, / "With my bow and arrow, / I killed cock robin"').

24 cockwise = motion of a weathercock (time symbol), reinforced by the echo of 'clockwise'; action of the penis in sex.

25–27 Who gave . . . coloured doubles = the God of creation ('time at flood') in his own image ('coloured doubles'), including the speaker ('my clayfellow').

28–30 O who is glory . . . walking circle = shifts from God's creation to the poet's role in an ongoing creation, as the created world is asked to provide images of process for the poet's body, reciprocating his efforts to create a world out of it.

Especially when the October wind (p. 67)

An early version in typescript, now in the British Library, is dated by Maud (1989) to late 1932, the period of the missing July 1932–January1933 notebook between *N2* and *N3*. It was revised for publication as 'Poem in October' in *The Listener*, 24 October 1934, and collected in *18P*.

The poem's speaker considers the extent of his absorption in language, and the degree to which this leads him to see the world in terms of words. The old idea of nature as the book of God's handiwork is overlaid by a post-symbolist notion of a textualised universe, governed by the conceit of words-as-things being circulated in the object world as blood circulates around the speaker's body, in Stanza 1. Stanza 2 describes a simultaneous, matching process, by which things in the object world are presented as a language. Words are made real, and the real is seen to speak, or write; as Thomas told David Daiches: 'When I experience anything I experience it as a thing and a word at the same time, both equally amazing.' The intertwining of word and world challenges their conventional separation according to which language merely denotes objects, feelings and ideas.

Thomas's response is to wish to communicate at a deeper-than-language level (of the 'beeches' in Stanza 2 and meadow and raven of Stanza 3). However, this leads him not to a retreat from language, but an ever more intense engagement with it, 'investing in the materiality of words in a way which aspires to transform them into *things* and so make words *real* and the real *speak*', as Harri Roberts (2008) puts it. Yet his aspiration to make language part of the real, and vice versa, is fraught with anxiety, as the repeated pleading to be allowed to verbalise the textualised world ('Some let me make you') shows. The return of the image of the heart in Stanza 4 reflects his ambivalence towards the possibility of fusing world and word. Having been equated with blood, and the spread of linguistic energy into the world, the final poem the speaker will 'make you' is that words have proved to be 'heartless', have drained and exhausted the heart, leaving only the ominous sound of winter birds. Courting greater linguistic fullness and presence, the poem seems to say, risks uncovering a more profound lack of it.

1 Especially . . . October = the poet is driven to think of the relationship of words to things by the bareness and clarity of the natural world in autumn; October was also a reminder of mortality as the month of Thomas's birthday.

3 Caught = given the shadow-casting context, this has a photographic sense (as in 'caught the likeness of'; crabbing = miserly; casting the poet's crab-like shadow; on fire = the glare of the sun on the sea and wet sand of the beach.

6 raven = a bird of ill-omen, as in Edgar Allan Poe's 'The Raven'; sticks = of its nest; the Sticks is also a grove in Llanstephan, mentioned in the story 'A Visit to Grandpa's'.

8 syllabic = blood is syllabic because the poem is; play on 'sibylline', referring to the prophetic action of the heart in pumping blood out.

9 tower of words = the poet's body, with the heart in it; the poet in the house where he writes; language as a tower imprisoning the writer is a common conceit in Thomas; mark = remark, mentally; mark on paper, write down; pun on Mark, the only gospel which records the miracle of Bethsaida (see l.10).

10 walking like the trees = the blind man cured by Christ says: 'I see men as trees, walking' (Mark 8:22–26).

11 wordy . . . women = talkative and much written about (seen in over-literary terms).

12 star-gestured children in the park = refers to children's games; rows = lines; arguments.

13 Some let me make you = 'some (poems) let me make (for) you'. The speaker wants to register the language of the outer world as strongly as his verbal inner life.

13–15 vowelled beeches . . . oaken voices . . . thorny shire = may allude to the Welsh tree alphabet, which included beech, oak and thorn; cf. 'Altarwise' VII.

17 wagging = the clock hand twitches as it moves, but it is a 'finger', and so can be said to 'wag' in an admonitory way.

18 neural meaning = meaning directly and non-verbally communicated to the nervous system by the external object world.

19 shafted disc = the face of the clock or the disc on a clock's pendulum.

20 windy weather in the cock = weathercock; also sexual (developed in 'neural', 'flies', 'shafted' and 'sins').

22 signal grass = grass starts to grow, signalling spring, with play on 'signs' in l.21.

23 Breaks . . . through the eye = a favourite image, probably with pun on 'I', as in 'Light breaks where no sun shines'.

26 autumnal spells = of weather, and of magic.

27 spider-tongued = alluding to Wales's two languages (like a spider's multiple legs, eyes, etc.); 'spider' also means 'opprobrious, cunning, or wily' (*OED*).

29 heartless words = 'heartless' in both senses; the words have left the heart, or inner world, and they do not themselves have a heart, are not alive.

30 drained = drained of blood; exhausted.

31 chemic blood = a typical (in)organic collocation; cf. Empson's 'chemic beauty' in 'Villanelle', and Thomas's story 'The Holy Six', 'man's chemic blood'; coming fury = the October wind presages the storms of winter.

32 dark-vowelled birds = in early Thomas usually birds of prey, associated with battlefield scavenging and hence the threat of war.

When, like a running grave (p. 68)

Written between autumn and December 1934; Thomas informed Pamela Hansford Johnson in late October 1934 that he was 'working very hard on a poem; it is going to be a very long poem; I've completed fifty lines so far; it is by far the best thing I've done'. It is likely that the material accumulated also produced 'I, in my intricate image'. 'When, like a running grave' has fifty lines, and very probably consists of what Thomas had written 'so far' in October 1934. It was published in *18P*.

The poem's framing image is that of a 'Cadaver' figure pursuing us through life, which is likened to a circular 'cinder' running 'track'. Verbally opaque and syntactically demanding, the poem opens with a sentence of over thirty clauses, over five stanzas (the flurry of short phrases underscoring the frantic plea for deliverance which is its theme). Stanza 1 is often cited as an instance of Thomas's surrealism, and the whole poem exemplifies his 'dialectical method' of composition. Its substance is a debate between a tyrant King Head and Queen Heart, and a Spartacus-like 'I' who, when the time is ripe and his forces (blood) are ready, will lead Cadaver to their overthrow.

The speaker is the self newly aware of its potential, anticipating a moment 'when' the 'you', 'head and heart', cautious rationality and evasive sentimentality, will be 'tracked down' (the opening sentence shifts from 'you' to 'I', from general mortal predicament to the recognition of the speaker that he shares this fate). He now claims freedom from his 'masters', asking for deliverance from timidity into life and love. But if the opening lines are directed against the immature self the speaker wishes to outgrow, this can be achieved only by embracing 'Cadaver', the destruction which accompanies growth, and there is an urgency about this because 'Cadaver's candle waxes thin', time is passing, and he wants to act while he is still in full 'force'. He must therefore reject the messages of his 'pickbrain masters' advocating 'despair' of 'blood', and faith in virginity. At l.26, heart and head dismiss his plans and his fears as an unreal 'fancy'. But he continues to reject 'lover skull' (deathly, idealised love) and 'hero skull' (deathly, idealised heroism); Cadaver is already telling the phallic 'stick' to 'fail'. 'Joy', he claims, is not the lively nation, the overcoming of illness, an idealised Christianity or nature, or the modern city: it is 'the knock of dust', accepting the inextricability of creation and destruction, life and death (particularly in sex), and this spells 'doom' to idealised attitudes, products of 'waxlights in your tower dome'. As against simplistic, idealist belief, 'everything ends', subjected to process, and you must love this 'trick', make or be 'happy' with 'Cadaver's hunger' as you 'take' the world, which is proof against your kiss and is proved in the kissing of it.

1–7 When ... Comes ... tailor age, / Deliver me = subject and main verb do not appear until l.7; running grave = pursuing open grave: cf. 'moving grave', Milton, *Samson Agonistes*, II, 102; suppurating grave.

2 scythe of hairs = the Grim Reaper, here scything hairs as we age; or, more surreally, a scythe made *from* hair.

3 gear = clothes; the gear of the 'hearse' of l.4; is = seems an active verb, love as a positive invading presence in the house, but rendered passive by 'hauled'.

4 Up naked stairs = uncarpeted stairs (prompted by 'gear' as clothes); epithet transposed to love stripped bare by ascending time; a turtle in a hearse = dead love, as 'turtle-dove'; the marine animal.

5 Hauled to the dome = with time and age, love becomes a thing of the mind.

6   like a scissors stalking, tailor age = tailors symbolise creation and destruction, measuring, cutting and sewing the cloth of our lives, like the Greek Fates. Here, the tailor has a knife, but embodies the fatal scissors in his own person, as in the tale of 'Little Suck-a-Thumb' in the then-popular children's storybook *Struwwelpeter*, where little Conrad foolishly ignores his mother's warning about 'the great tall tailor' who cuts off the thumbs of little boys who suck them. Following Freud, the tale was interpreted as expressive of castration anxiety, and as a warning against masturbation.

7   timid in my tribe = of sexually and emotionally inexperienced young men.

8   barer = pun on 'bearer'; Cadaver = first of six appearances in the poem by this figure of pursuing death; trap = mouth; snare.

9   foxy = cunning; Robbed = also the verb for 'footed tape'; footed tape = tape breasted by foot-race runners on a running track; tape measure used by tailors and undertakers, marked in feet.

10   bone inch = probably the thumb.

12   Cadaver's candle = the penis.

13   blood, spade-handed = each diastole-systole motion of the (spade-shaped) heart drives the blood round our bodies and us towards our grave-to-be.

14   Drive children up like bruises to the thumb = children are born and grow up to replace us as inexorably as hammering nails into a wall (with occasional 'bruises' to the thumb from a missed blow). Cf. 'And death shall have no dominion', where the dead 'hammer through daisies' into the world of the living.

15   maid and head = woman (maid) and head of the penis; play on maidenhead.

16   sunday faced = with a meek look; dusters in my glove = wearing gloves in compliance with polite society; knuckle-dusters in boxing gloves.

17   Chaste and the chaser = wordplay; the inexperienced pursuer of women is himself pursued by Cadaver; cockshut = twilight; cf. Francis Thompson's 'Before Her Portrait in Youth': 'I, faring in the cockshut-light, astray'; opposite of cocksure.

18   jacket = leads not just to 'coat of ice', repression by convention, but 'straight' in l.20, and the grave as a straitjacket.

19   virgin o = symbol of the nothingness of virgin honour held sacred by society; to John Davenport in 1938, Thomas denied the 'o' was a reference to 'raggletaggle gypsies o', as a critic had suggested: 'I meant a circle, a round complete o'.

22   morsing = tapping out a message, like Morse code.

24   Halt = halted; limping; nitric = nitric acid was traditionally used for embalming dead bodies; pun on 'night-trick', sex. Cf. 'A grief ago'.

26   Time is a foolish fancy = 'head and heart' try to dismiss the speaker's claims.

27–30   No, no, you lover skull ... Tells the stick 'fail' = head and heart, the 'skulls', are warned that time and sexuality cannot be deferred; descending hammer / Descends = cf. 'rainy hammer' in 'Before I knocked'; may also refer to aeroplanes landing; see 'hangar', l.29; entered honour = penetrative sex; Cadaver in the hangar = Cadaver is already telling the phallic joy-'stick' to 'fail' because of the speaker's failure to act; awareness of death prevents phallic take-off.

31–35   Joy is no knocking nation ... macadam = wordplay yields 'joy' from 'hangar' and 'stick' (the suppressed link term is 'joystick', used to control an aeroplane); the speaker tells his interlocutors what 'joy' is not (see above) before saying what it is; cancer's fusion = the overcoming of cancer (cancers *divide*, the opposite of 'fusion'); summer feather = metonymic for bird; Lit = alit; cuddled tree, the cross of fever = the cult of the Cross, symbol of death's 'fever'; man through macadam = macadam is a road surface (cf. the 'gravels' of the 'high-road' Cadaver lays in 'I, in my intricate image'); man's descent 'through', or as the son of ('Mac') Adam.

36, 41–45   tower dome, the tower ending ... leaning scene ... The actions' end = the tower symbolises isolation and cerebralism; here attributed to the 'masters' 'heart' and 'head' in their attempt to enforce conformity.

37–38   Joy is the knock of dust ... boxy shift = the realisation that death knocks for entrance at the moment of orgasm (from knock's sexual sense, as in 'knocking shop'); none of the properties listed in ll.31–35, joy (as sex) is wrenchingly paradoxical: on the one hand it intrudes into life as 'Cadaver's shoot / Of bud of Adam' (the penis), with ejaculation and conception as productive of death; on the other, 'Cadaver's shoot / Of bud' is regenerative, growth out of death, a green 'shoot' from the 'boxy shift' of the coffin we will all wear (and 'boxy shift' may also be the womb). 'Joy' is not just death knocking to enter, but a version of the Renaissance trope of the sexual act as a little death. This makes the 'shoot' a bud of Adam's stock, a spurt of Adam's semen, and also the gamekeeper's shot and the shot that kills him.

48   love for his trick = has no main verb; if the comma is seen as a stumbling block intended to trip us up, runners-readers, the sense is that we should accept death, 'Cadaver's hunger' for us, and the 'trick' of his dual nature.

50   kissproof world = a 'Kissproof' brand of lipstick was on the market in the early 1930s.

Should lanterns shine (p. 70)

Written autumn 1934, and probably among those sent to the journal early November 1934. *New Verse* published it in December 1935, with 'The hand that signed the paper' and 'I have longed to move away'; collected in *25P*.

The poem deals with an immature self, and its arrest between states, poised in midair like the ball of the final couplet. For Ralph Maud (2003), Stanza 1 tells how the 'boy of love' is able to adore a 'holy face' in the gloom, but unable to trust his attraction to 'the loved one' because he thinks she would wither up if light fell on her. The 'fall from grace' is a fear of 'getting attached to an unworthy person' (cf. 'In wasting one drop'). However, the initial concern is to pose a paradox – how can we trust reason if it is recommended by the irrational 'heart', or 'pulse'? The answer given is conventional; to answer the quickening pulse of desire by speeding up his 'actions' and 'defying time', so advancing more rapidly to maturity. Yet the terms in which this is presented – suggestive of Einstein's description of the way the universe appears as one approaches the speed of light – suggests relativity, not certainty; hence the speaker's hesitation, caught between an awareness of the need to advance, and the knowledge that childhood is not quite over.

1–2   the holy face / Caught in an octagon of unaccustomed light = in Holman Hunt's much-reproduced painting 'The Light of the World' (1851–53), Christ's face is lit from below by a faceted lantern.

3   wither up = cf. Browning's 'Bishop Bloughram's Apology': 'Under a vertical sun, the exposed brain / And lidless eye and disemprisoned heart / Less certainly would wither up at once / Than mind, confronted with the truth of him'.

4   Look twice before he fell from grace = reconsider commitment, or sexual intercourse.

5–8   The features ... expose an ancient breast = the speaker's belief that the 'holy face' of a lover will 'wither up' under the scrutiny of reason is likened to a scene in horror films in which a mummy's face disintegrates when exposed to daylight. There are Oedipal implications in loving a 'mummy' too old for a 'boy of love', and a Gothic whiff of necrophilia.

12–13   And, when it quickens ... lie level and the same = for Walford Davies (1972), this satirises 'a "Lawrentian" blood-programme ... in accents reminiscent of [Henry the Fifth's] harangue at Agincourt'.

14–15   time, the quiet gentleman / Whose beard wags in Egyptian wind = cf. the story 'The Mouse and the Woman': 'Consider now the old effigy of time, his long beard whitened by an Egyptian sun'.

16–19   I have heard many years ... reached the ground = a final admission of still being stuck in limbo. Before publication in *25P*, Vernon Watkins persuaded Thomas to 'cut the last two lines of the poem as it had appeared in *New Verse*. These two lines

Regard the moon, it hangs above the lawn;
Regard the lawn, it lies beneath the moon

seemed to me to echo Eliot, and indirectly Laforgue, and not to belong to the poem, whereas the previous two lines, with their hidden nuances, made a fine autobiographical ending.'

I, in my intricate image (p. 71)

Written October 1934–March 1935, along with (and possibly out of) 'When, like a running grave', with which it shares the Cadaver figure and a driving narrative style. Published in *New Verse* (August/September 1935) as 'A Poem in Three Parts'; collected in *25P*.

One of Thomas's most ambitious and daunting poems, this traces a narrative of growth, sea travel, symbolic death by drowning and rebirth, as part of a quest for selfhood and the secret of all natural life. However, large divergences in interpretation persist, and the meaning of some passages remains uncertain.

The 'image' of the 'I' of Part I is 'intricate', despite moving on just 'two levels' in a 'twin world' of matter and spirit, imaged as metal and ghost. It is an 'image of images' produced by the simultaneously burgeoning and blasting energy of process, driving the dual self into kinship with the natural world as it grows, and bringing about the creative androgynous 'fusion' the poet needs, but also the 'peril' of manhood, as sexual desire and worldly aspiration. The 'images' – projections of the 'I' – venture into the natural world, while the 'I' itself also becomes unrooted. In Part II the images embark on a longer journey, ascending to make macro- and microscopic (or 'scale') surveys of the operations of process in the world; they then descend to follow an oversea road laid down by death. A two-stanza aside arraigns death as 'instrumental', merely a means to the ends of process; but the images 'drown' nevertheless. Another aside negatively summarises the achievements of the 'I' and its images in an image of arrest.

Part III opens with the 'images' still 'suffering', but with the potential for rebirth. In a shift from the present tense to the subjunctive mood, they are exhorted to turn suffering into reincarnation, embrace the doubleness and singular 'ghost' they appear to have left behind, and submit to 'vision' and 'love'. They are reborn from the sea-womb and 'claw out' the 'crocodile' of death. Now, the previous history of thraldom to death is reviewed, in the past tense, and acknowledged as the 'god of beginning' – necessary to the images of final freedom to 'roar' and ascend. But since this, too, is cast in the past tense, the implication is that the psychodrama just traced is a continuous event. The stress throughout has been on a highly mutable and relativistic 'I', or self, projected on wildly varying 'scales', with the poem enacting a shifting, ceaseless process of poetic self-reinvention. It is, then, a poem about poetry, laying bare its procedures to ask how images represent 'images', and embodying Thomas's 'dialectical method' – even if the strain of reconciling these things is evident in the abrupt conclusion.

Form: three parts of six six-line stanzas, each stanza of four lines of twelve to fourteen syllables and two of five to eight syllables, differently arranged in each of the three parts. Seventy-two of the 108 lines are end-rhymed on vowel + letter l (with six exceptions); this was missed on first reading by Vernon Watkins, 'so subtle was the use of the variations and so powerful [the poem's] progress').

I

1 I . . . intricate image . . . two levels = a singular (rather pompous) 'I', resembling the numeral, is contrasted to binary and multiform conceptions of the self. The dual world of the creative mind is presented as a Hamlet-like speechifyer, integrated into physical reality, representing the poet's consciousness, and a protean unconscious energy which it tries to embody. The armour-clad ghost images this embodiment.

2 Forged in man's minerals = created, but a forgery – the poet is maker and faker; brassy orator = pushy; loud; metallic (from 'minerals') and machine-like; shallow. Cf. Auden's *The Orators*.

3 Laying my ghost in metal = 'ghost' is imagination, poetry and/or spirit. The image is of poetry being set in metal type in a printer's forme, rather as a spirit is exorcised, or 'laid', the first of several figurings of spirit with metal, as the most obdurate form of matter and externality. Pun on 'mettle'.

4 scales = *a* different perspectives; *b* balances (as used for weighing the souls of the dead according to Ancient Egyptian belief (see 'I have longed to move away'); also those of Libra, Thomas's birth sign; *c* musical scales (1.63); *d* climbs (1.74); *e* of the crocodile (1.91); on the double = on the 'twin world'; quickly.

5 My half ghost in armour = spirit-body, on 'two levels', with *Hamlet* reference: Tindall (1962) notes: 'half his ghost seems behind the "armour" of his persona and the other half behind type [the 'metal' of l.3]. Both shields are the "man-iron" of his indirect approaches'; death's corridor = life.

7 doom in the bulb = the seed of growth is equally the vehicle for decay and death (cf. 'The force that through the green fuse'); spring unravels = the season, but also clockwork (driven by a spring) running down.

8 her spinning-wheels = in Greek myth the Fates spun out the cloth of life and

cut it to its allotted span; colic season = babies suffer from colic; hints at the anxieties and immaturity lurking behind the 'brass'.

13   doom in the ghost = variant on 'doom in the bulb', suggests the spirit's knowledge that it is mortal because attached to the body.

14   Image of images = the 'intricate image'; an ultimate image, and a description of the poem itself; metal phantom = see note to ll.3 and 5.

16–18   My man of leaves = the images, with pun on 'leaves' of paper; bronze root = organic–metal collocation; twin miracle = the 'metal phantom' of the self, from a sexual 'fusion' of his female ('rose') and male ('motion') (cf. 'A grief ago').

20–21   A steeplejack tower . . . No death more natural = a phallic edifice 'railed' with the bones of those who have fallen from it; the death is the 'little death' of orgasm, here with anxieties about masturbation, which is 'natural', but immature.

22–24   Thus . . . The natural parallel = perhaps: because this natural sexual urge exists it can also lead to 'pictured' partners and the 'dead nuisance' of masturbation, a 'natural parallel' to the act of sex; anticipating 'damp dishonours', l.71.

22   shadowless man or ox, and the pictured devil = a notorious crux. The likeliest allusion is to Von Chamisso's *Peter Schlemihl* (1814), whose narrator sells his shadow to the Devil, is shunned by human society, and loses the love of his life: he seeks refuge in botanical discovery, travelling the world in a pair of seven-league boots, much like the adventuring images of the poem. It became an illustrated children's book, which may also account for 'pictured devil'. But there is no ox in the tale, and like other candidates for the reference, the full image-complex seems irresolvable; this may, of course, be partly the point.

25–30, 37–42   radical perspectival shifts.

25–30   My images stalk the trees . . . Hearing the weather fall = the 'images' are projected into the vegetable world, leaving the secret, timid self below; separation is signalled by distinct narratives and the initial sense that the gerundive 'Hearing' is the main verb for 'I', when it is 'mount'. This gives 'I' a temporary free-floating quality, anticipating how Part II will belong to the images. Vernon Watkins noted: 'It was characteristic of [Thomas's] taste at the time that his favourite lines in the poem were these [ll.28–30]'.

25   stalk = predatory advance; grass stalk.

28   wooden insect = wood(en)louse; insect in the 'tree of nettles'; the poem itself; tree of nettles = insect's-eye view of nettle; the Cross; cf. 'Altarwise' II.

29   glass bed of grapes = glass of wine; cloche; invalid self who remains behind

as the images depart; a 'glass bed' is one which is fragile (and devoid of privacy), and grapes are traditionally brought to those ill in bed.

31 invalid rivals = depending on the placing of the stress in 'invalid', rivals who are invalids or rivals who are not really rivals.

34 consumptives' terrace = the images resemble tuberculosis sufferers travelling south for their health; two farewells = because they still 'stride on two levels'.

35 Sail on the level = sail in a vertical plane; sail honestly.

35–36 departing adventure . . . sea-blown arrival = the beginning is simultaneously an ending; 'blown' refers to winds making sailing possible, but also means swollen in death following drowning. With wordplay on 'a rival'.

II

37 They = the images.

38 Twelve winds = the principal points of the compass; months of the year; white host at pasture = animals (perhaps sheep) feeding below the 'pinnacle'.

39 mounted meadows in the hill corral = 'mounted' is primarily 'climbed', but with 'corral' suggests horses; 'corral' also anticipates 'coral', l.83.

40 They see the squirrel stumble = disputing Henry Treece's claim that his poetry had 'no social awareness' in 1938, Thomas wrote: 'You are right when you suggest that I think a squirrel stumbling at least of equal importance as Hitler's invasions, murder in Spain, the Garbo-Stokowski romance, royalty, Horlicks . . . – but I *am* aware of these things as well'.

42 the windy spiral = ascending the dialectical 'spiral', the images look down on a process-driven world.

43 As they dive = the images descend into the sea, matching the ascent of the previous stanza.

44 cadaverous gravels = the cadaverous one (noun) lays a path ('gravels' as verb) over the sea; cf. 'When, like a running grave'.

45 seabear = seal.

47 petrol face = typical organic/inorganic collocation; from an iridescent slick on the 'highroad', possibly punning on 'petrel' for a marine equivalent; enemy = death.

49–60 (Death . . . under the conjured soil.) = this passage decries death, insofar as it brutally opens the eye to death in life, and views the child as something to be extracted from life by the grave-as-corkscrew; death is merely 'instrumental', an aspect of process.

49 instrumental = by the logic of pun, death must wield actual instruments, in this case surgical ones (it takes life, but, as understood by process, it heals too).

50 Splitting the long eye open = allusion to Luis Buñuel and Salvador Dalí's surrealist film *Un Chien Andalou* (1928), in which a woman's eye is slit with a cut-throat razor; play on eye/I.

50–51 the spiral turnkey . . . navel and nipple = agent (jailer) and instrument of death, the latter operating simultaneously alongside nurture, in the womb and at the breast, pulling the living into death like corks from a bottle.

52–53 neck of the nostril, / Under the mask = death as a surgeon, face masked between nose and neck, performing an operation; perhaps also a patient – one may be 'under' a mask and 'under' an anaesthetic.

53 they = death and its agents and 'instruments'.

54 antiseptic funeral = death and life-saving operation as a single event.

55–57 black patrol . . . monstrous officers . . . decaying army . . . sexton sentinel = death's agents, including clergy, viewed in terms drawn from WWI trench warfare; patrol = war image and play on 'petrol'.

58 cock-on-a-dunghill = emblem of false pride, boasting over something worthless.

59–60 Crowing to Lazarus . . . your saviour under the conjured soil = allusions to Jesus' raising of Lazarus in John 11:1–46, and Ecclesiastes, 12:7–8 ('Then shall the dust return to the earth . . . Vanity of vanities, saith the preacher; all is vanity'); those who present death negatively and falsely may decry life ('morning') to those dying/being born, but will receive a dusty answer.

61–66 As they drown . . . the tongues of burial = the images die; passing-bells ring out for them, they are imprisoned ('clapped in water') and a funeral service is read over them; with wordplay on 'diving bell' to create Thomas's drowned church image (cf. 'It is the sinners' dust-tongued bell').

63 Dead Sea scale = pun; 'Dead C', a musical scale appropriate for the dead.

67–72 (Turn the sea-spindle . . . The circular world stands still.) = an elaborate conceit, imagining the world as a phonograph. Land is the record, turned 'laterally' by the sea as its 'moon-turned [turn]-table' and central spindle, with lightning acting as a needle. The record it plays suggests the wet dreams of 'Our eunuch dreams'.

III

73   They = the images; undead water = the sea which drowned the images in Part II is womb- as well as tomb-like.

74–76   Come unto sea-stuck towers . . . the cell-stepped thimble = the imagery is increasingly that of sexual activity and conception; the images' voyage through death ends with their metamorphosis into the 'cell-stepped thimble' of an embryo 'scaling' and lodging itself in the 'fibrous' womb-wall.

77   double angel = perhaps the images united with the 'two levels' of the speaker; a gold coin (sense reinforced by 'lockers', l.78, a sailor's chest).

78   Sprout . . . like a tree on Aran = miraculously; the Aran Islands, off Ireland's west coast, are stony and treeless.

79   Be by your one ghost pierced = plea for 'they', the 'brass' and 'bodiless image', to unite; his pointed ferrule = brass tip, as on a teacher's pointing stick, symbolising the paternal authority of D. J. Thomas, and phallic symbol. The resurrection of the images is presented in terms of sex, conception and birth.

80–81   stick of folly / Star-set at Jacob's angle = 'stick' is also phallic (as in 'When, like a running grave'); the biblical reference is to Jacob's dream at Bethel of a ladder up to heaven (Genesis, 28:12; cf. 'Altarwise' II).

82   hophead = marijuana smoker; fuddled person.

83–84   the five-fathomed Hamlet on his father's coral . . . the iron mile = Hamlet-like Thomas junior, 'T(h)om(as) thumb', is submerged in D. J. Thomas's literary world; but sustained by what his father's bones have become and what he has made of them. This advances his still-limited 'vision' along the 'iron' road of poetic development.

85–90   Suffer the slash of vision . . . through the bed of eels = continues the foetal and incarnational imagery of the preceding two stanzas.

91–96   And in the pincers of the boiling circle . . . clawed out the crocodile = the narrator fights off death, imagined as the crocodile-headed devourer of souls in the Egyptian afterlife, and/or the armoured self, incapable of empathy or imagination, to achieve a violently imaged rebirth.

92   nicked in the locks of time = play on 'locked in the nick of time'.

97–106   Man was . . . mineral = 'was' makes clear that this is a description of past thraldom to death which the adventure of the images has overcome.

99   hourless houses = Egyptian pyramids and tombs of the dead.

102   All-hollowed = pun on all-hallowed; the Egyptian dead were 'hollowed', their internal organs removed, in the 'hallowing' mummification process.

103   Man was Cadaver's masker = man danced to the tune of death.

104   Windily . . . rotten fathom = man was dominated by the negative aspect of death; 'windily' is 'cowardly', as in 'And death shall have no dominion', since this version of death relies on fear.

107   god of beginning = the source of imaginative life ('images') is man's response to death, as 'Cadaver's masker', which by way of paradoxical compensation, denies mortality by creating 'heaven'.

108   heaven's hill = reused in 'Incarnate devil'.

Hold hard, these ancient minutes (p. 74)

Probably written early 1935; published in *Caravel* (March 1936), collected in *25P*.

In February 1935 Thomas temporarily retreated to Swansea from London. Most of his friends there had recently left for England. A past era – the 'ancient minutes' – had ended, and this poem seems to consider the 'hunt' of their future lives. The main conceit is time as a hunt across the landscape of the seasons, seen from April, 'the cuckoo's month' of maximum change. Syntax twists sense, but the addressees are the speaker's 'men' and 'children', and the object they are being urged to 'hold hard' to is 'the drive of time', riding *with* it. At l.6, however, time 'drives' them 'forth', hunted rather than hunters, as seen by the slip from '*county* man', whom time resembles in Stanza 1, and the '*country* children' of Stanza 2, whose realm appears to be 'summer' and 'game' (as play, not quarry). In Stanza 3 the scope widens from 'Glamorgan' as England summons them, as a 'four-stringed hill', violin-like, 'sets a rock alive'. 'Boulders' now unseat the huntsmen but also the hope of the 'children'. In Stanza 4 the unhorsed time, now a 'weather'-legged hound, continues to 'stalk' the children's faces 'with a tail of blood'. The final 'hold hard' is addressed to 'my county darlings', appropriate for 'my men, my children' (although 'county' was previously specific to hunters). But this poem, like others of the period, is as much about how an abstract 'sound of shape' makes a poem as it is a linear narrative.

1   Hold hard = the verb is completed, and its main object appears in l.3, 'to the drive of time'; the construction is repeated in l.10, l.18's 'hard-held', and l.22, so keeping a grip on every stanza; cuckoo's month = April (announcing spring).

2   folly = foolishness; an architectural conceit; Glamorgan's hill = the landscape resembles that of 'The Map of Love', a story containing the exhortation 'Hold hard, the children of love'.

5 vault = horse-jump (i.e. hedges and fences); tomb; ridings = hunt; internal county divisions (Glamorgan is divided into South, West and East).

7 sport = play, the hunt; quarry (as in l.24); the submerged link pun is 'game' (l.12).

8 seedy = sexually prime; degenerate (cf. 'I see the boys of summer').

9 fifth month = technically May, but April, if l.7's 'December' is counted; birds have flown = birds such as the cuckoo arrive, but the singing bird Thomas and his friends have flown the nest.

13–14 horns of England . . . four-stringed hill = England and Wales are analogous to the brass and string sections of an orchestra, tuning up like the earth in spring; snowy horsemen = winter; sound of shape = a favourite Thomas phrase.

14–15 four-stringed hill, / Over the sea-gut loudening = the country and the sea are set playing by the horns of 'England'.

18 hunter = one who hunts, and a type of horse suitable for riding to hunt.

19 scarlet = hunting pinks; the red of the Welsh dragon and the Union flag; bloody.

20 tail of blood = after their first hunt, a hunter has the blood of the dead fox applied to his or her face with the fox's brush.

21 harnessed valley = transposed epithet from horses; Glamorgan valley streams harnessed for power in the Industrial Revolution.

22–23 hawk descends . . . falling birds = the birds that 'have flown' are threatened by a bird of prey in an image suggesting hawking, another elite blood sport.

Now (p. 75)

Written in early 1935 (see note to 'How soon the servant sun'), published in *25P*.
    This was one of the two poems which, in May 1935, Vernon Watkins tried to persuade Thomas to drop from *25P* on the grounds that they presented 'a face of unwarrantable obscurity', and would give reviewers an excuse to dismiss the less difficult work in it. '"Let them have a bone", Thomas replied,' although, when asked about their meaning, 'he remarked of one of them that so far as he knew it had no meaning at all.' However, every negative in the poem opposes a negative, defeatist point of view, offering a qualified positive, as a Hamlet-like speaker adjures his near-suicidal inner self to overcome its negativity and direct its anger outwards. Suicide was a major concern in 1933–35, as rebutted in a letter to Pamela Hansford Johnson of 25 December 1933: 'But suicide is wrong; a man who commits suicide is like a man who longs for a gate to be opened and

who cuts his throat before he reaches the gate.'

Stanza 1 can be read: 'Now say no [you] dry lover and mine [explode; but also "belonging to me"] the base [in both senses] deadrock [play on 'bedrock'] of the self, and blow [let blossom] the flowered anchor of hope if he [the dry lover], drawn to the centre [tyrannical self-centredness], should hop in the dust and foolishly forsake the hardiness of [a generous] anger.' Stanza 2 declares death on 'The yes to death', and the suicide who would make his sister 'brotherless'. Stanza 3 rejects the idea of resurrection, and Stanza 4 imagines the cosmic disaster which would follow if the speaker gave in to self-destructive urges. In Stanza 5, the too-easy dismissal of his morbid and apocalyptic tendency is itself dismissed: 'Say no [to the attitude of] "a fig for the seal of fire and other gothic trappings associated with the doomy inner self"; both it and this speaking ego ["we"] make up the genuinely mystic, mysterious "me", just as much as things which are disposable and transitory.'

'Now' displays Thomas's love of pure 'sound of shape', yet it can be construed, and the syllables of the first four lines of each stanza add up to a pentameter. Part of its interest, therefore, lies in the degree to which it reflects Thomas's ambivalence towards different poetic modes; it is a tribute and a send-up, a parody of an avant-garde poem and the avant-garde poem as parody.

7 hardiness = capacity for enduring hardship, privation; courage, boldness.

14 handsaw = from *Hamlet*, 2:2, l.381, 'to know a hawk from a handsaw [heron]'. Thomas interprets it literally as a kind of saw, suggested by l.13's 'split'.

18 Yea the dead stir = both ghosts and resurrection are being denied.

20–21 He lying low ... upcasting from the fire = refers to the poisoning of Hamlet's father, in *Hamlet*, 3:2; the sense is to deny that the cock's cry warns the wandering ghost to return to the fires of Purgatory, or that it announces the resurrection, as the characters in the play surmise.

25 ball = the Earth.

26 mystic sun = the sun; Christ.

27 nought = vacuum of space; zero.

28 come-a-cropper = wordplay – the sun rides for a fall, and flowers will also be cropped; rider = invariably sexual in Thomas; hence, a reference to the sun's sexual penetration of flowers (and back to earlier 'flower'); a recognition of the prodigal excess of the natural world.

33 tapped ghost in the wood = fake spirit conjured up at spiritualist table-rapping séance (perhaps with play on drink, as in wine 'tapped from the wood'); another reference to the ghost in *Hamlet*.

How soon the servant sun (p. 76)

Probably written May 1935, published in *Programme* (23 October 1935); collected in *25P*.

With 'Now', this was one of two poems objected to by Vernon Watkins on the grounds of its obscurity when Thomas was assembling *25P* in 1936, and both were written in the same spirit of mocking tribute to avant-garde style (Thomas told Desmond Hawkins it was a 'stunt poem'). Its asides, opaque syntax and subject/object inversions are calculated to frustrate attempts to wrestle it into determinate meaning, but a growth-in-decay scenario can be traced.

Opening with the concessive clause (meaning 'as soon as'), Stanzas 1–2 state that once the sun/son and its agent, 'fog', can originate and set growing the speaker from the egg, the future ('Sir morrow') will 'tell' (enumerate) the rest of humanity. Attuned to 'serve the sun', in Stanza 3 the speaker questions a mouse-claw (mice symbolise sexual threat in early Thomas; cf. the story 'The Mouse and the Woman') and traps a mouse-like stone, uncaring whether the soil should protest that he is 'the biting man' (as a cat bites mice), and the dead 'inch out' of their graves. Stanzas 4 and 5 proclaim that when the speaker achieves a potency equivalent on his 'level' to that of the sun (a 'lamp' which generates 'clouds'), his phallic 'leg as long as trees' will cry and 'sweet hell' – sexual pleasure, even conception – will be able to 'Blast back the trumpet voice', answering the sun's affirmation of life with its own, creating life in the shroud-like flesh.

1   servant sun = because it serves the Earth and life (although it is 'lord' too).

2   Sir morrow = the future; mark = remark, take note.

3   time unriddle = straighten out, order time.

3–4   cupboard stone . . . bone = 'cupboard' with 'stone' is the womb and its body-making material, or flesh more generally (thus, the mouse of Stanza 3 is the 'long-tailed stone'). The lines allude to the nursery rhymes 'Old Mother Hubbard' and 'Humpty Dumpty'.

4–5   Fog . . . into meat = 'Fog' seems a partner of 'sun', energy which will 'trumpet' a dead bone into living flesh; if 'cupboard' is womb, 'bone' is also probably the penis.

6–7   Unshelve that . . . stand straight = the sun/time, using cupboard-womb and fog-bone-penis, unshelves the womb in order that the speaker can grow there, until he is born ('straight', unlike the curled foetus).

8–12   Sir morrow at his sponge . . . the sewing tides) = the future absorbs time as a sponge does water; nurse of giants = Ralph Maud (2003) glosses 'giants' as 'the human race in aggregate'; cut sea basin = womb; Swansea Bay; spring = water source; season; sewing tides = as if stitching sea and land together.

14 blows = blooms.

22 lord = the sun, to whom this final sentence is addressed.

24 Two heels . . . seed = the semen from a pair of testicles 'stamped' on the womb.

27 Erect . . . in the shroud = simultaneously creative and destructive, penis and womb-tomb images of sexual activity.

28–29 Invisible . . . long as trees = the penis' 'leg'-like appearance in arousal is usually 'invisible' or 'stump'-like.

30–32 This inward sir . . . womb-eyed = euphemisms and epithets for the penis.

34 trumpet voice = as in Stanza 1, a creative paean or fiat. This last stanza is a line shorter than its predecessors.

Do you not father me (p. 78)

A typescript version of September 1934 in three ten-line stanzas is among the Pamela Hansford Johnson papers at Buffalo. Revised in July 1935, and published in the *Scottish Bookman* (October 1935); collected in *25P*.

References to Cross, Christ and a shoreline suggest that the speaker is a Thomas-Christ-everyman figure, and that this is another poem of authorial isolation, in which the tower symbolises the writer and language, as in 'Ears in the turrets hear', with a Freudian take on family relationships added to the mix. As 'ascending boy' the speaker, at once father and sibling of his own children, overthrows and becomes his father; along the way, acceptance of the speaker's tower-self, as an 'erected crime', brings 'stain' and 'sin' to mother and sister. A phallic tower is simultaneously *raised* and *razed* by a 'stroke', both sexual and destructive; innocence is 'felled' as the penis is punningly erected. In Stanza 3 the assertions of Stanzas 1 and 2 are overthrown as the speaker is identified with the phallus, which he learns is as subject as anything else to the creative-destructive forces of process. Shock at this informs the near-accusation which opens Stanza 4, and the final query, which receives the parental answer that the speaker should outgrow his view of himself as centre of their universe and achieve autonomy, given that religious certainties no longer obtain and love and death 'lie all unknowing' of Christ.

2–6 tall tower's sake . . . tall turrets = cf. 'Ears in the turrets hear', 'Especially when the October wind' and 'When, like a running grave', in which the turret/ tower is one of the body, the writing self and of language, but also 5 Cwmdonkin Drive.

18 sacked the children's town = in Freud, the Oedipal struggle ends with the destruction of the (male) child's unproblematic unity with the mother.

19 Abraham-man = a beggar from Bedlam allowed out to beg; an erection.

22 wooden folly = a folly is an architectural caprice, often a tower, with no practical function (see 'Hold hard'); to be 'wood' is slang for having an erection.

24 wrack = seaweed; wreck (of the tower/penis).

29 widdershin = to go widdershins is to turn in an anticlockwise direction, as the Earth does upon its axis.

32 grave sin-eater = a sin-eater was someone paid to eat or drink food in a ritual which involved them taking on the sins of a dying or dead person, allowing them to rest after death. The greatest 'sin-eater' of all, because he is said to have 'eaten' the 'grave', or death itself, is Christ.

Grief thief of time (p. 79)

The poem's two stanzas derive from a revision of *N4* 'Five', 'Grief thief of time, crawls off' of 26 August 1933, beside which Thomas wrote 'Written and copied in later, August 1935. Glen Lough. Donegal', and *N4* 'Eighteen', Part II of 'Jack of Christ'. Published in *Comment*, February 1934; collected in *25P*.

By dropping the commas in the opening line of the original, Thomas deliberately set himself the task of creating a context which made sense of the change. In Stanza 1, time has to become the thief of grief, reversing the original scenario, and is said to 'steal off' the 'sea-halved faith' of youth (when time was briefly outfaced). However, the sense that 'thief of time' *is* a subordinate clause remains, the reader feeling that grief, as well as time, is a subject of the sentence. Thomas's change enacts more faithfully the argument of the original – that the old forget youth's griefs – and presents more forcefully their 'stumble' towards idealised, personified memory, the 'she' who 'lies' with the 'grief thief' time in a bed ominously like the grave.

In Stanza 2 a similar effect is created: what feels as if it ought to be a subjunctive exhortation – that the fathers should 'let' the 'crook' escape – actually states that they are allowing him to escape, although the more 'natural' sense seems to lurk, as in Stanza 1. The argument overturns that of 1; the fathers allow time as 'grief thief' to escape because, as the first version puts it, 'Grief is the price of peace', and must be confronted and accepted, not evaded. The thefts of the 'time-faced crook', described in masturbatory terms, may seem a grievous waste of time, but they paradoxically also 'free the twin-boxed grief'. Rightly understood, our time-bound sexual nature is the source of the mystery of the human condition and its metaphysical dimension. That mystery, symbolised by 'a rainbow's sex', cannot ultimately be rationalised away within the 'graveward gulf' of life.

1 Grief thief of time = 'grief' is an adjective of 'time', with the sense that

time is grief-making and steals one's time, in particular one's youth; lack of punctuation creates ambiguity; grief can be the thief of time, time the thief of grief.

2   moon-drawn grave = appositional phrase qualifying the thief as the sea, but also the womb / tomb; seafaring years = the years of adventurous youth, from life as a sea voyage (cf. 'I, in my intricate image', 'Altarwise', etc.). The sense is 'Grief . . . crawls off . . . with the seafaring years.'

7–8   castaways / Riding the sea light = idealised figures from the past.

10   albatross = bad luck, a curse.

12   stumble bedward where she lies = the old move towards the final sleep of death and the 'she' who personified their own eulogising of the 'high time' of their youth.

14   timelessly lies loving with the thief = 'she' embraces time outside of time's constraints; i.e. in the grave.

15   time-faced crook = time, as a kind of seedy, sexual thief, is allowed to get away with his masturbatory depredations because, in the long perspective of process, grief must be accepted and 'All shall remain'.

17   swag of bubbles in a seedy sack = sperm in the testes, contained in the scrotum, through masturbation or nocturnal emission, from mature sexual activity.

18   stallion grave = the grave has a legendary sexual virility, sex and death driving on life as part of process.

19   Bull's eye the outlaw . . . eunuch crack = shoot down ('bull's eye' as centre of a target) the 'she', or idealising tendency, through masturbation ('bull's eye' as the glans revealed by retracting the foreskin and 'eunuch crack' as a vagina guarded by emasculation and/or its imaginary nature).

20   twin-boxed grief = doubly suppressed; sperm in testicles.

21   No silver whistles = governed by 'let', l.15.

23–24   bites of snakes / And the undead eye-teeth = the 'swag' stolen by time will eventually bite back, so it is not worth pursuing him; 'eye-teeth' is proverbial for something extremely rare, while 'undead' is deathly and life-creating.

25   third eye = a mystical invisible eye which provides perception beyond ordinary sight; hence, do not attempt to 'probe' these secrets with mumbo-jumbo (the main verb is 'let', l.15); rainbow's sex = riddling, but also suggesting hermaphroditism.

Incarnate devil (p. 80)

'Thirty' in N3, entitled 'Before We Sinned' and dated 16 May 1933. Thomas reduced it by half for publication in the *Sunday Referee*, 11 August 1935, where it was titled 'Poem for Sunday'; collected in *25P*.

The poem presents a dualist world contested by God and the Devil, in which God is not yet omnipotent and the Devil may triumph: the final stanza is equally divided between the two. This mitigates humanity's burden of responsibility for original sin; how could it have opposed Satan, given his power in the world? 'Incarnate' also links Satan to Christ, and he seems to be more a trickster or Prometheus-figure than the traditional Father of Lies, who 'sting[s] awake' the circle of time and history which God would foreclose, acting as a catalyst for human agency and self-understanding. As elsewhere, Thomas exposes a God who claims to be merciful, but punishes man for his own negligence.

4   bearded apple = a Magritte-like image that blends patriarchal authority, Edenic apple and sexual temptation (the 'beard' on the 'apple' is pubic as well as facial). If sex destroys childhood innocence during 'the shaping-time' of adolescence, it is not a devil but 'bearded' Jehovah who falsely defines sexuality as hell. Destroying the possibility of innocence in sexuality, this deity then hypocritically gives himself credit for saving sinners from the clutches of the 'devil' he has invented.

5   fiddling = God 'fiddles' or manipulates while Eden is destroyed by the Devil, as Nero is said to have fiddled while Rome burned; also with the sense that God 'fiddles' the outcome of the Fall.

6   played down pardon = God provides salvation, in the form of Christ; however, he 'plays it down' in the sense of saying nothing about forgiveness in the Old Testament.

7   we = humanity.

10   eastern tree = tree of the Knowledge of Good and Evil, but the play on 'eastern'/Easter also makes it the Cross.

13   secret guardian = God, as hidden and secretive (adjectival sense of 'secret'), and as one with a secret (noun sense) – that he is a bigger 'fiddler' than Satan, using him in a plan that involves damning humanity, and then engineering its redemption by sacrificing his son.

A grief ago (p. 80)

Dated January 1935 in a typescript held at Austin; published in the Oxford-based journal *Programme*, 23 October 1935; collected in *25P*.

This poem was praised on its appearance by Edith Sitwell, although Thomas took issue with her reading (see below). Its obscurity meant that Ralph Maud (1963) took it as exemplifying Thomas's desire to 'distance the intimate', later claiming it was 'not about sex [but] DNA'. Yet the poem is also notable for its rueful tenderness, a sense of the lover as Other, and its concern with the emotional fall-out from sex.

Stanza 1 establishes a post-coital mood of sadness, and initiates a train of elaborate, euphemistic images of sexual activity, touching on outcomes of separation, sadness and possible pregnancy; Stanza 2 images the embryo itself; Stanza 3 introduces the themes of genetic 'heritage' involved in conception and its inevitable outcome in death (new life is destined for the grave); Stanza 4 asks who, after all these distancing, post-coital qualifications, the 'she' might be (now 'holding me', not just being held). Stanza 5, overcoming the speaker's fear of children as a 'plague', 'tell[s] her' that her future lies in reproduction. There is a turn in the poem from the solipsism of the first three stanzas to a recognition of the priority of the female over the male, in terms of the future of the human race.

1 grief = sexual act (cf. also 'Grief thief of time').

2 the fats and flower = female body and genitals.

3 lammed = hit (US slang).

5 cementing = pun: 'semen'-ting.

5–8 Various euphemisms and images for intercourse.

6 Rose maid and male = cf. 'rose and male motion' in 'I, in my intricate image'.

7 masted venus = pun on 'mastered', by the phallic 'mast'; reference to Botticelli's 'The Birth of Venus'; cf. 'My hero bares his nerves'.

9 grief = sexual partner, personification of the sexual act.

10 A chrysalis unwrinkling on the iron = literally, an insect chrysalis dropped on to a hotplate; metaphorically, the embryo unfolding on the wall of the womb after 'grief'. 'Iron' may be a phallic 'shooting iron', as in US slang.

11 fingerman = one fingering the trigger of his 'shooting iron'; also a member of a criminal gang who identifies the victim to his accomplices.

11–12 leaden bud / Shot through the leaf = ejaculate 'shot' past the leaf-like hymen; the embryo itself.

13 Was who was = (she) was (the one) who was.

13–16 the rod the aaron / Rose cast to plague . . . Housed in the side = Aaron was Moses' deputy, whose 'rod' (sceptre) conjured up the plagues of Egypt (including one of frogs) as Pharaoh reneged on his promises to free the Israelites; at one point, 'cast' down before Pharoah, it turns into a serpent (Exodus 7:9).

God also makes Aaron's rod burst into flower in Numbers, and the 'aaron / Rose' evokes the Rose of Sharon of the Song of Solomon. In *The Mabinogion*, the mother of Dylan ap Tôn is *Arianrhod*. The main sense is of a phallic rod that 'rose' serpent-like in sex to flower and cast the 'plague' of the 'frog'-like embryo.

17–20 she . . . Tugged through = subject and main verb of stanza.

18 exodus a chapter from the garden = post-coital state likened to the expulsion from Eden (Exodus is the book of the Bible after Genesis), prompting consideration of its outcomes – conception, birth and mortality.

19 lily's anger = the angel Gabriel bears a lily to Mary at the Annunciation, making it a figurative phallus; here it has 'branded' the ring of the womb, but also her marriage 'ring' from Joseph.

20–21 Tugged through the days . . . the wars of pardon = after sex, 'she' pulled at the genetic-psychic links to her forebears, the 'ropes of heritage' which signify feuds and 'wars of pardon' for the sin in Eden.

22–24 On field and sand . . . Engraving going = the puffing cherubs, denoting the winds at the twelve points ('triangles') of compass roses on old maps: the 'cherub' winds 'engrave' (make go to her grave) with their blowing on waste and fertile soils. This realisation of mortality is the poem's turning point, leading to the questions opening Stanza 4 and consideration of the future of 'she'.

26 The people's sea drives on her = the genetic inheritance of the population, or race, drives women on in their tasks of gestation and birth.

27 Drives out the father from the caesared camp = the 'father' (the male penis) is expelled from the 'camp' of the womb after sex/conception; there is also a suggestion of popular resistance to dictatorial takeover.

28–32 The dens of shape . . . Rise before dark = the womb, where the embryo is given shape; the grammatical sense of this clause is completed in the last line of the stanza.

31 The country-handed grave boxed into love = Edith Sitwell's review of *25P*, in the *Sunday Times*, 15 November 1936, glossed this as 'that simple nurse of grief, that countryman growing flowers and corn'. But Thomas demurred in a 1938 letter to Henry Treece: 'My image, principally, did not make the grave a gentle cultivator but a tough possessor, a warring and complicated raper rather than a simple nurse or an innocent gardener. I meant that the grave had a country for each hand, that it raised those hands up and "boxed" the hero of my poem into love. "Boxed" has the coffin and the pug-glove [boxing glove concealing a hand illegally wearing knuckle-dusters] in it.' The countries are those of the lovers' two sets of ancestors; the grave, or threat of mortality (being 'boxed' in their coffins), is what, like a boxer, bullies the lovers into bed.

33 night = death.

34 nitric shape . . . time and acid = image of death (nitric acid as embalming fluid) sexually 'leaping' on the lover; pun on 'night trick'.

35–36 suncock cast / Her bone to fire = rooster announcing individual death, as Day of Judgement.

37–38 Let her inhale her dead . . . Draw in their seas = let her draw on her ancestors and her genetic inheritance, by means of sexual intercourse.

39–40 So cross her hand . . . close her fist = thwart her personal fate as individual (the 'hand' of death which life deals us all) by resurrecting the ancestral/genetic past in her children ('eyes' as a characteristic sign of inherited family likeness), with 'grave' a reminder that they will also die; gipsy = fortune-tellers traditionally ask their clients to 'cross my palm with silver'; the speaker asks his lover to close her hand over the silver (her children), and thus secure her future.

Altarwise by owl-light (p. 82)

Probably begun Christmas 1934, since I and II are Nativity poems, and completed roughly a year later. Parts I–VII were published in *Life and Letters Today* as 'Poems for a Poem' in December 1935, and VIII–X appeared in *Contemporary Poetry and Prose* in May and July 1936. All ten appeared as the final work in *25P*.

'Altarwise' is, famously, Thomas's most obscure poem, its avant-garde nature signalled in his interim title for it, 'Work in Progress' (James Joyce's working title for *Finnegans Wake*). As late as mid-1936, he was unsure whether it was complete, but he told Denys Kilham Roberts that its parts were both 'entirely self-contained' and linked by 'a certain obscure narrative'. There is a general consensus that the 'obscure narrative' interweaves the poet's life (birth, growth, acquisition of language, onset of religious doubt, writing, growth of sexual awareness, etc.) with rough equivalents from the life of Jesus and other biblical and mythological personages. It begins with a Nativity (I) and infancy (II), III backtracks to the Incarnation, IV can be paralleled by Christ's questioning of the doctors in the Temple (Luke, 2:46–47), fasting and preaching occur in V and VI, respectively, VII mentions the Lord's Prayer, VIII is a crucifixion, IX a burial, and X includes the Gospel and St Peter. Thomas's 'young dog' persona in this sense emerges as the re-membered heir to the 'castrated Christ' of official religion, which Thomas describes in letters of the time. However, one must be wary: the most notorious case of over-ingenious speculation in Thomas studies is Elder Olson's 1954 attempt to tie 'Altarwise' to the legend of Hercules. Attempts to trace a coherent record of a struggle for, or loss of, religious faith come up against the poem's rapid tonal and thematic shifts, from profane to devout, flippant to momentous, and its unsignalled switches in speaker. On this issue, for example, several commentators take the resurrected Christ, who speaks the final couplet of I, to continue as the narrator of II; one believes he also speaks III; while Clark Emery (1962) feels he narrates the whole of the rest of the sequence.

Such lack of agreement on fundamentals indicates that, as with other experimental poems of the period, the undecidability of 'Altarwise' is structural, and represents a calculated testing of the limits of poetic meaning creation. The reader is deliberately teased into thought by both absence of overarching sense and local superabundance of meaning (generated via pun, reversible syntax, ambiguous punctuation and blurring of agents and events). In this sense, it should be thought of less as a poem about some*thing*, or by some*one*, than as the vehicle of a 'trickster' principle, driven by an 'outlaw' logic, as argued by Don McKay (1985/86). Thomas is to be regarded as a bricoleur, an inspired cut-and-paster, not a narrator in the normal sense, the poem seen as carnivalesque rather than devotional, flaunting its 'illusion and flamboyance', as 'each item declares itself, like an item in a Mardi Gras parade, momentous and momentary'. The 'items' may tease us to construct narratives, but these are almost immediately problematised (and the 'explanations' I offer below are no exception). The basic purpose of this provisional, decentred texture is to pull the timeless world of 'mythic pattern' into the flow of time, neutralising its imperatives, and eroding fossilised prejudice and authority.

Writing to Glyn Jones about 'Altarwise' in December 1936, Thomas defended its toughness: 'I'm not sorry that, in that Work in Progress thing, I did carry "certain features to their logical conclusion". It had, I think, to be done; the result had to be, in many of the lines and verses anyway, mad parody; and I'm glad that *I* parodied those features so soon after making them, & that I didn't leave it to anyone else.' Even this is too self-deprecatory, however, and should not be taken to detract from Thomas's extraordinary achievement of pushing one strand of his early poetry to a brilliant, proto-postmodernist culmination.

Form: ten inverted, pararhymed Petrarchan sonnets (the sestet precedes, rather than following, the octet, as in Donne's 'Loves Growth').

I (p. 82)

Christ appears in the tomb (but also womb and/or life), becoming Abaddon/ Adam. Ambiguous syntax blurs him and the speaker, allowing the 'dog' to both issue 'from' his 'fork' (crotch) and bite the mandrake 'from' it, midwife and castrator. Now dead, and risen, Christ 'scrapes' the speaker's cradle and declares his immanence in, and kinship with, the world and its primal coordinates of sex and death. The inter-identification of figures, rapidly shifting and informing (on) each other, sets the pattern for the poem. As Christ becomes the globe, he initiates the imagery grid and map, latitude and longitude which will also recur throughout, as 'cross-bones', ladders, rigging, antipodes, seasons, poles and 'atlas'. Cf. Donne's 'The crosse': 'thou spiest out Crosses in small things; / Look up, thou seest birds rais'd on crossed wings; / All the globes's frame, and spheares, is nothing else / But the Meridians crossing Parallels'.

1 Altarwise by owl-light = transposes 'altar light' and 'wise owl'. Christ *a* faces an altar; *b* is becoming an organised religion; and *c* is 'wise to' this fact; owl-light = dusk; cf. John Webster, *The Duchess of Malfi*: 'I'll go hunt the badger by owl-light'; halfway-house = *a* this world, between heaven and hell; *b* this life, between two unknowns; *c* the womb/tomb. Cf. Hopkins' 'The Half-Way House'.

2 The gentleman = Christ; furies = the passions which Christ-as-human acquired at his incarnation.

3 Abaddon ... Adam = Abaddon is death, the Angel of the Bottomless Pit in Revelation 9:11, and definitely 'a bad 'un'; hang-nail = torn fingernail; mortality, brought about by Adam's sin; nails by which Christ hung from the cross; cracked from Adam = active; '[that] cracked [itself]': (Abaddon) broke away from Adam as a result of Christ's 'hangnail' sacrifice; adjectivally, 'Abaddon in the hangnail [flesh] [who] was derived from Adam [and his sin]'; 'Abaddon in the hangnail [flesh] derived from Adam [human race, including Christ]'. Allowing for all these meanings at once, the line stresses death *and* redemption from it.

4–6 And, from his fork ... Bit out the mandrake = the genitals of Christ/Adam/Abaddon are bitten off, recalling Thomas's phrase in letters of this time, 'a castrated Christ'; fork = as noun, a groin; as verb, the 'forking' which produced the 'dog'; dog among the fairies = *a* Thomas as journalist chasing stories; *b* a heterosexual poet among the homosexual ones of the metropolitan literary world; *c* a trickster principle; *d* Christ ('dog' reversed to 'god').

5 atlas-eater = *a* the spread of Christianity makes Christ world-devouring; *b* the young Thomas wished to devour the poetic world; *c* 'atlas' is the first cervical vertebra supporting the skull of the child in the womb; *d* 'small atlas' is a paper size; jaw for news = cf. Thomas's response to Edith Sitwell's interpretation:

> [It] seems to me very vague and Sunday-journalish. She says the lines refer to 'the violent speed and the sensation-loving, horror-loving craze of modern life'. She doesn't take the literal meaning: that a world-devouring ghost creature bit out the horror of tomorrow from a gentleman's loins. A 'jaw for news' is an obvious variation of 'a nose for news', & means that the mouth of the creature can taste already the horror that has not yet come or can sense it coming, can thrust its tongue into news that has not yet been made, can savour the enormity of the progeny before the seed stirs, can realise the crumbling of dead flesh before the opening of

the womb that delivers the flesh to tomorrow. What is this creature? It's the dog among the fairies, the rip and cur among the myths, the snapper at demons, the scarer of ghosts, the wizard's heel-chaser. This poem is a particular incident in a particular adventure, not a general, elliptical deprecation of this 'horrible, crazy, speedy life.'

6   with tomorrow's scream = the bitten-out mandrake/future progeny of the castrated genitals intuits the horror of the future; mandrake = plant with a man-shaped root; it was reputed to utter a deadly scream when uprooted, so dogs were used for the purpose.

7   penny-eyed = pennies placed to close the eyelids of the dead; gentleman of wounds = Christ.

8   Old cock = *a* informal salutation to a male friend: *b* the penis; *c* the Holy Spirit; *d* weathercock; nowheres and the heaven's egg = God is born from an egg in several mythologies.

9   bones unbuttoned = sepulchral and sexual ('bones' as slang for erections released from an 'unbuttoned' fly-hole).

10   windy salvage = the world ripe for salvation; salvation on the windy hilltop of Golgotha; religion as 'windy' (cowardly) rubbish; one leg = like the Cross, but also the piratical trickster Long John Silver (echoing 'long world's gentleman').

11   Scraped at my cradle = Christ appears, crucified and castrated, to the infant speaker.

12   night of time = in the womb; darkness occurring at Christ's death on the Cross; Christward shelter = Bethlehem; the speaker's birthplace.

13–14   I am the long world's gentleman . . . Cancer = spoken by Christ; share my bed = he declares that his bed – the place of sex, birth and death – is the world, spanning opposites of time, space and experience: the winter and summer solstices, northern and southern hemispheres, life and death (Capricorn = the goat [lust and birth]; Cancer = the crab [illness and death]).

II (p. 82)

The newborn child grows up in a death-figured universe, identified with the world as a 'planet-ducted pelican' whose 'circles' are its lines of longitude and latitude. This cartographical image introduces the image of the child ascending a ladder of life made of Abaddon's rungs athwart Adam's 'verticals', New Testament aspiration 'rung'-ed with Old Testament damnation. Narrated by

Thomas-Christ, this sonnet critiques the human predicament created by God the Father, which betrays both Christ, man and, crucially, the Christlike potential in humans. The 'agent' is also this Thomas-Christ composite, 'hollow' because forced to follow a preset schema. In the last four lines Jesus's assurance that God the Father cares for each human being is said to be subject to process, here negative, as faith's 'groundworks' are overgrown and neglected.

1 Death is all metaphors = if man is metaphorically a microcosm for all things, all stories of man take death's shape and all metaphors are tainted by human mortality.

2–3 The child that sucketh long ... planet-ducted pelican of circles = links planets and suckling breasts. Traditionally the pelican was thought to suckle her young with her blood if no other food was available, and hence symbolic of Christ's sacrifice.

4 Weans on an artery the gender's strip = reverses 'wean *off*'; symbolically, Thomas-Christ is suckled on the blood (from an 'artery') later to be shed on the Cross, the latter growing the 'gender's strip' (genitals) previously bitten off.

5 short spark = coition; shapeless country = the womb; Wales.

7–9 The horizontal cross-bones ... You ... Rung = 'rung' is a verb, 'to make rungs for', applicable to 'the verticals', the ladder's uprights (perhaps the 'long stick' rising from the cradle in l.6); with pun on the skull-and-crossbones pirate flag.

8 You = probably God; cavern over the black stairs = dubious location; '*back* stairs' is a place for shady comings and goings and dirty deals, made here by God in setting up Christ as sacrifice.

9 verticals of Adam = appositive to 'horizontal cross-bones' of l.7.

10 manned by midnight = Jacob's ladder (below) crewed by darkness rather than angels; Jacob = verb: '(you) make ascend (the 'cross-bones')' as on Jacob's ladder (Genesis 28:12). God tells Jacob that the ladder symbolises his covenant with his chosen people, but here the ladder of Adam's skeleton is made of Abaddon's deathly 'cross-bones', and God is untrustworthy.

11–12 Hairs of your head ... Are but the roots of nettles and of feathers = God's love (cf. Matthew 10:29) simply means being returned to the natural cycle: as Thomas told Pamela Hansford Johnson in November 1933: 'The greatest description I know of our "earthiness" is to be found in John Donne's Devotions, where he describes man as earth of the earth, his body earth, his hair a wild shrub growing out of the land'; hollow agent = contradiction in terms; challenges the claim that God gives us free will.

13 groundworks = the foundation of human existence; pavement = the 'place that is called the Pavement' is where Christ was condemned by Pilate (John 19:13); ironic emblem of banal suburban modernity inhabited by 'the Rimbaud of Cwmdonkin Drive', Thomas himself.

14 hemlock = poisonous and 'hollow'-stemmed; wood of weathers = the ever-changing world.

III (p. 83)

Christ's sacrifice, as Lamb of God, is contrasted with the misdeeds of Adam, the 'wether', who 'horned it down' in being cuckolded by the serpent with Eve. What follows sounds like Christ describing his Incarnation; however, this occurred in spring, not winter, and the 'rip' seems more the 'rip and cur' of the young dog Dylan. This may be a play with the fact that Thomas's own 'incarnation' occurred not long after Christmas, the time of the Nativity, and a conflation of the two. Spring chimes 'twice' because on a global scale it does so – in southern and northern hemispheres – within a single year. The 'black ram' suggests Thomas as old Adam: he once opined that 'Christ was always the white sheep among the black, the superior, the natty gent in a tramps' ward'.

1 First . . . on knocking knees = Christ (Thomas) as toddler.

2 three dead seasons = trimesters of gestation.

3 wether = a bellwether is the castrated ram that leads a 'flock' of 'horns', or sheep; also the bad *weather* Adam created by his sin.

4 tree-tailed worm = Satan, twined around the tree of the Knowledge of Good and Evil.

5 Horned down = because Adam had cuckold's horns; also a sexual act.

7 Rip of the vaults = Christ as the harrower of hell and redeemer of the dead Adam; the (Dylan) speaker as product of the dead, with sense of the womb as tomb, and play on 'R.I.P.'; marrow-ladle = genetic material doled out by his ancestors.

8 Out of the wrinkled undertaker's van = your genetic material comes from those carried off in an 'undertaker's van', to rest in 'vaults' before you are born.

9 Rip Van Winkle = character in Washington Irving's tale of that name, who fell asleep for twenty years (from 'Van', 'wrinkle' and 'rip').

10 Dipped me = archaic reflexive form: 'I dipped myself'; breast-deep = Satan is 'breast-deep' in the ice of Lake Cocytus, the lake of traitors, in Dante's *Inferno*;

descended bone = in a hereditary sense; the 'descended bodies' in Lake Cocytus.

11   The black ram = play on 'black sheep'; the ram ('wether') is alone because the rest of the flock have been slaughtered.

13–14   We rung . . . and twice spring chimed = ironic; the 'rung' of the skeleton-and-Jacob's ladder of II evokes the longitude-latitude 'laddering' of the globe of I.

IV (p. 83)

The child Dylan-Christ-everyman asks the awkward questions young children put to adults. In retrospect, as the parentheses suggest, he realises they are deformed, and could have had no answers; they merely 'nag' the 'wounded whisper', Christ, and denote intellectual presumption. Even so, their bent question marks challenge straight ways of thinking, and their curiosity is a necessary aspect of the life process. Christ answers in the last six lines; demonstrating his power of penetrating appearances, he describes love in terms of the young embryo seeing those he will love after birth projected on to the wall of the womb, beings external to himself and his 'islandic egoism'.

4   My shape of age = my body in the shape it had reached at that age; an aside by the older narrator commenting on his younger self.

5   sixth of wind = in Dante's *Inferno*, one of Satan's six wings beats continuously to keep Lake Cocytus frozen.

6   (Questions are hunchbacks . . . poker marrow) = childish questions are bent compared to the straightness of poker-like adult ones.

7   What of . . . your acres? = do you have a man (in you) who is straight and upright? (But bamboo is also a 'hollow agent').

8   Corset . . . crooked lad? = Christ asks: should I straighten out (fear of) death for someone 'crooked' like you?

9–10   Button your bodice . . . shroud = however his interlocutor wraps up the 'hump of splinters' (bones in the grave/womb), Christ claims his vision will pierce it.

11–14   Love's a reflection . . . cutting flood = love is like recognising faces you saw long ago, in the womb, projected film-like against the womb-wall, which is food for the embryo; mushroom features = like a face seen in close-up, or an embryo's face. Cf. 'Then was my neophyte'.

12   Stills = freeze-frame pictures from a movie.

13–14   Once . . . the cutting flood = continues the image of film 'stills'; the amniotic 'flood' takes you from the womb-'wall' and its prenatal pictures (play on arc lamps in film projectors and the embryo-as-Ark on its waters); cutting the umbilical cord is analogous to an editor 'cutting' a film.

V (p. 84)

The filmic close of IV, and a pun on its 'poker' (as the card game), yields an opening scenario from a cowboy film; the archangel Gabriel appears as a saloon card sharp who 'trumps up' a dubious royal flush, and is followed by a drunken Bible-thumping evangelist or 'fake gentleman', a perverted version of Christ, who speaks l.5. The 'fake gentleman', the speaker, or both, may speak from l.6 on; the narrative fuses the trials of a number of seemingly incompatible figures, discussing, and demonstrating, the craft of illusion – sleights of hand (card sharping) and tongue (tall tales in religion and the Wild West). The appearance of Virgil also touches on the subject of poetry, suggesting the 'sirens' of writing, as well as of sexual desire.

1 the windy West = Wales; the Wild West; Gabriel = archangel who brings Mary news of the Annunciation.

2 Jesu's sleeve = where cards may be hidden by a card sharp; trumped up = *a* to trump the cards of other players; *b* to fabricate or forge; *c* to sound the Day of Judgement (one of Gabriel's tasks); king of spots = king of spades; the Devil.

3 sheath-decked jacks = new decks of cards are sheathed in a wrapper, but 'sheath' is also a condom and 'jack' is a phallus.

4 the fake gentleman in suit of spades = gravedigger, or death; with pun on 'suit' (in clothing and cards) and 'spades' (in card suits and for digging).

6 Byzantine Adam = the 'old [complex] Adam', rising like the penis at night.

7 For loss of blood I fell = detumescence; Ishmael's plain = Ishmael was Abraham's son by Hagar, sent into hungry exile after the birth of Isaac. This Ishmael morphs into the narrator of *Moby Dick*.

8 milky mushrooms = like the manna with which God fed the Israelites; hunger = perhaps Christ's, during his fast and confrontation with Satan.

10 Jonah's Moby snatched me by the hair = in *Moby Dick*, Queequeg pulls Tashtego back from the whale's mouth by his hair.

11 Cross-stroked . . . frozen angel = i.e. he swam to the angel; 'cross-stroking' the salt (licentious) Adam reverses masturbatory stroking. Cf. Donne's 'The crosse': 'Swimme, and at every stroake, thou art thy Crosse'; the frozen angel = Satan, frozen in the lowest circle of hell. Cf. III, ll.13–14.

12   Pin-legged on pole-hills = crucified; medusa = one of the Gorgons of Greek myth, whose fearsome appearance turned those who gazed on her to stone.

13   By waste seas where the white bear quoted Virgil = in Anatole France's *Penguin Island*, St Mael has a vision of a polar bear murmuring '*Incipe parve puer*', from Virgil's Fourth Eclogue, traditionally understood as prophesying Christ's birth.

14   our lady's sea-straw = Our Lady's Bedstraw is a 'cradle herb', believed to have been in Jesus's manger.

VI (p. 84)

The speaker is figured in graphic-textual terms ('cartoon', 'book', 'vowels', 'words') indicating his development as a writer, with hints of sexual and foetal development. The advice of ll.5–6 seems to concern how to take the sting out of the two chief sources of the Western canon, the classics ('medusa's scripture') and the Bible ('pin-hilled nettle') ('siren' and 'pin-hills' carry over from Sonnet V). The recommended plucking and lopping of the 'sea eye' and 'fork tongue' occur, but in reverse order, and with 'love' and 'old cock' performing each other's task. This renders the 'I' 'tallow' conveyed by Adam and the 'bagpipe-breasted ladies'.

1   Cartoon ... tide-traced crater = the speaker's womb-like environment (perhaps Swansea Bay) and his writing. An appositive clause, subject of the verb 'split through' in l.3, and/or a description of the 'He' (and/or 'book') of l.2.

2   book of water = one (in) which it is futile to write; womb; one which succeeds in embodying process; tallow-eyed = dark-eyed because up late writing by candlelight.

3   By lava's light = thanks to volcanic (poetic) outpourings; split through = may take l.1 as its subject, meaning 'split by using'; oyster vowels = part of an image train suggesting that language has been corrupted by seawater; however, 'oyster vowels' may contain poetic pearls.

4   burned sea silence on a wick of words = signals the effort to master or purify language.

5   Pluck, cock ... medusa's scripture = 'medusa' seems to be secular literature and sexual experience; the narrator is offered its 'sea eye', an aid for his journey, but this also sounds like a euphemism for the vagina; 'medusa' is a stinging jellyfish as well as a mythic figure, so care is required.

6 Lop, love . . . pin-hilled nettle = the Bible, speaking with the opposed messages of Old and New Testament, is a 'pin-hilled nettle', the summit of which is Christ's crucifixion on Calvary, whose message is painful to embrace; the speaker is asked to eliminate its 'fork-tongued' aspect in the name of 'love'.

7–8 love plucked out . . . Old cock . . . lopped the minstrel tongue = 'love' and 'old cock' (Christ, but the 'Old Adam' of sexual desire) perform each other's tasks, in a typically hybrid, transgressive fashion.

9 tallow I = echoes l.2, 'tallow-eyed'; wax's tower = a candle; 'waxing' phallus, with 'tallow' as its semen.

11 Adam, time's joker = as in III, Adam wears fool's motley; witch of cardboard = the joker (Adam) in a pack of cards.

12 evil index = can refer to 'Adam' and the 'seas' or the 'ladies'.

13 bagpipe-breasted ladies = the 'sirens' of V (cf. *Under Milk Wood*: 'bagpipe dugs of the mother sow'); deadweed = seaweed.

14 Blew out . . . wound of manwax = 'the "manwax" is the candle of fertility that appears a few lines earlier, and the wound is that of Jesus'; according to Korg (1965) the 'blood gauze' (as bandage on Christ's wound and veil covering the truth) is 'the sterile doctrine of continued life'.

VII (p. 85)

Cram something of huge ethical import into a tiny space, strip all the many-leaved and sacred leaves of the world's literature to a bare tree, and you are left with a child's alphabet, or pared-back 'scarecrow word'; let doom fall on those who deny 'wind-turned' process. What follows are the actions of the siren-like 'ladies' from VI, who, themselves suffering from 'heartbreak', inflict 'time's tune' on the poet-Adam. This deprives him of 'magic', as it has done since the 'beginning' of things, to all men; 'naked sponge' is a breast that reverses a breast's usual actions (accounting for 'milk'). The ladies give their heartbreak to the tune of time and it is embodied in the objects which follow; the point being that time, like a gramophone needle (or poem), 'tracks' the sound and shape of things simultaneously.

1 Now stamp the Lord's Prayer on a grain of rice = the most concentrated form of Jesus' teaching conceivable, but on a non-biblical foodstuff.

2–3 A Bible-leaved . . . Strip to this tree = perhaps '"A", Bible-leaved' (see below); reduce the myriad pages of the wood of texts to the Bible; written woods = wood is turned into paper, and therefore literally written on. In the Welsh tree alphabet, trees constitute writing.

3 a rocking alphabet = a child's ABC; wordplay: '[The letter] "A" [as its first letter] rocking [cradling the] "alphabet"'.

4 Genesis in the root . . . scarecrow word = Old Testament and New Testament (scarecrows are hung on crosses).

5 one light's language = the light of the Bible, the book of all trees (books).

6 Doom . . . wind-turned statement = suggests a weathercock, symbol of time and mutability; following a semicolon (as at V, l.6), this curse could be speech, a comment on the previous five lines rather than belonging to them.

7–9 Time's tune my ladies with the teats of music . . . fix in a naked sponge . . . Adam out of magic = time's tune *is* 'my ladies' (cf. VI), in whose 'bagpipe' breasts ('a naked sponge') the music of time is 'fixed' like a soundtrack, re-verse-suckling Adam into time and 'out of magic'.

9 Who = 'she who', if 'sucks' is 'gives suck to'; bell-voiced Adam out of magic = if 'bell-voiced' means 'buoy(ant)', the reading given for ll.7–9 applies; if it relates to Adam as a 'bell-wether' and 'time's joker' (VI), it seems more like a necessary demystification; but both may apply.

10 Time, milk, and magic, from the world beginning = appositional with 'Time' and 'magic': 'from the beginning of the world (the tune of) Time, milk, and magic has been fixed in the "naked sponge".'

12 bald pavilions and the house of bread = possibly the breasts and the womb (cf. 'bread-sided field', IV).

13 sound of shape = favourite phrase, and a definition of poetry (also 'shape of sound'); cf. 'Hold hard'; for 'tracking' cf. 'When, like a running grave'.

VIII (p. 85)

A crucifixion scene, in which the speaker is Christ, but with hints of Thomas and Mary as co-subjects; e.g. the pun at l.4, and use of 'Jack Christ' as if speaking of Christ, at l.7, suggests Thomas as 'Jack Christ' and Mary as em-pathic, suffering witness. The other interpretative crux, 'unsex the skeleton', may be understood as a typical double negative; the death of sex to death (the 'skeleton'), blasphemously asserting that Christ's sacrifice freed sex from the post-lapsarian curse of mortality, this being more significant than the belief that he conquered death. Goodby (2013) notes that Thomas 'restores the Renaissance's sexual reading of Christ's crucifixion as the nuptials of God and Man'.

2 Time's nerve in vinegar = Christ's death as Time's high/low point, winc-ingly alluding to the vinegar offered to him on the Cross; gallow grave = an

alliterative antithesis, contrasting the body above and below ground, playing on 'shallow grave' (it will not contain Christ for long).

3 the bright thorns I wept = Christ imagined weeping his crown of thorns.

4 God's Mary = possessive and contractive: Mary belongs to God; Mary is God (and her grief is God's); wordplay on 'God's *merry* in her grief'.

5 three trees = the crosses on Golgotha; bird-papped = soft, downy breasts (as in 'pelican of circles' in II, and Mary's impregnation by the dove-like Holy Spirit).

6 pins for teardrops = agonisingly painful tears.

7 Jack Christ = the Christ in humans, Christ as human; minstrel angle = pun on 'ministering angel', traditionally set in the 'angles' (corners) of depictions of the Crucifixion. The 'minstrel angle' is also a poet's interpretation of an event.

8 Drove in the heaven-driven = God ('heaven') has preordained the nailing of Christ to the Cross.

9 the three-coloured rainbow from my nipples = the nipples of Christ (or Mary) as the poles; the rainbow is in the three primary colours, red, yellow and blue.

10 snail-waked world = the world only grasps the significance of Christ's sacrifice very slowly.

11 I = compound of Christ, Mary and Thomas; all glory's sawbones = sawbones is slang for a surgeon – Christ as healer of sick humanity – but also the artist, whose works defy mortality, opening the kingdom of the spirit to humanity, even as he runs to seed by witnessing this 'sun'-like glory. 'Glory' is also orgasm (cf. 'A saint about to fall').

12 Unsex the skeleton = skeletons are genital-free, hence already 'unsexed', and symbolic of death, a condition beyond sex or gender; Christ's submission to death breaks the association of sex with death of the early poetry; mountain minute = a large or portentous moment; a tiny mountain.

13 blowclock = genitals of the 'gentleman'; dialect for the seed-head of a dandelion, used by children to tell the time.

14 Suffer . . . heartbeat = cf. Matthew, 19:14: 'Suffer little children, and forbid them not, to come unto me: for of such is the kingdom of heaven'.

IX (p. 86)

Crucified Thomas-Christ is embalmed, mummified and entombed, with Egyptian imagery temporarily breaking the Christian frame of reference.

'Rants' casts doubt on the reality of any 'resurrection in the desert'; scepticism is increased if Korg's point about 'blood gauze' bandages (cf. VI) is recalled. As well as the embalming effect of scripture, the burial rites also signify the mummification, in writing and print, of poems after their crucifixion-like birth (in VIII); as in 'How shall my animal', setting down the poem is seen as killing its essence.

3   queen in splints = mummies were placed between boards to straighten them.

4   Buckle = the main verb of the sentence as far as 'draw on', succeeded in turn by 'pour', which governs its final clause; natron = chemical used in mummification; footsteps = perhaps the stylised, foot-forward stance of Egyptian statues.

5–6   dead Cairo's henna . . . like a halo = mummies' hair was tinted with henna.

6   caps and serpents = royal headdresses placed on mummies often displayed a uraeus, or serpent, over the middle of the forehead, as a symbol of sovereignty.

7   resurrection in the desert = ironically echoes VIII in depicting the discovery of an Egyptian tomb, like Howard Carter's of Tutankhamen; all attempts to preserve power, wisdom, art and beauty will lead only to 'death', 'rants', 'dust and furies'.

8   Death from a bandage = deathly idea of everlasting life (scripture as mummy-bandage recurs in 'linen spirit')

8–9   rants . . . on such features = perhaps 'rants which . . . made gold'.

10–11   long gentleman . . . gentle wound = the terms return to those of I, as the Thomas/Christ figure, phallus and trickster principle are finally brought low.

12   triangle landscape = of pyramids south of Cairo.

13   With stones . . . garland = the Egyptian custom of placing talismans with the dead supersedes the Anglican burial service's 'ashes to ashes' (garlands were often offered for slain and resurrected fertility gods such as Attis and Adonis).

14   rivers of the dead . . . neck = the weight of ancestry; ancient Egyptians believed the dead had to cross a river in their journey to the Island of Osiris.

X (p. 86)

The speaker (now clearly Thomas) is resurrected after his stint in the tomb. As the sailor of the tale of Christianity, a survivor of its attempt to interpellate him, he prefers to balance the world on his poetry and stand off from the false harbour of faith, refusing to commit himself; magical 'winged harbours' (made of 'roc') see through the seedily 'blown word' of doctrine, and he prefers his hybrid images, impure blends of pagan and Christian, to any it has to offer. But he seems happy to let Peter (representing all believers) ask Christ who, exactly, has 'sown a flying garden' in the channel of the 'sea-ghost' (gendered as female, and meaning his voyage thus far). That 'who' is Thomas himself, the 'garden' 'Altarwise', or his poetic vision generally, which he hopes will paradoxically 'diving / Soar' to a regenerative Day of Judgement or revolutionary-sexual utopia.

1 the tale's sailor = Thomas; play on proverbial 'sailor's tale', or yarn (as by Odysseus, or Sinbad below); Christian voyage = the narrative of 'Altarwise', perhaps glancing at Fletcher *Christian*, leader of the mutiny on the *Bounty*.

2 Atlaswise = worldly-wise, rather than religiously 'altar-wise'; halfway off = more distant than the 'half-way house' of I; the dummy bay = false harbour of faith; 'dummy' is also a baby's soother.

3 Time's ship-racked gospel . . . I balance = I balance the world; the globe I balance = Thomas's poetry, the 'Altarwise' sequence.

4 rockbirds' = the roc is a giant bird in the tales of Sinbad the Sailor in *The Arabian Nights*. Roc(k) anticipates 'Peter' (l.7) and Jesus' pun in Matthew 16:18: 'thou art Peter (πέτρος), and upon this rock (πέτρα) I will build my church'.

5 blown word = the 'gospel' of l.3, blown, like a ship, across the seas from the 'bible east' to the 'winged harbours'; hollow; overblown; flyblown, dead.

6 December's thorn screwed in a brow of holly = blends Christ's crown of thorns and pagan midwinter symbols of life, as in 'I see the boys of summer'.

7–8 Let the first Peter . . . Ask = that is, let St Peter, not me, ask Christ what I am up to; quayrail = pun on 'key' (the Pope as keeper of the keys to the kingdom of heaven).

8 the tall fish = Christ; the tall, fishy tale/tail of Christianity.

9 rhubarb man = *a* hollow (cf. II's 'hollow agent', IV's 'bamboo man'); *b* emptily talkative – 'Rhubarb, rhubarb' is used by actors to simulate background talk; *c* man with a stick of (pink) rhubarb (penis symbol); foam-blue = Mary's colour is blue.

10 flying garden = poetry (a restored Eden); sea-ghost = the fly-'blown word'.

12 two bark towers = the trees of Eden and Calvary; that Day = Day of Judgement.

13–14 the worm builds . . . My nest of mercies = the main sense is of serpent, not grave-worm, coiled round the tree of the Knowledge of Good and Evil and building a nest atop the Cross. The trickster 'worm' can turn poison to positive use and is an agent of creation and destruction.

14 rude = *a* raw and rugged; *b* obscene (phallic); *c* homonym for *rood* – the Cross; red = the bloody Cross, but also penis, and with hint of socialist revolution.

The seed-at-zero (p. 87)

N4 'Six', dated 'August 29 '33', heavily revised March 1936. No ms survives and there was no periodical appearance; collected in *25P*.

'Six' derives from Johanna Southcott (1750–1814), the leader of a cult to whom she prophesied that she would bear Shiloh, the second Christ, foretold in Genesis 49:10 and Revelation 12. Thomas read her story through his process philosophy as the basis of a narrative dramatising the realisation of Christlike human potential (like 'Before I knocked', closely related to 'Six'), rather than as failed supernatural incarnation.

In revising 'Six', Thomas altered its pastoral and pantheistic imagery, using WWI-style metaphors of sexual conquest and tracing the male 'hero seed' to his ultimate 'harbour'. However, the idea of sex as (male) assault and (female) surrender is rebutted, the womb being fertilised by 'settling' fusion. This blend of fusion and dissonance is reflected structurally in four pairs of interlinked stanzas, the second in each pair modifying the first, with 'seed-at-zero' linking first and final pairs. In the final pair, what Maud (2003) calls 'panspermia' has left the womb to become the 'hero-in-tomorrow'. He does not 'thunder' on a 'star-flanked garrison' (Stanza 7) – the heaven promised by religion – but a 'foreign town', the 'grave-groping' city of death. Having warred on death, once he has occupied its citadel the 'seed-in-tomorrow' cannot 'range' his artillery 'from' it; he conquers mortality and by so doing succumbs to it.

1 seed-at-zero = a sperm, in its as-yet-unrealised potential; from 'zero-hour', in a military offensive (cf. 'A saint about to fall' for a similar scenario).

2 town of ghosts = womb haunted by potential human beings (ghosts; cf. 'A process in the weather of the heart', etc.); trodden = from 'treading', term used for the mating of birds. The replacement by 'manwaged' in l.9 is typical of the changes-in-repetition which constitute the poem.

3 rampart = part to be rammed; tapping = sexual; like table-tapping at a séance.

4, 11 god-in-hero = the Christlike potential of all human beings, made supernatural and literal in Johanna Southcott's claim.

5 tower . . . town = penis and womb; the image is that of a siege tower.

6 Dumbly and divinely = as child and god (perhaps the Christ-child).

7, 14 manwaging line . . . warbearing line = the terms interchange to produce 'war-waging' and 'man-bearing', as elsewhere.

16, 18, 23, 26 riddled = in ll.16 and 23, the seed is sifted (soil is 'riddled' through a sieve); in ll.18 and 26 it has the commoner sense of 'shot through with holes' or 'set riddles to answer' (cf. 'My world is pyramid').

17 Manna = in the Bible, a food which grows, or falls from heaven, overnight; an image of gentler sexual 'fusion'.

20–21, 27–28 guard ... key = virginity, at first obstructive and then overcome.

29–30, 36–39 May a humble village labour ... a green inch be his bearer = the answer is 'yes'; there is a chancy aspect to insemination. Like Christ's teachings, this is initially ignored, and then embraced, by the wider world.

32 green inch = a tiny fertile patch of ground; womb.

35, 42 thirsty ... drunken sailors = the sperm is hidden in the egg, which yearns for and is then intoxicated by it; with disguised pun on sailors ('seamen' as 'semen').

To-day, this insect (p. 88)

'II', 'To-day, this hour I breathe', in *N2*, of 18 December 1930 (see above); wholly rewritten, probably late 1935/early 1936, and included in a twenty-three-poem manuscript sent to Dent on 17 March 1936. Proofs were made, but a revised version was included in the final batch of poems Thomas sent to Dent, on 22 June 1936. Published in *25P*.

The 'insect' is, among other things, the segmented poem itself. It also has an archaic sense as 'snake', as in Stanza 2, while 'chrysalis' may figure the mutation of punitive Mosaic law, via Christ's 'flying heartbone', into the New Testament message of forgiveness ('blow[ing] Jericho on [the expulsion from] Eden'). However, this is in many ways a pretext for the punning and playful verbal excess, the process of writing the poem being its subject in at least equal measure.

The speaker has a divided sense of 'trust and tale', faith and fiction, describing his antithetical procedures but querying them too. 'Trust and tale' produce 'head and tail', 'double' of the more abstract terms, from tale/tail. 'Head' is equated with 'trust' grammatically, but is conventionally opposed to it (as rationality, contrasted with the heart's association with faith), and this means the 'murder' of faith, 'Eden and green genesis', which 'head and tail' (snakes seem all head and tail) created.

Stanza 2 refers to the Fall, but only to tell of the fall of belief in it. Its serpent is best seen as vivifying, an 'uncredited' trickster, testing the way in which fictions which set themselves up as truths deconstruct themselves: the New Testament relativises the Old Testament, and is, in turn, relativised by it. The gospels join other supreme fictions in Stanza 3, and, with that, their promise of eternal life vanishes. This is exemplified in the two single-line segmenting refrains, which worry at the meaning of 'certain'. But a poem is always a fiction, so the claim that it 'plagues' the Christian 'fable' is also dubious. It replaces religion's absolute promises with promises of the absolute, but death is the outcome of all such 'fibs of vision'. The 'madman' proclaims that his only certain end is the endlessness of his love for Adam, the type of Christ; if Death is certain, desire is 'endless', like writing. Crucifixion is therefore a cruci*fiction*, and 'certain' has drawn down the 'curtain' of art which conceals creative suffering, resists paraphrase and suggests that, as Don McKay (1985/86) puts it, 'ultimately, order and anarchy belong to the same poetic and cosmological enterprise'.

1   To-day = following *25P* and *CP52*, I keep the bisected form of the word; insect = from Latin *insectum* '(animal) with a notched or divided body', literal meaning 'cut into'; the world I breathe = as 'world' (or 'plague'), a periphrasis for the speaker's being-in-the-world, or existence.

2   outelbowed = imagination creates the space in which the poem can emerge.

4   sentence = a pun on the legal sense leads to 'guillotine' in l.6.

8   green genesis = story of Adam and Eve in the Garden of Eden.

9   The insect certain is the plague of fables = each word has at least two senses, but the main meaning of 'certain' is adverbial; opposed to dogma, poems plague 'fables' like that of Eden. But multiple meanings and syntax permit various interpretations.

10   This story's monster = the Genesis story imagined as the serpent that features in it; caul = a shell fragment on a hatching snake.

11   scrams = runs; blazing outline = perhaps of the 'story', now burning.

12   Measures his own length = to 'measure your length' means to fall down.

13   breaks his shell = the coherence of the story-as-serpent shatters; last shocked beginning = final awakening.

14   crocodile . . . chrysalis = the monster story is now a crocodile, incapable of taking off and flying (it is 'before the chrysalis').

15–16   flying heartbone . . . Winged like a sabbath ass = grotesque images for past faith, now extinguished. Cf. 'heartbone' in 'Then was my neophyte'.

17   blows Jericho on Eden = Jericho's walls collapsed when Joshua encouraged the Israelites to shout and the priests to blow their trumpets (Joshua 6:20).

18   The insect fable is the certain promise = only the poem (not religion or hyper-rationalist claims to 'certainty') can be relied on (but the ironic nature of the promise hints that death is the outcome of all the 'fibs of vision').

19 the nightmare madmen = Don Quixote, Odysseus, St John, Job. The deaths of their 'fibs' may suggest that the end of faith threatens the imagination, and its necessary suspense of disbelief, more generally.

20 air-drawn = drawn in the air (cf. *Macbeth*, 3:4, 61); drawn by the air, blown.

21 John's beast = probably that of St John the Divine in Revelation 12:3.

22 Greek in the Irish sea = the Irish James Joyce's Greek-sounding Stephen Dedalus, and use of Greek myth in *Ulysses*; from 'all Greek to me', idiomatic for incomprehensible.

25–26 All legends' sweethearts . . . the fabulous curtain = play on 'certain' as 'curtain', the illusions of art.

Then was my neophyte (p. 89)

Probably written April–June 1936, included in the last batch of poems sent to Dent for *25P* on 22 June 1936. It appeared, after the publication of *25P*, in *transition*, in autumn 1936, together with the story 'The Mouse and the Woman', and in *Purpose*, October–December 1936.

To Glyn Jones in December 1936, Thomas said: 'Nobody's mentioned it; perhaps it's bad; I only know that, to me, it is clearer and more definite, and that it holds more possibilities of progress, than anything else I've done.' The poem's conceit, as in 'Altarwise' IV and 'The tombstone told', is that our life-to-be – here filmed by God – is shown to us before birth, projected on to the 'tide-hoisted screen' of the womb-wall in Stanza 3. Vernon Watkins reports Thomas calling the poem 'a prophecy of his own melodramatic death, shown to him on a film which he, as a child, whose character has not been formed, sees unwinding and projected on a screen . . . under water'. God is also father and time, and the poem stages a clash between father and 'neophyte' sun/son, like '"Find meat on bones"' and 'I see the boys of summer'. The neophyte-foetus is Thomas and Christ, reluctant to enter the world of time and death, but lured into it by the images of love projected on the womb-wall by the father-creator until his 'heartbone breaks'. Birth leads him from the static deep sea of the womb to this world's 'dramatic sea' of tide and time, and the speaker's viewpoint moves between adult hindsight and foetal existence.

1 neophyte = newly planted, or newly converted to a faith; links the curled-up foetus with a novice praying 'on its knees'.

4 Ducked = immersed in the amnion and baptised; twelve, disciple seas = conflates Christ and speaker.

5 The winder of the water-clocks = Newtonian God who winds up the mechanism of the universe; 'water-clocks' are tides.

6   Calls a green day and night = in the womb, day and night are indistinguishable; God 'calls' the time 'green' because it is antenatal, immature, but also Edenic.

7   sea hermaphrodite = the embryo is initially genderless; a hermaphrodite brig is a ship carrying two kinds of sail.

8   Snail of man = snails are hermaphroditic; ship of fires = the body consumed by its passions.

9   burn the bitten decks = blends 'hit the deck' and 'bite the dust'. Cf. Felicia Hemans' 'Casabianca' ('The boy stood on the burning deck').

11   water sex = the embryo's gender is still fluidly indeterminate.

12   green rock of light = contrasting with undifferentiated 'green day and night' of l.6, this appears as a lighthouse-like phallus guiding the (now male) embryo.

13–15   these labyrinths . . . the lane of scales . . . moon-blown shell = the marine landscape of the womb.

14–15   tidethread . . . Twine = like the ball of thread Theseus used to escape from the Minotaur's labyrinth.

16–17   the flat cities' sails / Furled = a seaport (like Swansea) in the external world, encountered after birth; fishes' house and hell = the sea.

18   green myths = Garden of Eden; youthful illusions that life will not mean death or 'horrible desires'.

19   Stretch = as canvases on frames, for painting; salt photographs = taken or shown undersea/inside the womb.

20   The landscape grief, love in His oils = what the 'salt photographs' are of, but – given the lack of a comma after 'oils' – also subjects of 'mirror' in l.21.

21   Mirror from man to whale = give fullest enlargement to the existential 'landscape' (of 'grief' and 'love') so that the embryo can see what to expect after birth, in the form of a vision.

25   vanity = of existence as well as merely personal.

26   Shot = filmed; tilted arcs = arc lights, used for lighting film sets; rainbows.

28–29   Children from homes . . . Who speak on a finger and thumb = the Royal Cambrian Institution for the Deaf and Dumb was close to Thomas's family home.

30   the masked, headless boy = possibly the unformed face and head of the embryo, but with sinister suggestiveness; cf. 'When I woke, the town spoke'.

31–34 His reels . . . threw on that tide-hoisted screen = God projecting to the embryo the film of its life-to-be on the womb-wall.

33 ball of lakes = the Earth: cf. 'I see the boys of summer'.

35 heartbone = inmost 'bone' of love: cf. 'To-day, this insect', 'Vision and Prayer'.

37–43 Who kills my history . . . Time kills me terribly = a dialogue between the embryo and God couched in terms of film imagery. God answers its anxieties about its mortality with the disingenuous reply that because it is unborn it need not fear time and death; but the embryo has seen the film of its life, and is not deceived.

It is the sinners' dust-tongued bell (p. 91)

Written November 1936; published in *Twentieth Century Verse* (January 1937); collected in *TML*.

    Writing to Desmond Hawkins on 14 August 1939, Thomas called it 'very decorative . . . a poem, if you'll pardon me, on stained glass. There aren't many ornamental designs, but all, I hope, utilitarian. And I really can't get down to explaining it; you just have to, or just don't have to, let the poem come to you bit by bit through the rather obvious poetry of it. It's not a really satisfactory poem, but I like it. The blue wall of spirits is the sky full of ghosts; the curving crowded world above the new child. It sounds as though it meant the side of a chemist's bowl of methylated spirits, & I *saw* that too and a child climbing up it.' This offers little practical help, however, and autobiography has been resorted to in the claim that the poem stems from the gonorrhoea Caitlin Macnamara and Thomas picked up in 1936. 'Clap' in l.1 and l.29 (original version) gives credence to this; however, it would be reductive to view the poem as being simply 'about' disease. Its meaning lies more in its brilliant progression by contraries: a sinners' (not a saints') bell announces a devilish (not priestly) Time performing a Black Mass (parodic of the rituals of Holy Week). 'When', l.2, begins the poem's noting of the contraries of time as sex and its 'grief'-haunted outcomes; a narrative based on the sexual act emerges between them, figuring the Church as female sexual organs (Stanza 2), the excommunication of time-as-conception (Stanzas 3–5), another antithetical figure for the lovers' relationship. A characteristic paradox is enacted: sex releases us from time, but renews it because it fastens us (through its reproductive purpose, if not outcomes) more firmly to it: new life, real or projected, is the death knell of the living. The nature of art, as suggested by allusions in Stanza 2 and 'coral' in Stanza 3, is equally paradoxical.

1 dust-tongued bell = a passing-bell; glans of penis, whose sexual activity leads to death ('dust') by renewing the cycle of process; claps = grips; applauds; infects with gonorrhoea.

2 torch and hourglass = emblems of the passage of time.

4 marks = notes, but also brands; governs 'black aisle', 'Grief' and 'firewind'.

5 altar ghost = the Eucharist, into which the Holy Ghost enters in Holy Communion. What follows recalls the rituals of Holy Week, when communicants are 'branded' with ashes, the sacrament removed from the altar and fourteen candles extinguished, one being hidden behind the altar (thus darkening the 'aisle').

7 Over the choir minute . . . the hour chant = perhaps: above the timeless and ecstatic music of orgasm, the liturgical chant of time asserts itself. Cf. 'I know this vicious minute's hour'.

8–9 coral saint . . . salt grief . . . a whirlpool drives the prayerwheel = multiplying life (coral) and the suffering of existence (grief) blind us to death; only process has the status of religious truth. Yet coral can symbolise art, and a pun on 'choral' begins a chain of marine imagery.

10 sailing emperor = echoes of W. B. Yeats's Byzantium poems; tideprint = ship's wake; reflection.

11 death's accident . . . dashed-down spire = the spire is detumescent, following sex and the 'death's accident' of orgasm.

13 dark directly under the dumb flame = in a radio broadcast of 5 March 1958, Vernon Watkins commented: '[Thomas] came to my house one day and he said, "I've been reading a thriller, a very bad thriller, but I came on the most wonderful line in the middle of a lot of trash, which was 'the shadow is dark directly under the candle'". And he said, "Out of that line I'm going to make a new poem which is going to be my best, about churches."' The thriller has not been identified.

14 Storm, snow . . . fireworks = fireworks described in watery terms. Other contraries include 'calm'/'pulled [down]', exorcises/'christens', 'still'/'pacing'.

16–17 book and candle . . . bell = the phrase 'bell, book and candle' is from the Roman Catholic service of excommunication; after the phrase was uttered a bell was rung, a book closed, and candles extinguished or kicked over.

20 font of bone and plants = vagina-like font from which the 'baptised' child ascends; stone tocsin = warning bell from the excommunication of Stanza 3.

28 hyleg = 'ruling planet of a nativity' (*OED*); the position of the planets influencing the fate of the poem's 'sinners'.

29 Nutmeg, civet, and sea-parsley = a spice, perfume and herb; cf. *King Lear*,

4:5, ll.126–7: 'Give me an ounce of civet, good apothecary, sweeten my imagin-ation'; plagued = 'clapped' in *Twentieth Century Verse* version.

Two limericks (p. 92)

Andrew Lycett's *Dylan Thomas: A New Life* (2003) dates these limericks to the period of the affair with Veronica Sibthorpe in mid-1937.

From the Veronica Sibthorpe papers (p. 92)

Written April/May 1937, in albums belonging to Veronica Sibthorpe contain-ing occasional verses, sketches and miscellaneous items by herself and Thomas, some collaborative (now in the NLW).

In London in April 1937, with Caitlin Macnamara in Blashford, and nowhere to live, Thomas was given lodging by Veronica Sibthorpe, a disabled artist to whom he had been a neighbour in Cornwall the previous summer. They had a brief, open, amicable affair – her name for him was 'the angelic pig' – since Thomas was frank about his long-term commitment to Caitlin.

i. Three verses (p. 92)

a) Welsh lazy: one of three items titled 'Lazy', annotating cartoon by Sibthorp.

b) Poem to Veronica accompanies a doodle of a bee and someone in bed, titled 'Bear in bed'; its echo of 'the birds and the bees' and the bear/bare pun confirm its sexual nature.

ii. For as long as forever is (p. 93)

Thomas referred to the poem ('I scrapped a poem beginning with that line long ago') in the postcard containing 'Twenty-four years' he sent to Watkins on 24 October 1938. Autograph copies are held in the Veronica Sibthorpe papers and in Austin; I have generally followed the second of these, except for the final line, where 'shave' offers a full rhyme. First published, in the Austin version, in *CP88*, it is interesting as a transitional work and as a predecessor to 'Twenty-four years', which uses the germinal phrase more tellingly.

2–10   fox in the wave . . . heels of birds . . . partridge fence and the sea-duck rows . . . stag . . . snail's . . . she-bear's floes . . . cat's mountain = compare the zoomorphic transformations of 'How shall my animal' and the animal imagery of 'When I woke'.

8   a snail's gallop = a favourite conceit, probably from time-lapse photography; cf. the 'haring snail' of 'I, in my intricate image' and 'snail-waked world' of 'Altarwise'.

I make this in a warring absence (p. 93)

Written July–November 1937, although Vernon Watkins claimed it took 'rough-ly a year to finish' (*LVW*, 30). Thomas told Desmond Hawkins of *Purpose*, in September 1937, 'I can let you have one longish and very good poem, unprint-ed, for an immediate guinea. It is this week's masterpiece, it took two months to write, and I want to drink it.' Hawkins did not take Thomas up, and after more working and extension it was finally published in *Twentieth Century Verse* January/February 1938, with the title 'Poem (For Caitlin)'; collected in *TML*.

This is a difficult poem, and Thomas glossed it more than any other. After a reading at Goldsmiths College, London, on 27 January 1938, Hermann Peschmann wrote to ask for guidance. Thomas's reply began: 'I can give you a very rough idea of the "plot". But, of course, it's bound to be a most super-ficial, and, perhaps, misleading, idea, because the "plot" is told in images, and the images *are* what they say, not what they stand for.' He added: 'The poem is, in the first place, supposed to be a document, or narrative, of all the emotional events between the coming and going, the creation and dissipation, of jealousy, jealousy born from pride and killed by pride, between the absence and the return of the crucial character (or heroine) of the narrative, between the war of her ab-sence and the armistice of her presence.' A stanza-by-stanza account followed, incorporated in the notes below. In August 1939, preparing to review *TML*, Desmond Hawkins also asked for help, and Thomas responded again:

[Y]ou wanted to discuss . . . stanzas three and four of the poem beginning 'I make this In A W.A.' (Work of Art, Workshop of Agony, Witbite of Agenwar). The stanzas are a catalogue of the contraries, the warring loyalties, the psychological discrepancies, all expressed in physical and/or extra-narrative terms, that go towards making up the 'character' of the woman, or 'beloved' would be wider & better, in whose absence, and in the fear of whose future unfaithful absences, I jealously made the poem. I didn't just say in one line that she was cold as ice and in the next line that she was hot as hell; in each line I made as many con-traries as possible fight* together, in an attempt to bring out a *positive* quality; I wanted a peace, admittedly only the armistice of a moment, to come out of the images on *her* warpath. . . . Here, in this poem, the emotional question is: Can I see clearly, by cataloguing and instancing all I know of her, good and bad, black and white, kind & cruel, (in coloured images condensed to make, not a natural colour, but a militant peace and harmony of all colours), the emotional war caused by her absence, and thus decide for myself whether I fight, lie down and hope, forgive or kill? The question is naturally answered by the questions in the images and the images in the questions – if the vice versa makes any sense.

* 'negate each other, if they could; keep their individualities & lose them in each other'.

The poem's context is a marital row and temporary break-up. The speaker registers the temporary collapse of his confidence in the couple's splendid sexual world, and the qualities of the beloved are then recounted in terms that give a modernist-surreal twist to the Petrarchan antimonies of fire and ice, innocence and guilt, pride and humility. This is succeeded by his histrionic reaction to her 'absence', involving his imaginary murder of her, subsequent guilt and ruin in a Samson-like self-destructive scenario. Symbolic death by drowning, purgatorial purification, reincarnation, rebirth and a return to 'vision' from the 'blindness' of his anger follow. The psychodrama ends in reconciliation, with the beloved imaged as a raincloud bringing balm and nourishment. However, the speaker knows that this is only a truce; the very 'pride' which sustains their passion is storing up storms for the future.

Stanzas of alternately eight and seven iambic pentameters, with terminal words agreeing in a single consonant: 'n' in the first two stanzas, 's' in the third and fourth, 'n' in the fifth, 'd' in the sixth and seventh, 'n' and 'm' in the eighth, 's' and 'r' in the last.

1–8 Stanza 1 'The "I", the hero, begins his narrative at the departure of the heroine, at a time when he feels that her pride in him and their proud, sexual world has been discarded' (letter to Peschmann).

2 ancient ... minute = the phrase is from 'Hold hard, these ancient minutes'; stone-necked = initially seems to mean stiff-necked, but in retrospect, modified by images of harbour and anchor, takes on the meaning of secure, firm, reliable.

3 Harbours ... slips = the first verb is attached by an absent 'which' to 'season'. 'Slips' is governed by the subject 'minute'.

4–6 mast and fountain ... the handshaped ocean ... that proud sailing tree = images for womb and phallus, indicating the sexual pride the couple once possessed; pride = a key word, occurring nine times. Always with its standard sense, it puns also on the collective noun for lions, kingly beasts, and (as 'proud') the sense of 'standing clear of, erect', alluding to the couple's relationship and the speaker's phallic deeds and imaginings.

5 Sailed and set dazzling = transposed epithet (from 'set sail').

9–15 Stanza 2 'All that keen pride seems, to him, to have vanished, drawn back, perhaps to the blind womb from which it came' (letter to Peschmann).

16–30 Stanzas 3 & 4 'He sees her as a woman made from contraries, innocent in guilt & guilty in innocence, ravaged in virginity, virgin in ravishment, and a woman who, out of a weak coldness, reduces to nothing the great sexual strengths, heats, & prides of the world' (letter to Peschmann).

16–23 In his letter to Hawkins of 14 August 1939, Thomas confessed: 'Yes,

the syntax of stanza 3 is difficult, perhaps "wrong". *SHE* makes for me a net-
tle's innocence and a soft pigeon's guilt; she makes in the fucked, hard rocks
a frail virgin shell; she makes a frank (i.e. imprisoned, and candid and open)
and closed (contradiction again here, meaning virgin-shut to diving man**)
pearl; she makes shapes of sea-girls glint in the staved (diver-prised) & siren
(certainly the non-virgin) caverns; *SHE IS* a maiden in the shameful oak – :
(here the shameful oak *is* obscure, a mixture of references, halfknown, halffor-
gotten, nostalgic romantic undigested and emotionally packed, to a naughty
oracle, a serpent's tree, an unconventional maypole for conventional satyrate
figures). The syntax *can* be allowed by a stretch or rack-stretches; the difficul-
ty is the word Glint. Cut out "Glint" and it's obvious; I'm not, as you know
too well, afraid of a little startling difficulty. Sorry to be so conflicting and
confusing; I hope this is the only method, though; this rambling and snatchy
expansion.'

** 'This is adding to the image, of course, digging out what is accidentally there on purpose'.

23 Proud as a sucked stone and huge as sandgrains = Watkins noted: 'I sup-
pose that verse took him perhaps three weeks, and the last line three or four
days, of fairly continuous work, because he wanted an image of stability at
the end of the stanza after "Is maiden in the shameful oak". The last line that
I remember he put was "proud as a mule's womb and huge as insects", and
gradually "insects" was altered to "sandgrains", and about two days later the
other part was altered to "Proud as a sucked stone"' (BBC broadcast, 5 March
1958).

25–26 priest's grave foot . . . molten = Thomas's letter of 13 November 1937
to Watkins runs: 'I've used "molten", as you suggested, but kept "priest's grave
foot", which is not, I'm sure, really ugly.'

31–38 Stanza 5 'Crying his vision aloud, he makes war upon her absence,
attacks and kills her absent heart, then falls, himself, into ruin at the moment of
that murder of love' (letter to Peschmann).

31–36 I make a weapon . . . jaw-bone = the narrator's destructive impulses
suggest the 'new jawbone of an ass' (Judges 15:15) with which Samson slew a
thousand Philistines, as he presents himself as a blustering, asinine figure.

39–45 Stanza 6 'He falls into the grave; in his shroud he lies, empty of visions
& legends; he feels undead love at his heart' (letter to Peschmann). The image-
ry describes a death at sea which is also a drowning of the self prefigured in the
'approaching wave' of l.38; this is followed by mummification and burial, as in
'Altarwise', IX.

39 the room of errors = to Hawkins on 30 October 1937 Thomas noted: 'The
poem I have to revise. I thought it was perfectly correct – as to detail – before

I read it again early one morning. .... I saw that the third verse, which dealt with the faults and mistakes of death, had a brilliant and moving description of a suicide's grave as "a chamber of errors".' This was too close to 'chamber of horrors' for Thomas's liking.

43 hero's head . . . scraped of every legend = externally, as Samson's head was shorn of its locks by the treacherous Delilah; internally by a mental scraping-out (mummification involved the preliminary removal of internal organs).

46–53 Stanza 7 'The surrounding dead in the grave describe to him one manner of death and resurrection: the womb, the origin of love, forks its child down into the dark grave, dips it in dust, then forks it back into light again' (letter to Peschmann).

46 'His mother's womb had a tongue that lapped up mud' = the speaker is presumably 'love's anatomist' of l.44. Cf. 'He fed on the fattened terror', sent to Watkins 25 October 1937, which uses the same image.

50 fork = divide; graft; homophonic with 'fuck'.

52 taut masks = like the funerary masks on Egyptian mummies, but also like African ancestral masks; the dead are speaking here.

53 In the groin's . . . a man is tangled = there is no escape from the 'coil' (looped thread, but also 'quarrel') of sexual relationships.

54–60 Stanza 8 'And once in the light, the resurrected hero sees the world with penetrating, altered eyes; the world that was wild is now mild to him, revenge has changed into pardon' (letter to Peschmann).

57 With loud, torn tooth and tail and cobweb drum = cf. 'With biter's tooth and tail / And cobweb drum' in 'Your breath was shed' (see below).

61–68 Stanza 9 'He sees his love walk in the world, bearing none of the murderous wounds he gave her. Forgiven by her, he ends his narrative in forgiveness: – but he sees and knows that all that has happened will happen again, tomorrow and tomorrow' (letter to Peschmann).

64–65 A calm wind blows . . . turned to ice = on 13 November 1937 to Watkins, Thomas wrote: 'Lines 4 & 5 of the last verse might, perhaps, sound too fluent: I mean, they might sound as though they came too easily in a manner I have done my best to discard, but they say exactly what I mean them to. Are they clear? Once upon a time, before my death & resurrection, before the "terrible" world had shown itself to me (however lyingly, as lines 6 & 7 of the last verse might indicate) as not so terrible after all, a wind had blown that had frightened everything & created the first ice & the first frost by frightening the falling snow so much that the blood of each flake froze. This is probably clear, but, even to me, the lines skip (almost) along so that they are taken in too quickly, & then mainly by the eye.'

In the Direction of the Beginning (p. 96)

Probably written late 1937/early 1938; published in *Wales* (March 1938); collected in *A Prospect of the Sea* (1955) and *CS*.

Thomas originally intended this work to be included in what became *TML* and to provide the volume's title. Although he later withdrew it, because he came to feel it had potential for expansion, his earlier faith in its completeness and representative qualities testify to his high regard. It is the most experimental prose he ever wrote, and in subject and phrasing it has similarities with poems of the time; it fully matches J. Hillis Miller's description of it as a 'prose poem', which is why it is included here.

In its progression, it exemplifies what Thomas called his 'dialectical method' of composition. It is basically a myth of origin with folk-tale aspects – the birth of the poet-voyager 'in the direction of the beginning', and of a siren-like 'stranger', both with cosmic dimensions – which becomes a sexual quest-narrative. But the imagery suggests that this quest is indistinguishable from that of writing; the phallic mast is of cedar, used in making pencils, 'swinging field' and 'bay-leaf' are images for the page, and stone in its many forms figures text. The world described is that of the emergent poem, although it does not describe its own creation so much as make its readers co-creators of the work-in-progress.

He fed on the fattened terror of death ['Epitaph'] (p. 97)

Described as a 'four-line epitaph' 'just written' in a letter to Vernon Watkins of 25 October 1937 (in BL). An unpublished spin-off from 'I make this in a warring absence', l.2 is from Stanza 7 of that poem, while l.4 was later adapted for 'After the funeral'. It reflects Thomas's efforts to break his morbid fascination, or that of his poetry at least, with death and its 'terror'; the 'terrible' grave is one *made of* terror, rather than the real thing, and therefore a 'lesson' for the would-be 'suicide' who 'slits' his throat in an imaginative-creative sense, shedding the 'dry blood' of poems, and so perhaps (eventually) exorcising his morbidity. Thomas's letter to Desmond Hawkins of 30 October 1937, cited in the note to l.39 for 'I make this in a warring absence', above, and his presentation of his younger self in 'After the funeral', are part of the same cluster of thoughts and images. Suicide, and the grave of the suicide, clearly haunted Thomas; see 'O Chatterton' (June 1938) and 'I, the first named'.

O make me a mask (p. 98)

'Eighteen' in *N3*; a revision of the first nine lines of the forty-line original is copied on the facing page and dated 'Nov 1937 Blashford'. The rewording was extensive, though it did not much extend the original's basic premise. Following a request for work by *Poetry* (Chicago), Thomas revised four notebook poems, including this one; they appeared in the August issue. On 21 March 1938 he sent Vernon Watkins 'O make me a mask', with 'When all my five and country senses see', 'Not from this anger', the first part of 'After the funeral' and 'How shall my animal', to be typed out; *Life and Letters Today* published it in September 1938; collected in *TML*.

The *N3* original had stated that the mask was a defence against 'each pretty miss who passing / Smiles back confessing a treacherous heart', followed by a consideration of the impassivity of a snake's face. The revision eliminated misogyny and snake, and ambiguates the negativity; the speaker now also asks that he be given the power to not pierce others with his 'bayonet tongue', for example, and admits to a 'trumpet of lies'. Thomas preserves the original's wary tone, enters a plea for greater control over facial and verbal expressiveness in order to protect the inner self from intrusion, and to 'perceive' the pretence of 'others'.

2   enamelled eyes . . . spectacled claws = transposed adjectives.

3   nurseries = suggests the 'rape and rebellion' of the past, or that which is being incubated but suppressed in the present.

4   Gag = governed by 'O make me'; bare enemies = outright ('bare-faced') enemies – who may also seem 'naked' in the sense of honest and defenceless.

7   Shaped . . . dunce = the standard grammatical order is inverted to disorient the reader ('The countenance of a dunce shaped in old armour and oak / To shield . . .').

9–10   widower grief . . . To veil = the image is of a widow's veil to further cover the face of the speaker (who is male, hence 'widower').

10   belladonna = Italian for 'beautiful lady'; pretty but poisonous wild flower, deadly nightshade (eye-drops made from the plant were once used by courtesans to dilate the pupils, simulating desire).

The spire cranes (p. 98)

'IX' in *N2*, dated 27 January 1931; Thomas revised it in October/November 1937, and sent it to Vernon Watkins on 13 November 1937. It was one of the batch of four sent to *Poetry* (Chicago); collected in *TML*.

The letter to Watkins accompanying the poem described it as a 'little poem: nothing at all important, or even (probably) much good; just a curious thought said quickly. I think it will be good for me to write some short poems, not bothering about them too much, between my long exhausters.' Thomas seems not to have told Watkins that this, and the other shorter poems of the time, were revised notebook poems. Of all the revisions of this period, this was the one which remained closest to its original in terms of content; however, formally it is very different, the very short free-verse lines made into longer ones, compacted into an end-rhymed verse paragraph. It therefore belongs with the post-1933–34 poetry. The opening phrase plays on 'crane' as verb (perhaps applied to a sea-shore church) and as the name of a bird, with 'spire' and 'birds' being metaphors for the poet and poems respectively. The spire itself is adorned with 'carved birds', but these are unable to dive down to the gravel and water below, in contrast to the bell-chimes it sends out, bird-like, into the world, marking time for swimmers. On the other hand, stone birds are 'built', while the chimes 'pelter', dissipate. Since Thomas is not stigmatising the 'built voice', the choice is not a clear-cut one between songs which do not leave the spire and those that 'fly with winter to the bells' (the bells are in the spire anyway), but between poems which combine both virtues, and the 'prodigals' of the final line. As in 'Once it was the colour of saying', he suggests radical change, but is ambivalent about renouncing the past, combining past qualities with emergent ones rather than making an either/or choice between them.

2–3   feathery / Carved birds = the paradoxical. Walford Davies (1993) suggests that real birds live in the spire and are contrasted with the stone ones, claiming 'the carved birds are covered with the moulted feathers of the real birds'. However, Thomas blurs the either/or contrast this implies, and 'chimes' provide the chief contrast with the carved birds.

3–5   gravel ... Chimes ... = cf. 'Shall gods be said', 'Shall ... flung gravel chime?'

4   the spilt sky = water in the pool belonging to the spire.

6   that priest, water = allusion to Keats's 'Bright star' sonnet: 'The moving waters at their priestlike task'.

9   you = the speaker, or poet, himself.

When all my five and country senses (p. 98)

No ms or notebook version is extant, but this is likely to be a revision, in late 1937 or early 1938, of an earlier poem. One of four poems published in *Poetry* (Chicago) in August 1938 (see note to 'O make me a mask); collected in *TML*.

Thomas described this as 'a conventional sonnet'; it was revised with impending fatherhood in mind, and anticipates other fatherhood poems of 1938/39. The narrator appears to be an unborn child envisaging its post-natal future in ll.1–12, when it anticipates that senses other than sight will be subordinated to it, and forced to 'see'. As a result they will witness love, including that which arises from the embryo's current state of oneness with the cosmos, being stifled and destroyed within each sense's territory. Recalling Renaissance ideas about the component parts of the soul, Thomas follows Blake and Lawrence in attacking the limitations of sight (as opposed to vision) and its fetishisation by abstract, non-sensual rationalism. In the last two lines, the embryo anticipates its existence after death, when the full scope of the senses will 'grop[e] awake' once more.

1 five and country senses = on the model of 'sweet and twenty'; love (identified with the heart) is a continent made up of the countries of each of the interdependent, synaesthetic and various senses. 'Country' has undertones of 'down-to-earth' and also Hamlet's bawdy pun on 'country matters'.

2 forget green thumbs = play on proverbial 'to have green fingers', to be good at growing things; fingers, less rooted and vegetable-like than thumbs, will forget them, just as the prenatal stage will be forgotten.

3–4 the halfmoon's vegetable eye … young stars = *a* the 'halfmoon'-shaped belly of the pregnant woman, the 'eye' of which may be her navel or vagina, but also the 'vegetable' 'I' of the embryo; *b* the 'halfmoon'-shaped fingernails likened to shells out of which 'young stars' have hatched; *c* the embryo itself, curled like a 'halfmoon' and eyeing its fate. Thomas draws on the Renaissance notion of the 'vegetable', 'animal' and 'spiritual' components of the soul, the realisation of which corresponded to embryonic, worldly and after-death stages of existence.

4 handfull zodiac = 'handfull' is an adjective; the hand, containing 'halfmoon' fingernails, is a 'zodiac' which the embryo foresees himself 'marking' once he is born. It will also be 'marked' by the lines read by soothsayers, who read palms and use the zodiac in casting horoscopes. Either way, the hand represents fate, prefiguring the denial and death of love in the world.

5 Love in the frost is pared and wintered by = the syntax is 'How … Love is pared and wintered by'; 'wintered by' functions as a compound verb ('set aside under uncongenial conditions'), although appositional clauses surrounding it tease the reader into wondering whether 'by' requires a further complement. The general sense is that love has to hibernate in this life.

8–9 lashed to syllables = tied to (limited by) language; whipped (in)to fragments of language; tongue … fond wounds = a characteristic association of the tongue with wounds (cf. 'From love's first fever', 'Lie still, sleep becalmed').

9, 10 her = love.

11 witnesses = the senses, forced to see, are also 'witnessing', in a visionary sense, the future restoration of their uncircumscribed power after death.

13–14 And when … though five eyes break = when the 'blind sleep' of death falls, it will break the 'spying' forms the senses have been forced to adopt in this life, and the heart will be able to reintegrate all the senses in a 'sensual' mode once again.

Not from this anger (p. 99)

'Twenty Five' in *N3*, edited down from forty-two lines to fourteen, copied into *N3* and dated 'January 1938 Blashford'; one of the four poems published in *Poetry* (Chicago) in August 1938 (see headnote to 'O make me a mask), collected in *TML*.

The *N3* original describes a girl who is unfazed by the speaker's spurning of her offer of sex, and his anger with himself afterwards at his 'refusal' of her offer. The revision transposes this to different 'weathers', and inverts the original scenario; the 'refusal' is now that of the 'lame flower' which can only strike 'her loin'. Like other details, this suggests a flaccid penis. The speaker regards his 'anger' at his inability as pathetic and futile; it is not responsible for ineffectual lovemaking (Stanza 1) or the shame he feels on recalling his lover's indulgent smile (Stanza 2). However, the sense of the poem is by no means clear; it involves emotional as well as physical checks, and this is reflected in characteristic ambiguous negatives.

2–4 lame flower . . . strapped by hunger = 'flower' as penis, perhaps from the Lotos-eaters chapter of *Ulysses*: 'the limp father of thousands, a languid floating flower': it is bent like an animal under strain because of drought, like a drooping, unwatered flower or animal at a waterhole in a drought-stricken land ('strapped' suggests a tightened belt and punishment). The *N3* revision published in *Poetry* (Chicago) has 'In a land without weathers'.

6 tendril hands = what his hands have shrunk to through shame at his sexual inability.

7 two seas = the two protagonists; his partner's breasts.

10 golden ball = the circle of harmony made by the two semicircular smiles of the lovers when they are sexually satisfied.

12 bell under water = cf. images of drowned churches and cathedrals in 'I, in my intricate image' and 'It is the sinners' dust-tongued bell'.

13 breed = ironic; the smile (pitying, sympathetic perhaps) is all that breeds as a result of the speaker's failure.

How shall my animal (p. 100)

A complete rewriting of *N1* '42' (9 December 1930; see above) in the first half of 1938; published in *Criterion*, October 1938, and *New Directions in Prose and Poetry 1938* in the US; collected *TML*.

Receiving it in a letter of 21 March 1938, Vernon Watkins described this poem as an 'opus', along with Thomas's other 'long exhausters' of the time, to be contrasted with shorter 'opossums', such as 'When all my five and country senses'. It was sent as 'a new poem' to Henry Treece on 16 May 1938, with the gloss given in Appendix 2. Although he disavowed its 'beast & an angel' remark, the proximity of this poem to Thomas's famous account of his 'dialectical method' of composition, also sent to Treece, of 23 March 1938 (Appendix 2), suggests that it embodies that 'method', and reflects the struggle for a new style around this time.

Debate has centred on what the 'animal' might be. It seems at times to be a foetus, and the poem can more generally be read as concerned with sex, given the pervading phallic imagery in the form of sexual protuberances – octopus tentacles, snail horns, etc. Its narrative would then conclude with the 'little death' of orgasm. However, this is too limiting an interpretation of such a rich poem, and critics now view the 'animal' primarily as inchoate poetic energy in the throes of creative expression. The struggle to externalise the animal is cast in male vs. female terms, but these terms deconstruct each other; the poet/animal is both genders, and creation is an androgynous process, as elsewhere in Thomas.

The poem agonises over the fatal consequences of haling an inner energy into the outer world, but effectively does just that – the anxiety and guilt at treatment of the 'animal' being partially answered by the poem itself. Its language and mobility enact the difficulty of grasping the protean stuff of the unconscious through a series of zoomorphic mutations, and these echo a key element in the Welsh folk tale of Gwion Bach – an allegory of poetic inspiration, in which Gwion undergoes animal shape-shifting before being reborn as the great bard, Taliesin.

Form: four eleven-line stanzas in largely iambic lines of 6-12-12-12-12-6-12-6-6-12-6 syllables, with varied end-rhyme.

1 animal = animal nature; soul (*anima* in Latin).

2 wizard shape I trace = either the shape of the animal, or, like a pentagram traced by a wizard on the floor of his cell, or cave – which generates, by association, the caverns in which the beast hides.

3 Exultation's shell = like a conch shell.

4 the spelling wall = from Jerusalem's Wailing Wall, the 'wall' of language under which the animal will be buried (perhaps also teeth, against which words are spelled out); 'spelling' as 'casting magic spells'.

5 The invoked, shrouding veil . . . face = the 'wall' as a verbal shroud in which the animal will be wrapped; foreskin.

7 flailed like an octopus = octopus flesh is beaten to tenderise it before cooking.

9 outside weathers = implicitly opposed to internal weather, just as 'discovered skies' (l.10) are star maps by contrast with uncharted inner skies.

12–13 magnetize / Towards = the female 'animal' points compass-like towards the male; studded male = stallion at stud; man wearing armour ('studded *mail*'); maleness as learned ('studied'); blaze = fiery sexual energy; white facial marking on horses.

14 lionhead's = cf. Revelation 9:17: 'The heads of the horses were as the heads of lions'; also Max Ernst's surrealist collage work *La Semaine de Bonté* (1934), tracing the tempestuous career of a phallic, lion-headed protagonist; horseshoe of the heart = carapace which, like the 'heel', is melted by the 'animal'; also good-luck emblem.

16 haybeds of a mile = bucolic sexual experience.

17–18 Love and labour and kill / In quick, sweet, cruel light = inspiration; in sexual terms, satisfy ('kill') the male's sexual appetite.

20 bowels turn turtle = another metaphorical zoomorphic transformation.

22 parched = because 'raging', perhaps sermonising (cf. 'After the funeral').

23–24 Fishermen of mermen / Creep and harp = contemporaries, such as Auden, whose sorties into the sea of the linguistic unconscious were superficial ('mer*men*' may allude to their homosexuality).

26 Tongue and ear in the thread = bait for the animal/poem on a 'skein' of blood vessels, with a sense that poetry needs to be spoken and heard; temple-bound = refers back to 'cap of the face', and punningly anticipates the allusion to Samson, who was 'bound' and pulled down the Philistines' temple.

29–31 Nailed with an open eye . . . bowl of wounds . . . clap its great blood down = the bowl may be the 'skull', but the lines also seem to describe a sexual struggle.

32–33 atlas . . . poise the day on a horn = to adventure after its birth into this world (atlas means 'to map out', and with 'seas' and 'horn' suggests rounding Cape Horn; in a sexual sense, the male erection is temporary, unable to 'poise' the day).

34–35 Sigh long . . . stunned on gilled stone = 'sigh' and 'lie' are vocative; the other clauses describe the 'animal', metaphorised as a fish, dragged from the depths and killed (i.e.: the poem fixed in being written, or the wilting penis).

35–36 sly scissors ground in frost . . . love hewn in pillars drops = detumescent and castratory imagery, describing what language (or sexual activity) does to the 'animal'; with allusion to Delilah's shearing of Samson's hair (Judges 16:19).

Love 'drops' because the phallic 'pillars' droop; also suggests the pillars of the Philistines' temple.

37–38 the wrackspiked maiden mouth / Lops = language envisaged as an iron maiden (a medieval instrument of torture consisting of an internally spiked sarcophagus, one spike of which would pierce the victim's mouth).

38 a bush plumed with flames = like the burning bush out of which Yahweh spoke to Moses, Exodus 3:3, 2–4.

40 Die in red feathers = the 'animal' is finally a shot-down bird; flying heaven = poetry, imagination; cf. the 'flying garden', 'Altarwise', X.

44 dug your grave in my breast = the animal dies before it can be expressed in speech and find its own form and identity in language.

After the funeral (In memory of Ann Jones) (p. 101)

Written March/April 1938, as a major revision of *N3* 'Six'. A fifteen-line draft was sent to Vernon Watkins on 21 March 1938, and on 1 April 1938 Thomas told him he was 'completely rewriting [it] . . . I'm making it longer and, I hope, better than any of my simple poems'. Published *Life and Letters Today* (Summer 1938), collected in *TML*.

The poem's origins lie in the eighteen-year-old Dylan Thomas's rather unfeeling response to the death of his maternal aunt, Ann Jones, of the 'Fernhill' farm, where he had spent his childhood holidays, the location of 'Fern Hill' and the story 'The Peaches'. Thus, Thomas confessed to Trevor Hughes on 8 February 1933: 'Many summer weeks I spent happily with the cancered aunt on her insanitary farm. She loved me quite inordinately, gave me sweets & money . . . petted, patted, & spoiled me . . . But the foul thing is I feel utterly unmoved . . . I like – liked – her. She loves – loved – me. Am I, he said, with the diarist's unctuous preoccupation with his own blasted psychological reactions to his own trivial affairs, callous & nasty? . . . There must be something lacking in me.' *N3* 'Six', written at the time, reflects this state of mind in its rather callow mockery of Nonconformist hypocrisy, and concludes in the vein of the letter: 'Another well of rumour and cold lies / Has dried, and one more joke has lost its point.'

This suggests that the later poem makes amends for earlier unfeelingness. Thomas's problem lay in how to both praise Ann's loving kindness *and* critique her attachment to a narrow creed. His first attempt was too eulogistic, and he saw that its praise was as potentially hypocritical as the obstreperous mourners; as he told Watkins, sending him the final version, the 'facile &, almost, grandiosely sentimental' ending 'now becomes the new brackets', a self-critique. A new upsurge of praise follows, but it is one which transmogrifies and sets free Ann's emblems of staleness and restraint, the stuffed fox and fern in the parlour where her body would have rested before burial. In a pagan version of the chapel service, the speaker now assumes the role of courtly 'bard' (from Welsh *bardd*) – the poor, Welsh-speaking woman exalted as a medieval queen with a court – and, from her hearth, he invokes local seas and woods to celebrate her simplicity, warmth and dignity in death. In so doing, he creates a funerary statue of words for her grave; Ann herself becomes monumental, while the poet's tribute 'storms' him as perpetual reminder of her loving acceptance of life, and the cosmic process of death and renewal to which it now belongs.

   'After the funeral' marks an important stage in Thomas's development, linking the earlier elemental and later pastoral aspects of the 'green' strain in his work. It is also arguably his most Welsh poem; as well as its bardic details, it is clearly in the Welsh *cof* genre of laudatory memorial-biographical poem, while what Hardy (2000) calls its 'ecstatic metamorphoses of Christian church into wild green nature' recalls the Welsh poets Dafydd ap Gwilym and Edmund Prys.

1–4   After the funeral, mule praises ... in the thick / Grave's foot = the banal praises of Ann resemble the braying of the mules pulling the hearse. Their hooves are muffled, and this epithet transfers to the mourners, who 'happily' (they are still alive!) tap their feet as the 'peg'-shaped coffin is lowered to the 'foot' of the grave. Play on idiom 'one foot in the grave', near death.

5   spittled eyes = fake, artificial grief; the opening lines echo the mood and grotesque phrasing of Hamlet's account of Gertrude's hasty mourning rites. However, 'spittle' also initiates the water = life basis of the poem's redemptive imagery.

6–8   wakes up sleep ... dark of the coffin = the funeral merges into, and wakes the boy from, a nightmare of being imprisoned in the coffin and committing suicide.

8   sheds dry leaves = image of the boy's suicidal blood as the 'leaves' on which the 1933 poem was written; it is dry, by contrast with the water imagery that follows.

9   That ... judgement clout = 'That' is the 'spade' of l.6; the image seems to be of an old grave uncovered by the digging of the new one, exposing a bone, just as all bones will be exposed on Judgement Day. 'Clout' is to strike, but also shroud/swaddling clothes, in a typical birth/death image.

11   stuffed fox and a stale fern = 'The Peaches' describes a stuffed fox and 'a framed photograph of Annie, Uncle Jim and Gwilym smiling in front of a fern-pot' in the farm's front parlour.

14   hooded, fountain = Ann's overflowing love and kindness, like a woman hooded in church, was hidden; yet while Nonconformism was inadequate to

her generosity, Ann's personality was stultified by her faith and domestic circumstances.

15 parched worlds of Wales = spiritually arid (but a joke, given Wales' notoriously high rainfall); pun on Welsh *parchedig*, 'reverend', used of priests.

16 monstrous = exaggerated, but also grotesque; the image of the heart as a fountain which falls in puddles and drowns the sun is a strained metaphysical conceit.

20 druid = like the image of the bard, invokes less constrained religious and poetic eras in Wales, pre-dating Nonconformist dominance.

21 But I, Ann's bard on a raised hearth = the language is allowed to swell again as Ann's service and apotheosis are extended to include the natural world; Ann comes to resemble a dying god, becoming part of the regenerative cycle of nature.

24 ferned and foxy woods = Ann's 'wooden' tongue leads to a natural chapel in the living woods, containing a congregation of revivified forms of the fox and fern.

26 bent spirit = worshipful, but also crippled by its piety; four, crossing birds = cf. Donne, 'The Cross': 'Look up, thou seest birds raised on crossed wings'.

27, 36–37 this skyward statue . . . monumental / Argument = the poem as sculpture in sound becomes a funerary monument over Ann's grave.

36 These cloud-sopped, marble hands = gently mocking a belief in heaven, as exemplified in the uplifted hands of funerary statuary; cloud-like soap suds on Ann's hands as she performed domestic tasks. Cf. *The Tempest*: 'cloud-capped towers'.

38 In his letter to Watkins of February 1939, Thomas noted: 'The 38th line may seem weak, but I think I wanted it like that.'

39 twitch and cry Love = cf. Djuna Barnes's *Nightwood* (1936): 'if one gave birth to a heart on a plate, it would say "Love", and twitch like the lopped leg of a frog'.

39–40 stuffed lung . . . strutting fern = the revivified fox and fern of l.24 return to the stale parlour. The fox is described in terms of a fern, and vice versa, since the creative-destructive energy coursing through them is indiscriminate, all-embracing, and abolishes boundaries of kind, as of life and death.

O Chatterton and others in the attic (p. 102)

Included in a letter to Henry Treece of 16 June 1938; published in *TP71*.

In the letter to Treece, Thomas complains of extreme poverty, and the sense of the opening lines is that this will be sufficient to kill him without resort to the poison used by Chatterton.

1   O Chatterton ... attic = Thomas Chatterton (1752–70), Bristol-born poet who forged medieval manuscripts. On being exposed, he committed suicide by poisoning himself; he was just seventeen. He was idolised by the Romantics; there is a famous painting of him on his deathbed, in an attic, by Henry Wallis.

3   Jeyes' fluid = a cleaning fluid.

12   slap on = right upon.

20   dominies = teachers.

22   Love's a decision of 3 nerves = the reduction of love to the male sexual orgasm. Cf. 'My hero bares his nerves'.

26–27   he also serves / Who only drinks his profits = self-mockingly echoes Milton's sonnet 'On His Blindness': 'They also serve who only stand and wait'.

43   centaur = synonymous with lust.

On no work of words (p. 104)

N3 'Eight', dated February 1933; an extensive revision on the facing page is dated 'Laugharne. Sept. 1938'. Published in *Wales* (March 1939) and collected in *TML*.

In Stanza 1 Thomas berates his writer's block of the previous three months; in Stanzas 2, 3 and 4 three counter-arguments are set out; these expound his belief that human beings have a responsibility to reciprocate the creativity and generosity of the created world in creations of their own; to fail to do so is to suffer death twice, and one might as well revert to pre-human form. The narrative is loosely based on the Parable of the Talents. It is also one of the few poems Thomas himself explicated (see below).

1   On no work ... months = writer's block viewed as a kind of unemployment.

1–2   bloody / Belly of the rich year = the poem was revised in autumn as the leaves redden; 'rich' begins a series of money-related images and puns painfully appropriate for the poverty-stricken Thomases: 'purse', 'pounds', 'treasures', 'currencies', etc.

2   Belly ... big purse of my body = contrasting with 'lean' in l.1, references to Thomas's new stoutness are developed in food and eating imagery.

3   take to task = reprimand, but also, punningly, 'bring to the job in hand'; poverty and craft = imaginative poverty and the craft of writing poetry; but also reproved is the *craft*-iness of his excuses for not writing.

4   hungrily given = the world (or God) wants back what it lends us; life is only ever granted on a lease. Cf. the Parable of the Talents, Matthew 25:14–30.

5   Puffing the pounds of manna up = humans have a duty to return (inflated and multiplied) the gifts of life and 'craft' they are given, like a reversal of God's gift of manna to feed the hungry Israelites (some refused the gift, and it 'bred worms, and stank'; cf. Exodus 16:14–20). George Herbert's 'Prayer I' describes prayer as 'exalted manna'.

6   The lovely gift of the gab bangs back on a blind shaft = unused, the poet's gift returns as an insult ('bangs back') and wasted vision ('blind') to the world, like the refused manna of l.5; a good example of Thomas's approximation of *cynghannedd* effects (cf. 'I dreamed my genesis'), with a sonic mirroring around central repetition of 'b': *l g ft g b / b g b bl ft*.

7   To lift to leave = to pick up but then abandon, leave undeveloped, which is a kind of theft (slang 'lift'); pleasing death = a painless or flattering kind of death, but also pleasing *to* Death himself, who favours a wasted, death-in-life existence. Cf. Blake, *Milton*, First Book, pl.12, l.9: 'rest and pleasant death'.

8   rake = Death personified as a croupier, who will rake in the money of our selves laid down on the betting table of life, and count it in the 'bad dark' of oblivion.

10   expensive ogre = Death; twice = Walford Davies (1993) notes: 'Death takes not only the poet's body but also that body of poetry he failed to produce.'

11–12   Ancient woods . . . which is each man's work = a curse levelled at himself if he fails to perform his duty; as Thomas told Desmond Hawkins in a letter of 14 August 1939: 'The sense of the last two lines is: Well, to hell and death with me, may my old blood go back to the bloody sea it came from if I accept this world only to bugger it up or return it.'

11   woods of my blood, dash down to the nut of the seas = a de-evolutionary movement; 'woods' refers to the origins of humans as arboreal primates; 'dash down' can mean 'hurry down' and also 'throw down, break'; 'nut', as 'seed', is from the trees in the 'woods', bringing in the 'sea' in its evolutionary role as the origin of life. As Thomas told Hawkins: 'The oaktree came out of the acorn; the woods of my blood came out of the nut of the sea, the tide-concealing, blood-red kernel.'

12   If I take . . . which is each man's work = with 'to return' as its subject, this clause reads 'which is each man's duty'; with 'world', it means 'which is each

man's creation'. Thomas sees the world (and the poem as word-world) as continually created by the engagement with it by each human subject. If he merely consumes or throws the world back at itself ('returns', thanklessly) he shrinks it and causes regression; if he responds creatively it is reborn ('nut' becomes 'woods' again).

I, the first named (p. 104)

Enclosed in a letter to Vernon Watkins on 14 October 1938, and referred to in a letter to Henry Treece of 16 October 1938. Published, as 'Poem', in *Seven*, III (October 1938); collected in *TP71*.

This enigmatic quatrain proceeds by riddling self-definition. Its speaker appears to be a ghost, or double, of Thomas – perhaps a (dis)embodiment of the necessary self-consciousness and self-distancing the poet requires in order to write. The 'sir and Christian friend' is thus the bodily form of the self which 'writes these words I [the ghost] write', and the 'spellsoaked house' its head. In the final line, the bodily owner of the head-house is described as a 'lack-a-head ghost'; that is, the body is also viewed as a ghost by the 'ghost' of self-consciousness, doomed as it is to extinction in which the speaker will also perish (hence its 'fear'). The poem plays characteristically on the double sense of 'ghost' or 'shade', but foregrounds the distinction between mind and body Thomas usually questions.

1 I, the first named . . . sir and Christian friend = God and Christ are respectively the 'first-named' in Genesis and St John's Gospel.

The tombstone told (p. 104)

'Thirty Six' in *N3*, dated July 1933; expanded in a revision copied into *N3* dated 'Sept 1938. Laugharne'. Published in *Seven* (Winter 1938), *Voice of Scotland* (December–February 1938/39) and *Poetry* (Chicago), November 1939 (titled 'A Winding Film'); collected in *TML*.

Sent to Vernon Watkins in September 1938 as one of '2 short ones of mine, just done', and described as 'ballad-like', and (on 14 October) 'Hardy-like'. 'Thirty Six' is the tale of a woman who was 'wed on a wild March morning' but died in her wedding dress before the consummation of her marriage, and so was buried under both married and maiden names. The rewriting presents events from radically different subjective and chronological angles. In Stanza 1, the speaker happens on the church where the bride was married and buried, and reads her gravestone, telling us that her death took place long ago; in Stanza 2 we are told that 'before' her death but 'later' than it, the speaker heard the tale of her conviction, as she was dying, that she was naked and making love with Death. Stanza 3 claims the speaker saw this encounter projected, film-like, on the wall of the womb, and that he has heard her speak through the 'stone bird' carved on her tombstone. The last five lines are in the girl's voice, and endorse the story of her ravishment by death, depicted in terms of sexual climax, which is also imagined as a violent birth.

4 pouring place = it is raining in the graveyard; perhaps with pun on 'poring' over the inscription.

6 Before I heard in my mother's side = she died before I was in the womb, but I 'heard' about her there.

11 stranger's bed = the bride was taken ill on the way home after the wedding and goes into a nearby 'stranger's' house, where she dies.

14 Through the devilish years and innocent deaths = the notebook version has 'Through the small years and great deaths'.

15 a secret child = the speaker/Thomas himself; cf. 'My world is pyramid'.

21 hurried = 'winding' in previous versions. Thomas had rejected 'hurried' in his October letter – '"Hurried" film I just couldn't see; I wanted it slow & complicated, the winding cinematic works of the womb' – but reverted to it for *TML*.

27 bellowing = Thomas admitted to Watkins that 'perhaps it looks too much like a stunt rhyme with heroine, but that was unavoidable'.

29–30 A blazing . . . his hair = different climaxes – orgasm, death and birth – are fused. Thomas's September letter asked: 'I'm not quite sure of several words, mostly of "great" floods of his hair. I think it's right, though; I didn't want a surprisingly strong word there.' The 14 October letter admitted: 'A "strange & red" harsh head was, of course, very weak & clumsy, but I couldn't see the alliteration of "raving red" was effective. I tried everything, & stuck to the commonplace "blazing", which makes the line violent enough then, if not exactly good enough, for the last. In the last line you'll see I've been daring & have tried to make the point of the poem softer & subtler by the use of the dangerous word "dear". [It] fits in, I think, with "though her eyes smiled", which comes earlier. I wanted the girl's *terrible* reaction to orgastic [sic] death to be suddenly altered into a kind of despairing love. As I see it now, it strikes me as very moving, but it may be too much of a shock, a bathetic shock perhaps, & I'd very much like to know what you think.'

A saint about to fall (p. 105)

Written September/October 1938 and published in *Poetry* (London), February 1939, with the title 'Poem in the Ninth Month', suggested by Vernon Watkins; collected in *TML*.

Sending it to Watkins on 14 October 1938, Thomas said: 'Remember this is a poem written to a child about to be born – you know I'm going to be a father in January – and telling it what a world it will see, what horrors and hells.' It was provisionally titled 'In September', alluding to the signing of the Munich Agreement in that 'terrible war month', as Thomas called it, when WWII became all but inevitable. At first sight the poem seems to depict and address a child just about to be born, namely Dylan's and Caitlin's first son, Llewelyn. Thus, it clearly fuses a symbolic internal landscape with the estuarial one of Laugharne, where they were living, and Thomas referred in a letter to John Davenport of 24 August 1938 to the expected child as 'our saint or monster'. Glossing 'On the angelic etna of the last whirring featherlands' for Desmond Hawkins a year later, he noted:

> I wanted to get the look of this stanza right: a saint about to fall, to be born, heaven shifting visionarily [interpolated: 'changingly, the landscape moving to no laws but heaven's, that is: hills moving, streets flowing, etc.'] under him as he stands poised: the stained flats, the lowlying lands, that is, and the apartment houses all discoloured by the grief of his going, ruined forever by his departure (for heaven must fall with every falling saint): on the last wave of a flowing street before the cities flow to the edge of heaven where he stands about to fall, praising his making and unmaking & the dissolution of his father's house etc – (this, as the poem goes on to talk about, is his father-on-earth's veins, his mother's womb, and the peaceful place before birth): Standing on an angelic (belonging to heaven's angels & angelic itself) volcanic hill (everything is in disruption, eruption) on the last feathers of his fatherlands (and whirring is a noise of wings). All the heavenly business I use because it makes a famous noble landscape from which to plunge this figure onto the bloody, war-barbed etc earth. It's a poem written on the birth of my son. He was a saint for the poem's sake (hear the beast howl).

However, as suggested by both the poem's narrative and composition date (well before the birth on 30 January 1939), conception is the subject at least as much as birth. The 'saint' is so called because it is canonised by the ecstasy of its moment of origin, and there are in fact two 'falls'; in Stanza 1, from the 'heaven' of the sexual-orgasmic act; then, in anticipation, in Stanza 3, from the womb into the world.

7 his father's house in the sands = the father's erection is a 'house built on sand' – proverbial for a ramshackle construction, and alluding to the sandy Towy estuary.

8 chucked = patted lovingly; threw away (concealed pun on 'cast', as bells are).

11 On the angelic etna of the last whirring featherlands = the sperm is like a

winged (feathered) angel as it prepares to depart; pun on 'fatherlands'.

15–16   Sang heaven hungry . . . spitting vinegar = sang the satisfaction of the bliss of the sexual act (heaven) about to be satisfied by the bittersweet 'Christbread' and 'vinegar', with sexual climax as crucifixion (the vinegar given to Christ on the Cross).

18   Glory cracked like a flea = Thomas asked Watkins: 'Does "Glory cracked like a flea" shock you? I think you'll see it must come there, or some equally grotesque contrast.' Cf. Donne's 'The Flea', in which lovers' blood is mingled, as was believed to occur in intercourse, and a flea is 'cracked'. The line evokes the instant of orgasm, when conception was felt to occur; 'cracked' also refers to the female genitals.

22–24   boats bringing blood . . . a hold of leeches and straws = after ejaculation, the penis detumesces; cf. 'leech' in 'The force that through the green fuse'.

25   Heaven fell . . . beat the left air = as Ralph Maud (2003) notes, the heaven of orgasm collapsed as the saint fell from the father's penis and only a broken bell 'beat' the air abandoned ('left') by heaven at the end of coition.

26–34   O wake in me . . . brains and hair = addressed by the mother to the child, with the father returning to speak in l.35.

34   The skull of the earth is barbed with a war of burning brains and hair = to Watkins, Thomas noted: 'The last line of the 2nd verse might appear just a long jumble of my old anatomical clichés, but if, in the past, I've used "burning brains & hair" etc. too loosely, this time I used them – as the only words – in dead earnest.'

35   time-bomb town = of the womb (a bomb with nine-month fuse).

37   Throw your fear a parcel of stone = to forestall a prophecy that he would be usurped by his sons, the Titan Cronus ate all his offspring; to save Zeus, Cronus's wife Rhea gave him instead a stone wrapped in a baby's swaddling-clothes.

39   Lapped among herods = protected from modern massacres of the innocents, resembling that ordered by Herod (Matthew 2:16–18).

44   sponge of the forehead = sponge held to the forehead of the mother in labour.

48–51   Cry joy . . . girl-circled island = Thomas told Watkins: 'It's an optimistic, taking-everything poem. The two most important words are "Cry joy"', adding, 'The last four lines of the poem, especially the last but two, may seem ragged, but I've altered the rhythm purposely; "you so gentle" must be very gentle, & the last line must roar.'

Twenty-four years (p. 107)

Composed autumn 1938; sent to Vernon Watkins on 24 October 1938, and published in *Life & Letters Today* (December 1938), where it was entitled 'Birthday Poem'; collected in *TML*.

'Twenty-four years' takes its cue from Milton's sonnet on his twenty-fourth birthday, 'How soon hath time the suttle theef of youth'. Like Milton, Thomas begins with the reminder of mortality a birthday symbolises, but, in the parenthetical aside to himself in l.2, he dismisses regrets over the passing of time and missed ('dead') opportunities, and resolves to advance, as Milton also does, with a confidence that is all the greater for his uncertainty concerning the future. The image of the tailor-embryo, piecing together the fleshy 'shroud' of its death-oriented life-to-come, comes from a cluster of related symbols drawn from neonatal development, *Struwwelpeter* and tailoring. It leads to an outfacing of doubt and the inevitability of death, with life likened to someone dressed in their finery and out on a spree, with death as their final encounter. Existence is celebrated as necessarily self-spending, and Milton's Christian stoicism becomes a vitalist vision of life as sheer exuberant loss. Thomas himself was concerned about possible crudeness; on the postcard on which it was sent to Watkins, he wrote: 'This poem's just a statement, perhaps.' However, the last line transforms the poem's melodrama with a half-casual, half-resigned note; and a poem about death is ended with the verb 'to be' ('is'), reflecting open-mindedness about how 'long' the speaker has left (or whether eternity exists).

1 years . . . tears = the speaker's birthday reminds him of lost opportunities; the play years/tears reinforces the sense.

2 (Bury the dead . . .) = as in an aside in a Jacobean tragedy, the speaker cautions himself against the self-pity which might arise from thoughts of ageing (cf. Christ's injunction to 'Let the dead bury their dead', Matthew 8:22). To Watkins on 20 December, Thomas admitted: 'I do realise your objections to my line; I feel myself the too selfconscious flourish, recognise the Shakespeare echo (though echo's not the word)'; in labour = with difficulty; in the act of giving birth.

3 natural doorway = the entrance to the womb, from where life's 'journey' begins; I crouched like a tailor = tailors sat cross-legged and bent forward as they worked.

4 shroud = the flesh of the body; the winding-sheet in which the dead body will be wound. Cf. Donne's 'Death's Duell': 'Wee have a winding sheete in our Mothers wombe, which grows with us from our conception, and wee come into the world, wound up in that winding sheet, for wee come to seeke a grave'.

5 meat-eating sun = sun as destructive as well as life-giving.

6 Dressed to die = variant on idiomatic 'dressed to kill' (i.e.: dressed up in order to make a favourable impression, or sexual conquest; here it will be Death, who will conquer the speaker), with pun on 'die' as sexual climax; sensual strut = cf. 'the strutting fern' of 'After the funeral'.

7 red veins full of money = the disc-like blood corpuscles are coins the embryo will spend, once born; its 'veins' are ore which it will mine and spend.

8 elementary = death as the 'elementary' fact of life, punning on it as a kind of elementary school and return to the elements; cf. Sir Thomas Browne, *Religio Medici*, I, 37: 'Now, for these walls of flesh ... it is nothing but an elemental composition, and a fabricke that must fall to ashes'.

9 I advance = positive, despite describing a movement towards death (perhaps with financial sense of 'advancing' credit); for as long as forever is = also used in 'For as long as forever is' (see above). Sending the poem to Watkins, Thomas claimed: 'at last – I think – I've found the place for it: it was a time finding that place'.

Once it was the colour of saying (p. 107)

Probably a reworked poem from the same period as 'The spire cranes', written late 1938; published in *Wales* (March 1939) and collected in *TML*.

An account of the change in Thomas's style of 1938; revisiting the room inhabited by his teenage self at 5 Cwmdonkin Drive, he bids farewell to his early process poetic and explains what he feels might follow it. However, this is not quite what it purports to be, since Thomas's poetry became more, not less, obviously 'colourful' in the 1940s and 1950s, and some earlier verbal density was retained until 1941.

The melancholy tone flows from the risks Thomas knew he was taking in turning towards more discursive poetry, of a kind less prompted by the linguistic unconscious and more directly reliant on the ego and its biographical adventures. To represent this, he uses a template taken from the ultimate poetic *enfant terrible* and renouncer Rimbaud's sonnet 'Voyelles', which assigns a colour and a set of images to each of the five vowels. Thomas's version calculatedly falls one line short of the fourteen required; to Watkins' objection to this 'error of shape', he replied 'I see your argument ... but the form was consistently emotional and I can't change it without a change of heart.' The form flags up his distance from Rimbaud's radical, heroic stance and delimits his rebelliousness, like his self-description of 1941 as 'the Rimbaud of Cwmdonkin Drive'.

2 Soaked my table = the 'colour of saying' was like an ink-bottle overturned on his writing 'table'; this initiates a train of writing and sea imagery: the uglier

side of a hill = Cwmdonkin Drive is on a steep suburban hill, the other side of which was rural.

3 capsized = small (the size of a school cap); overturned, like a boat at sea, because the field is sloping; (fools)cap-sized writing paper.

4 black and white patch = playing field lower down Cwmdonkin Drive on which girls from the local school play in their black and white hockey gear; black and white poems (often about girls) on the 'patch' of paper.

5 gentle seaslides of saying = the earlier poetry.

6 That all the charmingly drowned . . . kill = (so) that all the things drowned by the (magical) charm of the earlier poems may return, like the sea giving up its dead on the Day of Judgement, to awaken the new poetry and 'kill' off the earlier sort.

7 mitching = Anglo-Welsh for truanting; reservoir park = a reservoir and a park lay opposite Thomas's house.

8 cold = originally 'close'; cuckoo = witless.

10 The shade . . . shades = play on the sense of the deeper shadow cast by the trees at night (into which the unfeeling boys throw stones hoping to hit the lovers beneath them), and on the multiple meanings of a word.

11 a lamp . . . in the dark = paradoxically, the trees' shade was like a light which permitted the perception of erotic truth; the 'poor' lovers are under the trees because they have nowhere else to go.

12 Now my saying shall be my undoing = a poetry based on my life will unmake me, use up me and my past.

13 every stone I wind off like a reel = Thomas's sense is made clearer if 'shall be' of l.12 is repeated after 'off'; the stones of poems he now casts off will not be like the irresponsible ones flung at the lovers, but like the castings-off of a fisherman's reel, made with the constructive aim of hooking something and reeling it in. There is also a lurking sense of film reel, and perhaps even a pun on 'real'.

Because the pleasure-bird whistles (p. 108)

Written January/February 1939 and sent to Vernon Watkins 4 February 1939; published in *Twentieth Century Verse* (February 1939) and *Delta* (Easter 1939) as 'January 1939'; collected in *TML*.

 Beginning with an image for the traditional belief that caged songbirds sang best if they had been blinded, Thomas surveys the disasters of 1938 (chiefly the Munich Agreement) from the vantage point of January 1939, a year promising even worse. Writing to Desmond Hawkins, he explained: 'The poem begins with a queer question about a bird and a horse: because one thing is made sweeter (qualify this word) through suffering what it doesn't understand, does that mean everything is sweeter through incomprehensible, or blind, suffering? (Later the poem has a figure in it standing suffering on the tip of the new year and refusing, blindly, to look back at, if you like, the *lessons* of the past year to help him; and the case, which is really a case for prayer, begins to make itself clear.)'

The 'prayer' is a grace, said for the book which 'Because the pleasure-bird whistles' opens. Usually said *before* eating, this one is for the meal of 1938 and its unlearnt 'lessons'. The speaker criticises the 'enamoured man', a version of Thomas himself, who has not yet faced up to the horror of his times. Refusing to be intimidated by the example of Lot's wife, however, he now takes responsibility for providing a symbolic meal for the year's victims. A self-critique, the poem seems to commit Thomas to exploring more openly the links between suffering and art.

2 blind horse = Gwen Watkins (2005) notes: 'The image of the singing horse came from a dream of Dylan's, in which a horse stood in a cage made of wires which gradually became red-hot, on which a man standing by said, "He sings better now."'

3–4 Convenient bird and beast . . . mood = the poem reflects on its processes; to Hawkins, Thomas explained: 'I, the putter of the question, turn momentarily aside from the question and, in a sort of burst of technical confidence, say that the bird and beast are merely convenient symbols that just have to suffer what my mood dictates, just have to be the objects of my mood (wit or temper? but here 'mood' alone) has decided to make a meal upon and also the symbolic implements with which I cut the meal and objects up.'

8 drug-white shower of nerves and food = play on 'snow'; here wintry weather, a drug (for 'nerves', 'snow' being slang for cocaine), and manna.

10 wind that plucked a goose = a wind bearing snowflakes.

11–12 wild tongue . . . red, wagged root = the mutilated voice of the post-Munich era (with allusion to the legend of Philomela, raped and mutilated in this way by Tereus, and turned into the nightingale); red tongues of fire which war will bring.

13 bum city = London, often negatively described by Thomas; the pun makes it a latter-day Sodom, in reference to the homosexual ethos of some of its literary circles.

14–20 frozen wife . . . salt person = Genesis 19:1–26 tells how God saved the family of Lot, warning them to leave Sodom before he destroyed it; although warned not to look back, Lot's wife did so and was turned to a pillar of salt; mauled = knocked about; painter's maul.

22–24 If the dead starve . . . rock-chested sea = if the dead of 1938 and their 'blasted place[s]' are not fed some 'fable' of recognition, their hunger will over-throw the 'upright' people, such as I believe myself to be, even though they live as far away as the other side of the world, and I am at sea on island Britain (while we may feel safely remote from Europe's troubles, such 'rock-chested' certainty is 'spray-based').

25 past table = of the past year.

'If my head hurt a hair's foot' (p. 109)

Written February/March 1939; published in *Poetry* (London) (April 1939); col-lected in *TML*.

Introducing the poem on a BBC reading in September 1949, Thomas ob-served that it 'tells of a mother and her child who is about to be born. It is not a narrative, nor an argument, but a series of conflicting images which move through pity and violence to an unreconciled acceptance of suffering: the moth-er's *and* the child's. This poem has been called obscure. I refuse to believe that it is obscurer than pity, violence, or suffering. But being a poem, not a lifetime, it is more compressed.' The unborn child speaks in Stanzas 1–3, and its mother replies in Stanzas 4–6. The child, fearing it may hurt its mother at birth, offers to be 'unravelled' back into her body, using metaphors drawn from mining and a miner's leisure pursuits. The mother responds by expressing her love for the child and anticipating feelings of loss after the birth, and sadness at the condition of mortality the child will enter.

1–2 If my head . . . downed bone = a 'hair's foot' is a follicle; the foetus would rather be absorbed back into its mother's body than hurt her in the least by being born. This is conveyed by proverbial '[I wouldn't] hurt a hair of your head' (ti-niest amount) and 'hair's breadth' (smallest measure), and via 'hare' the sense of brevity is also added; the hair's thinness has a counterpart in the hare's speed, the least measurable amount matched by the swiftest possible instant. A 'hare's foot' may also be a lucky charm ('If my birth is bad luck, unmake me').

2–3 unpricked ball of my breath = my as yet unbreathing head; Bump on a spout = hurt the urethra on the way out of the womb; let the bubbles jump out = let me drown now in the amniotic fluid. 'Unpricked', 'ball' and 'spout' also develop a phallic conceit.

4 drop = as on the gallows; the worm of the ropes = the umbilical cord; a noose by reference back to 'drop', but the plural leads to boxing-ring imagery.

5 ill = an adverb for 'bully'; the clouted scene = of birth; the midwife clouts (slaps) the baby if it is slow to draw breath, and clouts are also swaddling-cloths.

6 All game phrases . . . cockfight = the foetus says that the womb, shaped like a

boxing ring and cockpit, is apt ('fit') for talk of games, and does so; with sexual double entendre on 'ring' and 'cockfight'.

7–10 I'll comb the snared woods . . . Before I . . . bloody a loud room = s/he will do everything possible to evade time, and avoid inflicting pain on the mother. The 'woods' are the womb's, the 'snare' the route out of it, the foetus being likened to a poacher; glove on a lamp = applicable to boxer, miner and poacher.

8 Peck, sprint . . . duck time = s/he will dodge like a cock in a cock fight or a boxer.

9 ghost with a hammer = the South Wales coal miner and flyweight world boxing champion, Jimmy Wilde, was known as 'the ghost with a hammer in his hand'; air = as it is born, the foetus rushes the boxer-like pummelling air like its opponent.

10 Strike light = the newborn strikes light as a miner strikes a seam of coal; ignite a match (for a miner's lamp).

11–15 Realising it cannot dodge time for ever, the foetus gallantly offers to sacrifice itself.

12 making house = the womb.

13 cross place = a place for sexually conjoining, or argument.

16–17 Not for Christ's dazzling bed . . . particles and charms = the mother would not change this birth for the gentler birth of Christ or the slow process which creates mother-of-pearl.

24 grain = sperm and ovum, a symbol for man in general; grave = womb as well as tomb.

26 dust-appointed grain = our appointment with the dust of the grave; pun on 'disappointed'.

27–28 No return / . . . nor the skeleton's thin ways = there is no escape back into the 'fat streets' of the womb or through death.

29–30 The grave . . . And the endless beginning of prodigies suffers open = the mother's womb and death are as if blocked by a stone – you cannot escape through them, and the marvels of life have to be 'suffered' (in the senses of allowed and endured) at the opening of the womb.

Poem (To Caitlin) (p. 110)

Written spring 1939; published in *Life and Letters Today* (October 1939) as 'Poem (To Caitlin)' and *LVW* (1957); heavily revised in summer 1945 as 'Unluckily for a death' (see pp. 174–5, 397).

A hymn to the joys and travails of married life, this poem was written, Thomas told Vernon Watkins in sending it to him in May 1939, 'in a very enjoyable mood (or any other better word) of surly but optimistic passion'.

The basic premise of both versions of the poem is that the speaker has been saved by his beloved, the addressee, from the deathly temptations offered by two other female entities, a 'phoenix' and a 'widow', who call on him to 'shoo up the light . . . to heaven' or 'sing underground', respectively – that is, to prize the spirit at the expense of the body, or vice versa. 'Unluckily' for them, he sees the monstrosity, imaged in miscegenatory terms, of the 'Juan'-like behaviour involved in succumbing to them. Caitlin's love, 'got luckily', removes the polarised oppositions of the temptresses' 'black-and-white wedding', even though, in the last lines, it is acknowledged they continue to lie in 'wait' for him should he lapse.

1–28 Unluckily for a death . . . must wait my wish = 'Nor' (l.11) is governed by 'has not occurred' in l.7, and 'loving' in l.15 by the 'death' of l.1. Thus: although death desires the speaker's body, his 'ghost' 'fireworks . . . And weeps' at the breast of his beloved, and 'will never [therefore] . . . Arch . . . Or shoo . . . to heaven', forcing 'The . . . two [to] wait my wish'.

2 phoenix = legendary, long-lived bird, regenerated by dying on a pyre and rising from the ashes; here the lure of a false promise of resurrection.

4 thigh-describing wreath = pubic hair; sex as death. The earth is a 'continent-sheeted' bed in which the slow copulation of decay is consummated. Rejecting the 'phoenix' and 'widow' associated with it, the speaker rejects a morbid dwelling on this aspect of process.

13 continent-sheeted = pun on continence (see Stanza 3); animal rails = Thomas told Watkins: 'I am not sure of the word "animal" . . . it says more or less what I mean, that the rails, the frame, if you like, of the bed of the grave is living, sensual, serpentine, but it's a word I've used perhaps too often.'

16 burly body = refers to Thomas's new stoutness.

17 managed storm = natural phenomenon subjected to scientific understanding, common in Thomas's poetry; e.g. 'discovered skies', 'How shall my animal'.

27 shoo = to chase away; here self-reflexive; bird = the phoenix.

29, 36, 39 I see . . . Juan runs . . . I see through = the speaker 'sees' the plight of the 'tigron' and dissatisfaction of Juan, and thus 'sees through' the 'dust-drenched two'; tigron = cross between a tiger and a lion.

33–34 duck- / Billed platypus = like 'tigron', grotesque combination of seemingly incommensurable creatures; bush = Australian outback; pubic hair.

35   clot = blood clot; stupid or silly person.

42   Great crotch, and giant continence = Thomas told Watkins: 'I've also used [crotch], once fairly startlingly [in 'A saint about to fall'], but I'm afraid the word is quite essential here. Or so, at the moment, I think.' The line sums up the suggestion already given in 'cold as fish', 'want' and 'sexless' that the genuine sexual love the 'two' can give is in inverse proportion to their promises.

53   I chuck my armed happiness = Thomas told Watkins: 'With your annoyance at the word "chuck" I agree; and my use of it is sentimental. I have tried "cast" but that is too static a word; I'll find what I really want.' Like 'crotch', used in 'A saint about to fall'.

55   sycorax = adjective, like 'fair'; from the witch Sycorax in *The Tempest*.

56–57   We abide with our pride = Thomas informed Watkins: 'The jingle of "abide with pride" I'm retaining; I wanted the idea of an almost jolly jingle there, a certain carelessness to lead up to the flat, hard, ugly last line of truth, a suggestion of "Well that's over, O atta boy we live with our joy"; a purposeful intolerance – no, I meant an intolerance on purpose – of the arguments I had been setting against my own instinctive delight in the muddled world'; lump of mistakes = the world; to Watkins, Thomas explained: 'The last two lines I can see you disliking, especially the crude last lump. But that sudden crudeness is (again) essential to the argument, to . . . the philosophy. Perhaps I should have found a stronger & nobler adjective for the light, to be in greater opposition to the very real crudity of the lump of earth.'

To Others than You (p. 112)

Probably begun 25 May 1939, when Thomas was checking the text of the story 'The Orchards' (see note to l.15 below), and sent to Vernon Watkins in early June 1939: 'Here is a new short poem, nothing very much.' Published in *Seven* (Autumn 1939) and *DE*.

   The title accuses certain, unspecified friends of treachery, while absolving any particular friend reading the poem. Nevertheless, its target is usually taken to be Geoffrey Grigson, editor of *New Verse*, who turned against Thomas after 1936. The false friend is accused of deception, acting like a conjuror or card sharp; his eye is like a forged coin, he delved into the speaker's 'shyest secret', he enticed his sweet tooth for affection to bite 'dry' on betrayal. Playing on the meanings of 'familiar', Thomas 'calls out' the offender, using the legitimate magic of poetry, exposing him as a fraudster guilty of trying to smash the speaker's heart (as conjurors do with eggs and watches).

2   bad coin in your socket = as in a gas meter or a coin-operated machine; pennies were also placed on the eyes of the dead (in eye-'sockets') to keep them closed; play also on 'pocket'.

4   palmed = planted on the speaker, as if by a conjuror or card sharp.

5   Brassily = brazenly, shamelessly.

6   bits = as in drill bits; play on 'bit' as verb in l.7.

15   desireless familiar = friend who makes no untoward claims; but to be familiar can mean to assume an unwonted intimacy, and 'desireless' can mean 'indifferent'; a 'familiar' is also a supernatural creature which assists witches in the practice of magic.

20   friends were enemies on stilts = cf. *N3* 'Twenty Two', of 2 April 1933: 'A friend is but an enemy on stilts / Striding so high above the common earth . . . You cannot see his eyes or know his faults.'

When I woke (p. 112)

Written in Laugharne, June–September 1939, published in *Seven* (Autumn 1939) and *DE*.
   Thomas quoted a version of the opening line in a letter of 1 April 1938 to Vernon Watkins: 'I've got one of those very youthfully-made phrases, too, that often comes to my mind & which one day I shall use: "When I woke, the dawn spoke".' The original, 'You woke and the dawn spoke', was interpolated in *N3* 'Fifty One' of 1933. The context here is impending war; the speaker wakes from nightmares, presentiments of conflict, to the sights and sounds of a Laugharne morning. These briefly 'dispel' his fears, as he asserts his own ability to create the world. In the final lines, however, his fragile 'prophet-progeny' are shattered by a radio news bulletin, or perhaps even the announcement of war on the morning of 3 September 1939.

3–7   coiling crowd . . . pokers of sleep . . . woman-luck = nightmares, including a succubus (as well as a misogynistic association of women with bad luck).

8–12   a man outside with a billhook . . . beard from a book = outside a man is lopping a tree; he is bearded, and has a kind of scythe, and therefore resembles the figure of Father Time as traditionally depicted, although he is reassuringly 'warm-veined'.

9   Up to his head in his blood = blood is pumping healthily through the man's body, but the image is ominous too.

13–15   Slashed down the last snake . . . wrap of a leaf = the man disposes of the snake-like branches of the tree, with their snake-like leaves, comforting the speaker; the imagery is Edenic.

16–21 Every morning I make . . . Everybody's earth = knowingly over-grandiose description of how we 'come to' the world each time we awake, remaking it in consciousness; the 'godlike' phenomenological recreation is suggested by biblical allusion.

17 God in bed, good and bad = the second half of the line is a play on the first half.

18 water-face walk = cf. Jesus' walking on the Sea of Galilee (e.g. Matthew 14:22–3); also simply washing one's face in the morning.

19 stagged = various verb senses in *OED*, including stagger, stride, observe or spy upon, and '(of trousers) to cut short'; scatter-breath = from 'scatter-brained'.

19–20 Both lines may be read as a compound adjective applying to 'earth', l.21.

20 sparrowfall = cf. Matthew 10:9, in which the disciples are told that God marks even the fall of a sparrow.

25 erected air = radio waves of a broadcast, hinting at the machismo of sabre-rattling speeches on the eve of war.

28 No Time . . . no God = the clocks and church bells do the opposite of what they usually do with the realisation that the peace of the sea-town, and the world, is 'breaking'.

29–30 white sheet . . . shells = pennies are placed on the eyes of the dead and a sheet drawn over the body.

Paper and sticks (p. 113)

Probably written in summer 1939, and published in *Seven* (Autumn 1939); published in *DE* but, unlike the rest of *DE*, dropped from *CP52*.

Thomas wrote to Dent's on 10 September 1952: 'Proofreading the Collected Poems, I have the horrors of "Paper and Sticks" . . . It's *awful*. I suppose it's *quite* impossible to cut it out? I shd so like it, somehow, to be omitted.' Dent's obliged, but at the cost of moving 'Do not go gentle into that good night' from near the end of *CP52* to take its place. *TP71* and *CP88* restored the poem, and returned 'Do not go gentle' to its proper place.

Thomas may have felt that the slightness and atypical manner of 'Paper and sticks' would make *CP52* more vulnerable to criticism. However, it is an accomplished lyric in its own song-like, realist terms, in the voice of a servant girl seduced and deceived by a 'rich boy'. The '(news)paper and sticks' of the title are the materials with which she has made a fire, the 'shovel' a metonym for the coal which has been shovelled on top of them. Except for a final full stop, the poem is unpunctuated throughout.

Once below a time (p. 114)

Probably written late 1939; published in *Life and Letters Today* (March 1940) and originally intended for *DE*, it was excluded from that collection, but sent to Thomas's US publishers, New Directions, and appeared in its *New Poems* (1940) and *Selected Writings of Dylan Thomas* (1946). This may have reconciled Thomas to including it in *CP52*, where he specified a position for it among the poems of *DE*.

Written during Thomas's return to Wales in 1938–40, the poem reviews his youth in Swansea, mockingly charting his rise and partial fall as self-styled rebel, using the mixed line lengths, forms and rhythms typical of this time. Through the bruising loves, isolated struggles and idealistic voyaging involved in becoming an artist, the speaker tells how he modified the provincial suit of the self the 'tailors' made for him, emerging from the sea of self-reinvention to 'astound' them. In Part II, however, this 'silly' disguise is 'pierced' through by the eyes of the 'tailors' master', who sees the 'boy of common thread' beneath. But this does not mean that he regrets his earlier antics – even if he would now like to 'lie down'.

I

1   Once below a time = phrase reused in 'Fern Hill'.

3   bit = the main verb of Part I, whose direct object is the narrator. The sense runs: 'Once . . . when my . . . flesh bit [into me], [like an ill-fitting] suit [which I bought] for a serial sum . . . In common clay clothes . . . I astounded the sitting tailors . . .'.

4–5   serial sum . . . the first of each hardship = bought on credit, with payments due every month.

12   cloud swallower = on the model of 'sword-swallower'; so, someone who ingests insubstantial ideas and romantic notions.

13–14   bottlecork boats / And out-of-perspective sailors = as in a child's painting.

18   clock faced tailors = surreal representation of the fact that the tailors who make the body also determine how long it will live; cf. 'time-faced crook' in 'Grief thief of time'.

19   bushily = hints at pubic 'bush'; bear wig and tails = adapts 'top hat and tails'.

21   kangaroo foot of the earth = reference to D. H. Lawrence's poem 'Kangaroo', as he told Vernon Watkins in January 1940: 'Yes, the Lawrence calling-up-of-memory in the kangaroo lines was intentional, but if in any way it seems feeble, perhaps a little tame, in such a poem (strenuously resisting conventional associations) then, of course, I must change it.'

24 Up through the lubber crust of Wales = 'lubber' means 'awkward, stupid', as in the disparaging 'landlubber' for a novice sailor; Thomas mocks his own provincial origins, playing on W(h)ales and a whale's (b)lubber 'crust'.

26 squatters = traditionally, tailors squatted while they were stitching garments.

27–28 Shabby and Shorten . . . stitch droppers = an imaginary firm of tailors, whose name symbolises the provincial 'tailoring' of rebel instincts, and whose workmanship is shoddy.

II

30–34 coffin carrying / Birdman . . . hole for the rotten / Head = morbid attributes of Thomas's early self and poetry.

35 The cloud perched tailors' master with nerves for cotton = a god-like master tailor who uses thread made of 'nerves' to sew together the flesh-suit cut out in Part I.

37, 40 Columbus on fire . . . Cold Nansen's beak = explorers symbolising the young Thomas's taste for extremes.

45 cherry capped dangler = to lose one's cherry is to lose one's virginity; hence, sexual inexperience; green = naive.

47 Thomas told Watkins: 'I have put "Never never oh never to regret the bugle I wore" (all one line), so that the repetition, the pacific repetition, of "I would lie down, lie down and live" is loudly and swingingly balanced.' The bugle symbolises the younger Thomas's brassy assertiveness.

48 I blasted in a wave = like his namesake in *The Mabinogion*, young Dylan makes for the sea; 'blasted' may allude to 'The force that through the green fuse'.

There was a Saviour (p. 116)

Written January–March 1940, published in *Horizon*, 1:5 (May 1940); collected in *DE*.

To Vernon Watkins on 30 January 1940, Thomas announced he was 'working on a new poem, a poem which is giving me more pleasure than I've got out of any work for months, or even years', describing it as 'my austere poem in Milton measure'. Its form is that of Milton's 'On the Morning of Christ's

Nativity', a favourite poem, and it indicts organised Christianity's perversion of Christ's teachings to justify a complacent, otherworldly retreat from our responsibility to others. However, 'saviour' is broad enough to include other 'saviours' of the preceding decade, such as Hitler, Mosley and Stalin. Stanza 1 describes the believers who ignored growing injustice; in Stanza 2 they confess their faults; Stanza 3 addresses them, repeating the accusation; Stanzas 4 and 5 are spoken by the poet and one of the believers, with the poet confessing his own guilt. Psychosexual strains complicate the religious-political critique. In Stanza 2, the 'children' articulate the 'safe unrest' of puberty, showing a complex feeling towards a father figure whose 'murdering breath' conceals 'fears' and allows silencing to be 'done' within his 'shout' (like a speaker at a totalitarian rally). Stanza 3 describes delight in suffering, and suggests that this leads to displaced aggression, as followers identify with the deity for reasons resembling those that led to identification with demagogues. This leads to the benighted state of the 'brothers' of Stanza 4; they shelter in the Blitz blackout of a war which occurred because of the appeasement of fascism and hard-heartedness towards the poor. To escape, they must release the empathy and (sexual) loving kindness capable of eroding the stony barriers between us and the love 'exiled' in ourselves and others.

2   Rarer than radium = curative, but also threatening (it can kill, and allow others to see into you).

4   kept from the sun = kept from the literal sun and Christ's message (perhaps by being confined in Sunday school). In Freudian terms, the 'prisoners' expend so much energy repressing their desires that they cut themselves off 'from the sun', life as it might be enjoyed.

6   golden note turn in a groove = the saviour's glowing message, now distorted ('turned'), rote-taught and fixed, as on a gramophone record.

7–8   Prisoners of wishes ... smiles = (im)prisoners of the children's wishes locked up their vision and individuality (*I*s) in the smiles; but they too were imprisoned and cut off from the sun/Son by their 'wishes'; jails and studies = the prisoners link repression with the 'smiles' of the saviour, making them imprisoning structures; keyless smiles = echoes 'clueless': the saviour may not realise the repressive cycle he has begun.

15–16   Silence ... the tremendous shout = Winifred Nowottny (1962) notes that the building metaphors now suggest ferocity and concealment, madness and sanctuary, becoming 'much nastier' and yet 'more pitiful'.

22   Put a tear for joy ... flood = contributed to an escapist form of religion.

23   laid your cheek ... a cloud-formed shell = Thomas told Watkins: 'This harder word, "formed", balances the line, avoids the too-pretty internal rhyme

of "laid" and "made", and stops the too-easy flow, or thin conceited stream.'
The brothers rested on a Christ/leader who was vague, empty and ideal
only.

24 Now in the dark . . . yourself and myself = lost spiritually and intellectually
as well as in the darkness of war.

25 blacked = Thomas told Watkins: 'I like the word "blacked", by the way, in
spite of its, in the context, jarring dissonance with "locked". I had . . . the black-
out in mind, another little hindrance on the scene, and the word seemed, to me,
to come rightly.'

28–30 O we who could not stir . . . beating near and fire neighbour = the broth-
ers indict themselves for their indifference to the suffering of those at home and
abroad; near and fire neighbour = play on 'near and far'; ignoring the plight
of those near and far from us has brought the Blitz 'fire' 'near' (the allusion is
to Christ's 'Love thy neighbour as thyself'). From l.28 on, the poem is in the
brothers' voice.

31 wailed and nested in the sky-blue wall = took self-pitying refuge in religion's
otherworldly consolations rather than accepting kinship with the oppressed.

32 break a giant tear . . . fall = empathise with others' suffering, as opposed to
the better-known falls of Adam and Christ.

35 Brave deaths . . . never found = those killed in the war, perhaps indicting
indifference to the individual deaths.

37–38 dust / Ride = Thomas told Watkins: 'No, I can't see "seep" with
dust, & unless a better word can be made will remain true to "fly"', but added
in a postscript: 'For "fly" . . . I now have "ride". I'm sure of that: it's myste-
riously militant, which is what I want.' 'Ride', as elsewhere in Thomas, is
sexual.

39–40 Exiled in us . . . all rocks = proverbial; water wears away the hardest
rock; armless . . . love = play on 'dis-armed', meaning as without armaments
and like Venus (de Milo), goddess of sexual love; silk and rough = cf. Rupert
Brooke's 'The Great Lover': 'Then, the cool kindliness of sheets, that soon /
Smooth away trouble; and the rough male kiss / Of blankets'.

The Countryman's Return (p. 117)

Written spring/summer 1940, published in *Cambridge Front* (Summer 1940);
collected in *TP71*.
     No ms exists for the entire poem. *LVW* includes versions of ll.77–101, fol-
lowed by the complete poem, enclosed in a letter of 19 March 1940.
     The poem draws a contrast between London and rural selves; to Vernon

Watkins, Thomas described it as a 'half-comic attack on myself. . . . You'll see the heavy hand with which I make fun of this middle-class, beardless Walt who props humanity, in his dirty, weeping, expansive moments, against corners & counters & tries to slip, in grand delusions of all embracing humanitarianism, everyone into himself. The first "Cut" in the last verse is, of course, cinema. And a loud Stop. The heaviest satire against myself (or the figure I have made myself into) is in the 7th to the 13th line of the last verse. Then, in the very last part, by a change of rhythm I try to show the inevitability of my unrepentance that the rollicking attack has made. The whole thing's bristling with intentional awkwardnesses, grotesque jokes, vulgarities of phrasing . . . it's not the sort of poem to try to polish; in fact I've tried to avoid most slicknesses, which might have come so easily.' As this implies, in its 'melting' empathy and 'wanting sway' there is also something of the concerns of weightier wartime poems, in comic-surreal guise.

1 low-falutin = as opposed to highfalutin, aspirational (usually with the implication of getting above oneself), particularly as applied to speech.

6 Manuring popeye = bulging-eyed, with play on 'maturing'.

10 pintables = forerunners of pinball machines, common in pubs.

25 White feathering = during WWI, women presented white feathers to young men not in uniform as an accusation of cowardice.

27 Pedro's or Wendy's = probably bars or nightclubs.

33–36 I propped humanity's weight . . . all melt = the 'grand delusions' (see above).

38 under his eyes = literal interpretation of 'to have bags under one's eyes'.

57 great danes = also referred to in 'Two Epigrams of Fealty' (see pp. 203, 423–4). What appears to be Thomas's reminder to himself of Gawsworth's wartime accommodation difficulties, made on the reverse of a ms of this poem at Austin – 'Gawsworth has been living at at [sic] Stebbing in a house which boasted 14 Great Danes but little furniture' – seems to gloss this detail.

58 Bedsitting girls on the beat = a prostitute has a 'beat'.

59 metre = plays on 'beat' to suggest poetry, but puns on gas 'meter' (these were common in bedsits and had to be 'fed' with coins).

69 A singing Walt = Walt Whitman, with pun on 'single malt'.

70 jerrystone = jerry-built (shoddily) of stone.

72 Dean Street = in Soho; a centre of the film and advertising industry.

74   Twolegged and handbagged sparrows = Cockney 'sparrow'; sparrow as traditional symbol of lust, hence sexually available women.

79   paper-blowing tubes = of the London Underground.

91   dirtbox = London.

92   anachronistic scene = the countryside.

101 rich street = probably Dean Street.

Into her lying down head (p. 120)

Largely written between March 1940, when Thomas told Vernon Watkins he was beginning 'an ambitious new poem', and 5 June 1940, when he sent him its first version. Later in June he sent it to Robert Herring at *Life and Letters Today*, where it was published in November 1940. It was revised before being collected in *DE*.

Asking Watkins for help with a title, Thomas told him he had considered 'One Married Pair' and 'Modern Love' (the title of George Meredith's sequence charting a marital breakdown), revealing something of the poem's subject. His letter adds:

> For some reason, I wrote a note underneath it in my copybook: All over the world love is being betrayed as always, and a million years have not calmed the uncalculated ferocity of each betrayal or the terrible loneliness afterwards. Man is denying his partner man or woman and whores with the whole night, begetting a monstrous brood; one day the brood will not die when the day comes but will hang on to the breast and the parts and squeeze his partner out of bed. . . . It's a poem of wide implications, if not of deep meanings.

This closely echoes one of Thomas's favourite novels of the time, Djuna Barnes's *Nightwood*, in which sleep is described as the 'night into which his beloved goes . . . When she sleeps is she not moving her leg aside for an unknown garrison?' The poem concerns the sexual jealousy provoked by such dream 'betrayals' and fantasies about them by a partner.

In Stanza I, a man listens to his partner enjoying in her sleep the attentions of an imaginary or remembered lover. His jealousy seems to draw on a knowledge of how, at the age of fifteen, while Caitlin was modelling for the painter Augustus John, a friend of the Macnamara family, she was raped by him; 'thief of adolescence' (l.31), for example, in Stanza II seems too specific in this context to be a coincidence. Stanza II tells how the sleeping partner is 'enjoyed' by her dream-lover, while the speaker, cuckolded in fantasy, presents sex in caricatural terms, as a violation of the female, recalling the sexual activity preceding sleep as a 'raping wave'. The phallic and other stereotypes seem less his partner's than his own projections, in which both he and she are victims of her past (the luridly 'superhuman' images appear as *male* imaginings of female fantasy, tinged with a dark, grotesque humour).

The poem certainly has 'wide implications'. Its 'beast' is 'always anonymous' because lurking in every sexual subconscious, and Thomas's concern with the unity of being appears in the images of sand, shell, bird, stone and grass in Stanza III, where they magnify the 'needs, desires and severance' of the estranged couple. Married love and promiscuity, bliss and destruction, are set in the larger, amoral perspective of the natural world, a perspective humans are shown to be unable to attain in the last lines; though he views his partner as 'innocent', the speaker is 'torn up' by her behaviour.

Form: three twenty-three-line stanzas, with a syllable-count of 7-7-8-11-9-6-7-7-11-8-11-7-7-11-9-11-11-8-8-20-9-15-16, (with minor variations); rhyme scheme in Stanza 1 *aaabcbcccdbbbdbefggdfhh*, varied in 2 and 3.

1   lying down head = recumbent head; down-haired head which tells lies.

2   His enemies entered bed = the man's sexual rivals enter his partner's dreams.

4   the rippled drum of the hair-buried ear = the image surreally suggests the vagina, and the 'drum' of hymen, as well as that of the ear.

5   Noah's rekindled now unkind dove = the sleeping woman rejects the earlier flood of sexual passion (like the Deluge) with her partner, floating above it Ark-like, seeking the dry land of another lover by sending out a dove (sacred to Venus); play on 'bearing'/baring, and un-'kind' behaviour 'kindling' her treacherous lust.

7–8   Last night in a raping wave = during sex with her partner, the woman was already imagining violation by other men (Dylan ap Tôn, in *The Mabinogion*, identifies Thomas with the wave); Whales unreined = phallic in Thomas (pun on 'Moby Dick', a *sperm* whale); green grave = the sea; womb-as-tomb and font of life.

9   In fountains . . . gave up their love = ejaculated, like a whale spouting.

11–13   Juan = Don Juan, archetypal seducer; King Lear = in Shakespeare's play, Lear's speeches hint at a sexually active youth; Queen Catherine = Catherine the Great of Russia, famed for her sexual appetite ('Caitlin' is a version of 'Catherine'); Samson = Israelite champion, still with his hair, source of his strength and virility; often used by Thomas to figure himself.

16–17   dark blade . . . scythes of his arms = 'blade' is a dashing young man and a knife; the latter leads to 'sighing' as 'scything'; sighing = the sound made by corn being reaped as well as lovers; haycock = pre-Victorian term for 'haystack'.

18   Rode and whistled = sex ('rode') is compared to reaping, with the (male) lover like a whistling field labourer wielding a phallic scythe; scythes are also said to 'whistle' when cutting corn.

19–20 The 5 June 1940 version of this line reads: 'Enamoured Tahiti and shining Hollywood, Circe's swinish, coiling island'; Man . . . burning England . . . enamouring island = burning with passion; England about to burn in the Blitz, (reversing the standard symbolisation of territory as female); play on Isle of Man.

22   swaddling loin-leaf = combines covering for infants and adult genitalia; the woman is both childlike innocent and a sexually knowing Eve after the Fall.

22–23 Sleep to a newborn sleep . . . laid in the acorned sand = the dream-lover lulls the woman asleep, like a child, and makes her sexually receptive. 'Acorns' are food for pigs, symbols of lust, into which Circe transformed Odysseus' men; they are also seeds like those which, fertilised, will produce a 'newborn'.

24   There = in her 'lying down head'.

24–25 numberless tongue . . . male moan = imagined cries of the woman's fantasy lover(s) called up by her own cries of pleasure; the sound of their earlier lovemaking. The confusion is reflected in the lack of agreement between 'numberless' (imaginary lovers) and 'tongue'; their room = bedroom and vagina/womb.

27   baskets of snakes = symbolising revulsion, deceit and jealousy.

28   furnace-nostrilled = dragon-like, with grotesque-comic, as well as fearful, aspect.

45–46   foul wingbeat of the solemnizing nightpriest . . . always anonymous beast = she participates figuratively in a sexual black mass.

47–49   Two sand grains . . . Singly lie with the whole wide shore = the sand grains are the two lovers who, while separate, nevertheless 'lie together' (as a couple), and at the same time promiscuously 'lie . . . with' all the other grains on the beach.

50   The covering sea . . . no names = as in 'cover story' or 'cover up'; the sea/night rolls in, mingling the grains/lovers and anonymising their betrayals.

51   domed and soil-based shell = heavenly and mundane (contrast the 'cloud-formed shell', a falsely idealistic concept of Christ, in 'There was a saviour').

52–55 One voice in chains . . . dissolving under the water veil = the shell (the natural world) utters a single voice which is also collective, describing the fixed roles of male and female and their 'dissolving' and switching as the tide rises;

The female, deadly = cf. Kipling's 'The Female of the Species', in which women are 'deadlier than the male'; male / Libidinous betrayal = stereotype of men as naturally promiscuous. It is impossible to be guilty of *deadliness*, however; the woman is 'innocent' (l.65).

56–60 A she bird sleeping brittle . . . chirrup my bright yolk = the female calls to another male while her partner sleeps ('treading' = copulation); she is poised between bliss (her eggs' 'bright yolk' hatching out to 'chirrup') and destruction (the 'hawk'); nested treefork = where the nest is built; the groin, and the inextricable fusion of opposites involved in the sexual act.

61–64 A blade of grass . . . O she lies alone and still = Hardy (2000) observes: 'The last movement doubles images of grass and stone, not suggesting a pairing but with a scrupulous accuracy, solitude and anonymity for the stone, but company and membership for the grass blade.'

65 Innocent between two wars = the 'wars' punctuating the couple's relationship.

66 incestuous secret brother = the fantasy lover; perpetuate the stars = by begetting children (see l.69). Cf. 'Love in the Asylum', 'Suffer the first vision that set fire to the stars' (created the universe).

68 second comers = the fantasy lovers arrive at the woman after she has made love with her partner.

69 bury their dead = beget children. Echoes but alters the sense of the *Nightwood* passage Thomas used for '"If my head hurt a hare's foot"', 'Night people do not bury their dead' (see above).

Deaths and Entrances (p. 122)

Written summer 1940; published in *Horizon* (January 1941) and collected in *DE*.
Gwen Watkins (2005) reports that Thomas quoted the first two lines to Vernon Watkins in May 1940, told him the poem's title, and said it would also be that of his next collection 'because that is all I ever write about or want to write about'. It comes from Donne's last sermon, 'Death's Duell, or, A Consolation to the Soule, against the dying Life, and living Death of the Body'. This describes birth as an entrance from the womb, one kind of tomb, into this world, another kind: 'But then this *exitus a morte*, is but *introitus in mortem*, this *issue*, this deliverance *from* that *death*, the death of the *wombe*, is an *entrance*, a delivering over to *another death*, the manifold deathes of this *world*'.
In a letter of 8 August he told Watkins about '2 poems I want to write badly: both nightmares, I'm afraid', and in early September he wrote to him of being caught up in the first 'big raid' on London, and of suffering since from 'nightmares like invasions, all successful'. Later that month he had 'finished my poem about invasion, but it isn't shapely enough to send you yet'; this was 'Deaths

and Entrances', an 'invasion' poem anticipating the 'nightmare' of the Blitz, but completed after it had started.

This poem addresses those, including the speaker himself, on the 'eve' of death in 'incendiary' raids of the Blitz. A standard reading would take Stanza 1 to consider the death of someone near to the speaker (friends, lover, family); Stanza 2 the deaths of 'strangers' not known to him, who may or may not be on his side (the imagery suggests they are pilots); and Stanza 3, using the imagery of the death of a German bomber pilot, to consider Death (the 'One enemy') more generally. Yet there are allusions to Christ, and what appears to be an amniotic landscape in Stanza 2, while the figure of the betrayed and ambiguously triumphant Samson, often symbolising Thomas, 'looms' in Stanzas 1 and 3. In short, the poem is enigmatic; tortuous syntax, elaborate circumlocutions, and the slipperiness of the pronouns 'you', 'his' and 'one', make it difficult, if not impossible, to determine the identity of all the figures in it, or their relationship to the speaker, particularly in Stanzas 1 and 3. A nightmarish, evasive quality reflects the poem's origins and its deliberate blurring of self and others, combatants and civilians: 'near' inhabits 'far', 'stranger' 'friend' and 'deaths' 'entrances' at every point.

2 near deaths = of those near to you; almost-deaths.

3–4 When one at the great least of your best loved / And always known = 'great least' is a manipulation of the idiom 'very least'; the effect is to make the 'best loved . . . always known' a figure the 'you' likes to think isn't important, but who actually is – like death, which is inescapable, necessary even, but difficult to face.

5 Lions and fires = Samson slew a lion and set fires in revenge attacks on the Philistines (Judges 14:5–6 and 15:4–5).

9 One = also capitalised in ll.16 and 29; probably Death.

14 lips and keys = suggests rumours anticipating the attacks, and anticipates 'keys' at l.35; pun on the threatened 'quays' of the Port of London.

15 Locking, unlocking = with pun on Samson's long 'locks' of hair, and Delilah's 'unlocking' of him; murdered strangers = anticipatory, 'about-to-be-murdered'.

17 polestar neighbour = the Pole Star is distant – so, a contradiction in terms – but in a navigational and metaphoric sense it means 'reliable'; sun of another street = the 'sun' is a star, like the 'polestar', with a pun on 'son', the British fighter pilots or German bomber crews.

18 dive up to his tears = play on 'up to his ears'.

19 raining = pun on 'reigning'; the 'son' of l.17 is also the 'Son', Christ; the imagery of aspiring to the tears he 'rained' (l.18), and being bathed in the blood

of his sacrifice, recalls Metaphysical poetry and Nonconformist hymns (Samson is a 'type' of Christ).

21 wind his globe out of your water thread = the 'polestar neighbour' threatens to create his 'globe' out of the speaker's lifeline-like 'thread'; the imagery is uterine, but in the context of the Battle of Britain raging as Thomas wrote this poem, the German threat to Britain's global empire, based on the Thames and international seaways, also seems to be present.

27 near and strange wounded = future victims of the air raids; 'strange(ly)' could be adverbial, but also a play on 'near and far', especially if 'strange' has the archaic sense of 'distant' (as in l.12, 'estranging'); a not-quite oxymoron, like the poem's title ('near' things are not usually 'strange' to us).

29 One enemy, of many = 'of many enemies', or 'enemy of many', sounding like an anagram or palindrome.

30–32 Your heart . . . In the watched dark . . . thunderbolts = fire-watchers watched 'the dark' in shifts divided into watches, wore wrist*watches* with 'luminous' dials and hands visible in the blackout, and the treacherous heart, luminous with its desires and fears, 'will pull' the enemy to his target, which includes itself.

33 mount = with sense of sexual, as well as fatal, consummation; darkened keys = Thomas's letter to Watkins notes: 'I went to see a smashed aerodrome. Only one person had been killed. He was playing the piano in an entirely empty, entirely dark canteen.'

34 sear just riders back = the conflagration caused by the heart will drive away its rightful mates, as fire-fighters were driven back by Blitz fires.

35 that one loved least = probably the enemy, Death; but also God. Gwen Watkins claims: 'The last lines originally contained a hyena image suggested by one of [Thomas's] favourite passages from *Nightwood*: "For the lover, it is the night into which his beloved goes . . . that destroys his heart; he wakes her suddenly, only to look the hyena in the face that is her smile, as she leaves that company . . ."'

36 Samson = cf. 'Death's Duell': 'Stil pray wee for a peaceable life against violent death . . . but never make ill conclusions upon persons overtaken with such deaths . . . [God] received Sampson, who went out of this world in such a manner'; zodiac = Thomas told Watkins he was unsure of this word; it probably means 'fate'.

On a Wedding Anniversary (p. 124)

Probably begun in July 1940 (see note for l.3 below); a very different first version was published in *Poetry* (London) on 15 January 1941. Revised, probably just before Thomas returned the proofs of *DE* to Dent's on 18 September 1945; published in *DE*.

Thomas found this the least satisfactory poem in *DE*, and he told his publisher that it 'could be cut out' if necessary. The somewhat clumsy personifications and bald treatment of the theme of marriage under wartime stress suggest why; however, the poem is a good illustration of Thomas's search for a more limpid style during the war and of 'the Blitz sublime'.

3 three years = Thomas and Caitlin's third wedding anniversary was 11 July 1940.

5–6 their love lies a loss . . . Love and his patients = the couple have lost their love and become metaphorical 'patients' (possibly psychiatric); for the subject of madness in wartime, cf. 'Love in the Asylum'. Davies (1993) claims 'the horror of the bombing drives the man and his wife mad'.

7–8 true or crater / Carrying cloud = real cloud, or cloud of German bombers 'carrying' bombs which will leave 'craters'.

9 wrong rain = bombs 'raining down'; play on idiom, 'right as rain'.

Parodies from The Death of the King's Canary (p. 124)

Thomas was well known for his ability to impersonate his contemporaries. The best recorded examples occur in the comic novel *The Death of the King's Canary*, co-written with John Davenport while the Thomases were staying with Davenport at his country home, The Malting House, Marshfield, Gloucestershire, in July–December 1940.

The novel opens with the process of selecting a new Poet Laureate, Hilary Byrd, by the prime minister, who mulls over sample poems by eleven contenders. The rest of the novel concerns the antics of the guests at a country-house weekend hosted by Byrd to celebrate his appointment. The guests are lightly disguised members of the literary-artistic world of the 1930s, and the novel is a parody of the English country-house murder mystery novel; Byrd is found dead on the final page. Fear of litigation or giving offence meant that it was not published until 1976. Stylistic and other clues usually make clear who is being imitated. I have omitted five of the weaker pieces.

Lamentable Ode (p. 124)
by Albert Ponting

The ode form, the collection the poem is said to be from, *Claustrophosexannal*, and the reference to Balham, his birthplace, confirm this as a parody of George Barker, author of *Calamiterror* (1937).

3 huge davenport = escritoire; settee; joking reference to John Davenport's bulk (he weighed nineteen stone).

17 scolecophidian = misspelt 'scalecophidian' in *The Death of the King's Canary*: belonging to the genus of worms; see *N4* 'Twenty Four', 'Within his head'.

Brothers Beneath the Skin (p. 125)
by Wyndham Nils Snowden

Evidently W. H. (Wystan Hugh) Auden, the author, with Christopher Isherwood, of *The Dog Beneath the Skin* (1935). The poem is said to come from a volume called *Look, Dead Man*, whose contents seem to the prime minister to 'consist of a series of conversations; or rather, a series of lectures. They were all addressed to other, dead, writers. There was a long squabble with a tongue-tied Spenser in the metre of the *Faerie Queene*; a rap on the knuckles for Scott in the metre of *Marmion* . . .'

7 Woodbines = brand of cigarette.

36 Larwood = Harold Larwood (1904–95), leading English fast bowler.

42 tiffin = snack or meal; Anglo-Indian term typical of the British Raj.

Parachutist (p. 127)
by Christopher Garvin

A wickedly accurate impersonation of Stephen Spender's inappropriately excessive empathy and homoeroticism. Thomas read it to the Oxford University English Club in November 1941; Philip Larkin records that it 'had people rolling on the floor'. An undated *Horizon* proof sheet at Austin contains Cyril Connolly's note: 'Parody of . . . Spender by Dylan Thomas, set up by *Horizon* . . . but not published owing to lack of space – compassion to bard, & Empson published July 42 (Request to Leda)'.

Request to Leda (p. 129)
by William Dudley

Included in the novel, but published, though incomplete, in the William Empson special issue of *Horizon* of July 1942, with the subtitle '(Homage to William Empson)', and in Thomas's US collection *New Poems* (1943).

An incomplete villanelle (a form favoured by Empson), which convincingly mimics the private references and genial logic-chopping tone of much of Empson's poetry.

3 The worm . . . fruit = gently mocks Empson's style; the idea of a 'rational

worm' (Thomas's phallus-worms being anything but) is probably a joke at his expense.

7 Desire is phosphorous = Empsonian formulation, characteristic of his tendency to convert the sensuous into the abstract or scientific.

Ballad of the Long-legged Bait (p. 129)

Written January–April 1941, when the Thomases were living with Thomas's parents in Bishopston; published in *Horizon* (July 1941), the US-only *Selected Poems* (1943), and *DE*. Thomas's working title for it, 'The Ballad of Samson Jack', probably derives from a large (phallic) standing stone in North Gower called 'Samson's Jack'.

The poem is Thomas's longest, and one of his most impressive; however, it has proved resistant to explication. Thomas told William York Tindall that it was the tale of 'a young man' who goes 'fishing for sexual experience . . . but catches the church and the village green', while Brinnin (1956) tells of Thomas shocking a New York soirée by announcing that it described 'a gigantic fuck'. As this suggests, in broad terms it is a blend of symbolic-archetypal adventure and multi-layered allegory, of 'a young man', a single sexual act and, to a lesser degree, Thomas's career. There are literary sources in Coleridge's 'Ancient Mariner', Rimbaud's 'Le bateau ivre' and Donne's 'The Baite', and it marks a culmination of Thomas's poetry of sea voyages, distinguished by vivid marine imagery (Vernon Watkins noted it 'was so much a visual poem that [Thomas] made a coloured picture for it . . . of a woman lying at the bottom of the sea. She was a new Loreley revealing the pitfalls of destruction awaiting those who attempted to put off the flesh').

The ballad's trajectory arcs from the fisherman's setting sail, through arousal, sex and orgasm, to a more drawn-out phase of post-coital melancholy and the landing of his 'catch', after which sea becomes land, and he finds himself back at 'home'. But this is complicated by confusion of agency and speaking subjects. A series of speakers and (from l.85) impersonal narrator tell of the fisherman leaving a parental 'coast', phallic rod, anchor and mast erect. He throws a girl as bait into the sea, and she 'longs among' its creatures while he is lashed by a storm. He presses on, cocksure in his display of her, as she flees the phallic whales, and is present with other sea creatures as the bait enjoys a sexual climax with them. Soon, however, the bait is celebrating 'weddings' on her own account, a 'seal [kissing her] dead', probably sexually. At this post-orgasmic point the 'tempter' under the fisherman's 'eyelid' disappears, and he reels in his catch. It includes a chorus of 'long dead' 'fathers' clinging to the girl's hand, who warn that 'Time is bearing another son' and that it must be 'killed'. At this, God (likened to the sun) 'clings' to the girl's hair and 'weeps' among the 'liquid choirs of his tribes'. The fisherman's rod detumesces, 'divining land' (fused with the body of the bait), which now supplants the sea. The fisherman is led home, whether as honoured guest or sacrifice is unclear, although this is evidently a fall; the boat 'dies down', the bait is 'drowned', the anchor plummets through a church, and the fisherman finds himself back where he began.

Form: choppy and vigorous ballad measure, with stresses varying between three and five per line, and mixed rhyme schemes.

5, 18, 25 goodbye = the various parts of the shore are personified and say farewell to the fisherman, not the other way round.

6–8 anchor . . . by the top of the mast = images of tumescence.

20 stalked = a sign of the bait's own designs, and independence from the fisherman.

22 lips = vulval as well as facial.

24 dwindling ships = the line itself 'dwindles'.

32 hilly with whales = phallic Moby Dicks, suitors and lovers of the 'bait'; the Wales/whales pun is also one of Thomas's favourites.

41–45 He saw the storm . . , ram . . . rake   oil and bubble = the imagery is that of a naval battle in which a ship is sunk.

50 sick sea = queasily upends 'seasick'.

51 bushed = with pubic hair.

54 Jericho . . . lungs! = the trumpeting and shouting of the Israelites under Joshua brought down the walls of Jericho (Joshua 6:20).

60 Rose and crowed and fell! = a 'phallic vignette of the entire sexual action of the poem' (Parkinson, 1981).

68 bulls of Biscay = bull whales in the Bay of Biscay.

80 tread = act of copulation by male birds.

91 Oh all the wanting flesh his enemy = after the sexual raptures of Stanzas 14–22, the girl is 'the enemy'; 'wanting' means desiring and lacking (cf. 'A Winter's Tale').

107–8 Susannah . . . bearded stream . . . Sheba = like the two bearded elders spying on the bathing Susannah in the Old Testament Apocrypha, or Solomon giving the Queen of Sheba 'all her desire, whatsoever she asked' (1 Kings 10:1–18), the narrator has been inflamed with desire for the bait, but the only kings he sees attending her are those of the sea.

109, 215 the hungry kings of the tides . . . He stands alone = cf. Matthew Arnold, 'The Forsaken Merman': 'She left lonely forever / The kings of the sea'.

113–17 Lucifer . . . Venus = Lucifer and Venus are the same planet, as morning and evening star; an example of the shared identity, or marriage, of the bait and fisherman; bird's dropping = Lucifer either as a falling bird, or as guano.

116 vaulted = in a vault (crypt).

122 cast = sloughed off; cast a baited line; shaped or determined; scattered.

123 the fisherman winds his reel = see 'Once it was the colour of saying', l.13.

128, 181 catch = what the fisherman catches; the 'catch', or problem, with it.

129 six-year weather = the six years of Thomas's literary career to date.

140 The long dead bite! = the sharing of genetic material in sex involves one's ancestors in the act.

141, 142, 143 urn . . . room . . . house = womb/tomb.

159 walked the earth in the evening = after Adam and Eve ate the apple, they 'heard the voice of the Lord God walking in the garden in the cool of the day' (Genesis 3:8).

160 grains = dust; dialect for anything forked, including humans (Adam and Eve).

173–74 prophets loud . . . hold her thighs hard = the desert religions, repressive of female sexuality.

175 Time and places grip her breast bone = the bait is subjected to time and space after enjoying the freedom of the sea and unbridled sexual pleasure.

191 Sodom Tomorrow = play on Sodom and Gomorrah.

192 country tide = play on 'countryside'.

198–99 terribly lead . . . Lead . . . terror = chiasmus intensifies a sense of the fisherman's fatedness.

199–200 prodigal . . . ox-killing house of love = a fatted calf was killed on the return of the Prodigal Son (Luke 15:23–7), but the fisherman is about to be sacrificed too.

201 Down, down, down = cf. Matthew Arnold's 'The Forsaken Merman': 'Down, down, down!'

211 seven tombs = one for each of the seven seas.

212 The anchor dives through the floors of a church = image of detumescence induced by puritanical morality.

216 long-legged heart = cf. 'After the Funeral' for a similar image from

Nightwood. The image weds speaker and 'bait', and is inconclusively conclusive; a heart with legs may be arriving home, or readying itself to set off once again.

Love in the Asylum (p. 137)

Written February–April 1941; Thomas sent it to *Poetry* (London), at the end of April 1941, a poem having been promised them in a letter of 21 February 1941; published in the May/June 1941 issue and collected in *DE*.

Another marriage poem, figuring love as madness *and* as healing refuge from society and war. Thomas sometimes viewed his relationship to Caitlin as a creative madness, and here describes a 'stranger' who tricks her way into the imprisoning 'house' of the speaker's self; her apparently crazy behaviour 'deludes' its defences, allowing her to let in light and counteract his brooding. The concept is Blakeian – society is crazy, and only its outcasts are sane.

Form: six triplets in two sections of three, the first rhymed *abcabcabc*, the second *defdefdef*. In each section the first triplet has short first and third lines and long second line (5-12-5 syllables each), with the following two stanzas reversing this pattern.

3 mad as birds = birds are associated with madness ('cuckoo', 'birdbrain', etc.).

4 Bolting = securing; swallowing; her arm her plume = her arm is a wing (but also schoolboy French for 'pen'); the unstated image may be that of the 'she' as a winged angel, or muse.

5 Strait = straitjacketed; narrow; mazed = blends 'mad', circled, and 'crazed' written above it, in the autograph ms at Buffalo.

6 heaven-proof = the house of the self of the speaker, previously locked against happiness; with entering clouds = could belong to the 'house' or the 'girl', or both, while 'with' could mean 'accompanied by' or 'by means of' (i.e.: as a disguise).

7 walking the nightmarish room = counterposed to the 'entering clouds'.

8 At large as the dead = free and untethered, but ominously so.

9 rides . . . oceans = has sexual fantasies about the male inmates; wards = where male patients are segregated; the moving parts of a lock mechanism.

10 possessed = enraptured; bearing gifts; in thrall to madness or demons.

11 delusive light = deluding the defences of the house, and/or the speaker of the poem; the bouncing wall = the walls of a padded cell.

13 narrow trough = narrow is one sense of 'strait'; 'trough' could be bed or grave.

15 worn = originally 'raved', replaced following the use of 'raves' in l.13.

18 Suffer = originally 'bear'; first vision that set fire to the stars = the vision that started the universe going, as in Genesis; love. The Buffalo ms shows that 'brand' was considered for 'vision'.

On the Marriage of a Virgin (p. 138)

N3 'Sixteen', dated 22 March 1933. Rewritten summer 1941, with Thomas sending a version of Stanza 1 to Vernon Watkins in June 1941. Published *Life and Letters Today* (October 1941), collected in *DE*.

If the 1933 version was written in anticipation of the marriage of Thomas's sister Nancy in that year, the finished work is a poem of love in wartime, and reflects a turn towards the more douce Metaphysical poets – Marvell, Vaughan and Traherne, rather than Donne and Herbert. Its conceit is a typical Metaphysical one, blending pagan and Christian, spiritual and sensual, miracles of love. Stanza 1 is based on miraculous virginity (and birth as a result); the physical desirability of the woman, emphasised by the sun's sensual attributes, being spiritualised by the extension of the conceit to include the dove (the Holy Ghost), a god paired with God, opposition between pagan and Christian solved by an equivalence of miracles. In Stanza 2 the fundamentally pagan nature of the poem as an epithalamium (marriage hymn) is foregrounded, as the mortal lover who replaces the sun becomes the main subject of praise.

1–5 Waking alone ... Was miraculous virginity = celebrates the unmarried state of the girl, in whose eyes the sun, as a kind of lover, used to 'surprise' lingering images of his own 'golden' self, as she opened them to him each morning.

3 iris = part of the eye, but also Iris, Greek goddess of the rainbow, down which she travelled to earth. Note the pun on Mercury, another messenger of the gods, l.11.

4 this day's sun leapt up the sky out of her thighs = each new sun was like a son born from the previous night's coition; like the Virgin Mary's, therefore, the girl's motherhood was 'virginal and miraculous'.

5 old as loaves and fishes = i.e. as Christ's miraculous feeding of the five thousand (Matthew 14:17–21).

7 the shipyards of Galilee's footprints hide a navy of doves = the daily miracle of the sun/son's birth leads to consideration of how the moment of a miracle is permanently productive ('unending lightning'); the footsteps of Christ walking on the water (John 6:19) create not warships (it is 1941) but doves, symbols of peace and the Annunciation, sacred to Venus and profane love.

10–11 the avalanche / Of the golden ghost = the sun's former 'loving' of the girl is now likened to that of the shower of gold adopted as a disguise by Zeus when he visited his mortal lover Danaë.

11 ringed ... her mercury bone = the sun as a suitor placing a ring on the girl's finger (the ring that of the orbit of Mercury, the first planet). As well as Greek god, mercury is the male element; its shape-changing quality, and customary rise and fall in thermometer tubes, suggesting comparisons with the penis.

12 under the lids of her windows hoisted his golden luggage = the sun as a lover who used to illicitly move into the girl's apartment each morning; as Walford Davies (2000) notes, it is 'The cliché of "a moonlight flit" in reverse'.

14 unrivalled = because, although this is a poem of rivalry ('jealous coursing'), the sun himself cannot match the girl's flesh-and-blood lover/husband.

The hunchback in the park (p. 138)

Probably written June/July 1941, revising *N2* 'LVVV', dated 9 May 1932; published in *Life and Letters Today* (October 1941); collected in *DE*.

This is the last poem, except for a few lines in 'Holy Spring', to use the notebooks, which Thomas sold in 1941. Some lines survive intact, and many details are retained. The park is a version of Cwmdonkin Park, a favourite haunt near Thomas's childhood home. The opening conceit – which takes literally the child's notion that the park's contents do not exist until it is opened in the morning – raises questions about the relationship between imagination, reality and the self. These increase as the poem progresses. In Stanza 1, the hunchback's situation is presented through the eyes of the young child the speaker once was (the 'I' of l.10). The speaker's kinship with 'the truant boys' of Stanzas 3–5 is conveyed more obliquely. In Stanza 6, the hunchback is shown to transcend his persecutors by the daily creation of a faultless 'woman figure', and in a reversal of his lowly status, Stanza 7 reveals that everything in the park, except this figure, follows him to his 'kennel' at the end of the day.

The 'figure' is a compensatory fantasy, and, given her ability to defy 'locks and chains', also a muse, making the hunchback the poet in the modern world, ungainly as Baudelaire's albatross. The park may thus be a metaphor for that zone in which the artist creates, but which s/he must leave behind on re-entering the world. However, this is only one possibility; syntactical slipperiness created by minimal punctuation and switching viewpoints makes a complete resolution impossible – although it is notable that the rhyme 'park'/'dark' encloses the first and last stanzas.

Form: thirty-one free-verse lines were revised to make seven six-line rhymed and metrically irregular stanzas.

1   The hunchback in the park = the subject of a sentence whose main verb is 'slept' at l.11.

4   lock = lock on the park gate, opened and closed each day; metaphorically a kind of canal lock which lets the properties of the park enter.

5   That lets the trees and water enter = the subject that 'lets' could be the 'garden lock' or the 'hunchback; 'enter' is also double: 'trees and water' enter the park *and* the consciousness of the hunchback.

8   chained cup = chains are a common image in *DE*.

12   nobody chained him up = the rather cruel perspective of the past self associated with the 'boys'.

13–14   Like the park birds he came early . . . he sat down = from proverbial 'the early bird catches the worm'; the comparison of hunchback to 'water' and 'park birds' establishes him as a component of the park, which is an imaginative construct.

20   paper = newspaper; the abbreviated form links the hunchback to writing and the poet.

22   loud zoo of the willow groves = the boys played at being animals, but the willow branches they moved through are viewed by the older narrator ironically, as a cage.

31   bell time = play on 'bed time'.

32–34   A woman figure without fault . . . from his crooked bones = the deformities of the poet are a precondition of the perfection of his creations; 'figure' can also mean a poetic conceit.

35–37   That she might stand in the night . . . in the unmade park = the created figure, or poem, is not subject to the constraints on the hunchback, boys and other items in the park. It is now apparent that the poem is about the hunchback's problem of being locked out of the park at night and how he deals with it; his imaginative creation is more real to him than the reality of any objective park.

40   wild boys innocent as strawberries = transposed epithets.

Among those Killed in the Dawn Raid was a Man Aged a Hundred (p. 140)

Probably written summer 1941; published in *Life and Letters Today* (August 1941); collected in *DE*.

   In his first elegy for a Blitz victim, Thomas's use of a newspaper headline-style title ironically frames its sensationalist aspect, while at the same time showing his own fascination with the event and his desire to reimagine it in his own terms. Drawing on a real news item about the death of a centenarian in a bombing raid on Hull, the man's death outside the house in which he had been born, grown up and raised a family is presented as fulfilment of a natural cycle. The sestet of the sonnet rejects Christian ritual (depicted in the Daliesque image of an 'ambulance' drawn through the sky by a 'wound') and undercuts the sombre tone of elegy, as a pagan, sexual fecundity is extravagantly figured and embraced as a way of outfacing death. Its irreverence and incongruous linguistic display have led to divergent critical responses; the poem has been dismissed as heartless whimsy and praised as a mockery of the futility of war (all this firepower to kill a man of one hundred!). The tonal instability may, of course, be the point; an attempt to destabilise the usual discourse of mourning in a substitute rite which parodically compounds irony with affirmation.

1 morning . . . waking = puns on 'mourning' and 'waking' (as at funerals).

2 he died = not 'he was killed', emphasising a natural process, rather than social or personal tragedy.

3 The locks yawned loose = because of his great age, the man's door to death was already 'loose'.

4 loved = play on 'lived'.

6 street on its back = like the old man, the street in which he lived has been blasted flat; he stopped a sun = he was hit by a bomb; the sun for him literally went out; with pun on the Son, Christ.

7 the craters of his eyes grew springshoots and fire = the regenerative symbolism of wildflowers flourishing in bomb craters was common in wartime art and writing.

8 shot from the locks = the blast blows keys out of their keyholes just as the man's spirit is released from its mortal confinement; rang = death's liberation is celebrated as if by the ringing of church bells ('keys' as music).

10 The heavenly ambulance drawn by a wound = a hospital ambulance waiting to collect bodies after the raid imagined as the vehicle of the Christian promise of an afterlife 'drawn' (described and pulled) to heaven by Christ's 'wound', or sacrifice.

11 cage = ribcage.

12 common cart = in plagues during past centuries, bodies were thrown on carts for burial regardless of social or other distinction; 'common' also means 'Christian', the dead being lumped together regardless of belief; bombing

raids mean ambulances are all too 'common' a sight. Liturgically, the 'cart' is the Anglican Burial Service. The un-'common' nature of the centenarian, the poem claims, should give him the right to lie where he lived, loved and fell.

13 The morning is flying = far from being halted, the actual morning is quickened (in both senses) by the old man's death.

14 a hundred storks perch on the sun's right hand = by the violence of its coming, death frees the old man's imprisoned life force; each of his hundred years becomes a birth, the babies brought by storks, as in the tale told to curious children who ask adults where they come from.

On-and-on General Bock is driving a wedge among pincers (p. 140)

This verse-letter introduces a note to Thomas's friend and boon companion in Fitrovia's pubs, T. W. ('Tommy') Earp; it is dated 30 August 1942. This is the first surviving example of the genre; the allusions can be glossed and fleshed out by reference to biographies of Thomas and Fitzrovia memoirs. This example is a jocular quasi-fantasy, in which the governing conceit is the all-pervasive militarisation of wartime society, including Thomas's and Earp's drinking sessions.

1 General Bock = Fedor von Bock was a German field marshal; a 'bock' is also a drinking glass.

2 Timothy Jenkins = a wartime joke had it that the Soviet marshal Semyon Timoshenko had a Welsh grandmother, and that his name was a Russian corruption of Timothy Jenkins.

5 Talsarn = village in Cardiganshire, west Wales, in which Caitlin Thomas and sometimes Thomas stayed with a Swansea family, the Philipses.

6 spitfire sun = a Spitfire was a British fighter aircraft.

12 privates = 'Private' signs, and (as the camouflage is perceived) soldiers with the rank of private disguised as bushes, with pun on 'privates' as genitals and 'bush' as pubic hair; Nash parades = elegant Regency terraces in London built by John Nash.

When next shall we stumble to the stutter . . .? (p. 141)

Verse-letter to T. W. Earp dated 1 July 1943. Paul Ferris rightly calls it a 'crossword-puzzle poem'.

1 lewis-gun carols = the poems and songs Thomas and Davenport make up; play on Lewis gun and Lewis Carroll.

2   bombazine = shiny black fabric (cf. 'bombazine black', *Under Milk Wood*).

3   percies = perhaps from Percy Shelley; ladders = the Ladder club, London; banting = 'bunting' (in a London accent) and John Banting (painter and illustrator).

4   spoonered swiss pillars = a 'spoonerism' of 'piss [beer] swillers' ('swiss' is also the Swiss Tavern, a Soho pub and establishment of which the pair are 'pillars').

5   marcel-bound ... swine's way = cf. Marcel Proust's *Swann's Way*; ruth = perhaps play on 'root'; woman's name; many-johned = with many toilets.

6   Penny-fond = 'penny wise, pound foolish'; woman's name; antelope's cavern ... royal back-bar = play on pub names.

7   self-mabuses = play on *Dr Mabuse*, a 1920s German horror film, and 'self-abuses'; phelan = a surname, and pun on 'feeling'; withy = pun on 'with thigh'.

8   Peggy-legged = play on peg-legged; woman's name; bottle-dress = play on battle-dress; be hooved = be kicked, but also 'behoved'; Wardour-street smithy = centre of London film industry, with a drinking club whose owner was named Smith.

Lie still, sleep becalmed (p. 141)

Written 1944/45; published in *Life and Letters Today*, XLV (June 1945); collected in *DE*.

Thomas sent an earlier version to T. W. Earp in April 1944, and two identical drafts are held in Ohio and Austin. The sonnet takes the form of a dialogue between a 'we' (ll.1–8, 13–14) and a 'sufferer' (ll.9–11), although Thomas typically omits markers that would indicate the speakers. The draft suggests a sickbed scene – the 'we' at the bedside of the sufferer urging 'sleep', and concerned to silence his 'sea sound', while the sufferer answers with what may be a plea for help in dying, for cure, or for death-as-cure. Many critics interpret the poem biographically; Thomas referred to his father's cancer of the mouth as cancer of the throat (although there is no record of any recurrence after 1933–34).

The poem is about the war as much as any personal crisis, evoking as it does the figure of a torpedoed sailor adrift in the Battle of the Atlantic, and wrapping anxieties about a father and the war within those to do with wordshed as bloodshed, the poetic gift as a wounding. Mythic resonance is also thereby increased; the drifting, wounded singer seems Orphic, while 'slow sad sail' evokes the barge bearing Arthur to Avalon.

3   silent sea = cf. Coleridge's 'The Rime of the Ancient Mariner': 'We were the first that ever burst / Into that silent sea'.

4, 7, 12   salt sheet = bandage; bedsheet; sail; sheet of paper (on which the poem is written); rope (on a ship, a 'sheet' is technically a rope, not a sail).

8, 14   the drowned = the Day of Judgement in Revelation, in which the sea will 'give up its dead', is common in Thomas; here, the voices of the drowned also have something of the fatally alluring quality of Sirens, or the Lorelei.

9–11   Open a pathway . . . to the end of my wound = the notion of death as a sea voyage is an ancient one; the sufferer ambiguously requests help in dying, or to be cured; wandering boat = suggests Odysseus' voyage, in which he encountered Wandering Rocks; also Shakespeare, Sonnet 116: 'It [love] is the star to ev'ry wandering bark'.

From Wales – Green Mountain, Black Mountain (*film script*) (p. 142)

This film, produced in 1943, was part of the 'Pattern of Britain' series made by Strand Films; it is a survey of Wales at war and a synopsis of Welsh history, from the past wars with England to a present in which both stand united against the common foe. Near the end, a brief account of the Industrial Revolution and the Depression is followed by the excursion into verse. The poem was read over bleak 1930s footage of people scrabbling for coal on a slag-heap, shot by the documentary film-maker John Grierson. The anti-capitalist message of this section led to the film's rejection by the British Council on the grounds that it was unsuitable for overseas audiences. The Ministry of Information then took it up, but not before its Welsh Office had criticised Thomas as 'not a "real" Welshman', and proposed an alternative scriptwriter. This advice was rejected in London. A Welsh-language version of the film was also made.

Ceremony After a Fire Raid (p. 142)

Probably written just before publication, in April/May 1944, at Bosham; published in a special Lorca issue of Our Time (May 1944); collected in DE.

Writing to Vernon Watkins in July 1944, Thomas claimed, 'It really is a Ceremony and the third part of the poem is the music at the end. Would it be called a voluntary, or is that only music at the beginning?' The comment underscores the sense the poem gives of being the record of an attempt to construct a commemorative rite, set out at the beginning in the plea for the dead child to 'give' herself for an alternative service imaged in the interplay between fire and water, each with a destructive and creative, or purifying, aspect.

In Part I the jagged form and wrenching enjambements give a distraught aspect to the plea to the child by the 'grievers', now 'believers', that they be allowed to hold her death in a 'great flood' ahead of a service of renewal in which her spilt blood can be made to reanimate her 'dust'. Part II more calmly dwells on the levelling effect of the atrocity; the child's 'giving' of her death annuls the priority of other religions in which innocence is also sacrificed. These religions, like differences of gender and chronology, are subsumed by the enormity of her death; they die '*in*' the child's 'little skull'. Yet the speaker 'knows' that the discourse of Christianity cannot be 'silent' within his ceremony, 'legend' though he knows it to be. As a result, the child's death is figured ambiguously: as both a second Fall, a decreation leading to the 'serpent' triumphing in 'darkness' and 'wilderness', but also (insofar as she had the Christlike possibility of all humans) a potential reversing of the Fall, the child herself as the 'fruit like a sun'/Son. Part III extends the paradox of having to create a new religion from the ruins of the old by evoking the destruction of churches and cathedrals (such as that at Coventry) in the Blitz, a symbolic, purifying destruction of institutional religion which spills over into a new, fiery version of the Eucharistic rite, and an answering liquid resurgence.

The fires which killed the child are finally doused by the 'great flood' 'held' over from Part I, a tsunami-like manifestation of the future generations denied by her death. Baptism, amniotic gush and the spurt of conception all break apocalyptically in the liquid final line, dousing the fires, as Thomas prophesies sexual regeneration in the form of the baby-boomer generation.

I

1–4 Myselves . . . Grieve / Among the street = grammatical distortion produces several senses: *a* the poet is speaking for all the grievers, merging his identity with theirs; *b* 'myself' and 'street' stand for all 'grievers' and streets affected by such tragedy; *c* the nature of the self is multiple, not singular, and its splits are exacerbated by grief and loss.

6 kneading = pun on 'needing'.

8 dug = past-tense verb and noun (to enter the grave is to be taken to the 'dug', or breast, of mother earth).

12 Darkness kindled back into beginning = the 'kindling' is negative (with play on 'kind', as in 'A Refusal to Mourn'); see l.58.

14 A star = a bomb, in shocking contrast to the star of the Nativity.

15 centuries = the progeny which would have flowed from the child, down the centuries to come, had she lived (also the sense of 'blood', at l.22).

28 beyond cockcrow = beyond resurrection, but also beyond further betrayal by the adult world, in allusion to Peter's triple denial of Christ.

II

The ms version of Part II had the headline-style title 'Among Those Burned To Death Was A Child Aged A Few Hours'.

36–37 the chosen virgin / Laid in her snow = cf. Blake's 'Ah! Sun-flower': 'the pale Virgin shrouded in snow'.

49 service = ritual; use.

55–56 the serpent's / Night fall = the descent of the night created by the serpent (the Fall); the collapse of the night of the serpent.

56 the fruit like a sun = the forbidden fruit of the tree of the Knowledge of Good and Evil in the Garden of Eden; the child, 'a' (not 'the') sun/Son, both herself and in her progeny.

57 Man and woman undone = the Fall; humanity destroyed; distinction between genders abolished.

58 Beginning crumbled back to darkness = reverses l.12 while seeming to mean much the same thing; however, the death that was described there using an ironically positive verb ('kindled') is described here by a negative but potentially fructifying one ('crumbled').

59 nurseries = for plants and for children.

III

69 golden pavements = perhaps alludes to Golden Square, London, where Thomas worked for Strand Films.

73 masses = of water; services of (sexual) incarnation; the majority of the British population (associated with 'hovel and the slum' (l.68)).

77–78 Glory glory glory . . . kingdom = cf. The Lord's Prayer: 'For thine is the kingdom, the power and the glory, for ever and ever. Amen.' 'Glory' is noun (in its normal sense and as orgasm), a subjunctive verb ('[let] glory [be given to] the "ultimate kingdom"'), and a transitive verb ('Boast the wonder of').

78 The sundering . . . genesis' thunder = the conception or birth of any child is a 'genesis' (lower case), beyond that offered by religion (upper case), although it involves 'sundering' from the mother and subjection to the pains of mortality.

Our Country *(film script)* (p. 145)

Thomas sent the final version of this film script, written by April 1944, to Donald Taylor of Gryphon Films in October 1944. The film follows a sailor on shore leave as he travels around England, Wales and Scotland, from the point where he comes ashore in Dover, to his finding of a new berth on an Aberdeen fishing vessel. His journey symbolises national unity and common struggle, but the obviousness of this device is offset by the film's digressiveness, impressionistic text and atmospheric visual effects. Thomas expressed concern at cuts made after the matching of film and script, noting that these broke 'a literary thread, or, at least, a sense-thread' possessed by the original. He was also worried that the script might seem 'a little chaotic' or '"modern"' to those unused to contemporary poetry, and detract from the film's impact. In fact, 'Our Country', which premiered at the Empire in Leicester Square, was Thomas's most successful film.

51–52 his country's body . . . weathers of her eyes = phrases similar to those in poetry of the time, e.g. 'How shall my animal', 'Into her lying down head'.

107 troules = trundles.

Last night I dived my beggar arm (p. 152)

Written mid-1944; published in *Poetry* (London), IX (June 1944) with 'Your breath was shed' (see below). Omitted from *DE*; collected in *TP71*.

    With 'Your breath was shed' and 'On a Wedding Anniversary', the poem's spareness of vocabulary and syntax, and its subject – a love relationship – make it one of three very short wartime lyrics that test out more transparent poetic styles. Ferris (1977) cites an autograph copy with two pairs of alternative words, titled 'For Ruth', given by Thomas to the actress Ruth Wynn Owen with whom he had a relationship in 1942–43.

Your breath was shed (p. 153)

Writing to Pamela Hansford Johnson on 2 May 1934, discussing poems for inclusion in *18P*, Thomas disagreed 'heartily' with her support for 'Thy breath was shed', an early version of 'Your breath was shed', no longer extant. In 1944 Thomas rewrote it, publishing it with 'Last night I dived my beggar arm' in *Poetry* (London) (June 1944). Omitted from *CP52* and *CP88*; collected in *TP71*.

7–8 biter's tooth and tail / And cobweb drum = cf. 'I make this in a warring absence': 'With loud, torn tooth and tail and cobweb drum'.

Vision and Prayer (p. 154)

Completed summer 1944, and described as 'finished' in August, then reworked before being sent to Vernon Watkins on 28 October 1944. Published in *Horizon* (January 1945) and *Sewanee Review* (Summer 1945); collected in *DE*.

The poem brings together Thomas's vein of embryo/birth poems with his interest in the workings of belief, with analogues in Herbert's 'The Collar' and Francis Thompson's 'The Hound of Heaven'. The speaker runs from the (Christlike) child, but finds himself at its throne in Stanza 4, and, imagining himself in his sheltering but terrifying presence, declares he 'shall waken' to a vision of the Day of Judgement, as the 'bidden dust' of all the dead will rise up from the 'world'; he then 'dies' in its pain. Part II consists of three prayers. The first is for 'the lost', unbelievers who seek oblivion, that the child 'return' to the womb (the speaker does not wholly belong with these because he has experienced 'joy'). The second asks that the child leave alone those 'on the unchristened mountain' (pagans). The third prayer, in the name of the unbegotten, asks that the sun blot out the child's vivid 'martyrdom'. In Stanza 12, the sun burningly answers the prayers, and it seems that the sinner who wanted to escape the child has been hunted down by his love. But this resounding closure is ambiguous. To what extent is the child Christ simply the Christlike potential in all humans (and thus identifiable with Thomas's son/sun Llewelyn)? Does 'blinding / One' have the meaning of the 'oneness', as of the cosmic unity underlying the process poetic? Does the sun 'roar' to confirm the prayer or in opposition to it? Is the (Christian) Son being conflated with the (pagan) sun, as in 'Among those Killed'? In addition, like 'The conversation of prayers', the poem is framed in the future tense, as 'until' in Stanza 2 and 'shall' in Stanzas 3 and 5 suggest, despite its narration in the continuous present.

Form: the stanza forms mimics the Metaphysical shape-poem, notably Herbert's 'Easter Wings'; they have been likened to a lozenge, opening womb, diamond and teardrop (Part I), and a bobbin, cross, hatchet, flagon, chalice or hourglass (Part II). Two sections of six seventeen-line stanzas each, with a syllable pattern of 1-2-3-4-5-6-7-8-9-8-7-6-5-4-3-2-1 in Part I, with the sequence reversed in Part II. Rhyme (consonantal, assonantal and full) is partial and sporadic.

4 In the next room = Watkins remarked: 'Dylan told me, when he was just beginning to write it, that he had read a most wonderful statement of Rilke about God being born in the next room. (This must, I think, have been the poem "Du Nachbar Gott" from the *Stundenbuch*.)'

25 Casting = giving birth; as a shadow, of future suffering ('tomorrow like a thorn').

45 I shall run lost = as in Francis Thompson's account of his pursuit by Christ in 'The Hound of Heaven'.

49 cauldron = 'caldron' in *CP52* and *CP88*.

63 dumbfounding haven = cf. Hopkins, 'Heaven Haven': 'Where the green swell is in the havens dumb'.

65 high noon = hints at Hollywood Western cliché (Part I also has 'vultured' and 'canyons').

74–78 judge blown bedlam . . . With his flame in every grain = the Day of Judgement, when the sea 'shall give up her dead', summoned to judgement by Christ.

77 bidden dust upsailing = cf. George Herbert, 'Dooms-day': 'Summon all the dust to rise / Till it stirre'.

80–82 vultured urn / Of the morning / Of man = the earth, imagined as an urn bearing the ashes of the dead ('vultured' is 'stripped of dead flesh').

89 upright Adam = erect penis, as in 'I dreamed my genesis', 'Altarwise', V.

102, 177–90 In the name of the lost . . . in the name / Of no one / Now or / No / One to / Be . . . In the name of the damned = a prayer for the *un*holy or *non*-existent, *against* their salvation, is a double negative, and hence, in some way, a plea *for* their salvation.

107, 112 green dust . . . Like pollen = because the dust of the dead nurtures life.

115, 135, 181 I pray . . . I pray him . . . I pray = the three prayers of Part II.

136 That he let the dead lie though they moan = plea that the unsaved be spared the harrowing experience of salvation.

166 common lazarus = refers to Jesus' raising of Lazarus (John 11:1–45); here, a representative of all the resurrectable dead who prefers his unresurrected sleep.

169–70 For the country of death . . . shape of the eyes = death and lostness, not the terrifying demands of salvation, are what man is fitted for.

186, 187 interpreted evening . . . known dark = as in similar collocations, a natural phenomenon, subject to human reason, suggestive of restrictive ratiocination.

194 Christens = baptises in light.

198, 200, 201, 202 him, his, His, his = Christ, son and/or sun.

204 One = syntax ensures that this cannot be unambiguously assumed to be the precedent 'him' and 'his'; The sun . . . end = this apocalyptic, pun-charged sentence is at once pagan ritual, religious conversion and the birth of a son. Responding to criticism by Watkins, Thomas asserted: 'I liked the last line *for* the awkward stressing, for the braking, for the slowing up of the last two same-vowelled words.'

Poem in October (p. 160)

Begun summer 1944, finished 30 August 1944, and published in *Horizon*, February 1945, and *Poetry* (Chicago), February 1945. Collected in *DE*.

A version of the poem was started during Thomas's Laugharne sojourn of 1938–40, and according to Vernon Watkins the poem we now have had 'been contemplated for three years' before it was written. Thomas described it to Watkins as 'a Laugharne poem: the first place poem I've written' in a letter of 26 August 1944, sending it him on 30 August 1944, 'a month and a bit premature [for my birthday]. I do hope you like it, & wd like very much to read it aloud to you . . . It's got, I think, a lovely slow lyrical movement.' The lyrical sweetness is matched by the subtlety by which a birthday, a temporal boundary-crossing, is mapped on to other transitional states, topographical, meteorological and psychological. The speaker crosses the town 'border' to ascend Sir John's hill, where he emerges into sunshine while the town below, still waking up, remains rain-bound. This triggers a blurring of other border states, between meteorological 'marvel' and memory, vision and imagination, adult present and childhood idyll.

Thomas's fluid topography shows this to be a 'poem of place' in the sense that it explores the creation of a sense of place, rather than describing a specific locale; although belonging to the place-poem genre, it analyses some of its mechanisms. In doing so it invokes Blake and the Metaphysical mystic poets, such as Henry Vaughan, exceeding realism or Romantic evocation. Particularly important seems to be the ecstatic childhood vision of the created world in Thomas Traherne's *Centuries of Meditations*, 3:3, beginning: 'The corn was orient and immortal wheat, which never should be reaped, nor was ever sown. I thought it had stood from everlasting to everlasting.' This is a passage which John Ormond claimed was a 'keystone in Thomas's thinking', and it recurs in the later poetry. The 'truth' of the 'joy' of the childhood self is subtly linked with that self's death, and chastened by the wartime world of death in which it is being recalled.

Form: seven ten-line stanzas with a syllable pattern of 9-12-9-3-5-12-12-5-3-9, broken only in ll.55–56. Stanza 1 has an *abacabcbac* pararhyme scheme, varied thereafter.

2   Woke = the subject of this main verb in the stanza is 'morning', l.5.

5   The morning beckon = 'beckon' is an adverbial noun, 'morning' as an adjective qualifying it ('the morning's beckoning').

8   Myself = the object of 'beckon(ing)': 'beckon . . . [of] myself'.

12   winged trees = with birds in the branches, but also likening branches to wings; 'bare trees' in the copy sent to Watkins. Thomas noticed 'on copying out, that I have made the October trees bare. I'll alter later.'

19–20   And the gates / Of the town closed = medieval Laugharne was a walled town; vestiges of one gate survive.

21 springful = like an overflowing spring of sound; 'spring' also anticipates the later seasonal confusion.

23–25 the sun of October / Summery / On the hill's shoulder = the sun is shining on the top of the hill while rain continues to fall on the town below.

28–29 rain wringing / Wind = play on 'rain-bringing wind'.

32 the sea wet church = Laugharne's parish church, St Martin's, is not visible from Sir John's hill and is some distance from the sea; the townscape is an imaginary one, though it draws on the topography of Laugharne.

38–40 There could I marvel / My birthday / Away but the weather turned around = 'marvel' means 'bound by the superficial wonder of the meteorological spectacle'; 'but' introduces a deeper, visionary moment of the following stanzas; turned = a key term, repeated in various forms at ll.41, 46, 62 and 70, as the poem's final word; it creates internal rhymes with 'burned' and 'burning' at ll.52, 63, evoking the wartime context of other poems in *DE*.

44–45 apples / Pears and red currants = cf. the similar phrasing of Hardy's 'Regret Not Me', another poem of childhood happiness shot through with an awareness of mortality: 'Now soon will come / The apple, pear and plum'.

49 sun light = the splitting of 'sunlight' allows the suggestion of sun as son and Son.

51 twice told fields = 'told' means spoken of and counted; the sense is that the fields were counted / spoken about at the time, and are now in memory.

60 Still = motionless; quiet; even now.

66–67 summer . . . October = a last example of the poem's seasonal confusion.

67 leaved = originally 'brown'.

So much Meux has flowed under the bridges (p. 162)

A verse-letter of 1 September 1944 to T. W. ('Tommy') Earp.

1 Meux = a brand of beer.

2 drown London town, which would be just = the trope of London inundated as punishment for its decadence is common in Thomas; see 'Ceremony After a Fire Raid' and the story 'Prologue to an Adventure'.

3 religious = religiously.

6 Pera and pal = 'Pera' is an anagram of Earp; his 'pal' is Thomas.

8   Philmayicity House = Filmicity House was one of Strand Films' addresses; there may also be puns on May, the name of Earp's wife, Phil May the cartoonist, and Philip Lindsay, a fellow-scriptwriter at Strand.

10   Donald = Donald Taylor, Thomas's employer at Strand, and later Gryphon Films.

11   combs = short for 'combination garment', an all-body underwear item.

20   Heard = pun on 'hard' (short for 'hard labour', part of a prison sentence) and the name of Gerald Heard, a writer and friend.

21   de Polnay, Peter = Peter de Polnay was a novelist; the intended pun (if any) on his name is now lost.

26   Ockham = the name of Earp's residence was 'Ockham Cottage'.

27   Stephenson's machine = train drawn by a steam engine.

Dear Tommy, please, from far, sciatic Kingsley (p. 163)

A verse-letter of 21 September 1944, sent from Thomas's New Quay home to T. W. ('Tommy') Earp.

   In *TP71* Daniel Jones describes this as a 'parody of Earp's own verses', adding: 'When Earp, art critic, French scholar, lovable eccentric and hypochondriac (sciatica), solemnly read aloud the verses of his anagrammed protégé, Pera, no one ventured to laugh. In crabbed style, twisted syntax, far-fetched rhymes and vertiginous enjambement, "young" Pera out-Browninged, out-Cloughed them all. He was capable of writing . . . the line: "Embrace, my Sheba she-bear, me', which fortunately is the only trace persisting in my memory from Pera's extensive oeuvre.' However, if they are a parody, Thomas's verses are also a friendly tribute, evidently written without fear of provoking any 'solemnity' in Earp (who seems to have been able to take a joke).

1   Kingsley = the village in Hampshire where T. W. Earp lived.

2–3   Lee / And Perrins = Worcester sauce.

9   No-good = this seems to be a general personification (from the phrase 'up to no good'), but it later supplied the name Nogood Boyo in *Under Milk Wood*.

11   Buckley's = a Welsh beer.

12   Worthington = a London beer.

14   Playered gob = Players were a brand of cigarette. Thomas is referring to his habit of keeping a cigarette dangling from his mouth.

17   parchs = ministers (Welsh).

20   Mr. Jones the Cake = this puritanical hunter-out of sexual misdemeanour anticipates the figure of Jack Black in *Under Milk Wood*.

33   Augustus = Augustus John.

43   May = T. W. Earp's wife.

Back in the bosom, repentant and bloodshot (p. 164)

In a letter speculatively dated October 1944 to Donald Taylor, Thomas's employer at Gryphon Films (formerly Strand Films), and accompanying Thomas's film script for 'Our Country'.

2   draper-sly skies = in Wales, Cardiganshire people have traditionally been the butt of jokes alleging their meanness, cunning and propensity to work as drapers.

7   Gargoyle = London drinking club on Meard Street, off Dean Street, Soho (cf. 'The Countryman's Return'), to which Thomas and Taylor belonged.

Holy Spring (p. 165)

Sent to Vernon Watkins on 15 November 1944 with the comment: 'Here is a poem of mine which I started a long time ago but finished very recently, after a lot of work.' Published in *Horizon*, XI (January 1945); collected in *DE*.

   'Holy Spring' borrows lines from *N3* 'Ten', 'Out of a war of wits' (see above), the last published poem to use the notebooks in some way. Thomas's compositional struggles in autumn 1944 are charted by the existence of other versions of the poem, one of which, from the collection of James Gilvarry, was published in *CP88*; it has numerous minor differences with the *DE* version.

   Displaying formal and thematic similarities with 'Love in the Asylum' and 'Vision and Prayer', the poem recalls the Metaphysical poets in its use of an elaborate conceit and its shape. Its occasion is waking after a night of love during which a fire raid has taken place. The speaker finds he is unable to unequivocally praise the 'joyful' sunrise against the cruelly inappropriate backdrop of destruction, but can bless the 'hail and upheaval' of war and natural regenerative growth, insofar as it isolates him for the act of singing, 'If only for a time'.

   Form: two twelve-line stanzas, alternating short (irregular seven-syllable trimeters) and long lines (irregular fourteen-syllable heptameters), except at the opening of Stanza 1. The initial single-syllable lines of each stanza rhyme with each other, followed by stanzas rhyming *aabcbcbdede* and *aabaabacdcd*.

3   that immortal hospital = the 'bed of love'; sexual and spiritual renewal are one and the same.

4   cureless counted body = although bodies generally may be 'soothed' by

sex, the mortality of the individual body can never be offset by it; its days are 'counted'.

5–7 ruin . . . houses = the destructive progress of our mortality has been exacerbated by the war's effects on our wounded natures and the structures which surround it.

6 Over the barbed and shooting sea = the sea armed for defence and attack.

9 That one dark = death; proverbially, the debt we pay for our life ('the light').

10 Call for confessor . . . none = the speaker fruitlessly appeals for something 'wiser' than his own self-reflexivity.

11 god stoning night = the assault on the holiness of existence constituted by the raid, alluding to the first saint, St Stephen, who was stoned to death.

12 as lonely as a holy maker = play on *makar*, Scots for poet; here made to feel as 'lonely' as God by sunrise over the bombed city.

13–20 No / Praise . . . But blessed be hail and upheaval = the renewal of the morning and the city happens naturally, and thus cannot be cause for 'praise'; rather, the poet will bless the process of change itself.

14–15 all / Gabriel = in the Bible Gabriel warns of impending war (Daniel 9:21–27) and is the agent of the Annunciation (Luke 1:26–38); radiant shrubbery = bomb-crater weeds, symbolising regeneration.

16 woebegone pyre = smouldering ruins left after the attack.

18–19 My arising prodigal / Sun the father = play on 'prodigal son' (Luke 15:11–32) as a father, with allusion to God's prodigal sacrifice of his only son, and with phallic undertones. As father, the speaker is a returning wanderer full of creative force; as son he is a spendthrift who has been out at night, squandering his energies in the form of the fire raid.

19 quiver full of the infants of pure fire = sunbeams (with play on 'quiver' as verb); penis, ready to produce children like arrows; cf. also Psalm 127:4–5: 'As arrows *are* in the hand of a mighty man; so *are* children of the youth. Happy *is* the man that hath his quiver full of them.' The various identities – lonely poet, wastrel, anxious father, ruined son – are all Thomas's, though none are so exclusively.

22–23 husk of man's home . . . toppling house of the holy spring = 'home' and 'house' symbolise the complex relationship between human (but destructive) culture and impersonal (but creative) 'mother' nature.

24 If only for a last time = because the poet may be killed in the next raid; any moment could be our last, and this is the light in which we should regard existence generally.

Verses from Quite Early One Morning (p. 166)

Written late 1944 as part of the broadcast Thomas recorded on 14 December 1944, although not broadcast until 31 August 1945. Published in *QEOM* 1954.

Although only a series of comic-verse character sketches (based on inhabitants of New Quay, where Thomas lived at the time), these verses are a lively anticipation of *Under Milk Wood*.

A Winter's Tale (p. 167)

Probably begun winter 1944–45; sent to Oscar Williams and Vernon Watkins on 28 March 1945, with Thomas informing Williams that it 'has taken a great deal of time and trouble'. Published *Poetry* (Chicago) July 1945; collected in *DE*.

A hermit, near death, prays alone, at night, in the dead of winter, for release from the pains of existence. His selfless prayer magically thaws the frozen world into a remembered spring in which 'minstrels', 'nightingale' and other elements in the natural world 'sing' of rebirth. A 'she-bird' descends, animating the landscape, inducing him to pursue her. Either in reality, or imaginatively, he does so through the night. Dying at the end of his quest, his vision of the animated spring landscape dies with him; but, in a final gesture, the she-bird descends to embrace him and rise with him in a *Liebestod* union.

Shakespeare's title, proverbial for an inconsequential tale told to while away a winter's evening, is belied in his play and in Thomas's poem by the weighty subject matter of death, rebirth and a redemptive female presence. The hermit and the blank landscape of snow suggest the poet confronting the page, and may reflect Thomas's feeling that the poem 'doesn't, I think, come off, but I like it all in spite of that. It isn't really one piece, though, God, I tried to make it one.' Whether or not we concur, it works powerfully on several levels – folk-tale love story, allegory of romantic or sacred love, mythic-archetypal tale of rebirth – while the hypothermic-transcendent close sees the hermit submitting to the natural round, revealing the she-bird as process itself, amoral but holy.

5–10 breath . . . told = the poem's opening lines, with snow, prayer and hermit, evoke Keats's 'The Eve of St Agnes', as does the later ambiguous union.

14 scrolls of fire = one of many examples of Christian symbolism (valley as chalice, smoke the colour of the Lamb, etc.).

29 the quick of night = inverts 'the dead of night'.

33 May his hunger = the hermit prays for himself in the third person (see l.51).

42–43 the bread of water . . . high corn . . . harvest = snow is compared to manna, with which God fed the Israelites in the wilderness (Exodus 16).

50 the believer lost and the hurled outcast of light = with the desperation of one who has lost his faith, or 'outcast' Lucifer, brightest of all God's angels, he seeks a divine rebirth in the 'inhuman cradle' of l.49.

54–55 the fields ... flesh astride = the hermit prays to be removed from the cycle of sex, birth and death; but 'time dying flesh' may also mean 'flesh which overcomes time' (and the concluding union humanises the 'inhuman cradle' he desired); repeated with variation at l.103.

69–70 A she bird rose and rayed like a burning bride ... scarlet downed = the image of the burning she-bird combines various images: the dove-like Holy Spirit, or Paraclete; Christ as the bride in the Mystic Marriage; self-sacrificing pelican.

73 Exulting = earth's response to the hermit's invocation of process in his prayer and his own joy (in his vision of spring) at the answer to it.

113 villages of wishes = the vision of spring is a 'wish' of the hermit.

117 centaur dead horse = 'centuries-dead'; allusion to lasciviousness of centaurs.

121–30 The final stanzas reverse the violent, rapist's descent of Zeus at the close of Yeats's 'Leda and the Swan'; the 'she-bird' achieves ecstatic union with the hermit, in a descent which is simultaneously an ascent in his dying consciousness.

123 hymned = near-anagrammatical for 'hymen'.

125 woman breasted = in Genesis, the Hebrew for Almighty God, 'El Shaddai', means 'woman breasted'.

126 brought low = brought to ecstatic union with the bird; degraded like a beast.

128 wanting centre = both desiring and lacking.

128–30 folds / Of paradise ... flowering = heaven in Dante's *Paradiso* has the structure of a rose; the imagery is also vulval and sexual.

The conversation of prayers (p. 171)

Sent to Vernon Watkins with a letter on 28 March 1945; published in *Life and Letters Today* in July 1945, *New Republic*, 16 July 1945, and collected in *DE*.

This poem opens *DE*, introducing several of its themes: the adult relationship with childhood, innocence and experience, domestic spaces, the nature of suffering and prayer. It originates in a play on 'converse' as the root of 'conversation' (the *OED* has the usual sense of 'interchange of thoughts and words; familiar discourse or talk', and 'turned about, transformed'). From this comes the conceit of the switching prayers of the man and the boy, the man receiving the consoling answer the boy expected, the boy receiving his harrowing one. This echoes Thomas Hardy's 'On One Who Lived and Died When He was Born' (see 'Among those Killed'), and is enacted in the poem's self-echoing and criss-crossing rhymes.

The child and the man are also Thomas in his youthful and mature selves, as in Hardy's poem, as allowed by syntax: in l.2 the man is 'on the stairs', although the 'child going to bed' would also be there; in l.8 'the man on the stairs and the child by his bed' prompts the question of whose bed it is. The prayers are also two states of the soul, one unable to meet fear (and anxious about death), the other armed against bad dreams and evil (and death-defeating). It should be noted that it is not the sense of the prayers that 'turns' and converses, but 'the *sound*' of them, and that the 'sounds' are only ever '*about* to be said', never actually uttered.

Form: four stanzas of five roughly twelve-syllable lines, bound by internal and end-line rhyme in successive lines, except the last, where *stairs* rhymes only imperfectly with *prayer-care*, but (with *dead*) rhymes with Stanzas 1–3.

1 conversation = both 'discussion' and 'change', bringing about the 'converse' of the opening scenario by the final line; about = applies to prayers (*about* something) and the imminence of their utterance (to be said very shortly).

6 Turns in the dark . . . will arise = adapts the idiom of a conversation 'turning' on a particular subject; however, the event 'about' to occur is said to be conditional on a present-tense event ('turns'), and is then replaced in the future ('will'), suggesting that the poem's action is a projection into the future.

7 answering skies = ironic, like the 'unminding skies' of 'This side of the truth', 'The interpreted evening' of 'Vision and Prayer', etc. In one sense, however – as German V-weapons – there was an 'answer' from the 'skies' in early 1945.

17 climbs = transitive verb: 'makes climb'.

18 true grave = the Watkins letter version has 'made grave', which gives the link to bedtime, the child's grave waiting for him as certainly as his bed is made up each night. Cf. Herbert, 'Mortification': 'When boyes go first to bed / They step into their voluntarie graves'.

19 wave = like a wave of the sea; waving of a hand by 'the dark eyed'.

A Refusal to Mourn the Death, by Fire, of a Child in London (p. 172)

Composed probably October/November 1944; a partial draft, titled 'A Refusal For An Elegy', exists in Thomas's autograph in the NLW. It was revised in early 1945, sent to Vernon Watkins on 28 March 1945, and published in *New Republic* (14 May 1945) and *Horizon* (October 1945); collected in *DE*.

In the opening thirteen-line sentence, the speaker refuses to mourn the child, a girl killed in the 'Little Blitz' of 1944–45, until Doomsday, or his own death. The second sentence justifies this deferment: to mourn now would be to 'murder' the natural event which all must suffer ('mankind of her going') with a complacent promise of the afterlife, or revenge. Against this, the third sentence asserts the kinship of the dead girl with the 'first dead', and her 'mother' earth. The final line, a single sentence with strong caesura, sounds consolatory, but is highly ambiguous. It seems to assert that a form of eternal life begins with death, but calculatedly denies the 'second death' the Bible promises at the Last Judgement, and may even be understood to mean that utter extinction is all that awaits us.

As William Empson (1947) was the first to suggest, the poem may have its origins in Thomas's guilt at having written propaganda films during the war years. He also noted that it uses the rhetorical trope of *occupatio*; i.e. a poem that tells us what it won't do, but then does it. However, this straightforward reversal is complicated by extreme ambiguity and paradox. 'Never until', for example, is a deliberate solecism: 'never' means 'not ever' and there can be no 'until' about it. This opens up the undecidable temporal state within which the poem unfolds, in which 'breaking' is presented so that it can be taken to mean an ending or a beginning, and 'last' can, as Carson (1996) notes, 'take on the dignity of hope as well as the bitterness of despair'.

The impassioned simplicity, then, is deceptive. The dead child *is* mourned, and granted a monumental, Christlike dignity; yet religious doctrine – of atonement and the Last Judgement – is rejected. This is just one of several elements and levels (others include the mythic, historical, personal and literary) on which the poem works, accommodated in paradoxical tension with each other, as the eternity of death is granted without resolving the issue of whether it is eternal resurrection or oblivion. The poem manages to comprehend both cathartic mourning and paralysing melancholia as it tries to embody the incommensurability of this specific death and man's response to it, and thereby express the enigma of death more generally.

Evidence of Thomas's artistry is apparent in the richness of the intertextual mulch of the famous final line which includes lyrics by Wilfred Owen, Donne, Swinburne, Herbert, Lionel Johnson, Lawrence, Wordsworth's Lucy poems and Thomas himself (cf. 'I dreamed my genesis').

1–4   The subject of 'tells' is the originary 'darkness' out of which the world emerged, and which still 'humbles' the universe. Negatives and positives, active and passive qualities are paired in each clause (e.g.: 'Tells with silence'). Lack of hyphenation isolates the words describing the natural world, giving them autonomy.

2   Bird beast and flower = cf. D. H. Lawrence's *Birds, Beasts and Flowers*.

4   Tells with silence = paradoxical; 'tells' can also be transitive or intransitive – does the darkness simply record or 'tell' us about the 'last light', or does it tell

the last light something with its silence (as the echo of 'tolls' may suggest)?; last light breaking = a the end of the world, if followed by eternal darkness; b the dawning of the last day before this; c dawning of a (heavenly) day which will last for ever.

6 harness = the gravity of the moon, which controls the sea. Cf. 'Fern Hill'.

8–9 Zion of the water bead / And the synagogue of the ear of corn = ecumenical imagery renders the natural world sacred; 'water' and 'corn' are ingredients of the Eucharist, 'Zion' is a name for Nonconformist chapels, and 'synagogue' is Jewish. But 'Zion' is specifically Jewish too and with 'synagogue' constitutes an allusion to the Holocaust – news of which was reaching Britain as Thomas wrote the poem.

11 salt seed = tears, mourning; salt makes land infertile, and to sow land with salt is to condemn it to prolonged infertility. Oxymoronically, 'seed' suggests fruitfulness.

12 valley of sackcloth = sackcloth and ashes are signs of mourning, combined here with 'the valley of the shadow of death' of Psalm 23.

13 majesty and burning = oxymoronic and paradoxical; with a sense of the fires as purifying.

14 murder = travesty (by turning the death into a pious lament or government propaganda).

15 The mankind of her going = because death is in the nature of things; but since this one was unnatural, with emphasis on '*man*kind of *her* going', male militarism contrasted with mothering tenderness; grave truth = bitter pun on a weighty truth, or truism; b 'truths' about the 'grave' and afterlife found en*graved* on gravestones or war memorials; c truth about the child's shocking death and burial.

16 stations of the breath = a resembling the Stations of the Cross, the places where Christ rested his cross as he carried it to Calvary (hence, catches in the breath, sobs and sighs); b stations of the London Underground, used as air-raid shelters in WWII; c radio stations ('breath' as broadcast speech).

18 Elegy of innocence and youth = conflates Wilfred Owen's 'Anthem for Doomed *Youth*' and 'Dulce et Decorum Est' ('vile, incurable sores on *innocent* tongues').

19 the first dead = of London, or Adam and Eve, the first mortals to die; London's daughter = the dead child; cf. the 'Daughters of London' in Donne's 'Epithalamion Made at Lincoln's Inn'.

20 Robed in the long friends = enfolded by the 'grains' and 'veins' of those

already 'long' since dead, suggesting the kinship in death denied in life; cf. Ecclesiastes, 12:5: 'man goeth to his long home', which makes the 'friends' grave-worms.

21   the dark veins of her mother = the girl's mother; London, her mother-city.

23   riding Thames = 'riding' has a sexual connotation; the girl returns to the energies of soil, water and the vegetative cycle ('Thames' is also a near-anagram of 'Thomas').

24   After the first death, there is no other = echoes 'first dead', l.19; ostensibly, this is the reason given for not mourning; either *a* because no one can ordinarily die twice; *b* because, in dying, one passes into the cosmic cycle (albeit this is remote from a human concept of life); *c* because there is a Christian resurrection; *d* because the claim in Revelation (e.g. 21:6–8) that after the Last Judgement the damned will burn for eternity in 'the lake which burneth with fire and brimstone; which is the second death' is false – the underwriting of atonement and resurrection by the doctrine of eternal punishment is morally repugnant, incompatible with a loving deity.

This side of the truth (p. 173)

Probably written early 1945, and sent to Vernon Watkins 28 March 1945; published in *Life and Letters Today*, XLVI (July 1945) and *New Republic*, 2 July 1945; collected in *DE*.

  This poem is addressed to Llewelyn, the Thomases' first son (see 'A saint about to fall'), who was six at the time of writing, and had spent most of the war with Caitlin's mother in Hampshire. Like other Thomas poems, its main point is that 'good and bad', innocence and guilt, are human concepts, projected on to a morally neutral universe (see note to l.6). The same argument informs 'A Refusal to Mourn', with which it is exactly contemporary. However, as in that poem, while Thomas undoes the rhetoric of human presumption with which moralistic concepts are attributed to the universe and process, the amorality of the universe is subtly distinguished from the immorality of human behaviour; the universe's indifference, because 'unjudging', amounts to acceptance, and therefore to a paradoxical 'love'. To this extent, although less publicly than 'A Refusal', the poem reflects the recognition of the full scale of wartime atrocities occurring at this time; it acknowledges the necessity of childhood innocence, and is imbued with paternal tenderness for it and its inevitable loss, even as it appears to deny the objective basis for such tenderness.

1   This side of the truth = this side of maturity, or death.

4   blinding = because childhood is both ignorant of the 'truth' of the indifference of process, and because its innocence is dazzling to adult eyes.

5–11   That all is undone ... spilt ... Into the winding dark = an existentialist version of predestination; there is no purpose and point in the universe

6   unminding skies = the same ironic point about the indifference of the universe made by 'discovered skies' ('How shall my animal'), 'answering skies' ('The conversation of prayers') and 'interpreted evening' ('Vision and Prayer'), modified by the suggestion that it is a form of 'love' – a paradox the boy does not yet grasp, and which will always be unverifiable.

13   Good and bad = the subject of 'blow away', 'go crying' and 'fly'.

24   Fly like the stars' blood = unlike Christopher Marlowe's Doctor Faustus, who sees God's condemnation as 'Christ's blood streams in the firmament', the stars neither condemn nor applaud.

26   moon's seed = semen (cf. 'owl-seed' in 'Foster the light').

29   the wicked wish = creative or life impulse; 'wicked', like the preceding 'tears', 'rant' and 'rubbish', is a judgemental term which reflects the projection of human morality on to a neutral universe.

30–31   plants / And animals and birds = cf. 'A Refusal to Mourn' ('bird, beast and flower'); echoes D. H. Lawrence's poetry collection *Birds, Beasts and Flowers*.

32   Water ... light ... earth ... sky = the four elements of classical and medieval philosophy.

36   unjudging love = despite the non-Christian frame of the poem, this echoes Christ's 'I come not to judge' (John 3:17, 8:15, 12:48, etc.), and is another of its parallels with 'A Refusal', in this case Thomas's rejection of the Day of Judgement and its 'second death'.

Sooner than you can water milk, or cry Amen (p. 174)

Written late 1943; a revised version sent on 28 May 1945 to T. W. Earp; first version published in the 1978 edition of *TP71*, the second in *CL*.
   Daniel Jones titled the piece 'A Pub Poem', dated September 1943, and claims that it was co-written in a pub with Thomas's friend Wynford Vaughan-Thomas (whose copy he prints). The 1945 version is preferred because of the vagueness of Vaughan-Thomas's dating.

Unluckily for a death (p. 175)

A 'completely rewritten' version of 'Poem (To Caitlin)' of 1939 (see above), as Thomas informed Dent's, made between late May 1945, when he received the proofs of *DE*, and 18 September, when he returned them. Published in *DE*.

While it remained a love poem to Caitlin, the revision moves 'away from ironical, and towards religious, statement', as Vernon Watkins noted, introducing a swathe of devotional motifs, fused with erotic ones, to grant sexual love a transcendent, healing power. As before, two kinds of false love lurk, 'dedicate forever' (l.6) to tempting the speaker to believe either in immortality through resurrection, or an ascetic yet lustful love (it is clearer in this version that these are also inner aspects of the speaker and his 'Love'). 'Luckily' he asserts the 'ceremony of souls' he and his love enjoy in the here-and-now, knowing that his power to do so derives from his partner and 'the native tongue' of her 'translating eyes'.

This is one of the few poems in *CP52* without a consistent rhyme scheme, unlike the original version.

1–17   Unluckily for a death . . . My holy lucky body . . . is caught and held and kissed = the main subject and verb occur at ll.16 and 17; 'dedicate', l.6, is adjectival.

3   pyre . . . of my sins and days = the fading of his love and its acts for Caitlin.

4   shades = contains 'Hades'.

12   the order of lust = religious order; command. A distinction is drawn between genuine sexual passion and prurient desire.

13   sighs for the seducer's coming = the 'nunnery' 'sighs' for him to come like a 'seducer' to sexually thaw it out.

15   Loving = has 'wintry nunnery' as its subject.

16   holy = play on 'wholly' ('Poem [To Caitlin]' has 'Holy happy').

20   order of the quick = contrasting with 'the order of lust'.

21   heroic hosts = hospitable, not martial; the loved one's body is a secular Eucharistic 'host'.

22–23   the wound / Is certain god = 'wound' is female genitals, also Christ and love; play on W. B. Yeats's 'Song of the Happy Shepherd': 'Words alone are certain good'.

30   androgynous dark = the creative darkness of origin.

31   holocaust = the monstrous creatures are condemned to death because the speaker refuses the blandishments of the 'death biding two'.

32–33   The she mules . . . broody in a milk of birds = members of the monstrous tribe.

34   wanting nun saint = the 'woman in shades' who 'wants' the speaker, but is

also a saint of lack (cf. 'the wanting centre', 'A Winter's Tale').

40–41   full assemblage . . . monstrous or immortal = loving the 'two', rather than the 'living flesh', leads to the 'grave'; a more-than-physical death, since physical death is unavoidable.

47–49   Both shall fail . . . immortality at my side = to defeat the deathly alternatives, the speaker must earn the love of the 'living flesh', refusing either to 'bow' to his wife's 'blessing' or walk 'with immortality', to unreally sanctify the 'ceremony of souls' or devalue 'living flesh' by striving for eternal life; Christ the sky = false transcendence, contrasted with 'Christ the child', Christ-potential in this life.

53–54   she . . . vaulting bird = the temptresses; 'vaulting' is 'over-reaching' and 'tomb-like'.

54–56   the 'true love' is continually re-creating the emotional, sexual and spiritual world of the narrator; inch and glance = repeats l.22.

In my craft or sullen art (p. 176)

Written late summer 1945 and published in *Life and Letters Today* (October 1945); enclosed with 'Fern Hill' in a letter of 18 September 1945 to Dent's in which Thomas asked for it to replace another poem, perhaps 'Last night I dived my beggar arm', in the proofs. Collected in *DE*.

This deceptively simple lyric inverts the romantic exaltation of 'art' over 'craft' by applying 'sullen' to it, appropriately enough given the high degree of craftsmanship Thomas lavished on his own poems. The idea of poetry as solitary 'labour' leads to the word's secondary sense of giving birth, imaged in the moon – sacred to Diana, goddess of childbirth in classical myth – which also has its associations with poetic inspiration, love and madness (as in the moonlit forest of *A Midsummer Night's Dream*, 'The lunatic, the lover, and the poet, / Are of imagination all compact'). But while Thomas rejects the spiritualisation of art, the generation of 'wages', 'trade', 'pay' and 'labour' from 'craft' suggests that overemphasis on 'craft' may lead to an equally false reduction of poetry to the empirical logic of commercialism. In this sense, poetry as *either* inspiration *or* craft is a false choice, reflecting the situation of the poet in capitalist society.

The poet writes, therefore, not for reputation, fame, riches or even sustenance, but for the only other humans involved in activity as dissociated from these as his own, 'the lovers'. By romantic convention, poets who are rejected by society are cherished by lovers; in this poem, however, the lovers 'pay no praise or wages', and this gives his necessary isolation a more alienated, modern form. Even so, he will write for them, perhaps because the lovers' self-absorbed solitude mirrors his own, and is thus a paradoxical form of solidarity. Love, like art, has no exchange-value, and it is this absence he writes 'for', while the lovers' ignorance of him is the very reason why he can write only for them.

The poem's structure reflects this. Stanza 2 partly restates Stanza 1, but is a line shorter, and the last line's appearance of circular return is belied by its loss of 'sullen', the poem's most distinctive word. The stanzas are as complexly interlocked as the lovers, with rhymes ('art', 'arms', 'wages') and phrase-parts ('ivory' and 'towers') shared but altered, and the wartime context is hinted in the way 'griefs', on its return, applies to 'the ages' as well as lovers, hinting at 'arms' as weapons.

1 sullen = morose; solitary (in Middle English, from the Latin *solus*, 'alone').

2 Exercised = emphasises the physical labour of writing as 'craft' and a 'sullen', resistant 'art', with a pun on *exorcised*.

6 singing light = the light by which the poet writes, burning the midnight oil.

9 ivory = separated from 'towering', l.15 ('ivory towers'); possibly alludes to the ancient belief that true dreams came through the Gates of Horn, deceptive ones through the Gates of Ivory.

10–11 common wages . . . secret heart = love means the same for everyone, but is experienced as unique and personal in each individual case.

12 proud man = temporal authorities; with root sense of proud as 'raised above'.

14 spindrift = foam blown ashore by the action of wind on waves. This six-syllable line is a syllable shorter than the others, enacting the slight valuation the speaker puts on his own work.

15 towering dead = the great poets of the English canon (perhaps alluding to Yeats's Thoor Ballylee and collection *The Tower*).

16 nightingales and psalms = exalted themes of canonical poets, specifically Keats's 'Ode to a Nightingale' and Milton.

17–18 the lovers, their arms . . . griefs of the ages = comparison and contrast between the wars of love and the wars of arms was a commonplace in Latin and Renaissance writing.

Fern Hill (p. 177)

Written at Blaen Cwm, Llangain in Carmarthenshire, in late summer–September 1945. On 18 September 1945, Thomas returned the corrected proofs of *DE* to Dent's with 'Fern Hill' and 'In my craft and sullen art', new poems he asked to be added to the volume. Extra space had to be found for 'Fern Hill', but as Thomas explained, 'I very much *want* it included as it is an *essential* part of the feeling & meaning of the book as a whole.' Published in *Horizon* (October 1945); collected in *DE*.

The title is a version of 'Fernhill', the farm near Blaen Cwm owned by Thomas's aunt Ann Jones (cf. 'After the funeral'). It is a fitting climax to *DE*'s remembrancing of Thomas's childhood and elegising of childhood more generally, following the end of the war. It is his best-loved poem, and is unabashedly nostalgic, pulling out all the rhetorical stops – in particular a fluid, breathless-seeming syntax – to enact the unconstrained pleasures of childhood. Yet this success is only the precondition for a subtle manipulation of the child's selective vision and fantasies of omnipotence, adult recollection of these, and the irony implicit in the contrast between them. The result is complex and intensely bittersweet; in Thomas's words, it is 'a poem for evenings and tears' and 'that joyful poem'. Not just about how it feels to be young but how it feels to *have been* young, its easy-going manner belies its intricate constructedness; systematic phrasal manipulation, lexical repetition, colour-patterning, the use of leitmotifs, all indicate larger, cosmic and symbolic symmetries (it can, for example, be read as a six-day creation poem, in which the alternation of day and night is central, the sun appearing in every stanza). The narrative is that of growing towards death within a sacramentalised nature, an exploration of the nature of innocence, which became the theme of much of the later work, including *Under Milk Wood*, as Thomas leaves behind the more materialist and concrete aspects of his process poetic, and accesses the potency of religious feeling, if not of belief, more deeply than before.

The poem's Keatsian sensuous intelligence and partaking of the cult of childhood and the autumnal apple, its unashamed oral pleasures, make it seem purely Romantic. However, it is also a version of modernist pastoral, and its utopian 'anarchic paradise of play' presided over by the timelessness of the id, and its maternal cradling motion, have been linked by Stewart Crehan (1990) to the radical optimism of 1945 and the 'New Jerusalem' of Attlee's Labour government, elected a few months before it was written. It is also one of his first poems to make an open display of allusion to poems in the English pastoral tradition, as subversively signalled by the altered farm name – this manages to seem both more English- and suburban-seeming than its original and to indicate a more expansive, wilder greenness. English and Welsh stereotypes, places, names, religiosity and idioms are subtly interwoven to create a text which, in the words of James A. Davies (1998), is set in 'poetical marches . . . like the Welsh Marches . . . a place of great beauty . . . [and] cultural forces, often in tension, but that combine as much as compete'.

Form: six nine-line stanzas, with a syllabic count of 14-14-9-6-9-14-14 in the first seven lines of each stanza (11.6 and 52 have 15, not 14, syllables); final couplets of 7-9 (Stanzas 1 and 2); 9-6 (Stanzas 3, 4 and 5); 7-9 (Stanza 6). End-rhyme is assonantal (e.g. maiden-again-stable), and the tight, circular form approximates that of the sestina.

1 Now as I was = establishes the immediate timeless present of childhood, but 'now . . . was' creates a grammatical paradox, an ambiguous tense between past

and present, into which the poem emerges to mingle tenses and times; young and easy = from 'free and easy'; apple boughs = a central symbol; apples are the forbidden fruit in the Garden of Eden, the speaker is the apple of Time's eye, apples are both 'green' and 'golden'.

2 lilting = synaesthetic description of the house as musical; happy as the grass was green = from 'happy as the day is long', but sadly ironic: the day of grass is *not* long, and '*As* for man, his days *are* as grass', as in Psalm 103 and the *Book of Common Prayer*.

3   dingle = small wooded valley; cf. Auden's 'Look, Stranger' ('Doom is darker and deeper than any sea-dingle') and Matthew Arnold's 'The Scholar Gipsy' ('listen . . . From the dark dingles to the nightingales'); starry = as in Wordsworth's 'Immortality Ode', 'starry night'.

4 Time let me hail and climb = the image is of Time driving a 'wagon' loaded with apples, which the young boy signals ('hails') to stop, and climbs aboard.

5 Golden = suggests 'golden boy', but following 'green' also hints at autumn, soon followed by winter; heydays = days gone by; pun on 'hay' (harvest) days. Cf. Thomas Hardy's 'Regret Not Me', one of the poem's sources: 'I did not know / That heydays fade and go, / But deemed what was would always be so'.

6 prince = as in a fairy story; apple towns = apple orchards.

7 once below a time = inversion of the traditional fairy-tale opening, which has the child both out of time to all appearances and in time, subject of and to a time and future subject of another. It is also implied that if something can exist on the surface flow of time it may exist below it in the timeless present of the unconscious. This phrase is the title of a 1940 poem (see pp.114, 356).

7–8 I lordly had . . . daisies and barley = he decorated the orchard with garlands of barley and daisies. Like 'prince', the security of 'lordly' grows increasingly poignant.

9 windfall light = 'windfall' is fruit which has been blown down before picking, hence unripe; but also, metaphorically, an unlooked-for bonus.

13–14 Time let me play and be / Golden = the enjambement allows several senses; time lets the boy be golden; lets him exist; leaves him alone.

15 I was huntsman and herdsman = the boy's rapturous self-sufficiency resembles Thomas Traherne's in *Centuries of Meditation*: 'all the World was mine; and I the only Spectator and Enjoyer of it'.

16 Sang to my horn = from the nursery rhyme 'Little Boy Blue', but with a hint of childhood sexuality; foxes = wild animals, contrasted with the domesticated calves.

17–18 the sabbath rang . . . holy streams = indicates the Welsh context; the Oscar Williams letter describes a 'farm labourer who told me that the stream that runs by his cottage side is Jordan water and who can deny him'.

19 All the sun long = because the sun is the day to the child.

20–22 suggestion of the four classical elements of air, water, fire, and earth.

20 tunes from the chimneys = synaesthetic image for smoke rising and falling like musical modulations.

25 nightjars = nocturnal birds with a reputation for stealthy flight; also known as the fern owl.

30 Adam and maiden = not Eve, in order to stress that it was the boy's world alone, and its purity; cf. Vaughan, 'The Rapture', 'Only what Adam in his first Estate, / Did I behold'; George Meredith, 'Love in the Valley', 'Maiden still the morn is'. Self-sufficiency is enacted in a *cynghanedd*-like mirroring of vowels: *a d m / m a d*.

33 So it must have been = the adult speaker consciously tries to place childhood experience for the first time.

34 spinning place = because the earth spins.

36 fields of praise = alludes to Christian Eden and pagan Elysian Fields.

40 heedless = Thomas told Brinnin '*ran* my *heedless* ways! – that's bloody bad!', but it signals the more analytical, abstract adult consciousness initiated at this point.

42 sky blue trades = links the child's play to heaven.

43 turning = cf. 'Poem in October'; morning songs = cf. 'Our morning hymn is this', in Sidney's 'Ye Goatherd Gods'.

44–45 the children . . . Follow him out of grace = like the children who follow the Pied Piper of Hamelin.

46–47 time would take me . . . loft = the speaker as 'man-as-grass' anticipates being cut and stored in the hay-loft of death; lamb white = of Christlike purity (and sacrifice).

47 swallow thronged = cf. Keats's 'To Autumn': 'And gathering swallows twitter in the skies'; by the shadow of my hand = the subject of 'take me' in l.46.

53 held = applied to 'chains' in l.54, means 'chained up'; applied to 'mercy' in l.52 it means 'cradled', 'supported'; green and dying = 'green' still denotes youth and growth, but now also rot.

54   Though I sang in my chains like the sea = the sea sings in tides and waves because it is 'chained' by the gravity of earth and moon (cf. 'moon-chained', 'Ballad of the Long-legged Bait'). Thomas echoes Rousseau's 'Man is born everywhere in chains', but 'sings' the chains of mortality, defying them through the chains of his art. Cf. Donne, 'The Triple Foole': 'I thought, if I could draw my paines, / Through Rimes vexation, I should them allay. / Grief brought to numbers cannot be so fierce, / For he tames it, that fetters it in verse'.

In Country Heaven [fragment] (p. 179)

This incomplete forty-three-line draft, initially titled 'In Country Sleep', was written March/April 1947, just before Thomas's departure to Italy with his family in mid-April; first published in *TP71*.

In Italy, Thomas began a new poem, to which he gave the name of the draft poem he had recently abandoned ('Sleep' was later changed to 'Heaven' on the ms of the draft, to distinguish it from this later work). The date of composition can be deduced from the fact that when he sent a copy of the later 'In Country Sleep' to Margaret Taylor from Italy, on 11 July 1947, he told her that 'It isn't the [poem] whose beginning I showed you'. This must have been the draft, and he must have shown it her before leaving England.

Introducing a BBC radio broadcast of 'In Country Sleep', 'Over Sir John's hill' and 'In the White Giant's Thigh' on 25 September 1950, Thomas spoke of them as parts of a longer single work, to be called *In Country Heaven* (a recording of his introduction is included in *The Caedmon Collection*, 2002). Thomas published this BBC piece as a 'Note' sent to Princess Caetani for *Botteghe Oscure* later in 1950 (see Appendix 3). Both forms hint at the existence of the sequence's title poem (probably by then intended to be a link poem), some of which is said to be 'already written down on paper', while 'some of it is a rough draft in the head, and the rest of it radiantly unworded in ambitious conjecture'. Although the draft, at Austin, is incomplete, I include it among the finished poems because it is intertextual with three of the four most substantial later poems. It is also worth mentioning that Thomas made some corrections to the poems in his friend Ruthven Todd's copy of *ICS*; following *CP88* I have incorporated these as reflecting his final wishes. It is worth noting the point made by Daniel Jones in *TP71* that what is most striking about the *In Country Heaven* project is Thomas's indifference during his lifetime to the ordering of the poems which were to have made it up – the sequencing in the 1950 broadcast and in *CP52* is different (and in *CP52* the sequence is interrupted by two poems which do not belong to it), while to different correspondents he suggested that 'In the White Giant's Thigh' was the opening piece *and* that he had not made his mind up about where it would go. On this basis Jones notes that the idea of writing a long work 'suggested itself gradually and was often abandoned' and surmises that Thomas may have wondered whether he had the ability to create a large, overarching poetic structure.

Perhaps as a result of the September 1950 broadcast, Thomas reworked the opening lines as a sixteen-line fragment, in a notebook dated October 1951 at Austin. *CP88* includes this in the body of the poems, and the 1947 draft in its notes to the work. However, I view the first draft as more important than the short reworking of it, and have therefore reversed their placement. This is the reworked fragment of October 1951:

> Always when He, in country heaven,
>   (Whom my heart hears),
> Crosses the breast of the praising east and kneels,
>   Humble in all his planets,
>   And weeps on the abasing crest,
>
> Then in the last ward and joy of beasts and birds
>   And the canonized valley
> Where all sings, that was made and is dead,
>   And the angels whirr like pheasants
>   Through naves of leaves,
>
> Light and His tears dewfall together
>   (O hand in hand)
> Out of the pierced eyes and the cataract sky,
>   He cries his blood, and the suns
>   Dissolve and run down raggèd
>
> Gutters of his face: Heaven blind and black.

The similarity of all the versions, prose and verse, of the project suggests that 'In Country Heaven' would have set the scene in 'Country Heaven', where the 'heavenly hedgerow men' tell their tales of the destroyed earth, possibly linking these together. In the Caedmon recording, Humphrey Searle says that Thomas informed him that the poem was to describe 'shepherds on the moon' witnessing the atomic self-destruction of the earth. For Barbara Hardy (2000) it concerns 'a vastation, not a creation story . . . a tragic reversal of Genesis and St. John, not "Let there be light" [but] "Let there be darkness"', and it could be that this went against the grain of Thomas's habitual mode of praise and celebration, preventing the work's completion.

Form: four pairs of five-line stanzas, with regular syllabic pattern and interlinked by rhyme, as follows: 9a, 4b, 11c, 7d, 8e / 11b, 7d, 9e, 8a, 4c. Three lines only of the fifth pair had also been completed before Thomas left for Italy in mid-April 1947.

7   canonized valley = sanctified; pun evoking Tennyson's 'The Charge of the Light Brigade': 'Into the valley of death / Rode the six hundred . . . Cannon to the right of them, / Cannon to the left of them'.

11, 41   his tears glide down . . . glide of his tears = cf. Donne, *Holy Sonnets*, 'Divine Meditations', XIII ('What if this world present were the world's last night?'). Considering a similar apocalyptic scenario, Donne asks whether 'Tears in [Christ's] eyes quench the amazing light' of the sun and creation.

24   blackamoor = archaic for a black African.

31   the fifth element is pity = the Country Heaven of 'pity' for mortal things fashions a world which knows of, but does not itself contain, death.

35   Or twice dies = cf. 'A Refusal to Mourn'.

In Country Sleep (p. 180)

Derived from the unfinished 'In Country Heaven', which originally had this name (see above and Appendix 3). Beside an autograph copy in a notebook at Austin, Thomas has written: 'This poem begun May 1947. Rapallo & Florence & finished July 1947. Florence.' The date on the final page is 3 July 1947. Published in *Horizon* (UK) and *Atlantic* (USA) in December 1947; collected in *ICS*.

   The occasion of the poem is a father reading fairy tales (such as 'Little Red Riding Hood', 'Beauty and the Beast' and 'Snow White') to his daughter, as Thomas did for his daughter, Aeronwy. She is told not to fear the bogeymen and monsters of the tales, and to trust in the unthreatening and 'holy' natural world. Instead, she should 'fear most . . . the Thief', who approaches her as inexorably as the 'fall' of snow, hail, apples and other natural phenomena. This would suggest that the Thief is maturity and death, and ultimately to be accepted, were it not for his more menacing aspects. His name derives from 'the day of the Lord' that 'will come as a thief in the night' (e.g. 2 Peter 3:10), but there are satanic overtones in his 'pouncing', 'sly' ways, and 'beaked, web dark' suggests Zeus's rape of Leda, giving his threat a sexual aspect.

   The identity of the addressee is more ambiguous than first appears, too. Thomas once claimed the poem 'was not addressed to a child at all but to his wife', and details in Part II support this; certainly, a kind of magical realism uncovers the latent sexual content of the fairy tales, and this dramatises Thomas's conflicted paternal and spousal affections. Part II also reveals anxiety in an opening barrage of apostrophes, in which the pastoral, fairy-tale properties that offered a bulwark against the Thief now bear witness to his coming. The speaker understands that the sleeper somehow draws the Thief to her, and the tortuousness of the passage in which he grasps this (ll.87–95) enacts the difficulty of the realisation. He finally understands that the Thief does not come to take the girl's innocence or virginity; rather, her 'faith' is in the Thief coming to take her faith, and she needs the former in order to confirm the latter. Paradoxically, therefore, the betrayal would be if he did *not* come; her faith exists insofar as it is threatened, as conveyed by a complex series of double negatives.

The poem comes to be about grasping the paradox of belief, or faith. This is not specifically Christian, but more a faith in the self, one's work, the value of existence. When Thomas was asked whether the Thief was alcohol, he agreed, but added: 'Alcohol is the thief today. But tomorrow he could be fame or success or exaggerated introspection or self-analysis. The thief is anything that robs you of your faith or reason for being.'

A ms at Austin continues the poem in a Part III ('Who will teach you that the child / Who sucks on innocence / Is spinning fast and loose on a fiery wheel?'), but breaks off and is followed by prose paraphrase of the end of Part II:

> If you believe (and fear) that every night, night without end, the Thief comes to try to steal your faith that every night he comes to steal your faith that your faith is there – then you will wake with your faith steadfast and deathless.

If you are innocent of the Thief, you are in danger. If you are innocent of the loss of faith, you cannot be faithful. If you do not know the Thief as well as you know God, then you do not know God well. Christian looked through a hole in the floor of heaven and saw hell. You must look through faith and see disbelief.

Form: Part I has nine seven-line stanzas with *abcbaac* rhyme; Part II has eight six-line stanzas with an *abbcca* pattern. The fifth line of the stanzas in Part I and the fourth line of those in Part II are four syllables; the other lines range from twelve to thirteen syllables.

I

1   riding far and near = in dreams.

5   My dear, my dear = after the refrain 'O, my dear', in Yeats's 'The Three Bushes': Yeats's rather arch lewdness is deflected by the tenderness of Thomas's usage.

7, 13   eat your heart . . . honeyed heart = alludes to the troubadour legend of the lady tricked into eating her lover's heart, as in Dante's *Vita Nuova*.

29   robin breasted = folk tradition holds that the robin is red-breasted from the blood shed by Christ on the Cross; three Marys = the three Marys who were present at the crucifixion; Matthew 27:56.

30 Sanctum sanctorum = the Holy of Holies, innermost sanctum of a synagogue.

32 holt = an animal's lair.

38, 49, 93 Thief = the ambiguous image of the thief is common in the Bible.

41 prayer wheeling = like a Buddhist prayer wheel; along with the references to a synagogue, Protestant 'black bethels' and Catholic 'beads', makes the point that the holiness of the natural world is not monopolised by any one religion.

46 the roarer at the latch = the wolf in the tale of the Three Little Pigs.

51–54 until the stern bell . . . the soul walks / The waters shorn = until the end of time, or of the speaker's life.

59–63 pounded islands . . . cyclone of silence = allusion to Adam, 'wounded' in providing the rib with which God created Eve, leading via the 'apple' to the Fall and its 'seed' 'flowering' in mankind's side ever since. But nuclear weapons were tested at the 'pounded' islands of the Bikini atoll in the Pacific from 1946, and the Austin ms has 'melted islands'.

63 the cyclone of silence = cf. God's address to Job, 'out of the whirlwind', Job 38–41; aftermath of the atom bomb.

II

65 great roc ribboned for the fair! = the roc is the giant bird of Sinbad's adventures in the *Arabian Nights*; cf. also the nursery rhyme 'Oh, Dear! What Can the Matter Be?', in which Johnny goes to the 'fair' promising to buy his sweetheart 'a bunch of blue ribbons'.

66 And high, there = Hopkins, 'The Windhover': 'striding / High there'.

96 designed = emphasises purpose and control from this point on, as also in 'truly', 'ruly', 'surely', 'ship shape'.

96–106 he comes . . . to grieve he will not come = cf. Thomas Hardy's 'A Broken Appointment': 'You did not come . . . / Grieved I, when, as the hope-hour stroked its sum, / You did not come'.

111 Your faith . . . the ruled sun = A contrast is intended with the 'lawless' sun of l.105, perhaps a reference to man's 'ruling' of the nuclear forces which drive the 'sun'. However, 'outcry' also suggests Christ (as Son/'sun' 'ruled' by God to die) 'deathlessly' crying out from the Cross.

Over Sir John's hill (p. 184)

Written May–August 1949; published in *Botteghe Oscure* (December 1949), *Hudson Review* (Autumn 1950) and *TLS* (24 August 1951); collected in *ICS*.

Sir John's hill is a wooded promontory overlooking Laugharne, which can be climbed by a path from the town's main street (cf. 'Poem in October'). Thomas could see it across the estuary from his writing shed. The poem is quasi-allegorical, with birds serving as the vehicles for a consideration of the natural order, man's destructive impulses, innocence, guilt, judgement, death and the poetic act. This is articulated in two main image chains: destructive fire, appropriate to the 'In Country Heaven' sequence, and judicial execution, in which the hawk is likened to a hangman, the hill to a hanging judge. The narrator is presented 'reading' death in the natural world, intuiting a hierarchy in which hunted seem to collaborate with the hunter. As part of the natural order, 'all praise' must be offered to the hawk, as well as blessings to the smaller birds on which it preys. And yet he 'grieve[s]' their deaths, he says, 'tell-tale'-ing it as the 'guilt' of those who are 'led-astray'. Only at this point is God introduced and his 'mercy' invoked.

Arguably, the poem's subject is the human impulse to anthropomorphise animals and the natural world. The images personifying the hawk, hill and birds in their various roles are presented as a device by which this is done, and we are meant to understand them as such. In reality, however, man is separated from the natural world in the very act of trying to appropriate it in this way. The poem is restating – in a more elegiac and humane register – the 'dumbness' felt in 'The force that through the green fuse' of sixteen years before, as 'fuse' at l.28 hints. Particularly egregious is the case of the heron; although priest- and poet-like, the contradiction between it as 'stab[bing]' killer (l.19) and its later (presumed) grieving of the death of the birds (l.47) suggests that Thomas is using pathetic fallacy in order to expose its absurdity. In truth he knows that the heron, like the rest of the natural world, represents process, which is sufficiently holy without symbolism, while knowing at the same time that he (like other humans) cannot resist projecting such symbolism on to it.

Form: twelve-line stanzas syllabically patterned 5-6-14-14-5-1-14-5-14-5-14-14, with rare exceptions; full and assonantal rhyme scheme *aabccbdeaedd*.

2, 16, 27   the hawk on fire = both 'dynamically active' and reflecting the setting sun (the poem moves from evening, through 'dusk' and sunset, to night); hangs = the hawk hovers before stooping on its prey; executes; still = stationary before stooping; perpetually.

3   hoisted cloud, at drop of dusk = sky and landscape are imagined as the setting for the execution of the 'small birds'.

4   gallows = a verb; rays = the rays of sunlight by which the hawk sees the 'small birds' below him are imagined as ropes by which he 'pulls' them to his 'claws'.

6   Wars = the word's isolation highlights Thomas's fears of a new world war.

9   fiery tyburn = Tyburn was the main location for public executions in London

until 1783; it became synonymous with hanging, and its gallows was known as 'Tyburn tree'; with pun here on ty*burn*.

10 noosed hawk = the executioner is also subject to the round of death.

11–12, 18–21, 36, 47–48, 57–59 holy stalking heron = functions in a changing, richly complex way as the speaker's co-singer, surrogate, metaphor, and allegorical-symbolic cipher; but it is ultimately a predatory animal in the natural world.

12 river Towy = the rivers Towy and Taf flow into the estuary at Laugharne.

14–15 a black cap . . . Sir John's just hill dons = a judge would don a black cap before pronouncing the death sentence. The hill is the judge here, the hawk the executioner; gulled birds = a punning tautology; 'gulls' are birds, but to be 'gulled' is to be fooled, and a 'gull' is a dupe (cf. 'Poem on his Birthday').

21 sedge = as well as being a plant, sedge (as Thomas noted in his worksheets for the poem) is also the collective noun for herons; 'dilly dilly' = cf. the nursery song 'Mrs Bond': 'John Ostler, go fetch me a duckling or two; / Cry Dilly, dilly, dilly, dilly, come let us be killed'; loft = on high; origin late Old English, from Old Norse *loft*, 'air, sky, upper room'.

28 viperish fuse = the hawk is about to strike, as snakes do, and a fuse hisses like a viper.

28–29 brand / Wing = the wing's underside flares like a burning brand, or torch, in the setting sun.

33 We = the poet and the heron.

35 young Aesop fabling = Aesop is said to have written his animal *Fables* in old age; Thomas was thirty-four at the time of writing 'Over Sir John's hill'.

38 sea cobbles sail = the cobbled wharf seems to float on the sea; a 'coble' is a medieval merchant ship.

45 God in his whirlwind silence = God speaks to Job 'out of the whirlwind' in the Book of Job (e.g. 38:1–41; cf. 'In Country Sleep'); marks the sparrows hail = cf. Matthew 10:29: 'Are not two sparrows sold for a farthing? and one of them shall not fall on the ground without your Father'.

51 in the tear of the Towy = biographical evidence suggests that Thomas intended 'tear' as in 'rip', and this sound is taken up in 'wear-willow' in l.58. However, the fact that both senses and pronunciations fit suggests intentional ambiguity.

51–52 Only a hoot owl / Hollows, a grassblade blown in cupped hands = cf. Wordsworth, 'There was a boy! Ye knew him well . . .'.

58 Wear-willow = 'to wear the willow' (as a garland) meant to be in mourning. Cf. Desdemona's 'Willow Song' in *Othello*; grave = engrave – but the engraving is on stone, like the headstone for a grave.

Verse letter to Loren McIver and Lloyd Frankenberg (p. 186)

Written June–August 1950 as a verse-letter to two New York friends, the artist Loren McIver and the writer Lloyd Frankenberg, in whose flat Thomas had stayed on his first US reading tour. The ms of the original reads 'Now eleven weeks', dated from Thomas's return from the tour in early June; however, Thomas did not send it until November 1951. At this point 'Now fifteen months' was substituted in the ms. It was first edited and published in a limited edition in 1993 as *Letter to Loren* by Jeff Towns, who bought the ms at auction in 1992, and republished in *CL* (2000).

The poem is a greatly extended example of the wartime genre of verse-letters. A remarkable testament to Thomas's immersion in US literary and film-star gossip, it also bemoans the fact that Laugharne inhabitants are interested in the celebrities he met in the US, and his own antics there, rather than his 'odyssey' of readings, and presents the town in a dark, semi-surrealist fashion. It concludes with a set of improbable conditions to be fulfilled before he could ever return to the US, on a note of gloomily amused self-deprecation.

Form: eleven stanzas (4 and 11 have fourteen lines, Stanzas 5 and 10 have sixteen lines, the rest have fifteen), with a complex mix of pararhyme and full rhyme.

2 dome . . . pleasure = 'pleasure dome', from Coleridge's 'Kubla Khan', was the title of both a book and a collection of poetry recordings edited by Frankenberg.

5 queen e. = the liner *Queen Elizabeth*, or 'titan's canoe' / 'mastadon's sloop', on which Thomas returned to Britain.

6 bowery = the Bowery is a down-at-heel area of New York City; Thomas is joking that, having been in America for so long, Britons seemed as 'foreign . . . as freud' to him.

7 minikin = 'Dainty, elegant, sprightly. Now contemptuously: Affected, mincing' (*OED*).

8 milking his gnome = masturbating.

11 dominie = schoolmaster.

18 scrapered shores = the skyscrapered skyline of New York.

19 pettylike pretties = George Petty, US graphic artist, drew pin-up girls for *Esquire*.

28 tallulah = Tallulah Bankhead (1902–68), US film actress.

29 buttered with goosefat = cf. 'butter fat goosegirls', 'In the White Giant's Thigh'.

31 gables = Clark Gable (1901–60), British-born Hollywood film actor; brown derbies = fashionable soft felt hat for men; jane russell = Jane Russell (1921–2011), US film actress.

33 b. grable's pylons = Betty Grable (1916–73), US film actress noted for her shapely legs, or 'pylons' (reputedly insured for $1 million).

34 m. west . . . bette d. = Mae West (1892–1980) and Bette Davis (1908–89), US film actresses.

36 dylan's = the autograph copy has an accent over 'y', indicating a rhyme with 'pylons' and 'nylons'.

37–38 so clever / ly agented odyssey = the recent tour of the USA, for which John Malcolm Brinnin had been Thomas's agent.

39–41 cockles and mussel / s town = Laugharne.

41–42 boulevard . . . sunset = Los Angeles' Sunset Boulevard.

46 yale and harvard = New England Ivy League universities, where Thomas first read outside New York; o'hara scarlet = Scarlett O'Hara, heroine of Margaret Mitchell's novel *Gone with the Wind* (1936), and hugely popular film of 1939.

48 cold mutton = the penis.

49 holyoke = Mount Holyoke College, women's arts college in Massachusetts; t. bara = Theda Bara (1885–1955), US silent film actress.

50 'come into the garden Brynmawr maud / s' = reference to Bryn Mawr College and the opening line of Tennyson's *Maud*, XXII, famous as a parlour song in Michael Balfe's arrangement.

51 betty manhutton = Betty Hutton (1921–2007), US film actress; she had four husbands, accounting for 'man'; also a play on 'Manhattan'.

53 vassar = Vassar College, women's liberal arts college; chippies = US slang for a promiscuous woman.

56 gypsy lee roses = Gypsy Rose Lee (1911–70), US burlesque entertainer famous for her striptease act.

57 sweeny erect = c.f. T. S. Eliot's poem 'Sweeney Erect', about an invented figure for the contemporary philistine, John L. Sweeney, who edited Thomas's

Selected Writings (1946); tse-tse = play on T. S. Eliot's initials (the tsetse fly causes sleeping sickness).

58   loopy chicago = the Chicago Loop is the Elevated Transit System ('El') which serves the city's downtown area, but 'loopy' also means slightly crazy; aquinasses = from St Thomas Aquinas (1225–74), the leading medieval theologian, philosopher and teacher; with pun on 'asses', nit-picking academics and students.

59   sinused st thomas = Thomas as a put-upon St Thomas Aquinas.

60–62   Just as a blind man's nose . . . 'how d'you do, ladies?' = a crude joke; the blind man mistakes the smell of fish for that of women's vaginas.

64   hail croesus and meary = Croesus is a synonym for wealth; Meary could be the editor of *Poetry* (London), Meary James Tambimuttu; wordplay on the expostulation 'Jesus and Mary'.

70   ritas and hedies = Rita Hayworth (1918–87) and Hedi Lamarr (1913–2000), US film actresses.

75   oscar williams = Oscar Williams (1900–64), US anthologist and poet, friend and promoter of Thomas's work. Initial capitals in the ms; here lower-case in keeping with other proper names in the poem.

76   The inhaling bunion = the scandal-seeking nose of Thomas's interrogator.

79   derwood forest = allusion to Gene Derwood (1909–54), poet and painter, married to Oscar Williams, with play on Sherwood Forest (hence 'Robin Hood' and 'Friar Tuck' below).

82   schnozzle = Yiddish/US slang for a nose (mildly contemptuous).

83   vogues = the fashion magazine *Vogue*.

84   charles morgan = Charles Morgan (1894–1958), a prolific novelist, to whom Thomas took a permanent dislike after meeting him in Laugharne in 1938.

86   fannies = inoffensive (buttocks), US slang; ruder (female pudendum) in British slang; flairs = *Flairs*, a fashion magazine similar to *Vogue*.

87   weepers = eyes.

88   tennessee williams = Tennessee Williams (1914–83), US playwright.

89   st vitus 'em! = set them dancing uncontrollably (from St Vitus' Dance).

90   A truck called fuck = Thomas's cruder version of Tennessee Williams's *A Streetcar Named Desire* (1947).

97–98   gigl / I = Beniamino Gigli (1890–1957), famous Italian operatic tenor.

91–112   In this pretty as a stricture town . . . in the bloody vat = semi-surreal description of Laugharne and its inhabitants.

102   john peel = from hunting song 'D'ye ken John Peel?'

106   gabies = simpletons.

111–12   rack a jack crack / a jill = wordplay using 'crackerjack' (excellent) and the nursery rhyme characters Jack and Jill.

113   red market ration = play on 'black market'; meat was still rationed in Britain.

117   winkle pin = pin for extracting a winkle (sea snail) from its shell.

121–24   Must I stand in this public . . . themselves alone? = wordplay on uranium/urinal, alluding to notices found in Gents' toilets: 'Please Adjust Your Dress Before Leaving'.

124–25   to hell . . . cuntos = to mind ones p's and q's is to obey etiquette; 'these cuntos' are the stanzas of this poem, jokingly compared in their unwieldy complexity to Pound's *Cantos*; candystuck keys = of Thomas's typewriter, sticky with the sweets he was fond of.

127   watered street = Water Street, in Greenwich Village, New York.

128–31   if women's elbows and knees . . . are only glued together = cf. Blake's epigram: 'When a Man has Married a Wife, he finds out whether / Her knees & elbows are only glewed together'; rare bits to cheese = a Welsh rarebit is cheese on toast, but double entendres are probably intended.

133   theodore reothke = play on Theodore Roethke (1908–63), US poet and friend.

134   king kong's evil = 'the king's evil' is scrofula, traditionally believed to be cured by the touch of the British monarch.

136   dree this wierd = to dree one's weird (deliberately misspelt) is a Scots idiom for enduring one's fate; it leads to wordplay on 'drier than moth's wee / wee'.

138–39   stephen the seaman / 's bender = Stephen Spender (1909–95), leading 1930s English poet, bisexual (hence 'seaman's bender').

139–40   big chi / chi . . . hamingway = Ernest Hemingway (1898–1961), US writer famous for his macho lifestyle and writing; 'chi chi' and 'ham' mock this 'stewed ape' aspect.

142   john lehman = John Lehmann (1907–87), English poet, editor and leading metropolitan literary figure of the Auden generation; Thomas imputes bisexuality to him; leman = mistress.

144–46   peter . . . viereck = Peter Viereck (1916–2006), US historian, thinker, poet and professor at Holyoke College. Thomas refers to his conservative poetic stances ('toryballed').

146–47   e. / e. . . . cummings = e. e. cummings (1894–1962), US poet, admirer of Thomas and close friend of McIver and Frankenberg; his disregard for capital letters is adopted by Thomas throughout this poem; eimi = *Eimi* (1933) is cummings' critical account of his travels in the USSR; gorblimey = Cockney expletive.

148   trappised merton = Thomas Merton (1915–69), US poet and religious writer; Trappist monk since 1940.

150   dormouse room = cf. *The Enormous Room* (1922), novel by e. e. cummings; respectable mountains = cf. the Delectable Mountains in *Pilgrim's Progress*.

150–51   gee / gee jesus defend us from canter! emen! = play on child's term for a horse to produce Jesus, followed by a prayer to not be preached at, where the substitution of 'emen' for 'Amen' produces 'cantery men' (horses 'canter', preachers spout 'cant').

152–53   penic / illin = the wonder drug of the age. Although it rhymes with 'menace', 'penic' as 'penis' lurks here as Thomas forswears his 'cantankerous malice' as a kind of venereal disease (hence 'chancres') in this final stanza.

156   perry palace = the Frankenbergs' apartment in Perry Place, Greenwich Village.

160–61   once tennis / onian house = the once stately, now merely flippant structure of Thomas's poetry (from 'tennysonian' to 'tennis'-onian, a mere game).

166   cloaca and dagger = play on 'cloak and dagger' and cloaca ('sewer').

Lament (p. 191)

Probably written early 1951. On 20 March 1951 Thomas told Princess Caetani that it was 'nearly finished', adding that it 'will be about 50 or 60 lines long and is coarse and violent . . . a crotchety poem, worked at quite hard between the willies'. It was published in her journal *Botteghe Oscure* (November 1951), and in *Partisan Review* (January/February 1952). Collected in *ICS*.

Thomas worked simultaneously on 'Lament' and 'Do not go gentle' and they were published together, suggesting that he regarded them as complementary, but there are also several echoes of *Under Milk Wood*. Manuscripts at Austin show that the original title was 'The Miner's Lament', and include images such as 'skinbare pit' and 'moon shaft slag'; with surviving pit-related terms such as 'ram rod', this suggests the poem was once in the voice of a collier. It is a song in a working-class accent, reflecting popular culture of the time, but may also draw on the medieval Welsh genre of deathbed repentance poem (*marwysgafn*). Not to be mistaken for personal confession, it is a bawdy performance, chauvinistic yet self-mocking, of one aspect of Thomas's personality.

1 windy = full of empty rhetoric.

2 black spit = miners' spittle, black with coal dust; to be the 'spit' ('spitting image') of someone is to look like them, hence a dark likeness of the white lambs.

3 ram rod = like 'coal black', present in each stanza; rod used for tamping down explosives charges in mines; phallic image.

4 gooseberry wood = children asking where babies came from were once told that they were 'found under a gooseberry bush'. A 'gooseberry' is also someone who insists on accompanying lovers who want to be alone; cf. *Under Milk Wood*, 'gooseberried double bed of the wood'.

5 rude owl ... telltale tit = 'rude' because associating the indelicately named 'tit'.

7 donkeys' common = there is a Donkey Down in *Under Milk Wood*.

10 The whole of the moon = all night long.

14 beetles' pews = pious churchgoers, dressed in black, imagined as beetles.

19 Midwives ... midnight ditches = suggests the outcome of sex in illegitimate births; 'mid' imparts some of the illicit flavour of 'midnight' to the respectable 'midwives' who would attend them; 'grew' is as applicable to wombs as hedgerows.

28 bass = voice; Bass, a brand of beer.

43–48 At last the soul ... woman's soul for a wife = the epithet applied to 'mouse'-like women in Stanza 3 is now ironically applicable to the conscience, or soul, of the roué narrator.

54 a sunday wife = pious; sexually constrained.

56 Harpies = pests; angels with harps. As Siobhán Parkinson (1981) notes, this is 'a final wry comment on the tiresome nature of virtue'.

57–60 The suggestion is that this is a deathbed confession; yet the tone is tongue in cheek.

Do not go gentle into that good night (p. 193)

Completed May 1951 and enclosed in a letter of 28 May 1951 to Princess Caetani, to which Thomas appended the PS: 'The only person I can't show the little enclosed poem to is, of course, my father, who doesn't know he's dying.' Published with 'Lament' in *Botteghe Oscure* in November 1951, collected in *ICS*.

Addressed to his chronically ill father, the argument of this famous poem arose from Thomas's deep respect for D. J. Thomas's truculent temperament and independent, atheistic cast of mind. As he explained at a reading in the USA, his father 'went blind and was very ill before he died. He was in his eighties and he grew soft and gentle at the last. [He] hadn't wanted him to change.' The subject had been on his mind since at least 1945, when he wrote to Vernon Watkins: 'My Father is awfully ill these days, with heart disease and uncharted pains, and the world that was once the colour of tar to him is now a darker place.' Something of that grim humour survives, intensifying the poem's measured sonorities. To constrain the emotion of impending bereavement and his pity for his father's suffering, Thomas chose the notoriously demanding form of the villanelle, which uses just two rhymes (the words 'night' and 'day' end the opening two lines of the poem, impacting theme and form still further). As Golightly (2003) observes, there is a 'strained background bitterness in the poem that catches the experience in grief where flows of emotion run inexplicably both ways', and in this sense the poem enacts the opposite of what it ostensibly asks of the dying man; its rhythms and phrasing lull and soothe, as if to help him on his way, and in an elegiac tone which has already accepted his death.

1 Do not go gentle = 'gentle' is adverb and noun; 'do not go gently' and 'do not go, gentle one'; that good night = the final farewell. The sense that 'night' is 'good', opposed to the poem's ostensible argument, is allowed for by the splitting of 'good-night' into two words.

5 forked no lightning = cf. Byron's *Childe Harold's Pilgrimage*, Canto 3, Stanza 95: 'of all the band, / The best and brightest through these parted hills hath fork'd / His lightnings'.

8 in a green bay = in a hospitable world.

13 Grave men = serious, and (as good as) dead.

16 the sad height = of (Calvary-like) death. Asked by Watkins if this was 'a kind of transposition of Kierkegaard's learning that his father had once stood on a hill and cursed God', Thomas 'only smiled and remained silent'.

17 Curse, bless, me now with your fierce tears = cf. Blake's *Tiriel*, 1, ll.12, 16–18: 'His blessing was a cruel curse. His curse may be a blessing.' The doubleness, and halting rhythm of the punctuation, encapsulate the confusion of the son, who wants his father to be his 'cursing' self and, at the same time, wants him

to grant a final blessing, as only those who have accepted that death is imminent may.

Song (p. 193)

This drinking song, reflecting Thomas's occasional composition of impromptu pieces in pubs and clubs, was forwarded to the editor for verification in September 2013. It had been recently discovered in the papers of Anne Jarvis by her husband Fred Jarvis, and is thought to have been given to Anne's mother in Oxford in the early 1950s. It is written in pencil in Thomas's autograph on the verso of a sheet of headed notepaper for the Apollo Society, a concert society founded by Peggy Ashcroft and Natasha Litvin, with offices in Park Lane, London. Below the letterhead is written: 'This little song was written in Henneky's Long bar High Holborn by Dylan Thomas in 1951', followed by 'With the Secretary's compliments' in capitals and, in normal case, 'Dylan Thomas, Esq'. It has much in common with the songs of *Under Milk Wood*, and is an amusing reflection on British pub culture of the time. Watts-Ewers's name is a play on the standard formula for offering to buy someone a drink ('What's yours?').

In the White Giant's Thigh (p. 195)

Written summer 1949–May 1951. Thomas was probably referring to it in a letter of 12 November 1949 to Helen and Bill McAlpine: 'I have finished my poem, a hundred lines, but it may need a second part.' On 28 November he described it as '80 lines long', and it was sixty lines when published in *Botteghe Oscure* in late summer 1950. It was sent to Oscar Williams on 28 May 1951, described as 'only the first section of a poem', but also as 'recently finished'. Collected in *ICS*.

Thomas described this poem to Williams as 'conventionally romantic', but as his uncertainty about its completeness indicates, it is less straightforward than it seems. The giant of the title is a figure several hundred feet high (with a phallus to match) carved into the chalk of the hillside at Cerne Abbas in Dorset, within day-trip distance (43 miles) of Blashford in Hampshire, where Thomas and his family often stayed with Caitlin's mother. A fertility superstition attaching to it held that women who were infertile could conceive if they made love in the potent 'thigh' of the giant. The speaker imagines walking at night on the giant's hill, and communing with the spirits of the women. It is Thomas's most Hardyesque piece, and has a folk-tale tone; it interweaves the Dorset landscape with that of the Laugharne estuary, conflating the throats of the curlews on the hill and of the estuary rivers with those of the spirits. Thomas's choices slyly undermine any fixed sense of place still further, since the 'white giant' is a pre-Saxon, Romano-Celtic creation, while Laugharne is an anglophone outpost in Welsh-speaking Wales.

The speaker implicitly laments lost youth ('young as they'), but it is notable that he speaks for the 'daughters', identifying with them and celebrating their uninhibited sexuality. In its relish for bodily pleasure and poignant awareness of mortality the poem is simultaneously melancholic and carnivalesque. It is the 'daughters' to whom the speaker finally appeals for lessons in lasting love; even as the poem progresses gravewards, their ceaseless desire counters it, and they move from barrenness to being an eternal generative-destructive principle, flaring in the darkness of the dying year.

1 Through throats . . . curlews cry = streams of blood in the curlews' throats; a confluence of rivers near where they 'cry'.

2 conceiving moon = associated with Diana, goddess of childbirth.

7 waded bay = the Laugharne estuary, which could be waded at low tide; the wombs of the women.

9 curving act = the stars curve across the sky as the earth turns in a night.

10–11 unconceived . . . immemorial sons = the women's yearning holds long-dead, living and as-yet-unborn lovers within its force field.

12 gooseskin winter = geese are eaten at Christmas, roasted with crisp skin; winter cold brings out the skin in goosebumps.

14 wains = wagons.

17 lighted shapes of faith = the stars.

21–41 the central section of the poem imagines the lovemaking of the women with their partners ('swineherd', 'orchard man' and 'gander king').

24 bush = shrub; pubic hair.

28 ducked and draked white lake = 'Ducks and drakes' is the game of skimming flat stones on water, the winner being whoever can make their stone splash most times before it sinks.

29 hawed house = overgrown by hawthorn; pun on 'whorehouse'.

31 furred small friars = dormice, harvest mice, shrews, etc.

32–33 till the white owl crossed / Their breast = the menacing cross-shaped shadow cast by the wings of the hunting owl silences the 'furred friars'.

33 does = female deer; perhaps from verb 'to do', in its old sense of sexual congress.

34 torch of foxes = enraged by the behaviour of his wife and father-in-law, Samson fired the latter's wheatfields by tying torches to the tails of foxes and driving them through the crops (Judges 15:4–5).

35 linked night = night links past, present and future; a 'link' is also a torch.

37 gambo = Welsh English word for a farm cart; with a play on 'gambol'.

38 gander king = a non-violent equivalent of Zeus's union with Leda.

39 shippen = cowshed in which the geese gather.

42 veined hives = breasts.

43–44 Mother Goose's ground . . . Jacks = from fairy tale and nursery rhyme, hinting at the women's sadness at their childlessness.

45 Now curlew cry . . . their dust = the women's spirits plead with him to 'kiss' and reanimate their dust by memorialising them in the poem.

56 long desirers = worms; but also the 'hale dead and deathless' former lovers.

59 forever meridian = at their highest pitch.

60 daughters of darkness = hints at Lear's 'dark daughters' Regan and Goneril, and also *The Dark Daughters* (1947), a novel of sexual transgression by Rhys Davies; Fawkes fires = bonfires lit annually on 5 November to mark the foiling of the Gunpowder Plot of 1605, led by Guy Fawkes, to blow up the Houses of Parliament.

Poem on his Birthday (p. 197)

Started in October 1949 if l.8 is taken literally, although a worksheet at Harvard is titled 'Poem in October (1950)', and much of the writing seems to have taken place in summer 1951. The full-length poem was sent to Oscar Williams several weeks later, and published in *Atlantic* in March 1952. Collected in *ICS*.

Another of the birthday poems in which Thomas considered his mortality and the human condition more generally (see 'Especially when the October wind', 'Twenty-four years', 'Poem in October'). It is less clear whether it was intended to belong to *In Country Heaven*, but it is in the same Cold War pastoral vein, and makes explicit the underlying atomic fears of that work. A marine version of 'Over Sir John's hill', without the allegorical apparatus, it performs less of a flourish in portraying nature's acquiescence in the cycle of creation and destruction, and its creatures are more unknowing than in the earlier work. As Walford Davies (1985) claims, 'Finches now simply fly "in the claw tracks of hawks"; they don't cry "Come let us die" . . . We are in the world of emblems rather than of allegory.' Thomas gave Bill Read, John Malcolm Brinnin's partner, a synopsis that confirms this more self-centred, anguished, aspect:

[H]e, who is progressing, afraid, to his own fiery end in the cloud of an atomic explosion knows that, out at sea, animals who attack and eat other sea animals are tasting the flesh of their own death. ... He looks back at his times – his loves, his hates, all he has seen – and sees the logical progress of death in everything he has been and done. His death lurks for him, and for all, in the next lunatic war. And, still singing, still praising the radiant earth, still loving, though remotely, the animal creation also gladly pursuing their inevitable and grievous ends, he goes towards his. Why should he praise God and the beauty of the world, as he moves to horrible death? He does not like the deep zero dark, and the nearer he gets to it, the louder he sings, the higher the salmon leaps, the shriller the birds carol.

'Though remotely' reflects the poet's separation from the animal kingdom by his 'toils', and his awareness of its metaphysical dimension, signalled in Stanzas 5 and 6. Here, 'Why should he praise God?' is answered by a 'heaven that never was', and man after death joins the remains of his fellow-creatures and an equally pared-back, pre-Incarnation 'unborn God and His Ghost', who oversee 'young Heaven's fold'. Their status is problematic, however; the more the language of faith is used, the more ambiguous it becomes. As the speaker counts his blessings in Stanza 8, by way of praising the creation, something similar occurs, and the concluding stanzas offer Thomas's most unnervingly sublime vision of apocalyptic 'beauty' in the atomic age.

Form: nine-line stanzas, alternating six and nine syllables, with assonantal and full rhyme *ababcdcdac*.

1   mustardseed sun = small but hot (even in October) and the origin of life; in the parable told by Jesus (the Son/sun) in Matthew 13:32, mustard symbolises faith as 'the least of all seeds: but when it is grown, it is the greatest among herbs'.

4, 15, 25   house on stilts ... long tongued room ... house = the side-of-the-cliff shed next to his house in Laugharne where Thomas wrote.

12   The flatness of this line reinforces the sense of a passive, non-allegorised nature.

17   Toils = labours (as verb), with fainter secondary sense of snares (as noun).

18, 60, 81, 90   bless ... blessed ... blessings ... blessing = from Fr. *blesser*, 'to wound', and OE *bloedsian*, 'to consecrate with blood', as well as the usual sense.

23   wynds = alleyways.

25   racking house = because the speaker racks his brains in it.

32   serpent cloud = the atomic cloud, given a devilish aspect.

33   turnturtle dust = in their (predatory) life the dolphins inhabit their own death, with play on 'turtle', another marine animal.

38 angelus = in the Roman Catholic Church the angelus bell signals a series of prayers commemorating the Annunciation and Incarnation.

39 Thirty-five bells = for Thomas's thirty-fifth birthday.

41 falling stars = apocalyptic scenario, as in Revelation 6:13: 'And the stars of heaven fell unto the earth'; the 'falling stars' may be atomic bombs.

42–45 And tomorrow weeps in a blind cage . . . dark = the immediate future may be destroyed by atomic war ('terror'), but ultimately it will be freed by love and death. Walford Davies (1993) notes: 'What Thomas imagines from here on is not a Christian heaven, but a continuing process deprived of terror and uncertainty.'

48 fabulous = astonishing (assumes God exists); a fable (assumes God's non-existence).

53 Plenty as blackberries = cf. 'The Pardoner's Prologue' in Chaucer's *Canterbury Tales*, which describes the souls of the dead as having 'goon a-blakeberrying'.

62 Gulled and chanter = the poet will be 'gulled' (made into a bird) after death, hence '[a] chanter', or singer (like a 'chanter', the melody pipe on a bagpipes). The items' grammatical incompatibility blurs the identities of 'he' and 'God'.

65 the earth of the night = play on the 'night of the earth' threatened by the Bomb.

67 rocketing wind = missiles were tested at a Ministry of Defence range near Pendine Sands, along the coast from Laugharne, where explosions could be heard.

79 clouted aground = made to run aground.

94 tusked, ramshackling sea = the rough sea, white with foam, as a wild creature (possibly a boar) that makes 'ramshackle' what ventures on to it (with a glance at the ramshackle 'house on stilts'); 'shackles rams', or tames male energy.

105 mansouled fiery islands = cockle-pickers silhouetted on the mudflats of the Towy estuary; islands of the atom bomb tests in the Pacific.

108 As I sail out to die = cf. D. H. Lawrence, 'The Ship of Death'; Tennyson, 'Ulysses'.

Prologue to Collected Poems 1934–1952 (p. 201)

Written March–September 1952; published in *The Listener*, 6 November 1952, as 'Prologue'; collected in *CP52*, titled 'Author's Prologue'.

'Prologue' began as a verse-letter to John Malcolm Brinnin, Thomas's

US tour organiser, was then intended for Ruth Witt-Diamant, his hostess in San Francisco, and finally turned into the preface he had promised Dent for his *Collected Poems*. He told his agent, David Higham, on 28 June 1952 that he couldn't produce 'an ordinary prose-preface' and was writing instead 'a Prologue in verse: not dense, elliptical verse, but (fairly) straightforward and colloquial, addressed to the (maybe) readers of the Collected Poems, & full (I hope) of references to my methods of work, my aims, & the kind of poetry I want to write. . . . It will be about 160 to 200 short lines of verse, of which I have written about 80 so far.' Sending the completed poem off to his editor at Dent, on 10 September 1952, he observed: 'I set myself, foolishly perhaps, a most difficult technical task: The Prologue is in two verses . . . of 51 lines each. And the second verse rhymes *backward* with the first. The first & last lines of the poem rhyme; the second and last but one; & so on & so on. Why I acrosticked myself like this, don't ask me. I hope the Prologue *does* read as a prologue, & not as just another poem.'

'Prologue' develops the conceit of a collected poems as an 'ark', both Noah's and the Ark of the Covenant, built to preserve the Noah-like poet and his creations from the threat of a new world war, and mortality more generally. Despite his concerns, Thomas was clearly pleased with it and felt 'that it *does* do what it sets out to do: addresses the readers, the "strangers", with a flourish, and fanfare, and makes clear . . . the position of one writer in a world "at poor peace"'.

19–20 the cities of nine / Days' night = play on James Thomson's *The City of Dreadful Night* and the proverbial 'nine days' wonder', spectacular but short-lived.

20–21 towers . . . religious wind = Thomas has New York skyscrapers in mind.

23 I sing = the long-delayed appearance of the subject and verb of the first sentence (which continues to l.33).

44 bellowing ark = self-deprecating description of *CP52*.

46–49 As the flood begins . . . Molten and mountainous = as the blood-and-lava-resembling fear of nuclear war and annihilation starts to gush forth.

51 hollow farms = farms in hollows between the hills; repeated l.79.

56 deer = archaic for 'animals'.

57 bryns = 'bryn' is Welsh for 'hill' (plural 'bryniau').

65 Agape = open; pun on Greek *agape*, selfless love.

67 Heigh = heigh ho! is an exclamation; play on 'high . . . hill'.

73 On a tongued puffball = a puffball is a spherical edible fungus, hence a 'tune'

written *upon* and *about* the world, full of human voices; mocking Thomas's own stoutness and verbosity.

83 Felled = furred; my patch = place; ramshackle construction (as 'patchwork').

84–85 moonshine / Drinking Noah of the bay = play on moonlight as 'moonshine' (illicitly distilled liquor), alluding to the drunkenness of Noah (and the poet), and the legendary Welsh ruler Seithenyn, whose drunkenness led to the flooding of his lands.

88 noise = a verb.

94 water lidded = flooded; allusion to Keats's 'Bright star' sonnet, whose narrator identifies with the star 'watching with eternal lids apart . . . The moving waters'.

97 prowed dove = dove's thrust-out breast, like a prow; pun on 'proud'.

Two Epigrams of Fealty and *Galsworthy & Gawsworth* (p. 204)

Written early 1953; published 23 January 1953.

Each of the two items is a small pamphlet, consisting of single sheets folded to make eight pages, privately printed items for members of the Court of Redonda, the first consisting of two separately titled epigrams, the second of two untitled epigrams (but evidently 'Galsworthy' and 'Gawsworth'). The Kingdom of Redonda was a drinking-club joke created by the writer M. P. Shiel. In Thomas's time it was run by his successor as King of Redonda, John Gawsworth (Terence Ian Fytton Armstrong), who bestowed the title 'Duke of Gweno' on Thomas when he was admitted to the society in 1947.

Verses and songs from Under Milk Wood (p. 204)

The lyrics and songs of *Under Milk Wood* make manifest the fact that, as Walford Davies (1995) notes, 'the "play for voices" is closer to a lyric poem than a play'; they were probably written in 1951–53, although the idea for the work and for several of its characters goes back at least as far as the 1944 radio feature *Quite Early One Morning* (see pp. 166–67). *Under Milk Wood* was edited by Daniel Jones and published in 1954 and 1974; I follow the improved 1995 edition of Walford Davies and Ralph Maud.

Daniel Jones's account of Thomas's notes for *Under Milk Wood*, given in his 1974 edition, claims that Thomas was planning to add several more songs to it: 'I saw . . . fragments of ballads to be sung by some of the main characters, for example, Bessie Bighead; the evening, like the morning, was to be "all singing". Even from these fragments, it was possible to guess how the ballads would turn out: the style would be "mock sentimental eighteenth century", with some sexual innuendoes thrown in – like Mr. Waldo's song, in fact. Llareggub's evening was evidently planned to be a celebration of maudlin drunkenness and ribaldry, and the date of events . . . was to slip back still further into the eighteenth century, the century in which Polly Garter always had lived.'

i. Morning hymn of the Reverend Eli Jenkins (p. 204)

The 'hymns' are parodies of poems praising the locality or celebrating local events often found in small-town and county newspapers at the time As well as gently mocking Eli Jenkins's poetic ambitions they poke fun at Thomas himself, whose surrogate, to some extent, he is.

1 Gwalia = an antiquarian name for Wales.

9–12 Cader Idris . . . Plinlimmon = Welsh mountains.

14 Penmaen Mawr = promontory on North Wales coast.

17–23 Sawdde . . . *River Dewi* = Welsh rivers.

25 Carreg Cennen = spectacularly positioned castle in Carmarthenshire.

30 By Golden Grove = 'compared with Golden Grove'; a village near Grongar, celebrated in John Dyer's 'Grongar Hill' (1726).

ii. School children's song (p. 206)

An unsentimental reminder of the childlike innocence of all the inhabitants of Llareggub.

iii. Polly Garter's song (p. 206)

1–5 Tom . . . Dick . . . Harry = 'any Tom, Dick or Harry' is idiomatic for 'anyone', people whom you do not know, and who therefore mean nothing to you.

8, 12 little Willie Wee . . . Weazel = a nursery-rhyme name, with blatant double entendre on 'small penis'.

iv. Captain Cat remembers Rosie Probert (p. 207)

This was Thomas's favourite section of *Under Milk Wood*.

v. Evening hymn of the Reverend Eli Jenkins (p. 209)

See note to i above.

vi. Mr Waldo's Song (p. 210)

Unsentimentality, economy and blatant double entendre lend this song its authentic broadsheet flavour.

Elegy [unfinished] (p. 211)

Thomas's last poem, an unfinished elegy for his father, who had died 16 December 1952, was left unfinished at his own death in December 1953. One of the worksheets held at Austin gave Thomas's plan for the poem: '(1) Although he was too proud to die, he *did* die, blind, in the most agonizing way but he did not flinch from death & was brave in his pride. (2) In his innocence, & thinking he was God-hating, he never knew that what he was was: an old kind man in his burning pride. (3) Now he will not leave my side, though he is dead. (4) His mother said that as a baby he never cried; nor did he, as an old man; he just cried to his secret wound & his blindness, never aloud.'

Select bibliography and further reading

Books by Dylan Thomas

POETRY

18 Poems, Parton Press, London, 1934.
Twenty-five Poems, Dent, London, 1936.
The Map of Love, Dent, London, 1939.
Deaths and Entrances, Dent, London, 1946.
In Country Sleep, New Directions, New York, 1952.
Collected Poems 1934–1952, Dent, London, 1952.
The Notebooks of Dylan Thomas, ed. Ralph Maud, New Directions, New York, 1967 (reprinted as *Poet in the Making*, Dent, London, 1968).
The Poems, ed. Daniel Jones, Dent, London, 1971.
Collected Poems 1934–1953, ed. Walford Davies and Ralph Maud, Dent, London, 1988.
The Notebook Poems 1930–1934, ed. Ralph Maud, Dent, London, 1989.

PROSE

Portrait of the Artist as a Young Dog, Dent, London, 1940.
Quite Early One Morning, ed. Aneurin Talfan Davies, Dent, London, 1954.
Adventures in the Skin Trade and Other Stories, New Directions, New York, 1955 (repr. in *Collected Stories*, 1983).
A Prospect of the Sea and Other Stories and Prose Writings, ed. Daniel Jones, Dent, London, 1955.
A Child's Christmas in Wales, New Directions, Norfolk, CT, 1955.
Dylan Thomas: Early Prose Writings, ed. Walford Davies, Dent, London, 1971.

The Death of the King's Canary, with John Davenport, intro. Constantine Fitzgibbon, Hutchinson, London, 1976.
Collected Stories, ed. Walford Davies and intro. Leslie Norris, Dent, London, 1983.

DRAMATIC, FILM AND RADIO WRITINGS

Under Milk Wood, Dent, London, 1954 (repr. ed. Ralph Maud and Walford Davies, intro. Walford Davies, 1995).
The Broadcasts, ed. Ralph Maud, Dent, London, 1991.
The Complete Screen Plays, ed. John Ackerman, Applause Books, New York, 1995.

CORRESPONDENCE AND CRITICAL WRITING

See also *Quite Early One Morning* and *The Broadcasts*. Extracts from interviews and the letters are given in the Appendices.

'Replies to an Enquiry', *New Verse* 11, October 1934.
Letters to Vernon Watkins, ed. Vernon Watkins, Dent, London, 1957.
'Poetic Manifesto', *Texas Quarterly* 4 (Winter 1961): 45–53.
The Collected Letters, ed. Paul Ferris, Dent, London, 1985 (repr. 2000).

RECORDINGS

Dylan Thomas: The Caedmon Collection (11 CDs), with Introduction by Billy Collins, HarperCollins/Caedmon UACD 95(11) (2002).
Dylan Thomas: A War Films Anthology (DVD), with Introduction by John Goodby, Imperial War Museum, D23702 (2006).

Critical studies, Guides and Bibliography

The best short introduction to the poetry is by Walford Davies (2014), and the latest monograph-length study is by John Goodby (2013). William York Tindall (1996) and Ralph Maud (2003) offer poem-by-poem guides.

Ackerman, John, *A Dylan Thomas Companion: Life, Poetry and Prose*, Macmillan, London, 1991.

Barfoot, Rhian, *Liberating Dylan Thomas: Rescuing a Poet from Psycho-sexual Servitude*, University of Wales Press, Cardiff, 2015.

Davies, James A., *Dylan Thomas: A Referencee Companion*, Greenwood Press, Westport, CT, 1998.

Davies, Walford, *Dylan Thomas*, Open University Press, Milton Keynes, 1986.

Goodby, John, *The Poetry of Dylan Thomas: Under the Spelling Wall*, Liverpool University Press, Liverpool, 2013.

Hardy, Barbara, *Dylan Thomas: An Original Language*, University of Georgia Press, Athens, GA, and London, 2000.

Kershner, R. B. Jr, *Dylan Thomas: The Poet and His Critics*, American Library Association, Chicago, 1976.

Maud, Ralph, *Where Have the Old Words Got Me?*, University of Wales Press, Cardiff, 2003.

—— *Entrances to Dylan Thomas' Poetry*, University of Pittsburgh Press, Pittsburgh, 1963.

—— and Albert Glover, *Dylan Thomas in Print: A Bibliographical History*, University of Pittsburgh Press, Pittsburgh, 1972.

Moynihan, William T., *The Craft and Art of Dylan Thomas*, Oxford University Press, Oxford, 1966.

Tindall, William York, *A Reader's Guide to Dylan Thomas*, Farrar, Straus and Giroux, New York, 1962, repr. Syracuse University Press, 1996.

Essay collections

Bold, Alan, ed., *Dylan Thomas: Craft or Sullen Art*, Vision Press, London and New York, 1990.

Brinnin, John Malcolm, ed., *A Casebook on Dylan Thomas*, T. Y. Crowell, New York, 1961.

Cox, C. B., ed., *Dylan Thomas: A Collection of Critical Essays*, Prentice-Hall, Englewood Cliffs, NJ, 1966.

Davies, Walford, ed., *Dylan Thomas: New Critical Essays*, Dent, London, 1972.

Goodby, John and Chris Wigginton, eds, *Dylan Thomas: New Casebook*, Palgrave, Basingstoke, 2001.

Tedlock, E. W., ed., *Dylan Thomas: The Legend and the Poet*, Heinemann and Mercury Books, London, 1963.

Book chapters and journal essays

Aivaz, David, 'The Poetry of Dylan Thomas', *The Hudson Review*, VIII: 3 (Autumn, 1950), reprinted in Tedlock (1963).

Bayley, John, 'Dylan Thomas', *The Romantic Survival*, Constable, London, 1957.

Conran, Tony, '"I saw time murder me": Dylan Thomas and the tragic soliloquy', *Frontiers in Anglo-Welsh Poetry*, University of Wales Press, Cardiff, 1997.

Crehan, Stewart, 'The Lips of Time', in Bold (1990) and Goodby and Wigginton (2001).

Garlick, Raymond, 'Shapes of Thought', in *Poetry Wales: A Dylan Thomas number*, 9:2 (Autumn 1973), pp. 40–48.

Goodby, John, '"The Rimbaud of Cwmdonkin Drive": Dylan Thomas as Surrealist', in *Dada and Beyond*, ed. Elza Adamowicz and Eric Robertson, Rodopi Press, Amsterdam/New York, 2012, pp. 199–223.

────── 'Dylan Thomas and the poetry of the 1940s', in *The Cambridge History of English Poetry*, ed. Michael O'Neill, Cambridge University Press, Cambridge, 2010, pp. 858–78.

────── and Chris Wigginton, 'Welsh Modernism: Dylan Thomas, David Jones and Lynette Roberts', in *Regional Modernisms*, ed. Neal Alexander and Jim Moran, Edinburgh University Press, Edinburgh, 2013.

Gramich, Katie, '"Daughters of Darkness": Dylan Thomas and the Celebration of the Female', in Goodby and Wigginton (2001).

Heaney, Seamus, 'Dylan the Durable? On Dylan Thomas', *The Redress of Poetry*, Faber, London, 1995.

Keery, James, 'The Burning Baby and the Bathwater', in *P.N. Review*, issues 151, 29:5 (May/June 2003); 152, 29:6 (July/

August 2003); 154, 3:2 (November/December 2003); 156, 30:4
(March/April 2004); 159, 31:1 (September/October 2004); 164,
31:6 (July/August 2005); 170, 32:6 (July/August 2006); 171,
33:1 (September/October 2006).

McKay, Don, 'What Shall We Do with a Drunken Poet?': Dylan
Thomas' Poetic Language', *Queen's Quarterly*, 93:4 (1986), pp.
794–807.

——— 'Crafty Dylan and the Altarwise Sonnets: "I build a flying
tower and I pull it down"', *University of Toronto Quarterly*, 55
(1985/6), pp. 357–94.

Miller, J. Hillis, 'Dylan Thomas', in *Poets of Reality: Six Twentieth
Century Writers*, Harvard University Press, Cambridge, MA,
1966.

Mills, Ralph J., 'Dylan Thomas: The Endless Monologue', *Accent*,
XX (Spring 1960), pp. 114–36.

Nowottny, Winifred, 'Symbolism and Obscurity', in *The
Language Poets Use*, The Athlone Press, London, 1962 and
1975.

Pearson, Gabriel, 'Gabriel Pearson on Dylan Thomas', *The
Spectator Review of Books*, 20 November 1971, p. 731.

Phillips, Ivan, 'I sing the bard electric', *Times Literary Supplement*
(19 September 2003), pp. 14–15.

Riley, Peter, 'Thomas and Apocalypse', *Poetry Wales*, 44:3
(Winter 2008/09), pp. 12–16.

Thomas, M. Wynn, '"Marlais": Dylan Thomas and the "Tin
Bethels"', in *In the Shadow of the Pulpit: Literature and
Nonconformist Wales*, University of Wales Press, Cardiff, 2010.

——— 'Portraits of the artist as a young Welshman', in
Corresponding Cultures: The two literatures of Wales, University
of Wales Press, Cardiff, 1999.

Thomas, R. George, 'Dylan Thomas and some early readers',
Poetry Wales, 9:2 (Autumn 1973), pp. 3–19.

Williams, Daniel, 'Beyond National Literature? Dylan Thomas
and Amos Tutuola in "Igbo masquerade"', *New Welsh Review*,
60 (Summer 2003), pp. 5–12.

PhD theses

Golightly, Victor, *'Two on a tower': the influence of W. B. Yeats on Vernon Watkins and Dylan Thomas*, University of Swansea, 2003.

Hornick, Lita, *The Intricate Image: A Study of Dylan Thomas*, Columbia University, 1958.

Parkinson, Siobhán, *Obscurity in the Collected Poems of Dylan Thomas*, University College Dublin, 1981.

Biography and contexts

The two most recent biographies of Thomas are thorough and well written, although Ferris allows his dislike of his subject to colour his account. Neither Ferris nor Lycett has much appreciation of the poetry. James A. Davies does, and is highly recommended. Memoirs by John Malcolm Brinnin, Caitlin Thomas, Daniel Jones, Gwen Watkins and Vernon Watkins are revealing accounts of Thomas by those who knew him. The most recent life, by Hilly Janes, is a novel and highly absorbing account which reads Thomas back into the artistic milieu of his Swansea fellow-artists and friends.

Brinnin, John Malcolm, *Dylan Thomas in America*, Little, Brown and Co., Boston, MA, 1955.

Davies, James A., *Dylan Thomas's Swansea, Gower and Laugharne*, University of Wales Press, Cardiff, 2000.

Ferris, Paul, *Dylan Thomas*, Penguin, Harmondsworth, 1978.

Fitzgibbon, Constantine, *The Life of Dylan Thomas*, Dent, London, 1965.

Janes, Hilly, *The Three Lives of Dylan Thomas*, The Robson Press, London, 2014.

Jones, Daniel, *My Friend Dylan Thomas*, Dent, London, 1977.

Lycett, Andrew, *Dylan Thomas: A New Life*, Weidenfeld and Nicolson, London, 2003.

Thomas, Caitlin, *Leftover Life to Kill*, Putnam, London, 1957.

Thomas, David N., ed., *Dylan Remembered: Interviews by Colin Edwards* (two volumes), Seren Books, Bridgend, 2003 and 2004.

Watkins, Gwen, *Dylan Thomas: Portrait of a Friend*, Y Lolfa, Talybont, 2005.

Online resources

Essays by Victor Golightly, Richard Chamberlain, Nathalie Wourm, Harri Roberts, John Goodby and Chris Wigginton: www.dylanthomasboathouse.com/education/essays-academic-papers/

John Goodby, 'Dylan Thomas', *Oxford Bibliographies Online*: www.oxfordbibliographies.com/view/document/obo-9780199846719/obo-9780199846719-0057.xml?rskey=oop49f&result=41&q=

George Morgan, essay on 'In the Direction of the Beginning': http://revel.unice.fr/cycnos/index.html?id=84

Ruthven Todd, letter to Louis MacNeice concerning Thomas's death: www.dylanthomas.com/dylan-thomas-centre/exhibition/ruthven-todd/

The Boathouse, Laugharne, Dylan Thomas's last residence: www.dylanthomasboathouse.com/

Dylan Thomas Society of Great Britain: www.thedylanthomassocietyofgb.co.uk/

Andrew Dally, Dylan Thomas blog: www.dylanthomasnews.com and twitter feed @ dylanthomasnews

Dylan Thomas Birthplace, 5 Cwmdonkin Drive, Swansea www.dylanthomasbirthplace.com

Dylan Thomas Centre, Swansea www.dylanthomas.com/dylan-thomas-centre

Index of titles

Under Milk Wood

A Play for Voices

DYLAN THOMAS

ORIGINALLY COMMISSIONED BY THE BBC, and described by Dylan Thomas as 'a play for voices', *Under Milk Wood* is an emotive and hilarious account of a spring day in the fictional Welsh seaside village of Llareggub.

We learn of the inhabitants' dreams and desires, their loves and regrets. We meet Captain Cat, who dreams of his drowned former seafellows, and Nogood Boyo, who dreams of nothing at all. A unique and touching depiction of a village that has 'fallen head over bells in love', *Under Milk Wood* is a modern classic that continues to inspire readers and performers a century after Thomas's birth.

Paperback and ebook available

Portrait of the Artist as a Young Dog

DYLAN THOMAS

Introduced by Dylan Thomas's daughter,
Aeronwy Thomas

FIRST THE young schoolboy, gloriously immersed in
make-believe in a shabby farmyard, then the budding poet
with his thrilling dreams of fame and fortune. Finally, the
novice reporter roaming suburban Swansea in search
of momentous material.

In ten wonderfully evocative short stories, Dylan Thomas
explores myriad themes, from the celebration of everyday
life's complexities and eccentricities to his sense of
nostalgia for the countryside of his boyhood.

Paperback and ebook available

The Love Letters of Dylan Thomas

DYLAN THOMAS

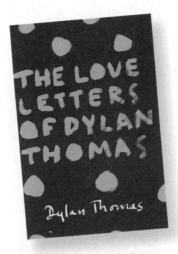

DYLAN THOMAS'S love letters to the many women in his life are among the most beautiful and lyrical ever to have been written. From wherever the poet's life took him, he wrote letters full of longing and painful separation.

This collection includes letters to Pamela, his first love, to Caitlin, his flamboyant wife, and to later loves, such as Elizabeth Reiter, the woman who was with him on the night of his death.

Like all great letter writers, Thomas had the gift of writing as if his correspondent stood directly before him. He used his letters to beg forgiveness, to cajole, to amuse and to give the impression of confidence and ease. Like so much of his poetry, they were designed to secure Thomas's place in his lover's heart and memory — as all true love letters should.

Paperback and ebook available

The Dylan Thomas Omnibus

Under Milk Wood, Poems, Stories and Broadcasts

DYLAN THOMAS

THE ESSENTIAL Dylan Thomas – a rich collection of his best-loved poems and stories, as well as pieces written for radio and magazines, including his play *Under Milk Wood*.

This selection spans Thomas's writing lifetime and shows the full range of this tempestuous and meticulous artist who once cheerfully claimed that he had beast, angel and madman within him.

Paperback available

Collected Stories

DYLAN THOMAS

Edited by Walford Davies

Introduced by Leslie Norris

THIS BOOK presents the complete span of Thomas's stories, from his first urgent hallucinatory visions of the dark forces beneath the surface of Welsh life to the inimitable comedy of his later autobiographical writings. The stories showcase his humour, his fine ear for speech and his exceptional narrative skills.

With *Portrait of the Artist as a Young Dog* and *Adventures in the Skin Trade*, Thomas found a new voice for his irreverent memories of lust and bravado in south-west Wales and London, leading to a sequence of classic evocations of childhood magic and the follies of adult life.

Paperback and ebook available

A Dylan Thomas Treasury

Poems, Stories and Broadcasts
Selected by Walford Davies

DYLAN THOMAS

'DISCOVERED' at the age of nineteen through a poetry competition in a London newspaper, Dylan Thomas became the object of immediate acclaim and criticism for his adventurous language and resonant verse. His famously reckless lifestyle belied his deep seriousness – manifest in his imaginative fascination with youth and his continual marvelling at the mysteries of life and death.

Along with startling images of pain and violence, Thomas's poetry and prose embrace touching childhood reminiscences and a spiritual yearning, from which he emerges, not as the loud bohemian of the personal legend, but as the careful and reflective artist of the poems, stories and broadcasts themselves.

Paperback available

For literary discussion, author insight,
book news, exclusive content,
recipes and giveaways, visit the
Weidenfeld & Nicolson blog and
sign up for the newsletter at:

www.wnblog.co.uk

For breaking news, reviews and exclusive competitions
Follow us 🐦 @wnbooks